T0302120

The Brandy Trade under the *Ancien Régime*

Regional Specialisation in the Charente

This study of the brandy trade and its merchants illustrates an intimate knowledge of spirits, the origins of which are relatively obscure and which were little traded internationally in 1600. Professor Cullen explores the emergence of cognac, the world's most famous spirit, as well as the evolution of its home region, the Charente. Brandy was part of the dynamic changes in alcoholic beverages in the seventeenth century, which a growing taste for spirits and novel surplus conditions in conjunction were to boost in the following century. Professor Cullen demonstrates that the brandy trade did not belong to a culture dependent on unstable agrarian surpluses and a precarious peasant viticulture, and illustrates that the French economy in the eighteenth century was more complex and dynamic than is often assumed. He shows that the brandy trade was based on a sophisticated regional economy, which, from the 1720s, was not only linked to the international market, but also supplied the imbibers of Paris with brandy and its bankers with bills drawn on foreign centres. Notwithstanding competition from cereal- and sugar-based products and from other brandy regions which emerging surplus created, regional specialisation in the Charente was an indispensable element in ensuring skill in distillation, quality of product and a stable output, and was recognised in the region's success in attracting foreign merchants who later became household names, such as Martell and Hennessy.

L. M. Cullen is Professor of Modern Irish History at Trinity College, Dublin

The Brandy Trade under the
Ancien Régime
Regional Specialisation in the Charente

L. M. Cullen

CAMBRIDGE
UNIVERSITY PRESS

CAMBRIDGE UNIVERSITY PRESS
Cambridge, New York, Melbourne, Madrid, Cape Town,
Singapore, São Paulo, Delhi, Mexico City

Cambridge University Press
The Edinburgh Building, Cambridge CB2 8RU, UK

Published in the United States of America by Cambridge University Press, New York

www.cambridge.org
Information on this title: www.cambridge.org/9780521592482

First published 1998

A catalogue record for this publication is available from the British Library

Library of Congress Cataloguing in Publication Data
Cullen, L. M. (Louis M.)
    The Brandy Trade under the Ancien Régime : Regional Specialisation
    in the Charente / L. M. Cullen.
        p.   cm.
    Includes bibliographical references (p.   ) .
    ISBN 0-521-59248-8
    1. Brandy industry – France – Charente — History.   I. Title.
HD9393.F83C483   1998
380.1′4566353′094465 – dc21   97-27258   CIP

ISBN 978-0-521-59248-2 Hardback
ISBN 978-0-521-89098-4 Paperback

To the memory of Síle Ní Chinnéide

Contents

Figures

Preface

This book grew out of what was originally research – still ongoing intermittently after more than forty years – into the Irish merchant community in France. I assumed that a one-day visit by motor car from Bordeaux to Cognac at the beginning of October 1976 would be the prelude to a further two or three days in Cognac at a later stage. The sheer scale of the Hennessy archive changed all that and my interest gradually widened to embrace other houses and the brandy trade at large. Cognac is a remarkable drink, perhaps the most remarkable spirit of all, and it is fitting that its records in all their richness should have the same uniqueness.

More than twenty years later, and after innumerable visits to the region, with the refrain 'Angouleme, Angouleme, deux minutes d'arret!' at the railway junction for Cognac still ringing in my ears, weighty obligations have mounted up. Two stand out. One is to Alain Braastad, proprietor of Delamain's, who guided me to many sources and discussed many problems; my major single debt to him is for help in sorting out the early technical development of brandy, in which a knowledge of brandy making is as essential as the documentary sources, in order to avoid slipping into error, and to both him and Marilise for hospitality and friendship. The other debt is to Maurice Richard Hennessy who, like his ancestor two centuries ago, looks after the Irish market and whose patient help and support have been forthcoming on numerous occasions. There is yet a third obligation to Jacques de Varenne whose interest and support have been unstinting and who also gave me the run of Augier's premises at weekends; Monsieur and Madame de Varenne's hospitality at midday on Cognac's winter days often compensated for the rigours of the numbing cold of unheated offices.

There are also obligations to others, often for access at short notice or in busy seasons. At Hine's they are owed to Brian Thompson, managing director in the early 1980s, and to Bernard Hine. At Hennessy's, over the years, they are owed to Frank Rochard, to Madame Jouannet and Monsieur Pestiaux in the archives, and to the genial and legendary Louis Bertin, sommelier of the house when the archives were stored with the bottles (in the customary cold conditions), who knew how to restore a researcher with brandy, claret and pineau. At Martell's Madame Evelyn Chapeau Woodrow, who was responsible for the excellent arrangement of the archives, and Mademoiselle Rousseau provided willing assistance over many years. Gérard de Ramefort, managing director of Otard's, provided much help, especially in relation to his researches on the difficult and interesting background of the Otard family, and both he and Madame Ludy Chapeau helped me in several visits to the firm. Madame Adole, to whom I was introduced by Monsieur de Varenne, provided me with information about her ancestor, Samuel Turner. The fact that two Samuel Turners resided in Hamburg at the end of the 1790s was, to say the least, disconcerting, and patient enquiry by Miss Ann Neary of the National Archives, Dublin, and, through the good offices of Dr Anthony Malcomson, by Miss Linda Johnston of the Public Record Office of Northern Ireland, provided information on one of the two Turners which was essential to resolving this problem beyond all doubt.

Professor Paul Butel of Bordeaux very kindly gave me a copy of his transcript of the brandy exports of Bordeaux and has often helped with his advice. Other debts are to Recteur Jean-Pierre Poussou, president of the University of Paris IV (Paris-Sorbonne) and to Professor Philip Loupès of the University of Bordeaux III. My wife spent a week with me in the Hennessy archives in 1978 and Matthew Stout of the Department of Geography, Trinity College, has very kindly drawn the graph and maps. The late Dr Peter Skrabanek of the Department of Social Medicine and Professor James McCormick, both of Trinity College, gave me advice from a medical perspective on the properties of spirits and brandy. I am indebted to Dr Jean-Louis Plisson for permission to reproduce details of the 1804 sepia sketch. I am also grateful to Professor T. M. Bartlett of University College, Dublin, for some invaluable detail on the Irish distiller Hilary Andoe. Finally a warm note of appreciation is in order to Richard Fisher at CUP, the production team and the anonymous referees. The dedication is to Síle Ní Chinnéide who introduced me to historical research in 1953 and whose suggestion of French trade as a dissertation subject was in a sense responsible for everything.

Twenty years is the time span in which a well-cared-for brandy reaches perfection; my hope is that some of this quality may have rubbed off on the book and that its twenty years of maturation may be a small repayment to many, not all mentioned in this preface, whose cooperation, unstinting help and unfailing courtesy have been drawn on. This volume deals with production and trade; it is hoped that a second book will appear shortly dealing with the families engaged in the *ancien régime* brandy trade.

Abbreviations

AAC   Augier archives, Cognac
AAE   Archives des Affaires étrangères, Ministères des Affaires
        étrangères, Paris
ACC   Archives of the Chambre de Commerce, La Rochelle
ADC   Archives départementales de la Charente, Angouleme
ADCM   Archives départementales de la Charente maritime, La
        Rochelle
ADG   Archives départementales de la Gironde, Bordeaux
AN   Archives nationales, Paris
CPA   Correspondance politique Angleterre
DAJ   Delamain archives, Jarnac
HAC   Hennessy archives, Cognac
HAJ   Hine archives, Jarnac
MAC   Martel archives, Cognac
OAC   Otard archives, Cognac
PRO   Public Record Office, London

Glossary

acquit	Revenue entry or declaration for payment of the *aides* (see below), also described as an *acquit à caution*, which means that the merchant had signed a bond for later payment of the duties.
aides	Excise or sales taxes collected at local level by the fiscal authorities. As such, goods destined for local consumption, inland trade and export were all liable to the charge.
Angleterre	In French usage, denoted the British Isles including the Isle of Man and the Channel Islands as well as Ireland (in this sense the term is used in italics in the text).
anker	In French *ancre*, a small measure used by smugglers. It was as small as 12 gallons (HAJ, letter book 1771–5, 22 November 1773; 22 January 1774). Such ankers were illegal under revenue law in Britain or Ireland. They were also discouraged in France, and there was opposition as far back as 1729 by the officials of the *aides* to *ancres* below 60 pintes (ACC, La Rochelle, no. 3601). As a result they were not readily available, and Irish smugglers sometimes brought ankers out with them from Ireland. An *ancre* of 64 pintes was, however, made in the Cognac region. This would amount to 16 gallons, English or Irish measure.
banquier	A banker. However, unlike the term 'banker' in English which was used sparingly, the term '*banquier*' was used widely, and the nearest equivalent is the informal term 'correspondent' or 'friend', denoting a house which handled bill business, often as a sideline to other dealings. In essence a *banquier* or correspondent, neither of whom nec-

essarily conducted a full range of banking func-
tions, did – or could – create credit by allowing a
provincial merchant to draw on him before he had
negotiated such bills as were passed to him for disposal. No French *banquiers* issued notes payable to
bearer, whereas English, Scottish and Irish bankers
did (though by the end of the eighteenth century
bankers existed in London, Edinburgh and Dublin
who had ceased to issue notes payable to bearer).
Banquier is an elastic term referring to function and
to houses, some highly specialised, some not;
'banker' in English is a rigid term confined to
houses issuing notes or, where notes were not
issued, creating credit on a wide scale.

barrique
: In La Rochelle a measure containing 27 veltes, in
Bordeaux 32 veltes.

Borderies
: A region to the north-west of the town of Cognac
producing the best of the sweet wines of the region
and also a brandy which was held to be almost the
equal of brandy from the Champagne. See map 2.

canton
: A market. The Saturday canton in the town of
Cognac was the main market for brandy. Though
larger distillers sold direct to *négociants*, it remained
important, especially for the smaller distillers. The
name survives to this day in the Place du Canton in
Cognac.

Champagne
: A region on two sides of the town of Cognac. The
modern distinction between Grande Champagne
and Petite Champagne was never made by eighteenth-century merchants. See map 2.

Cinq grosses fermes
: A customs union formed in 1664 embracing north-
central France and reaching the sea in the Aunis
(La Rochelle) and Poitou on the west coast and in
Normandy and Picardy on the north coast. It had a
common tariff on trade with other provinces and
with foreign countries. Provinces outside the Cinq
grosses fermes were termed Provinces réputées
étrangères.

couper (or *coupe à la serpentine*)
: See also rectification. This process was used to
create a better brandy. The flow of inferior brandy
out of the *serpentine* (worm or cooling coil) was
directed into a separate receptacle and later

returned to the still. In addition, the very first stages – the *tete* or, in English, the foreshots – of a distillation second pass contained highly volatile and unwanted elements and were directed into a separate receptacle. The final flow – the *queue* or tailings – was also diverted from the main receptacle. The object of the *coupe à la serpentine* was to eliminate a flow of brandy of intermediate quality – *seconde* – which was formerly admitted into the finished liquor.

état   Summary returns of foreign trade, usually of a *généralité*. More detailed returns survive very rarely.

farmers-general   *Fermiers-généraux* in French, they were the main tax-farming body, their duties *inter alia* including the collection of *aides* and *traites*. Their activity was determined by a series of successive contracts and they enjoyed a quasi-official status.

Fins Bois, Bons Bois   Regions outside the ring of Champagne and Borderies districts. A clear distinction between Fins Bois and Bons Bois was not made in the eighteenth century although merchants made occasional reference to 'woodlands' and 'best woodlands' brandy in their letters. The reference to woods implied that they had been mixed regions of woods and varied agriculture, whereas the Champagne regions had acquired their name centuries previously as intensive cultivation had already left them comparatively denuded of woodland. The Bois Ordinaires or Bois Communs were regions beyond the Fins Bois and Bons Bois, still more mixed in activity and producing a brandy that was not highly regarded. While under modern legislation brandy from the districts defined as Bois Ordinaires, Bons Bois and Fins Bois enjoys the style of cognac brandy, the term 'cognac' was restricted in eighteenth-century usage to Champagne, Borderies and a region covering the Fins Bois and Bons Bois in later times. Brandy from the Champagne regions, usually designated as such, was increasingly the basis of the London trade. While some brandy from the Fins Bois and a little from the Bons Bois regions did enter into brandy bought for the London market, both regions and especially the Bons Bois provided a 'best cognac' which was quite distinct from and inferior to the Champagne and Borderies cognac.

généralité   Administrative district supervised by an intendant. It usually embraced several historic provinces, and was the basic unit for the compilation of the statistics of the *balance du commerce*. As such, each *généralité* contained several 'bureaux' (in British customs' parlance 'creeks').

muid   a variable measure, used for many dry goods, but not regularly used commercially for liquids. It seems to have been used in the *balance du commerce* as a common measure to which to convert other measures of brandy or wine. It amounted to 1⅓ of a la Rochelle barrique of 27 veltes or 144 *pots*. A decree of 2 July 1784 noted it as a measure of 36 veltes 'pour constater l'exportation et servir à la formation des états de la balance du commerce' (ACC, La Rochelle, no. 3666). Its use can be confirmed by detailed scrutiny of the figures in AN Paris F^{12} 1666. While the *pot* was a variable measure, the revenue *pot*, like the revenue muid, seems to have been a fixed measure, used for coping with the varied local measures.

négociant   The equivalent of merchant, and like merchant in the eighteenth-century usage of that term it denoted a position of prestige. *Négociant* derived from *négocier* (to negotiate) and indicated a trader who regularly negotiated or marketed bills, his own or those of others. It thus meant a merchant of standing and credit. As the century went by, merchants in this position ceased to describe themselves as they often had in the past as *marchand*, and used the more prestigious term.

octrois   Municipal or town duties but with the proceeds usually going to the state.

pièce   A large measure, the largest used in shipping brandy, generally the equivalent of 81 veltes or 3 barriques. A large *pièce* of 85 veltes was a recognised measure (AAC, letter book 1727–8, 1 November 1727). In Bordeaux the *pièce* was a measure of 50 veltes.

pinte   Four pintes were the equivalent of 1 gallon.

pipe	The term was in declining use in both English and French in the brandy trade. It seems to have been an alternative and archaic expression for the *pièce*. In 1763, there was reference to pipes of 85 veltes (MAC, letter book, 28 March 1763), and in 1768 to pipes of 180 to 190 gallons (DAJ, letter book, 13 August 1768).
pot	A small measure containing 4 veltes.
Provinces réputées étrangères	Provinces outside the Cinq grosses fermes. Goods paid tariffs on entry or exit from them and at identical rates, whether to or from each other, the Cinq grosses fermes or overseas. The level of duties also varied from one province to another.
puncheon	In French, tierçon. A measure amounting to two barriques, and the most common type of barrel for brandy shipments to England or Ireland (the smaller and more tightly bound barrique was favoured for longer voyages). Though in theory containing 54 veltes, its size grew (as a means of minimising charges) and after mid-century it universally contained 60 veltes, even running to 66 veltes.
rectification	Enhancing the alcoholic strength of brandy by one or more distillations beyond the two distillations which were normal to reach an acceptable strength. The term was also used to denote the strengthening of brandy in a second distillation by cutting off the flow through the worm or cooling coil before the alcoholic strength began to fall off, thus achieving a total accumulation in the receptacle at the outflow from the worm of a very high strength. This process was known as the *coupe à la serpentine* (see above). As it became widespread, the term 'rectification' was increasingly confined to the raising of brandy to a higher strength by a third or even further distillation. Specialist rectifiers emerged in Bordeaux and in the Languedoc who routinely raised brandies of indifferent strength to the desired strength by further distillations.
régie	Direct collection of taxes by state officials rather than by the tax farmers (i.e. private interest who contracted to collect taxes for an agreed sum,

receiving a surplus as their profit or income). The collection of the *traites* by a *régie* became effective in 1783, though the *fermiers-généraux* were employed as the commissioners charged with administering the *régie*. That helped to draw on the state itself some of the hostility already directed against the farmers.

soumission Declaration in order to obtain an *acquit* (see above).

tierçon French for puncheon.

Traite de Charente *Traite* signified the customs duties payable on entry or exit. The *Traite de Charente* was the duty payable at the ports of the provinces of Saintonge, which were principally Tonnay-Charente, Rochefort and Mortagne. In the *Traite de Charente* the customs duty levied on brandy was 11 livres compared with 3 livres levied in the Cinq grosses fermes. Other charges also accrued before the total duties, amounting to 19 livres at the beginning of the 1780s, were determined.

velte Or verge. Widely used as a measure of content, the equivalent of 2 gallons. Hence it contained 8 pintes.

Terms in French are indicated in italics only when they have a special meaning, e.g. *Angleterre*. *Pièce* is written in italics, whereas barrique, used as a standard measure in the text is not. In general, measures are given in *ancien régime* units, rather than, as in modern French practice, converted into metric equivalents. The use of *ancien régime* measures reduces the ambiguities of processing uncertain or variable measures, and, more importantly, remains a more convenient mode of comparison for historical purposes with figures as quoted in both older and modern sources in English, where metric usage is very recent.

For the conversion of the Republican calendar into the Gregorian, M. Lyons, *France under the Directory* (Cambridge, 1995), appendix I, pp. 239–40, has been used.

In accordance with current practice, the French in this book does not include circumflexes.

1 The emergence of brandy spirits

The rise and significance of the brandy trade

Spirits were an almost unknown product in 1600, and where they did exist, as in Ireland or Scotland, they were the subject of curiosity to the visitor from the outside world. Their story is later one of growth, at first in modest and obscure stages, and finally and rather dramatically, a rise to a major place in alcohol consumption in the north of France and in northern Europe. If key periods have to be singled out, they are, obscurely, the 1670s–1680s and, with a wealth of detail, the 1710s–1720s and the 1760s. It is, at one level, the story of both the development and refinement of a product (and of the matching taste which was the motor force for it). At another level it involved the creation of the necessary centres of supply to meet an emerging market. That supply could come from local grain, from wine-based alcohol from farther afield or even from sugar-based rum from outside Europe. They are all interlinked, and the products were in competition with one another on the emerging consumer markets. Surplus in grain was as important as the earlier surplus in wine, which had for a long time been the long-distance beverage trade of Europe. It was precisely the fluctuating supply of cereals – in demand for bread as well as for alcohol – that accounts for the precocious prominence of brandy in the international spirits trade, just as new-found surplus in grain as well as in rum from outside regions was necessary to keep the prices of spirits low enough, once an expanding market for them was created, to prevent an excessive price rise from choking off any expansion in consumption. Brandy also had complex internal currents within its marketing: for instance, prices along the coast or the immediate hinterland in wine-producing regions could be affected by the greater or lesser abundance of rum and gin (or whiskey) on foreign markets, just as frost damage to the vines along the Loire could lead price-insensitive Parisians to outbid the agents of foreign merchants who could often replace brandy with cheaper competing spirits from home or from across the Atlantic.

If brandy was part of the larger and worldwide story of different spirits, it also had its own history of specialisation in types of product (variously

1

mediocre and of high quality) and of a changing pattern of localisation in which specialist regions thrived to cater for more stable and predictable markets, and production contracted in the less convenient locations in an older and more diffuse pattern of brandy making. In other words, the eighteenth-century brandy trade reflected robust developments within the economy and within brandy itself as marginal producers and regions declined relative to the more specialised producers and districts. Hence the trade admitted of increased sophistication either by way of a better quality product for less price-conscious markets or by innovation in organisation to market a low-grade brandy distilled by more industrial methods. In districts close to the Loire, in Armagnac, and above all in Cognac, the former response was the one adopted. Elsewhere, in Languedoc, which was less conveniently placed for markets in the north of France, the response took the form of producing an inferior brandy, rectified by specialist distillers in central points rather than throughout the region. In Bordeaux's hinterland, with its large coastal and foreign trade in wine, the brandy business contracted from the early decades of the eighteenth century and, beyond the ups and downs of port distilling, never picked up again. Armagnac, on the fringe of the larger Bordeaux region, alone resisted the trend. In Languedoc, farther from the international markets for wine, brandy both grew and absorbed normally the greater proportion of wine output within the region. The combination of a rising trade in wine to the Toulouse region and of a growing switch in a rising total output from wine to brandy should in fact have resulted in an increase in the aggregate purchasing power of what had hitherto been one of the most disadvantaged regions of France. The response was a perfectly rational one to the situation of a region whose wine prices had been among the lowest in France.[1]

At the outset brandy comprised a comparatively unstable and small traffic. However, if the brandy trade was to expand, it needed not only to replace a loose business pattern with a better-defined and more solid one but to acquire an effective financial framework to ease the execution of external transactions. In essence both developments were greatly accelerated in the 1710s and especially at the end of the decade. La Rochelle began to lose its place as the distribution centre of foreign commissions as houses in Charente and Cognac began to process direct commissions from abroad. Financial speculation in 1719–20 and spiralling prices also created financial links from Cognac with Bordeaux to replace La Rochelle which was too small a market to cope with demands for soaring

---

[1] On prices, see George Freche, *Toulouse et la région Midi-Pyrénées au siècle des lumières (vers 1670–1789)* (Paris, 1974), pp. 726–8.

credit and foreign exchange needs. Paris was also increasingly used to underpin, with the proceeds of foreign bills, the provincial bills which financed much of the trade, and Bordeaux became the centre in which to acquire, by the sale of bills on Paris or on London, the specie necessary for the ultimate purchase of brandy. In time, with the continued growth of its financial market, Bordeaux rivalled Paris as an outlet even for bills on foreign centres.

Thus the brandy trade was not a simple peasant product, devoid of a coherent market context. It was characterised over the century by significant patterns of market specialisation. One pattern was for viticultural regions to shift into or out of brandy distilling over time. Another was specialisation by quality, whether a high-quality product in Cognac or a rectified one on the quays of Bordeaux or at focal points in the wide rural tracts of Languedoc: both responses reflected the changes in the international market and maximised the comparative advantage of the respective regions. There was also a significant redistribution of wealth and power from La Rochelle to its hinterland and a concomitant rise in the importance of Cognac, Jarnac and Angouleme, and of smaller centres like Aigre and Ruffec on the older and newer routes respectively to Paris.

Merchants in brandy regions also increased in wealth and confidence. The growth of trade reflected the strengthening of the local economy. The cognac markets in Paris, supplied overland, and the coastal regions of the north of France, supplied by *cabotage* (coastal sailings), were at a record level in the 1780s. A recovery in the coastal trade to some extent mitigated the bad fortune that La Rochelle, in contrast to the inland suppliers of the Paris market, had experienced in the 1760s and early 1770s. The export trade too, which had lost its lustre in these years, recovering in the 1780s from the gravitational effects of high prices in the north of France, competed on more equal terms with alternatives on foreign markets, whether in London or in Dunkirk (at two contrasting levels of quality the prime international markets for spirits). The overall export total for 1783 compared favourably with all but a handful of exceptional years during the century and the level was even higher in 1789, despite the countervailing pull of Paris. Within the total, the key business with London was on an unprecedented scale in the 1780s, and Martell's benefited disproportionately precisely because they had already become the dominating house in the London trade.

The changes inevitably also translated into close ties between the bigger houses and the prime Paris banks of greatest repute, ever closer links with Bordeaux from the time it entered into its great boom from before mid-century, and into participation by brandy merchants in fashionable freemasonry and, through that, some association with the region's noblemen. As late as the 1740s Augier, though at that time the leading house in Cognac, had been eager to leave the town, since buying by Paris houses was putting brandy out of reach of exporters. However, over the longer term, confidence increased, and the deprecating tones in which merchants spoke of themselves and their town ceased. The growing strength of local families is reflected in the fact that, while outsiders had played a powerful part in the trade from 1718 to the 1760s, no outsiders, that is those not already in the region by the end of the 1760s or not drawing on existing ties, made a mark later. This was the basis which made it possible for the Otards and Dupuys, the Hennessys, and with some lag the Martells, to do surprisingly well out of the economic upheavals of the 1790s. How much benefit the ordinary peasants drew from all this is harder to say. What can be said with confidence is that brandy itself was not a passive force in the region, a mere receptacle for surplus or glut in the Labroussian sense, but a positive force for development. No doubt here as elsewhere economic change was a double-edged phenomenon for the humble tillers of the soil, conferring some gains and bringing some drawbacks. On balance, the combination of more stable markets and the premium in the market for quality or for strength helped to create a stable custom for wine and generated a demand for foodstuffs from other regions, as specialist viticulture and distilling emerged.

The origins of brandy and early trade

The origins of spirits as a consumer beverage are obscure. The earliest reference to brandy on a vessel in Bordeaux is in 1513, and on a vessel for Ireland in 1519.[2] In the celebrated Sound registers – the record of tolls levied from 1494 on commodities passing into the Baltic through the channel dividing Sweden from Denmark – brandy featured infrequently and in small quantities in the cargo details from 1562. Only in the 1610s for the first time did the quantities become somewhat more important.[3] However, after very modest peaks of 200 pipes (600 barriques) in 1625 and 295 pipes (885 barriques) in 1638, they entered into a valley period again. Only in 1657 did they regain ground when 270 pipes were reached.

The term *brandwijn* itself may cover spirits other than wine-based ones. In most years up to 1660, the principal source of supply of spirits to the Baltic was Holland: it remains uncertain as to whether this was French or

---

[2] Jacques Bernard, 'The maritime intercourse between Bordeaux and Ireland *c.* 1450–*c.* 1520', *Irish Economic and Social History*, 7(1980), p. 14.

[3] N. E. Bang, *Tables de la navigation et du transport des marchandises passant par le Sund 1497–1660* (Copenhagen, 1922).

Spanish brandy transhipped or spirits made in Holland. Apart from uncertainty as to whether in practice *brandwijn*, despite its etymology, invariably implied brandy, the hint at a Dutch role in the origin of brandy suggested by the word *brandwijn* (later anglicised as brandy) may be quite misleading. The term may have simply originated in Dutch recognition of a new and exotic product from abroad. The term used in Bordeaux in 1513 was *eau ardente*, which still remains a word for strong brandy in Spain (*aguardiente*). *Brandwijn* then became the word to designate imported spirits in northern Europe; and in customs usage in England and Ireland, where it was already archaic, it seems to have been used well into the eighteenth century to denote all categories of imported spirits. If the Dutch contribution was largely linguistic, the technical origins of the emerging wine/brandy distilling of the early decades of the seventeenth century owed nothing to the initiative of the Dutch despite their ubiquitous presence as traders.

Despite the later versions, vague and confused in detail, of a Dutch role in the French origins of brandy, from as early as 1568 small quantities of brandy from Spain and on occasion even Portugal or Italy passed through the Sound. The widespread, even if obscure, diffusion of spirits in early modern Europe embraced both the sixteenth-century Mediterranean, where the Dutch presence came only at the very end of the century, and the remote Gaelic-speaking fastnesses of Ireland and Scotland, where, in total isolation from the currents of international trade, spirits had become the festive drink of the rural upper classes. Of course the role of the Dutch later became important because their growing taste for spirits reached both foreign and domestic products. This evolution was made easier by the presence of Dutch trading communities in Nantes, La Rochelle and Bordeaux, and of Dutch paper manufacturing families in the hinterland of the Charente. What the Dutch (or Flemings) contributed was simply the word used by later foreign buyers, and which early on was also taken into English to differentiate imported spirits from *uisge beatha*, the festive drink of the Celtic fringe already known to visitors or administrators from non-spirit-drinking England.

References to brandy occur in La Rochelle notarial acts from the sixteenth century onwards, though acts such as those of 1549 and 1571 provide no evidence of wide activity.[4] The first sustained reference in the

---

[4] P. Martin-Civat, 'Le monopole des eaux-de-vie sous Henri IV et le départ du cognac', *Actes du 100e Congrès national des sociétés savantes* (Paris, 1977), pp. 187–8. See also E. Trocmé and M. Delafosse, *Le commerce rochelais de la fin du xvᵉ au début du xviiᵉ siècle* (Paris, 1953). Another source for later decades from the Angoumois are the references cited in G. Delaye, *L'Angoumois au temps des marchands flamands (17ᵉ siècle)* (Paris, 1990), pp. 188–97. The book reflects the widely held view that brandy was more important than wine (p. 191).

west of France occurs in 1604–10. In 1604 a decree by the council of state created a monopoly for ten years in the export of brandy out of the kingdom from the *généralités* of Tours, Poitou, Languedoc and Guyenne in favour of Isaac Bernard. More strikingly still the monopoly was intended to embrace distillation as well as sale. However, new letters patent obtained by Bernard in 1605 referred to Flemish merchants and others who distilled brandy and 'cherchent tous moyens de continuer le dit transport ... tant par charroy que par bateaux'. This dispute also provides the first evidence of activity in brandy in Cognac as the council of state, responding to Bernard's complaints, ordered that Jacques Roux, Michel Levesque, Jacques Ranson, Guillaume Haguenon and Pierre Gilles, inhabitants of Cognac and Tonnay-Charente, 's'expliqueront au sujet des rebellions et voies de fait qu'ils auraient commises en violation du privilège accordé à Isaac Bernard, trésorier des Mortes paies de Bretagne seul fabriquer et faire transporter de l'eau de vie dans les généralités de Tours, Poitiers, Toulouse, Guyenne, Limoges et dans les comtés de Nantes et de Blois'.[5] Vested interests in the *comté* of Nantes had caused Bernard to renounce his privilege in 1610, and the absence of further mention of it may suggest that resistance to his pretensions led to the abandonment of it elsewhere. Despite a broad geographical diffusion, market penetration by the product was shallow, thus making monopoly theoretically plausible, not only in trade but in production, even if in the event opposition quickly made it impossible. Reference to Flemish merchants may even suggest that some rise in foreign trade had provided the urge to monopolise. There was some upturn in brandy traffic through the Sound in 1605–6.

The projected monopoly embraced a region running from Languedoc via the Atlantic coast as far north as Nantes, in other words corresponding to the full extent of the future diffusion of the industry within France. While the 'folklore' about the origins of distilling visualises a crisis in wine sales along the Charente in the seventeenth century, in reality the hinterland of La Rochelle enjoyed enormous prestige for its celebrated sweet wines, much sought after by the Dutch, especially from the inland districts of the Borderies and Champagne, later the most intensive and prestigious brandy districts in the region. The reverse of a glut in wine existed. Salt and wine were the basis of La Rochelle's trading prosperity. Like Saint-Malo, it enjoyed an early and precocious prominence in the exploitation of France's new world across the Atlantic, and in the number of vessels on long voyages La Rochelle easily surpassed Bordeaux until the end of the seventeenth century.

[5] AN, Paris, E, t.25, no. 15268, quoted in Martin-Civat, 'Le monopole', p. 191.

The brandy trade in the second half of the seventeenth century

Even if activity in brandy paled by comparison with later times, a transition was evident, and from early in the second half of the seventeenth century the quantities passing through the Sound exceeded earlier levels. In 1681 and 1682 the total was 1,430 barriques and 1,330 barriques respectively. Moreover, the provenance began to change, with 'brandy' direct from France gradually replacing 'brandy' from Holland. Of the 1,330 hogsheads in 1682 for instance, a mere 25 had come from Holland. Whether this was a replacement of other spirits by grape brandy or simply the result of more frequent direct shipments because the growth of a real market made larger consignments worthwhile is a matter of speculation. By 1700, 2,769 hogsheads coming from France were recorded as passing through the Sound, a further 159 hogsheads coming from Holland.[6] The shift in the pattern within the Sound registers may hint at a broader rise in brandy relative to grain spirits. If the Irish parallel is relevant, the growing taste of the upper classes for spirits in the second half of the seventeenth century was met by imported brandy, not whiskey. Moreover, as French brandy grew in prominence, it became more dominant in international trade. The small quantities of brandy from Spain in the early registers, as was the case for brandies of Dutch provenance, were not a prelude to a later trade through the Sound. Nor did Cognac or La Rochelle at this stage assume the mantle of the leading sector in the French industry. The thin wines from the hinterland of Nantes and the embarrassingly large surplus of red wine with a short keeping life from the huge Bordeaux hinterland watered by the rivers Garonne and Dordogne made both regions the focus of distillation at this stage, doubly so as both ports had regular connections with northern Europe. In contrast, the sweet white wines of La Rochelle, which were produced by an art encouraged by La Rochelle's early leadership in long-distance voyages, were still sought after for their durability. Around 1700, Nantes is said to have exported 7,000 *pièces* or 21,000 barriques of brandy.[7] This is a large

[6] N. E. Bang and K. Korst, *Tables de la navigation et du transport des marchandises passant par le Sund, 1661–1783* (Copenhagen, 1930–53). Trade in brandy was given in the Sound registers mainly in hogsheads (barriques) and *pièces*. Brandy in other measures, apart from pipes, is ignored in calculating these totals, as the amount involved was insignificant. It is assumed that the *pièce* amounted to its more or less standard eighteenth-century size in Charente of 81 veltes. If it was smaller, for instance containing 50 veltes (the figure Huetz de Lemps employs for his Bordeaux calculations, and which is confirmed later in ADC, Angouleme, 5C5 and in AN, Paris, F^{12} 1666), the volume of trade would have been significantly smaller. This would, however, simply reinforce the argument of this chapter: i.e. that the growth of the brandy trade occurred late and strongly. [7] P. Jeulin, *L'évolution du port de Nantes* (Nantes, 1929), pp. 2–44.

quantity, equalling or exceeding Bordeaux's exports, except in a year of great wine surplus like 1700–1 when Bordeaux's exports were 34,000 barriques of brandy. In the two preceding years Bordeaux's shipments, even if coastal shipments are added to the total, were only 12,500 and 12,917 barriques. The 1700–1 brandy exports were the consequence of the remarkably abundant vintage of 1700: wine exports in that year were exceeded only in a single year in the following half-century.[8]

If brandy shipments are added to exports and estimated home consumption of wine in Bordeaux and its hinterland, the figures would suggest that almost 9 per cent of the vintage in the region was destined for the still, a proportion which rose to 22 per cent in 1700–1.[9] Outside the port of Bordeaux, distillation centred on the middle reaches of the Garonne and on the Gers where the vine occupied the poorer ground and was cultivated in conjunction with other products.[10] The absence of a stable distilling base in the hinterland was from the outset reflected in speculative distilling within the port itself or more precisely in the Chartrons just outside the walled town: in 1700 some 5,000 to 6,000 tons of wine 'qu'on ne put pas vendre à cause de la mauvaise qualité' were said to have been distilled into brandy.[11]

This crude estimate suggests that as many as 4,000 barriques of brandy (6,000 tons of wine would distil into approximately 4,000 barriques of brandy) may have originated in the port itself. Distilling in the Bordeaux region was a highly fluctuating business, destined to recede in the course of the eighteenth century, and to survive mainly as a port-based activity. Shipments never reached the 1700–1 level again, and even the level of the

[8] Christian Huetz de Lemps, *Géographie du commerce de Bordeaux à la fin du règne de Louis XIV* (Paris, 1975), pp. 101, 104–5, 216–17, 231. Huetz de Lemps gives the quantities of brandy shipped in hectolitres. From the total shipped in 1700–1, the amount of 8,400 hectolitres shipped along the coast (*Géographie du commerce*, p. 217) should be deducted in order to arrive at the quantity exported. For purposes of comparison, both contemporary and international, these have been converted back into barriques. In his glossary (p. 650) Huetz de Lemps gives an equivalence of a velte equalling 7.258 litres. In fact, in his text, the equivalence he uses seems to be 7.52 litres (see p. 216), and various conversions in his text are consistent only with a barrique (the Bordeaux barrique of 32 veltes) based on this rate of conversion and therefore containing approx 240 litres.

[9] Based on a total of 200,000 tons of wine for domestic consumption and shipment (Huetz de Lemps, *Géographie du commerce*, p. 103, and similar estimate for the *sénéchaussé de Bordeaux* in J. Savary des Bruslons, *Dictionnaire universel du commerce* (1742 edn)), and the optimistic assumption that 6 barriques of wine were required to produce 1 barrique of brandy. These calculations ignore local consumption of brandy, assuming that it was not significant. If the conversion ratio for wine into brandy was less favourable, say the more probable rate of 8 barriques of wine to 1 barrique of brandy, then the importance of brandy would be further reduced.

[10] 'La distillation parait n'y avoir été le fait que d'un petit paysannat dont la viticulture n'était pas toujours l'activité essentielle et qui se trouvait établi dans des secteurs un peu marginaux et à l'écart des voies navigables'. Huetz de Lemps, *Géographie du commerce*, p. 223.   [11] *Ibid.*, p. 223.

two preceding years was not passed again until late in the first decade of the century and then only briefly. Another upswing occurred in the years 1717 to 1721 and peaked at 27,000 barriques in both 1720 and 1721.[12] It was a final upturn, a short-lived response to the new-found international buoyancy in the spirit trade in and after the mid-1710s. Exports halved during the remainder of the 1720s.[13] With its great waterways and burgeoning demand for food and wine in a large port and in expanding overseas plantations, the hinterland switched either to specialist wine production, successfully making longer-lasting wines in the process, or to cereal and animal husbandry. Only in Armagnac, itself barely on the fringe of the Bordeaux region, did a brandy business thrive. By the 1760s Armagnac was for the first time being designated as a distinct brandy in the letters of merchants in Cognac, and in 1789 almost as much brandy was shipped through Bayonne, the outlet for Armagnac, as through Bordeaux.

Rapid expansion in distilling within the closing decades of the seventeenth century would explain why, against the historical evidence as far as we know it, there was a belief, for instance in Bordeaux in the early eighteenth century, that the industry had originated within the preceding hundred years.[14] In Cognac the later assumption was that the industry emerged around 1622. This fact itself, given the vagueness of early recorded knowledge of the first stages of the industry, suggests a recollection within the generation living in 1700 of a transformation of the trade in the preceding generation. In whatever way the belief emerged, the date seems plausible enough as marking the timing of significant change in brandy making. As far back as the 1640s exports of brandy from Bordeaux were a sizeable 3,000 barriques.[15] In Cognac by 1681–6, regular market quotations for brandy existed. This is evident from the earliest sustained record for brandy, the letter book of the Augiers for those years: however, even there brandy still took second place to wine.[16]

The brandy trade, 1680s–1720s

According to the Augier letter book, at the sharply increased prices of August 1683 (reflecting a poor outlook for the vintage), 500 to 600 *pièces* (1,500 to 1,800 barriques) would be available on the Cognac market. August represented a point in the calendar of the distilling year three

---

[12] *Ibid.*, pp. 235–6.
[13] ADG, Bordeaux, C 4268–4271, 4385–4390, *états de la balance du commerce*. I am grateful to Professor Paul Butel who gave me a copy of his detailed breakdown of the brandy exports from the port.   [14] Huetz de Lemps, *Géographie du commerce*, p. 219.
[15] *Ibid.*, p. 220.
[16] AAC. The letter book, 1681–6, a small one, has been badly damaged by water stains in several places. Some of it is difficult to read, and a few sections are now completely illegible.

months ahead of the opening of a new season: the preceding season's distilling would have come to a halt in April. What Augier seems to be saying in modern terms is that the total stocks on the local market towards the end of the old season were of the order of 1,500 to 1,800 barriques. Within the preceding year Augier purchased about 200 *pièces* (600 barriques) of brandy, a small volume compared with the purchases of an established Cognac house in the 1710s or 1720s, but if we understand the stock position aright, a significant proportion of turnover in his day. If we assume crudely that the amount of brandy still on hand would be sold before the new distilling season began and that as much again might be sold within the season itself, we may be talking of 3,600 barriques as the approximate shipments from Cognac in a year. This is not an implausible figure, though it may err on the high side given the modest scale of Augier's buying. We would of course have to add production in the Aunis and on the islands of Ré and Oléron. That could double or more than double the grand total.

Brandy quotations were given fairly regularly, but the active market itself was limited. Even in abundance and with no demand in March 1686, 'il y a peu de gens qui veuillent se résoudre à vendre'.[17] Wine was a more regular item in commerce: the terms 'champagne' and 'borderies' as such were specified by Augier only for wine, not brandy. That explains both the speculative withholding of brandy and the bunching of Augier's brandy orders, either in the autumn (in August and September) when the fate of the new vintage was predictable and speculation warranted either the sale or purchase of older brandy, or in December or in the following months, when the effective outcome of the wine trade had determined the prospects for distilling wine into new brandy. The level of activity within these restricted seasons fluctuated from year to year. For the same reason, the pattern of supply varied widely: thus there were large supplies from Ranson in nearby Jarnac in September 1682, and in May 1683, with brandy scarce, Augier offered a price in far-off Angouleme. In the abundant vintage of 1685 Augier's activity seems at first to have been exclusively in wine, brandy quotations disappeared until December, and actual brandy dealings seem to have resumed only in February. He then handled only 28 *pièces*. The predominance of wine over brandy was mirrored contemporaneously in the minutes of La Rochelle's great mercantile *étude* of the notary Teuleron.[18] In overseas trade with northern Europe, even in the late seventeenth century, salt overshadowed wine at least in bulk, and

[17] AAC, letter book 1681–6, 3 March 1686, to Theodore Tersmitten.
[18] ADCM, La Rochelle, Teuleron *étude* (notarial minutes), 3E 1294–1319 (1645–81). This *étude* is exceptionally informative on maritime trade, and the minutes are also very comprehensive.

brandy on the evidence of notarial minutes must have been subsumed into the 'autres marchandises' often noted in the minutes. Thus, despite the presence of English and Scottish merchants and the growth of a very large Irish colony, trade in brandy remained a subsidiary affair.[19] The switchover to brandy specialisation in the Champagne and Borderies districts had not yet seriously begun in the early 1680s: their repute still rested, especially in the Borderies, on sweet, white wines, prized for their ability, especially by the Dutch, to last on long sea voyages.

The brandy trade in the 1680s still lacked specialisation. The distillers had to compete with the counter-attractions of a foreign market for wine, and only a fraction of the vintage was converted into brandy. The Champagne and Borderies districts, later reputed for their brandy, not only produced wine, but its prestige rested on its being denominated by the names of the districts. A letter from Augier to Tersmitten in Amsterdam on 8 December 1685 seems to show that the brandy supply would consist of distilling what was left when the wine trade had subsided after the first rush of autumn and winter sales of wine (by implication, brandy was made from the same grape variety as the wine for export): 'je ne suis point d'avis qu'elles baissent, car quoique les vins vendent bien du moins de cette qualité on en chargera beaucoup et ainsi il en restera moins pour bruler. Le temps le plus favorable pour en faire des achats sera au mois de Janvier et Février.'[20] The variable character of the market seems borne out in the fluctuations in the Paris account of the Augiers. Their account with Tersmitten of Paris for 10 months in 1684 was for 10,604 livres: later accounts with Le Couteulx of Paris were for 18,626 livres (September 1686–December 1687), 44,508 livres (December 1687–January 1689), 43,151 livres (January 1689–3 January 1690), and 22,742 livres (January–September 1690). Augier's account with Theodore Paget in La Rochelle, was smaller – below 10,000 livres for irregular accounting periods of less than a year. As Augier had few external dealings, some business could have been funded without recourse to the bill market covered by the Paris and Paget accounts. However, if we take an average – 47 livres – of the highest and lowest brandy prices (34 to 60 livres) recorded, we would get for the brandy accounts (adding Paget to the Paris accounts) a theoretical maximum volume ranging from 439 barriques to 1,181 barriques. In fact, this greatly inflates the size of

---

[19] An account of La Rochelle's merchant community will be set out at a later date. For a preliminary account, see L. M. Cullen, 'Galway merchants in the outside world 1660–1800', in D. O'Cearbhaill, ed., *Galway: town and gown* (Dublin, 1984), pp. 63–89. The scale of the incoming traffic is well illustrated in the account book of sales by an anonymous merchant 1699–1707 in ADCM, La Rochelle, 4J 2283.

[20] AAC, letter book 1681–6, letter to Tersmitten, Amsterdam.

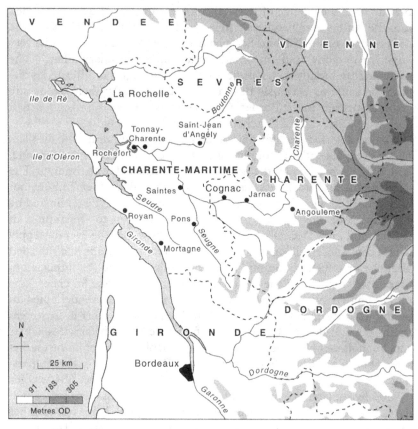

Map 1 The Bordeaux and La Rochelle hinterlands. (The boundaries indicated are of post-revolutionary *départements*.)

brandy dealings because so much wine was handled. His turnover would already have been a large part of the 3,600 barriques speculatively suggested as the possible turnover.

The story of the La Rochelle and Bordeaux *généralités* is one of contrasts. By 1723 Bordeaux's exports of brandy had been halved to 13,763 barriques. They failed to rise substantially above that figure in the best remaining years of the decade, and thereafter the 1723 level was exceeded only once, in 1762, in the wake of the bumper vintage of 1761. By contrast, exports from the *généralité* of La Rochelle rose decisively from 17,582 barriques in 1718 to 23,430 in 1723, and they exceeded 28,000 barriques in seven of the nine subsequent years, which proved the most sustained period of activity in the region's foreign trade in brandy. Even

Bordeaux's short-lived boom around 1720 was markedly less impressive than La Rochelle's. The 1720 and 1721 figures of 27,000 barriques (Bordeaux barriques) were outstripped by La Rochelle's which amounted to 42,023 barriques in 1720. These were the highest exports for any port in the eighteenth century. The collapse in the French currency which cheapened brandy to the Dutch and English explains the rise. A rise on this scale, fuelled by hectic buying in the spring, in other words quite late in the distilling season, would have been possible only through a switch of production from existing markets: in other words, in 1720, from an already not insignificant home market. The inland market had even more significance for Nantes, which was closer to Paris. Yet even with a Paris market to supply Nantes still exported 18,636 barriques in 1728, and was clearly ahead of Bordeaux.

Thus in a crude fashion a hierarchy in descending order of La Rochelle (Cognac), Nantes and Bordeaux existed in the 1720s. However, so rapid and recent was the change, especially in the Cognac region, that Savary's account in his book of 1723 was already out of date, seeming to give the order in reverse with Bordeaux and Nantes ahead of Cognac on volume, and Nantes ahead on quality.[21] Savary gave little attention to La Rochelle or, within its hinterland, Cognac. Exports from Nantes were said to be 7,000 to 8,000 barriques; the figure for Bordeaux twice that, and other places simply in proportion. Even the quality of cognac merited no special mention. The brandies of Nantes and Poitou were said to be 'les plus estimées . . . ce sont de celles là dont il va plus grande quantité à l'étranger'. This statement is ambiguous as to whether Savary meant that they were the best brandies in France or simply the best in the hinterland (as he noted brandies from elsewhere in Nantes's hinterland, Anjou, Touraine and Orleans, which went to Paris and Flanders). Yet the reality was that cognac had elsewhere become the recognised superior product, and that Savary was reflecting a somewhat outmoded Parisian perspective of the brandy world. Two decades earlier, in a sale of prize wine in London newspapers during the War of the Spanish Succession nineteen out of ninety mentions of brandy distinguished cognac from Bordeaux, Entre-deux-mers, Rochefort, Oléron and Nantes brandy.[22] Its price was moreover the highest in a hierarchy of French and Spanish brandies.

---

[21] Savary des Bruslons, *Dictionnaire universel du commerce*, vol. I (Paris, 1723), cols. 1785–90. The article on 'eau-de-vie' in the 1742 edition is almost identical to that in the 1723 edition. It repeats the same hierarchy of volume and quality, though elsewhere in the 1742 edition cognac is recognised as the best brandy.

[22] René Pijassou, 'Quelques aperçus sur le commerce des eaux-de-vie en Angleterre au début du xviiiᵉ siècle', in A. Huetz de Lemps and Ph. Roudié, eds., *Eaux-de-vie et spiritueux* (Paris, 1985), pp. 119–20.

14   The brandy trade under the *ancien régime*

With a novel dynamism emerging in the market, important structural changes, triggered by international trade in the product, began to alter its hitherto amorphous and undifferentiated character. Bordeaux with its good waterways shifted decisively towards wine. Nantes became progressively more reliant on Paris, as the kingdom's largest consumer market, close at hand, acquired a taste for spirits. As Bordeaux and Nantes brandy receded from outside markets other sources met the deficiency, not only maintaining but enlarging the stream of supplies. The Aunis from La Rochelle and the islands of Ré and Oléron satisfied coastal demand in the north of France; Cognac within La Rochelle's hinterland concentrated on the quality market abroad; Languedoc and Spain emerged quickly as suppliers too, though at the outset they were secondary to the Atlantic coast. In 1699 Sète, although at the time far removed from the main currents in Atlantic trade, already exported over 5,000 barriques of brandy. The resources of its vast hinterland which embraced Montpellier, Béziers, Narbonne and Nimes, would provide the basis of enormous expansion after 1750.[23] Another interesting index of this development is that some 43 per cent of the brandy mentioned in auction notices of prize brandy in the London press in the first decade of the eighteenth century was described as 'Spanish brandies'.[24]

Whether a widespread increase across northern Europe in distilling was a result of the emerging surplus in wine and cereals or of an increase in real incomes (simply another way of looking at surplus), or alternatively arose out of improvement in distilling techniques remains to be seen.[25] Grain spirits and wine spirits were not in themselves cheap; more accurately they were not cheaper than beer and wine respectively. While there was little loss of alcohol in the process of distilling, the actual quantity of alcohol in a second-distillate brandy, for example, represented the alcohol drawn in from at least six times the bulk in wine. To this had to be added the direct and indirect costs of conversion. In consequence a given quantity of pure alcohol absorbed by a consumer in brandy or whiskey should cost more than in wine or beer. Only two considerations could offset this: first the production of spirits either from marginal quantities of wine or cereal thrown on the market below general market prices or from undrinkable wine or decaying grain (ignoring for the purpose of argu-

[23] L. Dermigny, *Sète de 1666 à 1880: esquisse de l'histoire d'un port* (Montpellier, 1955).
[24] R. Pijassou, 'Quelques aperçus', p. 119. It is also possible that as some trade in French commodities was conducted under the disguise of Spanish or Portuguese trade, some of the brandy described as Spanish was actually French. See AN, Paris, F[12] 51, 54, 55, minutes of *conseil du commerce* (council of trade); J. S. Bromley, 'Le commerce de la France de l'ouest et la guerre maritime, 1702–1712', *Annales du Midi* (1953), pp. 52–65.
[25] L. M. Cullen, 'The early brandy trade 1660–1760', in E. Aerts, L. M. Cullen and R. G. Wilson, eds., *Production, marketing and consumption of alcoholic beverages since the late middle ages* (Leuven, 1990).

ment the likely deficiency in alcohol strength in using inferior raw materials); and, second, the saving in transport costs from the concentrated bulk of alcohol in the form of spirits. If exports by sea fluctuated widely, it was simply because in bad years inland demand rose more sharply than foreign demand which could more easily switch to cheaper alternative sources of supply (grain spirits and, in quantity for the first time in the 1730s, rum).[26]

In contrast to the demise of Bordeaux's hinterland, distilling in the upper Loire not only survived on the basis of the Paris market but thrived. In Cognac, even the prize vineyard districts were converted from the grapes which made the sweet white wines to the *folle blanche*, the source of a thin acidic wine which proved excellent in the region's distilling. The distillers were specialists, and three layers of specialisation took shape in La Rochelle and its hinterland: the central regions produced the justly famous champagne brandies, the eastern and northern fringes began to supply the growing Paris market, and the coastal stretches supplied the mouth of the Seine (with some of the brandy destined also for Paris), Normandy and Picardy. The rapid spread of distilling in the hinterland of Sète after 1750 was a response in a hitherto marginal region to the opportunities created by the growth of international and national markets in spirits. It resulted in an expansion of production which by the 1780s exceeded cognac output and over a shorter span of time. In 1786 output was said to be 150,000 barriques.[27] The *généralité* of La Rochelle (the provinces of Aunis and Saintonge) had an output of 100,000–110,000 barriques and probably more. To this figure, should be added, in order to arrive at a regional figure, an estimate for Angoumois output which was expanding rapidly at this time (and of which small quantities were beginning to appear in foreign trade): no guess is feasible on present knowledge. The growth in Languedoc accounted for the expansion of Sète and for the emergence inland of Béziers as the centre of distilling. Even in the case of Languedoc, while the foreign market was a major outlet, it took second place to a significant market in Paris (supplied by sea and the Seine) and in the northern provinces.[28] Further east, Toulon developed an export trade.[29]

[26] John J. McCusker, 'Distilling and its implications for the Atlantic world of the seventeenth and eighteenth centuries', in Aerts, Cullen and Wilson, eds., *Production, marketing and consumption of alcoholic beverages,* p. 23; McCusker, *Rum and the American Revolution* (New York, 1989).
[27] See Dermigny, *Sète de 1666 à 1880,* p. 33n, where output was said to be 50,000 barriques of 70 to 80 veltes. These are clearly *pièces,* and the barrique scale has been calculated simply by multiplying the number of *pièces* by three.   [28] *Ibid.,* p. 48.
[29] In 1753, a high year, Toulon shipped 3,200 *pièces,* and its Paris trade (also supplied by the maritime route) grew with time as well. Charles Carrière, 'Le commerce des eaux-de-vie à Toulon au xviiiᵉ siècle', *Provence Historique,* 12, fasc. 47 (January/March 1962), pp. 34, 39, 41n., 50.

The fact that early distilling was not a consequence of an equation of poverty and surplus (the producer poor because he had otherwise a virtually unsaleable product, the consumer poor because he could consume only if prices fell) corresponded to a general pattern of spirit consumption in which everywhere they were purchased for cash and often from afar: wine and beer, on the other hand, had originated literally in the household and almost invariably, unless shipped by sea, were consumed locally. Spirits were at first appearance the drink of the better-off and of festive occasions when expense was not spared, either acquired by cash purchase, or, if made in a rich household, by hiring the services of a specialist distiller. The Irish upper classes, either absentee or going to England on long visits, frequently came ashore at Chester in the 1680s with two or three gallons of whiskey or *uiscebagh*, forerunners of the modern tourist clutching his precious duty-free. In 1683 on no less than forty-seven occasions whiskey or *uiscebagh* was brought ashore from the packet boats at Chester, mostly by people with prominent Anglo-Irish names: they included the earl of Ardglass, and two titled ladies, the countess of Arran and the lady Mildmoy.[30] It was, it should be added, a new fashion and had not been evident in the port books even twenty years previously. Oats, even when brewed with the advantage of a bigger turnover in towns, made a bad beer (castigated by English and continental visitors in the seventeenth century), but produced a better whiskey: into modern times the belief has survived in Irish distilling that the presence of oats among the distillers' grain added to the flavour of the whiskey. The diffusion of cash in the eighteenth century was a vital factor in widening the social circle buying spirits in the Irish countryside. In urban society sales depended, as in Paris, on vigorous selling on street corners or in London on a novel investment of capital and effort by the distillers themselves in publicity.[31]

The great consumers, importers and makers of spirits in the seventeenth century were the Dutch, the richest people of their day. The brandy-sodden Dutch sailor moreover (a symbol of the downward social move of spirits) was already a reality by 1690.[32] Holland itself was the most advanced centre of both the seventeenth-century distilling industry and of the taste for imports which went hand in hand with it. Not only was brandy not a consequence of cheap surplus, but it corresponded to increased expenditure on the regular intake of alcohol. Just as the main

---

[30] PRO, London, port books Ireland, E190/1345/1/16, December 1682–3.

[31] On spirit sales in Britain in the 1720s and 1730s, see P. Clark, 'The "mother gin" controversy in the early 18th century', *Transactions of the Royal Historical Society*, 5th series, 38 (1988), pp. 63–84.

[32] E. Kaempfer, *History of Japan* (London, 1727), vol. I, pp. 51, 52, 56.

makers of spirits in the north were Dutch, they were also the main buyers from further afield: around 1700 Holland accounted for between two-thirds and three-quarters of the total quantity of brandy loaded aboard vessels, ocean-going and coastal alike, on the Garonne.[33] In the 1720s they still took more than half the brandy exported from the La Rochelle *généralité*, then the leading centre of the brandy business.

If we take the shift from Holland to France in the Sound registers as part of a wider pattern, it seems likely that the Dutch taste for spirits as it accelerated could not be satisfied solely from grain-based supplies and that brandy began to loom large in their buying and consuming pattern. In other words, insofar as surplus is relevant as the basis of a spirit industry, it is not surplus in an absolute sense, but surplus in wine relative to surplus in cereals. The key importance of the Dutch for the brandy districts is not a personal role, either in distilling or even in the diffusion of methods, but a taste – or thirst – for spirits in a rich and growing home market which progressively outran traditional grain-based supply by the late seventeenth century. Perhaps England might have become a large-scale buyer except for its French wars which raised its already high duties against French goods further in the 1690s, and which helped to ensure that its emerging mass market almost exclusively rested on home distilling rather than on imports. The importance of England as a pioneer of large-scale commercialised grain distilling is worth noting – a consequence of slow population growth combined with emerging grain surplus in an improving agriculture in the late seventeenth century as well as of high tariffs.

These issues are important because speculation has often been made as to whether the Dutch were behind the rise in brandy distilling, even as far afield as the Mediterranean.[34] Insofar as consumption promoted commercial distilling – and Dutch buying was vital in turning a small, widely diffused activity into a commercial enterprise – the answer has to be that they were. However, the Dutch were to be found not in brandy distillation itself: their presence in the ports and in paper manufacturing inland gave them easy access to the product. At the time there was little local consumption in the south-west of France, in the Mediterranean regions, or at first even in Paris, despite the city's corporation of *sauciers-vinaigriers* acquiring, in 1514, the privilege of becoming distillers. In the hinterland of La Rochelle the only Dutch families had been drawn in by the paper manufacturing industry, and though some of them married into local business families, no group of Dutch brandy buyers has been found in

---

[33] Huetz de Lemps, *Géographie du commerce*, p. 219.
[34] C. Carrière, 'Le commerce des eaux-de-vie à Toulon', pp. 35–6.

inland districts, and neither did Dutch distillers make an appearance. Orders spread out from the Dutch traders in La Rochelle itself, and were then serviced inland by local houses. The 1604 dispute over monopoly revolved around local names, even if orders by 'Flemish' merchants also entered into the story.

A few statistical measures of the growth of the international brandy trade are possible for the decisive decades on either side of 1700. The most extended measure is in fact for Irish imports of brandy. In 1665 imports amounted to 65,638 gallons, the equivalent of 1,200 La Rochelle barriques. They were already a subject of adverse comment as a novel form of luxury expenditure by 1670.[35] In 1683–6 average imports from France alone had risen to 88,352 gallons, and in the peace years at the end of the century imports, almost exclusively from France, grew from 82,917 gallons in 1698 to 271,796 gallons in 1701. Despite its whiskey industry, Scotland was an active importer of brandy, more from Bordeaux than from La Rochelle, after as before 1707.[36] The effect of low duties in Ireland and much higher ones in England can be seen in the presence of a distilling industry in England and a weak one in Ireland: total imports to England and Wales of spirits in 1701 were a mere 64,964 gallons. On the other hand, the excise figures for England and Wales suggest a fourteen-fold increase in output between 1684–6 and 1743–6. Between 1684–6 and 1699–1702 output doubled from 529,000 gallons to 1,118,000 gallons. By 1711–14 it had doubled again to 2,075,000 gallons.[37] In Ireland at the beginning of the 1720s output, according to excise figures, was below 200,000 gallons, and the illicit distilling that became notorious at a later date scarcely existed, judging from the absence of concern in the revenue commissioners' minutes.

Philippe Augier, who had spent a number of years early in the new century in Holland, regarded the prospect of war as likely to increase prices, and recalled the years of low prices that had ruled from the ending of a previous war until the late 1710s.[38] However, there is no direct link at that time between war and spirit consumption, especially as naval and army consumption appear at this time to have been, and to have

---

[35] National Archives, Dublin. Wyche documents, 114/41, 'Some reasons demonstrating the prejudice that the importation of brandy occasions to Ireland'. For statistics of Irish overseas trade in 1665, see PRO, Calendar of State Papers, Ireland, 1663–5, pp. 694–8; British Library Add. MS. 4759; PRO, Customs 15.

[36] See Scottish Record Office, General Register House, RH/59/5, RH/54/4; CS96/1575, CS96/3264, CS96/3309, CS96/3815.

[37] B. R. Mitchell and P. Deane, *Abstract of British historical statistics* (Cambridge, 1962), p. 254.

[38] In February 1727 he observed that 'en général pour notre commerce d'eau-de-vie je regarde le temps de guerre plus propre que celui de paix'. AAC, letter book 1726–7, 10 February 1727, to Voigt, Hamburg.

remained, low. Whether war of itself had played a part in increasing output or not, it had certainly coincided with an increase in output in England at a rate which was not equalled later, even in the notorious gin mania of the 1730s and 1740s. What the increased taxation in the 1750s did was merely cut back the production of gin: roughly half the shortfall in the production of gin was offset by a rise in legal rum and brandy imports (and there was also, from the 1770s, a growing contraband trade in the south-east of England). The measures made gin more expensive for the urban working class, but consumption above that level must have held its own or even risen. Scotland, with only half the population of Ireland, produced a larger quantity of spirits so the consequences were superficially far more disastrous: output in the short term, at least on the basis of tax returns, was virtually annihilated.

While Irish and English figures give some long-term guidance as to trends, study of French trends is more problematic, as very little is known in quantitative terms about the volume of brandy exports up to 1720. The individual high points in exports may well have been the 40,288 barriques (34,000 Bordeaux barriques converted into La Rochelle equivalents) exported from Bordeaux in 1701 or the 42,023 barriques from La Rochelle in 1720. The huge La Rochelle exports in 1720, promoted by the dramatic fall in the external value of the French currency in 1720, depended on an upsurge in Dutch purchases in particular. In Bordeaux brandy distillation virtually collapsed in the hinterland of the port, as the demand for wine firmed up in the 1720s. In Bordeaux port activity was kept going by erratic brandy surpluses from the hinterland. It never greatly expanded, and when it attempted to do so in the 1770s brandy supplies proved hard to get for the rectifying stills. In the 1780s, Bordeaux merchants and rectifiers alike were increasingly buying from the fringes of the greater Cognac district across the Garonne estuary, and from a very diffuse hinterland to the south (including brandy from afar carried on the Canal du Midi).

The transient character of Bordeaux's brandy exports can be seen in the fact that the thrust had spent itself by 1723, and the brandy export trade of Nantes did not preserve a momentum beyond the early 1730s, as its business became ever more closely linked to the new and relatively near Paris market. In the 1720s there was already direct purchasing on the fringes of Cognac, either inland at Aigre and Angouleme or on the coast – a trade whose prior existence was an essential condition, given the fact that merchants carried few stocks, for the spectacular elasticity of the region's exports in the exceptional conditions of 1720. The growth in depth of the Paris market can be crudely measured in the collapse of exports from Nantes after the 1730s and in a continued rise in the regularity of consignments from the northern fringe of the cognac region to Paris in the 1740s. The bad vintages in the terrible seasons of 1739–41 account for an abrupt slump in exports from the *généralité* of La Rochelle to external markets, i.e. the advent of price-insensitive Paris demand resulted in a fall in the volume of brandy exports on the Atlantic coast.

The pan-European story of brandy becomes more complex in the second and third quarters of the century. The reason is that while a growing market for spirits encouraged production – and Atlantic-coast France was the earliest beneficiary of this trend – it also encouraged both production of alternative spirit products within importing countries, and the emergence, to cater for the export market, of new producing centres of brandy in Languedoc and Spain, and, by the 1730s, even more importantly, the production of rum in the West Indies and New England. In the early 1720s prices were high, and the shift to cognac seemed to augur well for the export trade. Prices were on a new plateau compared with the past. While prices in the 1680s had varied from a high of 60 livres per barrique to a low of 35 livres, the higher marks were uncharacteristic. In 1700 they were as low as 25 livres and they were under 50 livres in 1707–8.[39] A later account in 1731 recalled that 'pendant plus de 40 ans jusqu'en 1698 on l'a vu de 24 à 27 livres les 27 veltes et depuis ce temps-là souvent de 30 à 36 jusqu'à 50'.[40] From the mid-1710s a firm trend emerged which raised prices above 50 livres per barrique. In 1717 they were above 60 livres, and from 1720 to 1728 the official valuations in the La Rochelle *généralité* never fell below 80 livres. A measure of the upward thrust in trade is offered by the Irish figures for brandy imports from France. They achieved a new peak of 397,984 gallons in the year ending 25 March 1724, itself in turn exceeded in the year ending 25 March 1730, when they reached 524,330 gallons. That was to be a level not exceeded until the Seven Years War. In 1724 Augier, who had just returned to trade after several years of misfortune, enthused to a fellow Huguenot in Amsterdam that 'la consommation de cette marchandise augmente de jour à autre partout où elle se transporte'.[41]

The Dutch demand for cognac was still rising in the 1720s and even the oversanguine Martell, though a newcomer and literally a learner, hoped in 1720 that he could break into the market. Moreover, the Dutch market was supported by an important Hamburg market. The Augier letter

[39] Huetz de Lemps, *Géographie du commerce*, pp. 239, 241n. The account book of an unidentified Saint-Jean d'Angély merchant gives prices ranging from 77 to 84 livres a *pièce*, or 26 to 28 livres a barrique, in 1659–60. ADCM, La Rochelle 4J 3630. The higher prices of the early 1680s may well be a plateau between two periods of lower prices.
[40] ACC, La Rochelle, no. 4245, 2 May 1731.
[41] AAC, letter book, 1724–6, 2 December 1724, to Balguerie, Amsterdam.

books which begin in 1717 show that despite the close connection of Hamburg with Bordeaux, Hamburg orders in Cognac were already well established in 1718. While Dutch orders in Bordeaux contracted from 15,474 barriques in 1718 to 6,466 barriques by 1723, they rose in La Rochelle. Leaving 1720 aside, they had climbed to 19,146 barriques in 1725, and fell below 13,572 in only one year before 1736. In contrast to the 1680s when wine was the main commodity sought, and brandy was – on the evidence of the Augier letter book – a mere adjunct to wine cargoes, entire shipments of brandy had now emerged.[42] In the 1730s a distinction must be made between small consignments to other markets and entire cargoes to the Dutch market. In July 1735 Régnier, writing in a year in which exports were the third highest since statistics for the La Rochelle *généralité* began in 1718, noted that 'j'ay eu cette année plus de ¾ des vaisseaux à mon adresse qui estoient frettés en entier d'eau-de-vie'.[43]

The appearance of a literature on spirits coincided with the rapid development of spirit drinking in the 1720s. From the outset increased spirit consumption involved controversy. There were two strands in the literature: one a recognition of the merits of spirits, the other alarm caused by the moral questions of increased public drunkenness in the wake of cheap, accessible and potent alcohol. This contrasted with earlier views of spirits which on the whole saw them as a benign product with a medicinal value. A French map of Ireland in the sixteenth century noted the use of spirits by the Irish to cope with stomach fluxes, 'à quoi ils résistent par le moyen de l'eau-de-vie, qui n'enflame pas tant que la notre, mais desèche davantage'.[44] P. Shaw's *The juice of the grape* appeared in 1724, indeed at a time when brandy drinking was becoming prominent in a rising general consumption of spirits in Britain. George Cheyne's *Essay on health and long life*, also of 1724, could see the good point of 'double-distilled spirits' just as another pamphlet in 1736 was entitled *Distilled spirituous liquors the bane of the nation*. The concern over spirit drinking emerges in Hogarth's famous engravings of Gin Lane and in much contemporary writing. The moral tone in such writing influenced M. D. George in her influential *London life in the eighteenth century*: it in turn coloured other historians. Even the economic historian T. S. Ashton speculated later that alcohol may have been responsible, by reducing the birth

---

[42] Huetz de Lemps observed, on the evidence of the admiralty records for Bordeaux even for the year 1699–1700, that 'dans la plupart des cas, il est vrai, l'eau-de-vie n'était qu'un élément de la cargaison, et généralement pas le principal'. Huetz de Lemps, *Géographie du commerce*, p. 216.
[43] HAC, Régnier letter book, 1735–6, July 1735, to Vantongeren.
[44] *Le royaume d'Irlande* (late sixteenth-century printed map, in private hands).

rate in the 1730s, for depressing English population growth.[45] However, any relationship between spirit drinking and population growth seems fanciful: rural whiskey drinking in Ireland a century later went hand in hand with rapid population growth and with concern about excessive spirit drinking. A moral dilemma, and the high tone of debate, made it possible for those with a vested interest in moral reformation to exaggerate the effects of what they condemned by attributing almost all the ills of society to it. Spirit drinking involved novel commercial publicity by the distillers and a concerted effort to push sales; spirits required more disposable income than beer (though hostile critics, who tended to see an increase in prices as a means of combating the evil, tended to stress how cheap spirits were); regular consumption in the towns, combined with fair-day purchases for cash in the countryside, created a novel problem of public and mass drunkenness.

If concern about addiction can be laid aside (and eighteenth-century writers had a class bias, as what concerned them was the novelty of public drunkenness and their perceptions of the consequences of the discretionary disposal of income in popular purchases for cash), the merits of alcohol were frequently recognised. Corporal Trim in Laurence Sterne's *Lives and opinions of Tristram Shandy* saw brandy as a source of health. The *London Medical Journal* (1786) had the same opinion and W. Sandford in 1799 wrote *A few practical remarks on the medicinal effect of wine spirits.*[46] The first Irish concern specifically addressed to spirits was voiced almost a generation later than in London in Henry's pamphlet of 1753. In France, where spirit drinking had a counterpart in Paris and in northern France to Hogarthian London, concern in public policy with the harmful effects of spirit drinking became evident from an early date, and was deep-rooted. The distillation of the lees or *marc de raisin*, for instance, had been prohibited by declaration on 24 January 1713 in the belief that 'l'usage des eaux de vie qui en proviendrait seroit prejudiciable au corps humain'. Even as late as 1784 its distillation was still permitted only in some provinces.[47] A decree of 13 February 1728 tightening up revenue administration in regions where *aides* (excise taxes) were levied was said, three years later, to have been prompted not simply by the

[45] T. S. Ashton, *An economic history of England: the eighteenth century* (London, 1972), p. 7.
[46] See R. Porter, 'The drinking man's disease: the prehistory of alcoholism in Georgian Britain', *British Journal of Addiction*, 60 (1985). I am indebted to a former colleague, the late Dr Peter Skrabanek, Department of Social Medicine, for having brought this paper to my attention. Edmund Burke's defence of the medical and social value of spirit drinking in his famous 1795 pamphlet, *Thoughts and detail on scarcity*, should also be borne in mind. The text is readily available in A. P. I. Samuels, *The early life, correspondence and writings of the Rt. Hon. Edmund Burke* (Cambridge, 1923), p. 291n.
[47] ACC, La Rochelle, no. 3666, 21 July 1784.

growth of the retail and wholesale trade but by opposition to 'l'excessive consommation d'eau de vie'.[48] While a literature on the evils of drink did not develop as it had in England, reflecting the economic importance of distilling, a technical literature did emerge. The dates of the prime works, one written in 1766 but published only in 1770, the other appearing in 1776, corresponded to a key period in the development of the product.[49]

Serious recognition of the merits of spirits required wide availability of well-made spirits. The standard Aunis brandy with its incredibly large dose of *seconde* (the increasingly undesirable flow of brandy of declining quality in the pass of liquid from the still) was not only weak but must have been distinctly unpalatable: the international sale of such a product is itself an oblique comment on how unappetising were the pioneer products in general. Adverse comment on spirits, however paranoid, thus had an element of truth and a writer like Henry, as late as 1753, seized with relish on an account of mass deaths from badly-made spirits. The repute of cognac lay in the early recognition by its makers of the need to control the amount of *seconde*, and of the merits of ageing. Spirits, however elementary the technology and equipment, were not simple to make. Great care was required in controlling the distilling process and close attention was also necessary to hygiene and to ullage from the casks: above all, if a perfect product was to be made, a radical separation of *coeur, première*, or *eau de vie bonne* (brandy of acceptable quality) from *seconde* had to be made. The latter challenge was the most fundamental one, and because it seems logical now, it is easy to underestimate the uncertainties at the time. The lesson was all the harder to learn because there were several intermediate solutions and because the economies necessary to keep costs down ran counter to adopting the most radical of them, the *coupe à la serpentine* (see glossary) which entirely eliminated *seconde* from the product. Indeed only the challenge of reducing transport costs for the Paris market moved producers towards a wider reliance on this radical solution. Most brandy, even for London, was brandy at an intermediate strength, thus containing some or much *seconde*, strengthened as necessary, after its making, by the addition of *esprit*.

Expansion of the brandy trade 1720–1750

A host of developments promoted the new patterns. While some of the factors were external to the classic brandy-producing country, i.e. occurred outside France, others were internal, notably the rise of French

---

[48] *Ibid.*, no. 3614.
[49] E. Munier, *Sur la manière de bruler ou de distiller les vins* (1770; new edition, Paris, 1981); Abbé Rozier, *De la fermentation des vins* (Lyons, 1776).

consumption. This was already sizeable at the start of the century. Some 3,500 barriques were sent from Bordeaux by coast to the north of France in 1700–1.[50] Paris was the key point in the growth of this traffic. As early as 1723 Savary had graphically described the Paris market in which, in catering for the growing demand, the sedate *marchands épiciers* were replaced by vigorous selling by street vendors:

qui chaque jour dès le matin, et lorsque les boutiquiers commencent à s'ouvrir, et que les manouvriers et artisans vont, et se mettent au travail, établissent ces petites boutiques aux coins des rues, ou parcourent la ville, en portant tout le cabaret, bouteilles, verres et mesures, dans une petite manne pendue à leur col. Ce sont les femmes qui sont sédentaires, et les hommes qui vont criant leur marchandise.[51]

In Savary's comment that brandy 'n'est guère d'usage que parmi le peuple et le soldat' there is a re-echo of contemporary Hogarthian London. More importantly, Paris was prepared to pay high prices when the regular Loire brandy supply faltered in a bad season and the high demand, caused by the absence of alternative spirits, pushed prices up in La Rochelle. In 1720 the existence of an inland market had already made possible soaring exports under the artificial conditions of a declining exchange rate and helped Dutchmen to outbid French buyers. Under more normal exchanges the growing inland market had the reverse effect. This was first seen in the abrupt fall in exports in 1726. The events of this year may have had serious consequences. It was in the wake of this crisis that London importers became restive with their Guernsey intermediaries and bypassed them. It was also the first year of a collapse in Dutch buying, and may have quickened their growing reliance on other sources and other spirit products. The pattern of a sharp fall in export trade in 1726, repeated in 1736–7, became progressively more marked. Pronounced in 1739–41, it was even more protracted over 1746–52, creating a new nadir in exports in 1748. Exports sank below that record low level once more in 1772 and yet again in 1778. Moreover, these dips were less a measure of economic crisis than of a soaring internal market.

The date of the peak in the Dutch trade – 1728 or 1729 – was significant. From 1729 to 1738 the official brandy price communicated by the chamber of commerce for the *balance du commerce* statistics for the La Rochelle *généralité* was never above 65 livres per barrique. A real malaise existed in 1731, when it was possible simultaneously for the merchants to point to low prices and for the farmers-general to point to a rising volume of business and to a much higher level of prices than in the more distant past.[52] In June and July 1732 prices fell to 42 and even 38

[50] Huetz de Lemps, *Géographie du commerce*, p. 217.
[51] Savary des Bruslons, *Dictionnaire universel du commerce*, vol. I, col. 1787.
[52] ACC, La Rochelle, no. 4245, 2 May 1731.

livres, the lowest for any point after the first decade of the century.[53] An indicator of the fundamental change in the market is that after the mid-1730s shipments to Holland, once the driving force in the French brandy trade, began to decline rapidly everywhere on the west coast. This points to a crucial development. The Dutch were now engaged in a twin operation of turning to new and cheaper regions, and consuming more home-produced spirits made from grain and sugar derivatives.[54] Régnier's business at Charente, largely one with Holland, illustrates the process very well. The second half of the year 1735 foreshadowed the onset of real crisis: brandy prices rose from 44 livres in July to 63 and 64 livres by the end of the year. Prospects of a poor vintage in Nantes, Blois and Orleans led to large commissions from Paris to Cognac and Saint-Jean d'Angély as early as July.[55] Ships from both Amsterdam and Rotterdam were already conspicuously absent from the Charente in July.[56] As always, when a price rise occurred or, as in mid-1735, was simply anticipated, merchants responded either by sending commissions to other markets as the Dutch invariably did, or in the case of those determined to stay in the market, by spreading their commissions over a larger number of houses. Thus as early as July Régnier gained both by a first commission from Rasteau who was buying for the Dutch market and from enquiries from an established London importer, Michael Hatton. Régnier compensated in part for his loss of business in the Dutch market by a rise in his business with less price-sensitive customers in England.

Leaving out the quantities shipped in 1720 when an artificially low French foreign exchange sent foreign purchases soaring, shipments to Holland peaked in 1728 when 19,870 barriques were consigned there from the La Rochelle *généralité*. If the quantities for the Nord (Hamburg, the Baltic and Russia) (3,691 barriques) are added to the consignments to Holland the two markets would have accounted for 83 per cent of total shipments of 28,845 barriques in that year. This was to prove the peacetime peak for shipments to Holland; and 1735 which excited Régnier in Charente was the last peacetime year of good business, just as 1744 after the bumper vintage of 1743 was the last good wartime one.[57]

In Bordeaux post-1713 shipments to Holland peaked at 8,011 bar-

[53] *Ibid.*, nos. 4246, 4247, 4248.
[54] On sugar derivatives, see John J. McCusker, 'Distilling and its implications'.
[55] HAC, Régnier letter book 1735–6, 26 July 1735, to Michael Hatton.
[56] *Ibid.*, 7 July 1735, to George Boyd, Bordeaux.
[57] The high shipments to Holland in 1744, second to those of 1720, however, have to be interpreted in the context of a total absence of shipments to England in that year. The figure of 20,771 barriques in all probability contains a sizeable quantity intended for re-export to Britain. In the case of La Rochelle, shipments to Holland for the entire period 1718–36 amounted to 267,525 barriques and to the Hansa towns 86,501 out of total shipments of 489,929 barriques, average 25,827 barriques (ADC, Angouleme, 5C6).

riques in 1729, and then collapsed even more rapidly than in Cognac. In peacetime in the late 1740s and in the first half of the 1750s Dutch orders from the La Rochelle *généralité* scarcely exceeded 4,000 barriques in the best years, and in the 1770s they were below 1,000 barriques a year. In Bordeaux the trend was no different, and the orders of magnitude of shipments about the same as in La Rochelle. In Nantes, which in the 1720s was as important to the Dutch brandy buyers as Bordeaux, buying virtually ceased altogether.

A sign of changing times was the fact that the initially smaller market in the north of Europe, Hamburg in particular, was more stable. Though Germans did not settle as buyers in Cognac, active shippers with German names can be traced through the minutes of the notary Cherpantier as residing in Tonnay-Charente in the 1740s and 1750s. The Englishman John Baker, moving from La Rochelle to Cognac around 1730, worked up both the Isle of Man business and custom with Hamburg, forming a partnership with Pierre Bryan. While peacetime shipments from Bordeaux to the north were depressed after 1731, exports from La Rochelle *généralité* grew up to 1737 when a total of 8,087 barriques was dispatched. Ignoring wartime peaks (as reflecting the peculiar circumstances of neutral Hamburg), they were still at the same level in the 1750s and significantly exceeded it only in 1765 and 1766. Moreover, northern buyers were abandoning the Charente, as they purchased in Bordeaux in both years. Indeed they were already going further afield, probably to the Mediterranean, as shipments through the Sound were too large to have been drawn solely from La Rochelle and Bordeaux. In 1750 4,445 barriques from France passed through the Sound and 15,484 barriques in 1765.[58] As only part of the quantities shipped for the Nord, Sweden and Denmark took this route, the fact that the figures for the Sound exceeded shipments from La Rochelle and Bordeaux both in 1750 and in 1765 underlines the fact that the northerners were already buying in the Mediterranean world. At a later date – the first half of 1783 – no less than 7,135 barriques were shipped at Sète for Hamburg alone.[59] In 1789 exports from Sète at 24,776 barriques were second only to the Charente's.

By the 1730s the Dutch interest in other sources of supply and in other products began to bite in earnest. The Dutch addiction to spirits and their growing market was as easily satisfied by increased grain spirits (a trend which Cognac merchants recognised in the 1720s) or spirits likewise distilled in Holland, but made from sugar syrup – the residue of the

[58] The quantities were down to 9,448 barriques in 1775.
[59] ACC, La Rochelle, no. 3663, 13 February 1784.

molasses used in the expanding sugar industry of both Holland and Bordeaux.[60] Moreover, the rise of domestic production in Holland was paralleled in Ireland and in England.[61] Domestic production in all these countries, imports from new centres of supply, and rum – not a new product in the Antilles, but virtually so in Europe – all enjoyed the stimulus of the novel demand for spirits. English imports of brandy had risen sharply to 1,145 tons (4,580 barriques) in 1723, and to a significant peak of 4,325 tons (17,300 barriques) in 1733. This is also borne out in the fact that the La Rochelle figure of 8,438 barriques exported to *Angleterre* (the French designation for the British Isles) in 1731 was the last high recording for over two decades to come. In 1733 rum imports to England and Wales reached a level which was not to be exceeded until 1748. Thus the momentum evident in the international trade in wine brandy in the 1720s lost pace from the beginning of the 1730s.

Spirit production in England and Ireland

Retained imports of rum in England and Wales, negligible in the first two decades of the century, attained a level of half a million gallons for the first time in England in 1733. In Ireland direct importation of rum, first permitted in 1731, was followed by expansion, and, reflecting the modest scale of the indigenous spirit industry, the level of imports was not much below that to England. The year 1733 was the peak year for brandy imports to England (and the level was not to be reached again until the 1780s); it was also for a decade and a half a peak for rum. Perversely, imports of rum and brandy, in boosting the growing taste for spirits, promoted a powerful expansion in domestic distillation from cheap domestic grain in the 1730s and 1740s. The decisive factor was the rise in gin production, in England somewhat more belatedly than in Holland, which kept rum as well as other spirit imports at bay. In Ireland, too, domestic whiskey output rose. In Holland syrup direct from the sugar islands or reshipped from Bordeaux, where its conversion into rum was prohibited, was an added ingredient of spirit output. The striking feature of the British spirit consumption pattern is that, in contrast to Ireland, imports of spirits (brandy and rum combined) fell far short of domestic consumption. In the 1730s, for instance, imports accounted for less than 20 per cent of consumption, and in the 1740s, when domestic output soared, the proportion was even less. From the mid-1730s to the mid-1750s spirit

---

[60] McCusker, 'Distilling and its implications', p. 15.
[61] In England output peaked at the huge total of 8.2 million gallons in 1743. In Ireland output grew steadily from the modest figures of the early decades of the eighteenth century to a peak for the pre-1760 period in 1752 of 623,000 gallons.

imports to England and Wales were stable in absolute amounts: the main change in imports was that rum retained the ground it had gained from brandy in the 1730s.

In Ireland, a country with an insufficient cereal supply, the situation was entirely different. Before 1731 imports of spirits consisted almost exclusively of French brandy, at twice the level of domestic spirit production. Moreover much of the output of Irish spirits, as of the country's execrable beer, had depended on oats: in the 1730s rising imports of barley malt as much as a rise in output pointed to the early stages of modernisation in the archaic beverage industries. In contrast to England, where the rise in rum imports halted in the 1730s and 1740s, imports did not lose their buoyancy in Ireland, and accounted for 30 to 50 per cent of total Irish spirit consumption. From the late 1730s rum imports consistently exceeded brandy imports until the disruption of the rum market by war in the late 1750s: that combined with the phenomenal rise in the taste for spirits in the 1760s for a time restored the fortunes of brandy. At best as a result of some remarkably benign harvests within the three four-year periods ending in March 1734, 1746 and 1750, home distillation accounted for 39.2 per cent, 50.2 per cent and 46.3 per cent respectively of the total spirit market. Given Ireland's high import dependence on spirits, this was in itself quite remarkable, and underlines how even in Ireland domestic spirit production was expanding. The change in whiskey production had already been sensed by Samuel Madden in 1738 when he declared that 'our distillers make excellent spirits, from our own grain of aqua vitae, which are as palatable and vastly cheaper, and wholesomer, and do also furnish us with an usquebaugh, which no nation can come up to'.[62] By 1753 another writer, Henry, alarmed by the spread in the consumption of whiskey, noted the impact of domestic production on French brandy itself.[63]

In the past, according to Henry, whiskey or *usquebagh* had been used 'by the great in their feasts'. That rather special outlet apart, there was only an inferior spirit, *balcaan*, 'a fiery spirit made from black oats' for the lower orders. The term 'bulcaan or worse sort of aqua vitae' was noted by Dunton in 1698 when he was entertained by the chieftain O'Flaghertie in Connaught.[64] Nor, noted Henry, was the use of spirits general: 'they were mostly confined to the coast of the Shannon, Lough Erne, the Bog of Allen',[65] a somewhat quaint way of specifying the northern half of Ireland. In 1754 Dublin was the furthest south of the eight revenue dis-

---

[62] S. Madden, *Reflections and resolutions proper for the gentlemen of Ireland* (Dublin, 1738).
[63] W. Henry, *An earnest address to the people of Ireland against the drinking of spirituous liquors* (Dublin, 1753), p. 31.
[64] Dunton in E. MacLysaght, *Irish life in the seventeenth century* (2nd edn, Cork, 1950), pp. 329–30, 337–8.   [65] Henry, *An earnest address to the people of Ireland*, p. 2.

tricts making the largest revenue return in whiskey.[66] To the north whiskey drinking was already entrenched. Hugh Faulkner, on the completion of the bleach works at Wellbrook in Co. Tyrone in the 1760s entertained all his men with whiskey, and he himself wrote an exuberant and flattering account of the powers of whiskey.[67] By way of contrast, while references to whiskey were common in the Gaelic folk poetry of the north, there is little mention of it in the abundant references to alcoholic beverages in the poetry of Munster. In the north, whiskey consumption and the economic boom of the early 1750s had gone hand in hand: 'the price of labour and spinning, is within these three years, since the abounding of spirituous liquours, risen more than a third in the north'.[68] In a letter of 1772 a land agent from Strabane noted that as crops were good, whiskey inroads on grain supply would not harm food supplies: in consequence 'this year of plenty as I hope I may call it, distilling might not hurt us, for the people will have spirits at any rate . . . that crop [barley] being remarkably good'.[69] Of course there was also whiskey which did not pay duty, either distilled in comfortable homes for family consumption (and distillation for private consumption was not prohibited until 1779) or illegally made for sale. However, such abuse was not a serious preoccupation in the early decades of the century: in the revenue inspection conducted by Edward Thompson in 1733 a revenue preoccupation with either the use or abuse of spirits was absent.[70] In 1753 the very novelty of whiskey-induced drunkenness on fair and market days was one of the things which upset Henry.[71]

In the years 1756–67, however, the upward trend in distillation in Ireland was seriously disrupted. Bad harvests in 1755 and 1756 and a novel prohibition of distillation reduced supplies well into 1758. In 1756 these factors had been reflected in a novel demand for brandy satisfied first through neutral Ostend, and when Ostend lost its neutrality through Rotterdam. Rum imports, which could have made good the shortfall, fell during the Seven Years War, and deficiencies in rum supply, particularly in the years ending March 1760 and 1761, reinforced the switch to brandy. The result was a significant rise in brandy imports, a change helped by the exceptionally good vintages and favourable prices of the late

[66] *Journals of the House of Commons (Ireland)*, vol. VI, app. xxvi.
[67] Faulkner papers in the possession of Mrs Amy Monahan, Castletown, Co. Carlow.
[68] Henry, *An earnest address*, p. 20.
[69] Public Record Office of Northern Ireland, Abercorn papers, agents' letters 1772 (no. 66), James Hamilton, Strabane, 15 November 1772.
[70] National Archives, Dublin, 'A registry of reports by the Honorable E. Thompson Esq. Anno 1733'.
[71] Henry was obsessed with spirit-induced addiction, and wrote at least four pamphlets on the subject in the 1750s. E. Malcolm, *'Ireland sober, Ireland free': drink and temperance in nineteenth-century Ireland* (Dublin, 1986), p. 42.

1750s and early 1760s. After bad harvests in 1765 and 1766 domestic distillation was again prohibited, and shortage combined with soaring demand in years when a rising taste for spirits reinforced the rise in brandy imports. Poor harvests in 1769 and 1770 perpetuated the shortage in spirit supply. The domestic component of consumption fell to 21.5 per cent in the four years ending March 1767 and to 22.2 per cent in the four-year period ending March 1771. Over the four years ending March 1767 imports of French brandy were once more to recreate the pre-1731 pattern of imported brandy exceeding domestic output. In the three individual years ending March 1761–2, 1764–5 and 1766–7 the peak brandy imports of the century occurred: 733,175 gallons, 757,105 gallons and 770,319 gallons respectively. In the first of these years the figures included large imports of Spanish brandy; in the other two years the imports were almost exclusively French. The most sustained boom in brandy imports in the eighteenth century took place in the five years ending March 1768. The import trend at large spent itself in the four years ending March 1771: while brandy imports were below the level of the preceding four years, rum imports peaked, and overall spirit imports were the largest of the century. Rum imports peaked in 1770–1, and only thereafter began to fall.

After 1771 domestic production, aided by rapidly expanding cereal cultivation, began to overhaul imports. The previous peak in home distillation in the four years ending March 1747 was well and truly exceeded in a comparable period ending in March 1783. The change was a function of the growth of agriculture, especially of barley production. A barley surplus was essential for the rise both in whiskey distilling and in beer brewing of a standard which matched the quality of imports from London. Ireland was now entering the era of its famous whiskey distilleries and of its great porter breweries.[72] Significantly the rising fortunes of the whiskey industry preceded revival of the brewing industry whose prosperous years began in the 1780s and 1790s. In the 1760s and 1770s consumers were said to prefer rum. By the 1790s the preference for whiskey as opposed to other spirits was quite well established. Even in the south of Ireland a successful whiskey maker like Hewitt in Cork catered to quite a sophisticated and discerning clientele.[73] In Scotland a comparable experience can be seen in the rapid spread, for the first time, of whisky at the end of the century to and through the Lowlands.[74] Illicit distillation in Ireland would not greatly alter the picture. From the 1780s allowance for it as a major activity in its own right would serve to reinforce the trend of home products replacing imported ones.

[72] See L. M. Cullen, 'Comparative aspects of Irish diet 1550–1850', in Hans J. Teuteberg, *European food history* (Leicester, 1992), pp. 47–8.
[73] Cork Archives Council, Cork, Hewitt letter books.
[74] The *Old statistical account of Scotland*, written in the 1790s, has many graphic illustrations.

Ireland and England as a motive force of the spirit trade

An illuminating comment on the loose structure of the early trade was the way in which a single group of merchants from the tiny island of Guernsey for a time acquired the leading role in the new currents of trade. This first grew out of their privateering activity in the long wars of 1689–97 and 1702–13: success in taking prizes at sea went hand in hand with a more conventional though miscellaneous trade even in wartime. Apart from the Irish and the Scots, who both had their own quite distinct commercial interests catering for their home markets, the Guernseymen were the main buyers from the British Isles in Bordeaux.[75] With peace in prospect, exports from Bordeaux to *Angleterre* were a high 16,850 barriques in 1712–13. The speculative Guernseymen, well aware from their success in acquiring prize brandy of the qualities of cognac, quickly moved from Bordeaux to both Nantes and La Rochelle, as trade channels became more orthodox and stable.[76] The trade figures of both Bordeaux and La Rochelle, the only two near complete runs for this early period, illustrate the change in the trade from the 1710s onwards.

Table 1. *Exports from the* généralités *of* La Rochelle *and Bordeaux to* Angleterre *(in barriques)*

Date	La Rochelle	Bordeaux
1717		3,516
1718	3,841	5,477
1719		3,425
1720	9,842	4,862
1721	7,105	3,524
1722	7,204	n.a.
1723	8,557	2,639
1724	7,903	4,025
1725	7,876	n.a.
1726	5,066	n.a.
1727	3,707	n.a.
1728	4,003	1,588
1729	6,902	3,098
1730	6,894	4,050
1731	8,438	2,977

[75] Huetz de Lemps, *Géographie du commerce*, p. 235.
[76] Exports from Bordeaux to *Angleterre* were only 5,340 ht (2,373 barriques) in 1714–15, and even in the very favourable circumstances of 1717–22 ran at no more than between 3,500 and 5,400 barriques.

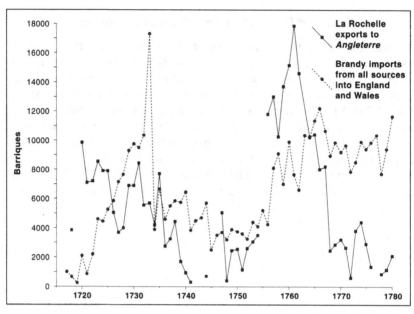

Figure 1 La Rochelle brandy exports to *Angleterre* and England/Wales brandy imports from all sources, 1717–1780. The figures for *Angleterre* include shipments to Flanders in 1756–7 and 1779–80, and to Holland in 1758–62, largely for entrepot for the British Isles. *Angleterre* as a destination in French customs entries includes shipments to Ireland, Scotland and Guernsey as well as to England and Wales. The large excess of shipments to *Angleterre* over imports into England and Wales in the early 1720s points to the very varied activity of the Guernsey houses in cognac at that time which is only incompletely recorded in returns for England and Wales.

The Guernseymen were a new business interest, relying on the backing of the handful of islanders who in wartime had successfully penetrated the magic circle of big business in London and acquired in the short term a large stake in both wine and brandy which it was difficult to hold on to in peacetime. They were vulnerable in the stable conditions of peacetime as, with demand remaining strong, brandy buyers were tempted to transform themselves into importers on their own account. The boom in English demand was largely a post-1722 phenomenon: import figures reveal a sharp upturn from 1723. The result was that the Guernsey interest, which had already pioneered direct buying in Cognac for the British market in the mid-1710s, was undermined in and after 1727 by the very London brandy houses they had supplied in the past. The Martell business virtually folded up for more than a decade, and London was supplied

Table 2. *Exports from the*
généralités of La Rochelle,
Nantes and Bordeaux to
Angleterre *1728 (in barriques)*

La Rochelle	4,003
Nantes	3,341
Bordeaux	1,558

on London account by the long-established Augier houses and a few lesser or transient houses. The conversion of the recent pattern of an excess of La Rochelle exports to *Angleterre* over the inspector-general's figures in London for imports to England and Wales into a shortfall is further testimony to the eclipse of the Guernsey interest. In 1728 import figures (the equivalent of 7,656 barriques) were not far short of the combined exports of Nantes, Bordeaux and La Rochelle for *Angleterre* despite the fact that Nantes had virtually no dealings with England, and Bordeaux had only a limited trade with London.

In the case of Nantes and Bordeaux, *Angleterre* meant markets other than England itself. Nantes had a large Irish market, sustained by rising Irish exports of beef and even wool. Bordeaux's brandy exports to *Angleterre* were now primarily directed to Ireland and Scotland as well as to the Isle of Man. The La Rochelle *généralité*, with its once large Irish trade withered and with only one house holding an interest in the Isle of Man (Baker, which failed to make a breakthrough into the London trade), had become the real measure of the effective English market.[77] The recovery in the exports of the La Rochelle *généralité* in and after 1728 corresponds to the establishment of the new nexus.

---

[77] Figures for shipments from Bordeaux to *Angleterre* were at first larger than the corresponding figures in London-compiled statistics for brandy imports from all parts to England and Wales alone: the import data reached 334 tons (1,336 barriques) in 1714 and, apart from 1720, did not rise before 1723. In 1723 they reached a novel 1,145 tons (4,580 barriques) (sources: for France, *balance du commerce* data in ADG, Bordeaux, 4268–71, 4385–90 and ACC, La Rochelle, cartons 21 and 27; for Bordeaux 1717–20, Huetz de Lemps, *Géographie du commerce*, p. 236; for England and Wales, E. B. Schumpeter, *English overseas trade statistics 1697–1808* (Oxford, 1960)). If La Rochelle's growing exports, largely London-directed, are seen as the basis of exports to England and Wales, the correspondence is closer. Ireland, with an active trade with Nantes and Bordeaux, and Scotland (like Ireland comprehended in the rubric *Angleterre*) with a more active traffic in Bordeaux wine than England, would have relied primarily on Bordeaux. The sharp decline after 1713 in La Rochelle's Irish community, and the growth of a large Irish colony in Bordeaux and the continued presence of some Scots there, would underline the direction of some of Bordeaux's surviving brandy exports.

The changes – a rise in English imports and the emergence of an effective London importing, as opposed to final buying, interest – corresponded to a revolution in English tastes for spirits. It might seem to have been an augury of a bright future for spirit imports. What happened was, with a short time lag, quite different. Home spirit production, already highly elastic on the evidence of revenue data from the 1680s onwards, and helped by cheap grain in the 1730s and 1740s, soared. The contrast between English and Irish patterns is instructive. Essentially it reflected differences in the taxation of imports. English duties were high and favoured domestic production. Irish duties were low, and thus, although Irish whiskey was a longstanding and familiar product, the growing taste for spirits was satisfied from imports, first of brandy and then of both brandy and rum, rather than from domestic output, more particularly in the southern half of Ireland. The pattern in Ireland was decisively reversed only in the 1780s. With high duties, English purchases were small and concentrated on quality; lower duties in Ireland resulted in larger absolute purchases but, in the main, of ordinary brandy. When London wholesalers supplanted their Guernsey suppliers and ordered direct from Cognac, it made more sense to ship regularly in small quantities to Dunkirk (but declared on the customs forms for *Angleterre*, and hence recorded for the final destination in the trade statistics), rather than to arrange large and infrequent direct shipments from Charente. From Dunkirk it was then ferried to London as occasion demanded. Full-cargo overseas shipments of brandy from the Atlantic coast were either for Holland or in Nantes for Ireland.

The buying of spirits outside La Rochelle or, beyond Europe, in the West Indies, which supplemented and at times probably exceeded purchases in La Rochelle in the short-lived upsurge of English demand for spirits in the late 1720s and 1730, was temporary. It had been prompted by a contraction of uncommon severity in exports in 1726–7 as Parisian buyers invaded La Rochelle's hinterland. It tailed off once the boom in spirit imports ended in the mid-1730s in the wake of the expansion in domestic output. From that time on, La Rochelle exports and English imports in peacetime corresponded more closely. They point at one and the same time to the general collapse of broad-based English spirit buying abroad, and to its reduction to a single but strong core of demand in London. Rich trade though it was, the brandy trade from La Rochelle was too small to provide a livelihood for more than one or two Cognac houses. The English statistics of brandy imports and La Rochelle figures of exports are not very far apart over most of the period from the mid-1730s to the mid-1750s, a correspondence which hints at the fact that the import trade in spirits had reduced itself to little more than the carriage of one type of brandy – cognac – to a single market – London.

While the English market for spirits contracted from the mid-1730s, the Irish and Isle of Man markets, certainly if combined, were expanding. Ireland was supplied especially through Nantes. Irish imports peaked at 538,316 gallons or a huge 10,000 barriques in 1729–30 and were halved or more than halved in the 1730s. A significant trade from Nantes survived up to the late 1730s. In 1738 eighteen vessels declared for Ireland, and no less than thirty-nine Irish vessels declared for other, largely fictitious, destinations.[78] These figures, twice the level of legal exports to Ireland at the time, work out at an average of almost 100 barriques per vessel, which means in effect that brandy was either the sole or major item in most cargoes. The Isle of Man was supplied fitfully from Nantes, more permanently from Bordeaux (a member of the Irish house of Black in Bordeaux became a partner in a key house in the island), and very modestly through Cognac where the house of Baker played a role. Direct business, legal and illegal alike, was, however, hard to maintain, because the Isle of Man increasingly replaced France as the immediate source of supply, and drew its supplies from increasingly varied continental bases reaching beyond Bordeaux, a constant resort of the Irish brandy interest even as early as the 1750s, into Spain and Languedoc. Smugglers like the O'Connells of the Iveragh peninsula or the O'Sullivans and others of Bantry, supplying remote markets like Kerry and west Cork from France, were still in business in the early and mid-1750s, but the market at large was now supplied from the Isle of Man. The decline in Bordeaux's trade in low-grade brandy was contained, and the port continued to do a smart traffic with the Isle of Man especially in peace years: exports to *Angleterre* ran in the 2,000 to 4,000 barriques range into the mid-1750s, a figure not much different from La Rochelle's exports to the same technical global destination of *Angleterre* (though primarily of course merely to London).

Ireland offered a sharp contrast to England where domestic production successfully excluded brandy imports and reduced the trade in effect to the high-cost and high-quality London demand, supplemented by a small but sophisticated custom from Bristol, Leeds and Newcastle. Ireland's dependence on imports produced a dramatic distortion in the comparison of statistics in the 1750s and the 1760s. French exports soared, a trend which has to be measured in wartime from shipments briefly to the Austrian Lowlands (modern Belgium), thereafter to Holland (exports to Holland, which in the preceding decade had become negligible, immediately jumped as an entrepot base for Ireland). War meant, in the interest of French exports, departure from the established French revenue practice of recording the final destination of goods, a departure all the more inevitable as false invoices conveying neutral ownership of goods were

---

[78] Archives départementales de la Loire Atlantique, Nantes, Amirauté, B4694¹.

equally tolerated. At its peak in 1761 the exports from La Rochelle to 'Holland' were 17,800 barriques; English imports of brandy were then 1,910 tons (or 7,640 barriques) from all sources in a period of rising English imports. The balance of 10,000 barriques would crudely approximate to Irish imports. This figure would amount to 540,000 gallons of brandy, and is thus close enough to the Irish customs returns for imports. As England imported brandy from locations other than La Rochelle, the proportion of the actual discrepancy between the two sets of figures absorbed by the Irish trade was even larger. In the four years ending March 1763 imports of brandy from all sources, according to Irish statistics, averaged 500,000 gallons, and from then up to and including the year ending March 1768 they were to run at a level just above or below 700,000 gallons (approximately 15,000 barriques). Given the modest Irish business with La Rochelle in the past, the fact that Irish buyers congregated there and in its hinterland in 1761 reflected the dominant place that Cognac now held in the export brandy trade on the Atlantic coast.

This, though certainly not the first boom in Irish brandy imports, was the first one in La Rochelle business for Ireland. It was in part made possible by the coincidence of great French vintages, a temporary halt in Irish distillation and a concurrent wartime shortfall in rum. The interrelated circumstances of relatively firm prices, a spirit shortage in Ireland and abundant vintages in France resulted in a Dublin upsurge in imports. The years 1757–65 equalled the legendary sequence from 1727 to 1735 in duration, and exceeded those years in both volume and price. More extraordinarily, despite increased encroachment by Paris demand and soaring prices, export buying remained high in 1766 and 1767, mainly because of the Irish market where a whiskey shortage and distilling restrictions recurred. This would have been a rare case of Irish customers outbidding London and Paris customers, a phenomenon which shows how with the change in tastes in Ireland, demand had become for the first time much more inelastic.

English imports of spirits at large were also at high and near-record levels between 1763 and 1767, though 1766 itself was a crisis year for cognac importers in London. The collapse of La Rochelle exports in 1768 simply reflected the disappearance of the Irish market: the continuing La Rochelle exports to England remained close to the levels of the period preceding the disruptive markets of the late 1750s and 1760s: or put in simpler language the stable London demand remained substantially unchanged. The highest La Rochelle export for *Angleterre* of the years 1749–54 was 3,499 barriques in 1754; the 2,470 barriques exported in 1768 compared with 4,404 barriques in 1774, the highest of the period 1768–76. Given some market in the Isle of Man in the 1750s and early 1760s, the figures of the late 1760s and 1770s relating to years

in which that business no longer existed, imply in all probability a rise in
the effective London market. This is consistent with the general pattern
in England in which distilling remained at a reduced level, and brandy
and rum imports held up well. With a belated revolution in barley
growing there, Ireland continued to afford contrasts with England: spirit
output rose in the 1760s and 1770s. Inevitably imports fell, first of
brandy, and after 1770–1 even of rum.

In spite of the waning of the Irish market, England's pattern fits into the
context of an international trade in spirits growing strongly in the late
1770s and still more markedly in the 1780s. With good vintages, though
lower prices, demand was very strong even in Cognac from 1778 to the
end of 1780. Another sign of change was that the Dutch had become very
large buyers again in 1778–80, although that was a temporary phenomenon and may have represented a disruption in supplies of syrup. The
higher British taxes from the 1750s were also reflected in a growth in
smuggling: official figures underestimated consumption to a greater
extent than in the past because brandy smuggling had grown to new
heights. The Dunkirk and Boulogne figures from the 1770s are startlingly
high: Dunkirk exports in 1772 were estimated at 6,020 pipes (18,060 barriques); in 1778 the port was said to receive 18,518 barriques of brandy
each year; in April 1782 the merchants of Boulogne claimed that their
stocks were 7,518 barriques of brandy and gin, and in 1789 exports from
both ports amounted to the equivalent of 26,897 barriques of spirits.[79]

Table 3. *Imports of brandy and
gin to England and Wales (in
barriques)*

1783	6,868
1784	9,928
1785	3,172
1786	12,232
1787	27,636
1788	21,468
1789	28,644
1790	28,208

[79] AAE, CPA, 499, f. 238, Memoir by the Chevalier Ruthledge of Dunkirk, 4 April 1772, to
d'Aiguillon; CPA, 514, ff. 274–5, Considérations sur la ville et le port de Dunkerque 1776;
CPA, 536, ff. 284–5, 2 April 1782; AN, Paris, F12 1666. There are lists of the English mer-
chants in Dunkirk in 1773 in AAE, CPA, 503, ff. 11–12, 14. There are some details on
Johnston, head of one of the major houses in AAE, CPA, 530, ff. 293–5, Hamilton to de
Rayneval, 22 September 1778. On the Johnston house, see also L. M. Cullen, 'Smuggling
and the Ayrshire economic boom of the 1760s and 1770s', *Ayrshire Archaeological and
Natural History Society*, Ayrshire monographs, 14 (September 1994), pp. 38–9.

The fact that Dunkirk and Boulogne exports were about as large as the total legal imports is a pointer to the underlying force of changing tastes and to the circumstances that made the smuggling trade in spirits probably for the first time a serious force to be reckoned with in England. Martell's own exports in 1789, virtually all for England and for a legal market, were a huge 16,165 barriques. The actual exports to *Angleterre* from Tonnay-Charente were 27,584 barriques, or, combined with Rochefort's trade (for exports to Ireland) 29,805 barriques.[80] Other Cognac houses would have helped to bridge the gap between Martell's shipments (16,165 barriques) and total shipments in the French statistics, mainly to England and Wales (27,584 barriques): Hennessy and Turner, now launching their new partnership, provided some 1,500 barriques; Delamain and several other houses would also have provided their share. The gap between shipments from Tonnay-Charente to England and Wales (27,584 barriques to *Angleterre*, less a small but unknown component to Ireland) and total imports, as recorded at the English end, for England and Wales (28,644 barrels) would have come from several sources: a little from the great reservoir of spirits in Dunkirk (though the smugglers would of course have taken most of that), the balance from Languedoc, Spain or Holland. The total from such sources would not have been large in 1789, but, given a lower level of activity in cognac for London in 1790, sustained imports in that year point to a rise in dealings with the Mediterranean, whether Languedoc or Spain. Dunkirk, as the warehouse for speculative and inferior goods, also increased its role in an ever tighter market. In 1789 exports from Dunkirk and Boulogne to *Angleterre* had depended heavily on gin, which accounted for 18,835 barriques out of a total of 26,897 barriques of spirits, and which would have been largely imported.[81] Dunkirk's role can be seen also in coastal shipments to free ports which are recorded in the French statistics of 1789. Some 7,251 barriques, mainly from Charente and from Sète, were recorded. The importance of Charente is significant, and underlines Dunkirk's notoriety in mixing spirits which were then passed under the name of cognac.

As trade grew the contrast between the best brandy and more mediocre brandies sharpened. The houses in the Cognac market, shipping direct to London in the 1780s, took pains to distinguish their product from others

---

[80] These figures differ from those in chapter 2, page 48 which are for all destinations and for the *généralité* as a whole which includes other revenue 'creeks' as well as Tonnay-Charente and Rochefort.

[81] In Boulogne the provenance of spirits is clearly distinguished; in Dunkirk, a free port, it is not. The total is based on the assumption that all Dunkirk's gin, like Boulogne's, was foreign.

by assurances that there was no mixing. contrasting with Cognac, Loire ('Nantz brandy') and Armagnac brandy as the best products, both Languedoc and Spanish brandies found their place in the trade at the lower end of the market. The poor quality of Spanish brandy, like that of Bordeaux, meant that it had difficulty in securing a firm toehold in the trade, and its place, like that of Bordeaux, was most secure in the smuggling trade, which supplied the bottom of the market. Thus, in the regular Irish import trade, Spanish brandy entered in a big way only in 1760–62, when a shortfall of rum made spirit supply tight, and again in 1770–1 and 1771–2 when French exports dried up because of calls from the Paris market. Virtually none was imported in other years, even in years of relative shortage. The main regular outlet for Spanish brandy seems to have been Dunkirk with a trade in spirits in the 1780s catering for the bottom end of an expanding market, often sold with the help of a dubious concealment of origin. Though a marginal product, a combination of rising demand for spirits and poorer vintages in France boosted foreign custom for it. The chamber of commerce of Picardy in 1787 claimed that the cellars of Dunkirk, Saint-Omer, Calais and Boulogne were full, and that supplies were expected in Saint-Valerie-sur-Somme.[82] The chamber thought that little would be available for export. With much greater imbalance in 1789–90 references to Spanish supply multiplied in the correspondence of the Hennessy house. A somewhat later report quantified the imports to Dunkirk from Catalonia for England at 1,200 *pièces* (3,600 *barriques*).[83]

Trends in brandy distilling and trade

The fluctuating Irish brandy market was largely a thing of the past by the early 1770s. It recovered fleetingly only in a grain crisis in the early 1780s and in another round of restrictions on distilling: in the two years ending March 1784 and 1785, high, though not record, imports of French brandy occurred. Other markets had been lost by the French even earlier. In the 1730s La Rochelle lost for all practical purposes its Dutch custom. After the early 1730s, it also lost the miscellaneous buying in the *généralité* by the Guernseymen who had played with so many ways of selling – and buying – brandy. What Cognac – Cognac district itself, not the La Rochelle *généralité* at large, it should be stressed – succeeded in holding was the London demand for cognac. This was a quality demand, largely

[82] AAE, CPA, 559, ff. 55–60, 'Précis sur les représentations de la chambre de commerce de Picardie', 17 January 1787.
[83] AN, Paris, F¹² 1646–50, a report regarding the re-establishment of free ports, 9 Thermidor, an 9.

confined to Cognac itself, and was a relatively limited trade in volume. It was of course of incalculable importance, because some of the brandy was aged, adding to the profits of local distillers, and because it was the centre of innovation or quality in the business. It was around this London market, successor to an Amsterdam one, that ageing and quality revolved. It was characterised by trends towards a more careful weeding out of the deleterious *seconde* from the early flow in a second distillation.

No less impressive than the trends in spirit production abroad or in international trade was the general reordering of French production and trade in response to changing tastes at home and foreign competition. Nantes and its hinterland, close to Paris, were the key to the early growth of the metropolitan brandy market. While La Rochelle had supplied the sweet, long-lasting wines much sought after by the Dutch, the absence of a large market in La Rochelle for the products of northern Europe meant that relatively few foreign vessels touched there and freights were higher than in Bordeaux. In other words, it made more sense for the Dutch and German wine buyers to shift ever more of their wine buying to Bordeaux, especially as Bordeaux's importance as a great European port was quickening and offered freights inwards as well as bulky wine shipments outwards. In turn the Cognac region switched to brandy. Thus in response to cost factors and its own dynamic expansion, Bordeaux increasingly dominated the wine trade, not only as the largest ultimate source of supply, but by providing the wine directly for foreign markets, rather than, as was so common even well into the seventeenth century, at second hand through Calais, Saint-Malo and other ports.

Exports of wine to European markets were 52,280 tons in 1700 and 59,667 tons in 1701; coastal shipments were also large; 30,000 tons in 1700 and 34,000 in 1701.[84] Regular figures for coastal shipments are not available after the early 1700s, but the tonnage of *cabotage* may reflect a rise in volume, especially when set against the inflated figures of 1700–1. Total *cabotage* averaged 52,000 tons in 1720–4; it was 37,837 in 1745–9,[85] though this figure is probably depressed by wartime privateering harassment of French shipping. Wine exports from the late 1710s and 1720s were around 60,000 tons (not including shipments to the colonies); moreover the quality of Bordeaux wines improved and Hamburg and Irish merchants revolutionised business in the Chartrons from the 1720s onwards. The eighteenth-century colonisation of the hitherto underdeveloped Médoc region in Bordeaux was a response both to a stronger export market and to a demand for a more carefully made

---

[84] Huetz de Lemps, *Géographie du commerce*, pp. 42–4, 101, 104–5, 124.
[85] P. Butel, *Les négociants bordelais, l'Europe et les îles au xviiie siècle* (Paris, 1974), p. 17.

wine. It was in the Médoc that the new wines – darker and stronger – sought by the Irish and British market developed. A first wave in the opening of Irish houses in Bordeaux occurred in the 1720s and 1730s, followed by another at the end of the 1740s. Significantly, the temptations of the wine business attracted Martell from Cognac to settle in Bordeaux in 1723. The addition of *cabotage* (assuming with some exaggeration that all *cabotage* related to wine) would suggest total shipments of around 100,000 tons. In 1765 exports peaked at a huge figure of 151,245 tons[86] and, if *cabotage* was, say, 50,000 tons, total shipments could have been around 200,000 tons. In fact *cabotage* was 47,186 tons in 1773 and 61,000 tons in 1788.[87] Bordeaux's prospering wine trade, expanding cereal cultivation to supply a growing urban market and booming plantations in the West Indies, all made the brandy trade more marginal. While the poor vintages of the 1770s depressed exports, they recovered in the following decade: exports even on the basis of the figures used by Labrousse were no lower than in the 1760s, the quite exceptional year of 1765 apart. Moreover, *cabotage* averaged 53,000 tons between 1782 and 1787.[88] Nor were the prices lower. As in the case of brandy, that depends on regarding the prices of the 1780s as a reversal of the long-term price trend: in other words the fact that the high prices of the early 1770s or of 1777–8 were exceptional must be recognised.

Significantly there were only two branches of distilling activity that survived commercially to the south of the Cognac region. The first was distillation in the port of Bordeaux, which from 1773 to the late 1780s even attracted foreigners: the Irishman Hilary Andoe in 1774,[89] Richard Hennessy in 1776, and Casey and Dowling in 1789, and even, after 1800, the Dubliner, Exshaw, who married a daughter of the Nairac branch in Dublin. It had something of a captive market in Bordeaux's colonial trade and in the many Irish vessels which called there, some of which, in years of high brandy prices, wanted a quick dispatch for the home market. However, speculative and intermittent port-based distilling was hardly a

[86] E. Labrousse, *La crise de l'économie française à la fin de l'ancien régime* (Paris, 1944), pp. 530–1. In Labrousse's table, the figures for exports excluding colonies and exports including colonies have become inverted in the columns. The muid contained in the figures used by Labrousse has been converted on the basis of its being one-third larger than the barrique.

[87] P. Butel, *La croissance commerciale bordelaise dans la seconde moitié du XVIIIe siècle* (Lille, 1973), vol. I, p. 369.

[88] P. Butel, *L'économie française au XVIIIe siècle* (Paris, 1993), p. 73.

[89] In Wilson's Dublin directory, John Andoe was recorded as a distiller in Hammond Lane from 1751 to 1766, and Hilary Andoe in Russell's Court from 1767 to 1773. Thereafter the name disappears. On Andoe's Bordeaux sojourn from 1774, see PRO, Home Office papers, HO 100/43/251–267, c. March 1793. I am indebted to Professor T. M. Bartlett of University College, Dublin, for this reference.

guarantee of quality. Bordeaux brandy had a very bad reputation. The second branch, and the only brandy in the port's hinterland with a reputation, was in Armagnac, shipped through Bayonne. By 1789 total exports were as large as those of Bordeaux. In 1789 shipments at 11,337 muids (15,116 barriques) were little short of shipments of indigenous or Guyenne brandy through Bordeaux (16,385 barriques). However, the Bordeaux figure was inflated by 3,271 barriques of Angoumois brandy, which brought Bordeaux's total exports to 19,656 barriques. The appearance of Angoumois brandy, including some *double*, in Bordeaux's exports is an illustration of the development of the Angoumois industry, though it is more a reflection of the remarkable demand in 1789 for brandy from any source in disregard of cost.

Understanding spirits: new uses, strength, quality, moral issues

The widening use of brandy in the navy, army and long-distance navigation came quite late, growing out of increased civilian awareness and acceptance of spirits. At the beginning of the century, wine in France and beer in England were the drink of navies and armies. Around 1700 brandy dispatched for the naval arsenal at Brest from Bordeaux was modest compared with the huge quantities of wine.[90] The arsenal at Rochefort may have been victualled with brandy from the Charente valley. However, a demand for brandy either from the East India Company or from the arsenal at Rochefort, is never mentioned in the surviving Cognac records for the first half of the century, and it would seem that naval demand was not significant at this time. The attitude of army administrators seems to bear out this conclusion. One of the most striking illustrations is in the correspondence of D'Avaux, the French ambassador in Ireland in 1689–90, who had the responsibility of organising supplies for the French expeditionary force which supported the exiled King James. The main emphasis as far as alcohol was concerned was on wine, which is frequently mentioned, and on beer. Brandy is sometimes mentioned but only in passing; on one occasion d'Avaux went so far as to say that 'l'eau-de-vie est ce qui est le moins pressé'.[91]

In the British navy spirits were taken only on voyages in distant waters, in the French East India Company they were used only on the return leg, and the senior officers were favoured with long-lasting and expensive wine rather than brandy. In the British navy the allowance, as printed

[90] Huetz de Lemps, *Géographie du commerce*, p. 234.
[91] *Négociations de M. le Comte d'Avaux en Irlande 1689–1690*, ed. J. Hogan (Dublin, 1934), p. 529.

from 1731 onwards, of a gallon of weak beer could be replaced in distant waters by a pint of wine or a half pint of brandy or rum.[92] From 1750 to 1757 brandy purchases by the navy amounted to 351,692 gallons,[93] a mere 1,000 barriques of spirit a year for the period. In the French East India Company the brandy for the return voyage was 17 centilitres for the crew, 25 for the sailing officers; higher officers, entitled to the best treatment, still had wine.[94] In the surviving records of the 1730s in Cognac, the company appears as a purchaser of the region's sweet wines, not of its brandy. In the 1770s Thomas Sutton, perhaps more experienced than any other civilian in France in the needs of long voyages, stressed his doubts about the keeping qualities of red wine.[95] Moreover, for cruises south of the equator in the hot season, his maxim was that 'une croisière dans cette saison exige des rations de liqueur forte plus souvent que de vin'.[96] In fact only the expensive red wines for the British Isles and Hamburg had any real keeping qualities, and given the demand for strong, dark wines, and the abiding Bordeaux problem of recurring thin vintages, the *coupage* or mixing of Bordeaux and Spanish wine in defiance of law reflected a persistent conflict of interest between the local sellers of poor wines and the export houses in the Chartrons. Mixing Spanish wine with Bordeaux wine to turn it into an acceptable product was, despite vested interests and prohibitions, a longstanding practice, and controversy on the subject was as lively as ever in the 1780s.[97]

Outside Holland spirits had not yet acquired maritime significance in

[92] N. A. Rodger, 'The victualling of the British navy in the seven years war', *Bulletin du Centre d'Histoire des Espaces Atlantiques*, new series, 2 (1984), p. 42.   [93] *Ibid.*, p. 40.

[94] Ph. Haudrère, 'Ravitaillement et ration alimentaire à bord des vaisseaux de la Compagnie Française des Indes en Asie au xviiie siècle', *Bulletin du Centre d'Histoire des Espaces Atlantiques*, new series, 2 (1984), p. 61. On the general problems of victualling, see L. Sueur, 'La conservation des vivres et des boissons sur les vaisseaux au long cours appartenant au roi de France et qui se dirigeaient, à la fin du XVIIIe siècle vers les Indes Orientales', *Revue Historique*, 117th year (January–March 1993), pp. 131–40.

[95] See letters from Thomas Sutton in the Lamaignère et Delaye papers, Archives départementales du Morbihan, Vannes.

[96] Thomas Sutton to Antoine Delaye, Lorient, 2 December 1779, *ibid.*

[97] ACC, La Rochelle, no. 3496, 1 March 1790. This report is very specific, though containing some exaggeration, on the practice: 'Tout le monde sait la grande réputation des vins de Bordeaux, tout le monde sait également qu'il en sort bien peu qui ne soit coupé avec les vins violents et couverts d'Espagne; jamais le parlement de Bordeaux ne s'est avisé de défendre l'introduction de ces vins d'Espagne, il est trop éclairé pour cela, la plus part des grands crus appartiennent aux membres de cette cour souveraine.' See also T. Malvezin, *Histoire du commerce de Bordeaux* (Bordeaux, 1892), vol. III, pp. 282–3. The practice was already well established in the 1740s, and the Irish wine merchants, faced with a demand for fuller wines than the often thin vintages of Bordeaux, were leading figures in the practice. See PRO, State Papers, Ireland, SP 63, vol. CCCCVIII, correspondence under cover of Duncannon to Newcastle, 24 August 1745. See, at a later date, *Correspondence of the Rt. Hon. John Beresford illustrative of the last days of the Irish parliament* (London, 1854), vol. I, pp. 247–9.

1689. As the century progressed this changed; naval, military and commercial consumption of spirits rose. The change is very evident too in the military treatise of Count O'Rourke in 1778 which specified brandy provision as one of the main professional preoccupations of a commander. His advice was that:

the moment your army enters an enemy's country, you must seize on all the brewers of beer and spirituous liquors in your neighbourhood; and above all, you must order a quantity of brandy to be distilled, that the army may never stand in need of a beverage which it cannot do without.[98]

Spirits were often added to water: whether this was an empirical grasp of the sterilising properties of alcohol or simply a practical awareness of the stable qualities of spirits we cannot as yet say. Military men had long been well aware of the dangers of bad wine, and more particularly the perils of hastily made beer or ale, which could result in dysentery. Brandy or rum, stable once it was distilled, had none of these dangers, and added in generous quantity to the suspect water supply, it was seen, though from empirical knowledge rather than exact understanding, as a therapeutic. By 1811 the Russian naval captain Golownin in his tortuous negotiations with the Japanese in the Kurile islands produced bottles of French brandy with some abandon.[99] For armies also, as the treatise of Count O'Rourke reveals, it had become an indispensable item in their liquid stores. We were now far removed from the world of d'Avaux.

For the inhabitants of the West Indies or of mainland America or for the Indians (who were introduced by Europeans to the charms of firearms and firewater), brandy was never an important item, as rum was available. Even if rum was not permitted in the French islands in theory, it was in practice made in or imported to them. Despite its huge colonial trade, Bordeaux's shipments rarely exceeded 2,000 barriques of brandy for the French West Indies (îles françaises de l'Amérique). La Rochelle's shipments, in contrast to Bordeaux's, fell to a very low level in the 1760s and early 1770s. On the other hand it made very large shipments especially from 1773 to 1776, when the slave trade was the main export outlet for brandy from the *généralité*. Slaving expeditions, on their outward leg, involved long voyages along the coast of Africa, in some cases as far afield as Madagascar, and for them, more than for the shorter voyages to the West Indies, the appeal of spirits was more central. Almost certainly some of these quantities were intended for other ports, especially Bordeaux which provided very little brandy for the slave traffic. The relatively large quantities in the 1770s for the colonies and the slave trade (*traite des noirs*

[98] John O'Rourke, *A treatise on the art of war* (London, 1778), p. 14.
[99] V. Golownin, *Narrative of my captivity in Japan during the years 1811, 1812, and 1813* (London, 1818), vol. I, pp. 25, 30, 37, 64.

or Guinea trade) compared with the modest quantities in Bordeaux, France's greatest port for the colonies, hint strongly at this. The East India Company ordered its brandy variously in Bordeaux and in La Rochelle, and its purchases can be followed in the company records. Army use created a huge demand for the great levies of the revolutionary period. Hennessy's, because of the steady nerve of two young men, Samuel Turner and James Hennessy, who directed the fortunes of the house at the time, were quicker to do business with the revolutionary governments in the 1790s than any other house.

The growth of spirits is one of the phenomena of the age. In Cognac itself by the 1720s the ageing of spirits was well understood, and a hierarchy of qualities existed. The principles determining the strength of spirits in distilling were well recognised by the 1680s both in France and abroad.In France, apart from some unenforced aspirations in 1687 and the 1740s, the taxing of brandy in proportion to strength first emerged in 1771 in the wake of the spread of an effective hydrometer, and became universal in 1782. However, while the taxation of spirits in proportion to strength already existed in England, Clark's hydrometer was given legal authority only in 1787; the authority until 1800 depended on annual renewals. French taxation regulations in 1771 and 1782, while allowing of derogations for coastal trade in 1771 and export trade at both dates, were ahead of British legislation by from sixteen to five years in giving permanent statutory authority to the readings of a measuring instrument.

The sending of brandy to Paris at a higher strength, as it developed after the end of the 1730s, had an important consequence on the quality of brandy, and the physical structure or chemical composition of spirits began to change. Brandy could be made up, as in the past, of a mixture of early flow from the second distillation and some of the inferior spirit or *seconde* in the later stages of the same distillation. However, if it was to be sent at higher strength, transport costs were lower. As up to 1771 there was no fiscal incentive to raise the strength of brandy (the law did not in practice tax *esprit* at a higher rate than brandy), this illustrates how vital transport and the importance of the Paris market were for change in the product. The brandy was then diluted with distilled water on arrival to meet consumer taste, and the distinctions between brandy one-third, three-fifths and one-half – all indicating the proportions of water to add to reduce the proof to standard – entered into vogue in recognition of the wide range of practices that had emerged.[100] The phenomenon coincided with the sharp rise in overland carriage of brandy to Paris from the late

[100] The existence of brandy one-third and brandy three-fifths can be traced in the Augier letter books in the late 1710s and 1720s. The latter is described in the letters in Dutch as *verloop*. On this identification, see Savary des Bruslons, *Dictionnaire universel du commerce* (1742 edn), article on 'eau-de-vie'.

1730s. It is hard to trace its emergence with precision as the 1740s is one of the least well-documented decades of the century. This brandy of higher alcoholic content could be achieved by adding a dose of stronger brandy, in proportion to the strength desired, to a mixture of first flow and *seconde*. However a stronger brandy could also be achieved in the second distillation by retaining less or none of the *seconde*, in other words by a *coupe à la serpentine*, either radically eliminating the *seconde* altogether to make a very strong brandy or by admitting only some of it. While the original purpose was purely economic, to cut down on transport costs, it was recognised by 1771 that the consequence was a much superior brandy to taste. Some of these brandies approximated to modern brandy, and would, subject to any variations in the amount of syrup added to sweeten and colour the liquid, probably have a recognisable taste for today's imbibers.

2   Brandy and the French economy

The expansion of output in the eighteenth century

Foreign demand for brandy, which first reached significant proportions in 1680–1720, grew afresh in the late 1750s and 1760s. Inland markets in France had also developed. The consequence of the pull of Paris was that export business on the Atlantic coast either fell or shifted between ports. A highly rational regional specialisation took shape. The regions closest to Paris developed a dependence on that market (Nantes's hinterland almost completely, the *généralité* of La Rochelle partially); Bordeaux shifted from brandy to wine, in part because its vast shipping meant that freights were lower than in La Rochelle. Overall exports overseas fell on the Atlantic coast, and a temporary revival in the late 1750s and 1760s apart, became increasingly confined to the central districts of the Charente catering for the quality-conscious London market. However, that should not detract from the fact that London demand was stronger than ever in the 1780s, and that inland demand in France more than compensated for the loss of external trade. Moreover, with strong English demand for cognac, and with sustained growth in Bayonne and even more in Languedoc (augmented also by a short-lived boom for the Irish market in 1782–5 and by an Irish-driven port distillation business in Bordeaux in the 1780s), exports from France were 98,352 barriques in 1784. In 1789, difficult year though it was, with foreigners bidding against equally determined Parisians, exports were, even excluding colonial trade and re-exports, a remarkable 106,739 barriques. Re-exports of spirits, mainly through Dunkirk and Boulogne, and to a lesser extent Calais and Roscoff, totalled a further 21,555 barriques.

One would not sense this state of affairs from the various memoirs in 1782 and 1784 from the Charente which represented the brandy trade in the most pessimistic terms possible, not altogether surprisingly perhaps, as they had been drafted expressly to support the case for fiscal concessions in favour of the brandy districts of the south-west. One memorial from the merchants of Cognac, Jarnac and Pons suggested that exports overseas were a mere 12,000 barriques, while another put the figure at

15,000 barriques.[1] The reality was that exports, the special circumstances of war apart, were actually higher in the 1780s than in the immediate past, and the case was made plausible only by concentrating on the quite dramatic fall in exports to Holland, itself more a feature of past decades than a new one. In 1783 exports from the *généralité* amounted to 31,519 barriques.[2] From Charente and Rochefort, the exports were 510,320 and 88,326 veltes respectively, in all 598,646 veltes or 22,172 barriques. The figure had been exceeded only in six previous years, and outside the heady days of the 1720s and 1730s only in two years of near legendary abundance, 1744 and 1761. In 1789 total exports from La Rochelle *généralité* at 38,183 barriques[3] were actually second only to the unique and quite unrepresentative exports of 1720. The contrast with the past was that Tonnay-Charente now dominated foreign trade: it accounted in 1789 for 31,343 barriques of the total, of which 27,584 were destined for *Angleterre*.

In the 1780s brandy distillation must have become even more general in the Saintonge and beyond it in the Aunis and Angoumois. At an earlier date, the maps of the period suggest that the vine had substantially invaded the bulk of the soils. The first great impulse had followed the expansion of the brandy trade in the 1710 and 1720s. According to the farmers-general, who were rebutting pessimistic claims by the chamber of commerce in 1731, the demand 'a au contraire si fort augmenté depuis plusieurs années que presque tout le terrain de la généralité a été mis en vigne à un point que le pays n'a plus assez de bleds pour nourrir ses habitants'.[4] According to the comte de Jarnac in 1782, wheat was not sown on the poorer soils, and the indigenous supply would only meet three months' needs.[5] Labour shortages also existed. As early as 1763 representations from La Rochelle referred to a 'multitude de journaliers que la récolte attire du haut et bas Poitou, du Limousin, de l'Auvergne'.[6] In 1745, according to a petition of the merchants of La Rochelle, 3,000 families made a living from the brandy trade: the figure seems to relate not simply to the Aunis but to the neighbouring provinces as well.[7] Moreover, in addition to the distillers and various support workers, it multiplied employment for the carters not only of the brandy, more of which moved

---

[1] ADC, Angouleme, 5C5, 5C6.

[2] Two *états* of brandy exports in 1783 in ADC, Angouleme, 5C5. This comprised 851,080 veltes, made up of 760,638 veltes to Europe plus 90,442 to America and Guinea.

[3] Exports in 1789 do not include exports to the colonies or for the slave trade. They are included in the 1783 figure when they amounted to 3,348 barriques.

[4] ACC, La Rochelle, no. 4245, 2 May 1731, Observations by chamber of commerce on comments of the tax farmers and deputy tax farmers.

[5] ADC, Angouleme, 5C5, comte de Jarnac and accompanying letter, 20 June 1782.

[6] ACC, La Rochelle, no. 3553, 7 October 1763.   [7] *Ibid.*, no. 3709, 20 January 1745.

overland, but for the outside goods which local wealth now brought into the region in a new profusion for the beneficiaries of these developments. The growing carting trade was a supplement to agricultural income: in the month of June, for instance, carters were not available as they were taken up in haymaking.[8]

The rise of brandy bills in the Paris foreign exchange market

The importance of the brandy trade is also reflected in the growing economic significance of the trade in the foreign exchanges. The London brandy importers were uniquely solvent; failures among them were few, and Cognac houses compared Irish importers very adversely with them.[9] Their status was inevitably reflected in the growth of the repute of bills drawn from the Charente on London. In consequence, the accounts of the Cognac houses dealing with London were sought after by the best Paris houses. The brandy accounts of several Charente *comptoirs* had a major place in the bill business of the Mallet Bank in Paris. The business of the Martells, the largest of the Charente houses, had a no less vital place in the portfolio of their main correspondents, the Cottins. Moreover, there was a switch from the *rescription* or exchequer acquittance (a receipt for monies paid over in Paris into the royal exchequer which would be converted at a later date into cash by a *receveur* in the provinces) which was onerous, arbitrary and uncertain for the merchant, to the more efficient inland bill of exchange. In the 1760s only recent arrivals such as Laurence Saule or Hennessy made extensive use of them: established houses such as Delamain or Martell primarily relied on the bill of exchange.

The Charente had always run a payments surplus. The trade also provided the main sources of bills on London for much of the hinterland of La Rochelle. There was a close link between the houses and the revenue receivers with regard to the remission of money between the Charente and Paris. The sale of the London bills in Paris by the brandy houses created credits which financed the inland bills they drew to the order of the *receveurs*. Cognac houses also opened Bordeaux accounts. These arrangements gave them the alternative methods of paying for purchases (usually the larger ones) by inland bills financed by the sale in Paris of bills on London or (usually for their extensive piecemeal acquisitions) with specie sent from Bordeaux in return for similar bills. The volume of

---

[8] HAJ, Delamain no 2 letter book 1793–8, 16 June 1794 (28 Prairial, an 2), to Obry *ainé*.
[9] MAC, letter book 1774–5, 19 March 1774, to Cottin et fils.

business shifted between the Paris and Bordeaux accounts, and transfers between accounts occurred regularly. Thus, the brandy trade played an important role in arbitraging the exchanges between the two great centres, Paris and Bordeaux, which quoted exchange rates for France's trade with its maritime partners.

The business of the region provided a stream of inland bills earned in brandy sales in Paris and the north of France, and of foreign bills on London generated by exports to England and Ireland. The sale of these bills in turn financed the region's own imports. The bills on London occupied a distinctive and privileged place in the finances of the Charente. These bills, in the main on large London importers, conducting a sure and solvent business punctuated by remarkably few bankruptcies by the standard of the age, were the safest in the entire Anglo-French trade. Delamain, the principal merchant in Jarnac, was at one stage the largest customer of the Mallet house, arguably the most representative of the Paris commercial banks, and certainly the one most respected in commercial circles.[10] The bills on London were taken in blocks by the Mallets and other Paris correspondents, and they disposed of them to houses in the capital. From these houses in turn, if they did not use them to augment their own balances in London, the bills passed to other Paris houses requiring credit on London. This pattern of business was very evident in the region's boom in the 1780s: disposed of by Paris houses which prized the accounts of their Cognac customers, the bills feature very prominently in the paper on London acquired by the Compagnie des Indes, which desperately needed cash in London.[11] At this stage, the Martell house, at the peak of its eighteenth-century turnover, engaged regularly in drawing and redrawing operations between Paris and London (a vital technical element in keeping the exchanges in the two centres in alignment), a measure of the status, scale and sophisticated perceptions of the house in exchange business.

In the past Cognac houses had sold much of their paper on London in La Rochelle. The purpose of sales in La Rochelle as in Bordeaux was in part to supplement the supply of specie by acquiring coin by the sale of bills on Paris to local houses: the cash was then taken by safe hand to Cognac. In the case of paper sold in Paris, the balances could be used to finance inland bills on Paris. Their sale in turn would provide specie, and the advantage of this was that a local supply of specie purchased by these bills had none of the inconvenience and expense of carrying it from La Rochelle or Bordeaux. Local houses (i.e. houses outside the major ports)

---

[10] AN, Paris, 57 AQ1–AQ8, Mallet archives.
[11] AN, 8Q 179, 217, 218, 230, 231, 239, Compagnie des Indes, archives of the 'third' company.

ready to take paper were, however, few, and revenue collectors predominated among the purchasers. That put the brandy houses at a disadvantage, as these houses required paper only seasonally or else took
advantage of their monopoly position to beat down the terms on which
they took bills. Thus in their strong position they were frequently able to
force brandy merchants to give them bills before they themselves supplied
cash in payment for them; the revenue *receveurs* moreover had a poor
record for solvency as well as punctuality.

By mid-century the growth of the economy meant that paper could be
disposed of more easily. As early as the 1740s the sale of paper in
Bordeaux had grown rapidly, and it became still more marked in the
1760s and 1770s. The sale of the enlarged mass of paper was not primarily to get specie, but in a roundabout way to get funds in Paris which by
their conversion into inland bills sold in the interior provided specie for
brandy buying. Significantly, as further proof of the fact that the poor vintages and shrunken exports did not create a corresponding banking crisis
(and that the economy was not as weak as the export statistics taken at
their face value would suggest), the exchanges functioned very well in the
late 1760s and early 1770s. When Bordeaux merchants were short of
funds in Paris or in London, they could buy bills in Cognac, and Cognac
in turn was a beneficiary of the growth of the huge Bordeaux foreign
exchange. This exchange moderated the swings in the inland exchange on
Paris which in the past often plunged to a large discount. The process of
arbitraging the market generated a larger demand for bills; the advantage
of a more closely arbitraged exchange was that inland bills rarely sold at a
heavy discount, and that sale of paper on Paris rarely departed from the
face value of a bill by more than 0.5 per cent per usance, which, given the
legal rate of interest, was in fact the equilibrium rate in an effective
market. Significantly, it was in the course of the assured Martell dominance of Cognac's London business in the mid-1770s that Theodore
Martell opened a house in Bordeaux. As advantage and convenience dictated, the large sales by Martell's of prime bills on London switched
between Paris and Bordeaux.

The financial business was quite elaborate, and was part of the process
of keeping exchanges in line in a country which had not only two main
centres of foreign exchange (three if Lyons is included), but in which the
importance of the second one – Bordeaux –rapidly grew as the city's
foreign trade soared. The switching between Bordeaux and Paris helped
to steady the exchanges. If bills on London were plentiful in Paris, they
could be sold in Bordeaux; equally if they were scarce more were sold in
Paris. If inland bills on Paris were scarce, the inland exchange rose
towards a premium; if they were plentiful, the discount widened beyond

0.5 per cent per usance. If bills on London were scarce in Paris, the sale of such bills in Paris to profit from their higher price funded the drawing of more inland bills. That in turn kept the inland exchanges from rising to a premium which would result if few bills on London were sold in Paris. If bills on London were plentiful in Paris, a poor price led to their sale in Bordeaux; the decline in negotiation of such bills in Paris meant that fewer inland bills could be drawn, and the reduced supply of such bills reduced the discount on them. A reduced discount made it attractive to sell them, and in order to have the funds to draw them, the negotiation of bills on London was switched back to Paris. In this fashion movements in the Bordeaux and Paris exchanges on London and Amsterdam were brought into line, and in the process the expanded or reduced offer of inland bills on Paris prevented the swings in the inland exchange from taking the form of large and disconcerting swings from a discount to a premium: in other words the inland exchange steadied around the equilibrium point of 0.5 per cent. This point corresponded to the legal rate of interest for a month, and any significant widening of the discount beyond that point was ruled out by the fact that if it occurred, the alternative strategy of moving specie between the provinces and Paris became attractive.

Of course arbitraging could not of itself steady the rate at which Cognac sold inland paper on Paris if demand for the paper did not grow also. A growing market for paper on Paris was an essential ingredient in keeping the exchanges near the equilibrium point. This demand came from houses in the region. Tax receivers had always taken the paper but the demand was much more varied and complex in the 1770s. Angouleme had taken over the role that La Rochelle had played in the past, and La Rochelle was reduced to a peripheral position. The rise of Angouleme as a business centre taking Cognac and Jarnac paper is one of the dynamic features of a changing economy. The increase in the number and resources of the houses taking paper, the shift of the axis inland and a steady discount, reflected a demand for paper from the region's importers. The demand could in theory have stemmed from the demands of tax receivers for bills. This was the position in the 1720s, but they are far less central in the 1770s and 1780s. It could also in theory arise from the demands of noblemen in the region who lived in Paris and who required incomes to be remitted to them. But few bills were sold by the merchants to noblemen. Delamain, for instance, though he acted as the local agent for the comte de Jarnac provided him with few bills on Paris. In other words, if bills were in demand, it was only in part because tax receivers sought them; noble demand was insignificant. The rising source of demand came from importers in the region, paying either for goods imported from abroad or provided by other regions in France.

From one point of view this meant that living standards rose, though how the benefits were distributed between the well-to-do and the labourers and *manoeuvres* at the base of society is another question. From another point of view, it reflected the presence of more and larger merchant houses, and the overshadowing of houses in La Rochelle, once the dominant force in the region, by houses not only inland but progressively further so. Angouleme had replaced La Rochelle as the local business centre by the 1770s. Moreover, as these changes took place, the brandy houses became more powerful in their financial role, deepening contacts with Bordeaux by the move of family members or associates there. By 1800 the pattern was set for the effective dominance of business in the early decades of the new century by the two houses of Hennessy and Martell, challenged in a real sense only by the house of Otard.

Brandy and the French economy

While historians have been prone to see the 1760s and 1770s as crisis decades, whether in the context of the domestic economy in France or England or of the great wave of migration across the Atlantic, the truth of the matter is that the 1760s and 1770s were a novel period of unparalleled economic growth punctuated by correspondingly severe and in some respects novel depressions. A new and unfamiliar world, closely linked to great cities like London and Paris and supported by unprecedented ties in trade and movement with North America, was in the process of coming into being.[12] The study of the brandy trade, a cog in these relationships as well as in the mass of paper which arbitraged the Paris–Bordeaux exchange, is bedevilled by an assumption made in the economic history of wine-producing regions that distillation was a business motivated solely by the need to mop up surplus wine production.

The belief that distillation was essentially a response to surplus and that a rise in activity in distillation reflected conditions of surplus, low prices and hence agricultural crisis is one of the themes of Labrousse's celebrated *Crise de l'économie française à la fin de l'ancien régime*. Distillation had a large place in the logic of the Labroussian equation of surplus and crisis. If distillation existed, it proved that there was already a tendency to surplus; if brandy prices fell, that proved that the crisis was worsening

[12] See L. M. Cullen, 'The Irish diaspora of the seventeenth and eighteenth centuries', in N. Canny, ed., *Europeans on the move: studies on European migration, 1500–1800* (Oxford, 1994), pp. 113–49; Cullen, 'History, economic crisis and revolution: understanding eighteenth-century France', *Economic History Review*, 46, no. 4 (November 1993), pp. 636–57; Cullen, 'The economic crisis of the end of the Ancien Regime', in J. P. Poussou, ed., *Crouzet festschrift*, forthcoming.

because wine producers unable to sell their goods moved into brandy production. The brandy trade was thus, in Labrousse's view, one of the great measures of agricultural crisis: 'produit substitutable, l'alcool tend donc, en fin de période, à aggraver par ses progrès exceptionnels la crise des revenus paysans'.[13] Some rise in brandy exports in the 1780s – which Labrousse concedes – is even taken as a proof of the crisis in wine, as brandy 'constitue pour les vins à la fois un débouché et une concurrence'.[14] Where, as in Bordeaux's immediate hinterland, brandy distillation did not grow, the reason was attributed by Labrousse to a shortage of wood as fuel.[15] However, the events of the 1780s cannot be related to some progressive impoverishment caused by low prices (and high rents) in the rural economy coming to an inevitable point in 1788 and 1789, when harsh weather and crop failures added to a downward spiral of misery. It was simply France's misfortune that its progressive political and fiscal crisis coincided in 1788 and 1789 with the more transient circumstances of remarkably bad weather and of crop failure, the effects of which became evident in the respective springs of 1789 and 1790.

The crisis of 1789 and 1790 was no different in nature from the paralysing economic crisis of 1770 and 1771 which occurred at the end of the greatest decade of economic growth in the century, and in some respects was significantly less serious. Vintages fared much worse in the late 1760s and early 1770s, and this source of cash income was less savagely reduced in 1789 and 1790 than in the years around 1770. The boom in the inland brandy trade in the second half of the 1780s was a real one, and in contrast to the late 1760s and early 1770s when poor vintages meant that soaring inland trade virtually annihilated export trade, the active inland trade was accompanied by an active export trade in brandy in the years 1788–9. These were years of prosperity in foreign trade.

In the 1780s there is little evidence of the long-term decline claimed by Labrousse in consumer demand consequent on impoverishment as a result of a fall in the price of wine. Labrousse made much play of the lower prices in the 1780s. The contrast is in some respects false: the high prices of the 1760s were explained first by a remarkable surge in trade in wine and brandy – the strongest of the century to that date – as part of a great international boom in the 1760s and then by years of dramatic failure over a singular weather cycle in the late 1760s and early 1770s. To Martell's in 1774 it seemed that there had been a succession of seven bad vintages.[16]

Labrousse, with his artificial creation of cycles, made too much of high

[13] Labrousse, *Crise de l'économie française à la fin de l'ancien régime* (Paris, 1944), p. 607.
[14] *Ibid.*, p. 346.   [15] *Ibid.*
[16] MAC, letter book, 1774–5, 18 July 1774, to Cottin, London.

wine prices in the late 1760s and 1770s and low prices in 1778–83. Brandy prices on the Charente in 1783 rose sharply from a trough in 1780 and 1781, and the poor vintage in 1783 reinforced the trend. There was a pronounced upturn in late 1783 and in 1784 and prices were high. The specialist distillers in the port of Bordeaux, benefiting from the regularity of sailings from Ireland, profited in particular in 1782–4 from the poor harvests there which drove consumers from whiskey to brandy. Indeed a pinnacle of expectations was probably reached at the outset of 1785, judging by Hennessy's rash investment (with other and much younger merchants) in a dining club in the Lormont hills.[17] Late 1785 and 1786 was a bad business period, in part because of poorer external conditions. The trade then moved to boom in 1787 and while brandy prices eased later in the year, they picked up again at its end. A poor vintage in 1788 and a harsh winter created a shortage of brandy in 1789, prices rose, and in the aftermath of another bad vintage reached extraordinary levels in 1790.

Labrousse's price perspective was coloured by the high wine prices of 1767–72 and again by the quite exceptional prices of 1777 and 1778 (his own index was higher for 1778 than for 1771).[18] In consequence he saw prices in the 1780s as low. If we ignore these peak prices, support for the Labroussian concept of surplus does not emerge even from his own price index for wine; there were two periods of significant price rises (1783 and 1784, 1787 and 1788), both following intervening troughs (1781 and 1782, and 1785 and 1786). The troughs, moreover, merit comment. The first one was prolonged because of the American war and the immediate post-war recession;[19] the second one was short-lived. Labrousse read his evidence of brandy activity in part from the fact that the export trade appeared to collapse in 1778. With higher prices for the inland brandy trade, exports contracted in 1778 in the manner of 1772: the inland trade soared through 1778. Inland trade also benefited from war which made both coastal and foreign trade hazardous. In November 1778, at the outset of the distilling season of 1778–9, one merchant on the Charente went so far as to comment on 'our trade in a more flourishing state than for some years past'.[20] Brandy prices did fall to a nadir in 1780 and 1781, but the fall was less a consequence of the surplus–depression equation of Labrousse than of the crushing wartime credit crisis of 1780 which gets

[17] HAC, letters from Richard Hennessy, Bordeaux, to John Saule, Cognac, 1785.
[18] Labrousse, *Esquisse du mouvement des prix et des revenus en France* (Paris, 1933), p. 275.
[19] Labrousse recognised the existence of price recovery in 1783, but deployed every possible argument to minimise its significance. *La crise de l'économie*, pp. 326, 350, 355.
[20] HAJ, Delamain no. 1 letter book, 1778–81, Delamain to Falk and Lovelace, 7 November 1778.

no recognition in his pages, and the importance of which falsifies Labrousse's attempt to find a neat pattern for a cyclical switch from high prices to low prices.

The later crisis of 1788–9 did not grow out of the conditions of the 1780s, and was in no way anticipated in the voluminous surviving correspondence of merchants for the preceding years. This emphasises that rural conditions were less the centrepiece of the story than Labrousse assumed. Indeed the credit crisis of 1788 is in some respects the key problem. The economic system in the Charente region showed no signs of serious difficulty until the fiscal crisis in 1787–8 began to bite. If bills of exchange could be negotiated with ease, it meant that there was a firmer demand than in the past for paper on Paris. Unless there was an increased demand from tax collectors for paper on Paris (and the revenue was static), it means that the region was importing more. In other words there was more consumption, not progressive impoverishment. The onset of a credit crisis in late 1787 was rather abrupt, its timing influenced by the fear of war with England by the two states taking the side of a different faction in the internal affairs of Holland.[21] In November Delamain complained that 'we are so stinted for money in this country that it is hardly possible to take time to profit of advantageous circumstances'.[22] However, despite this, the exchange on London steadied and it was still possible to conduct a brandy business which rose to record proportions in 1789. Brandy prices rose despite the crisis, and in early 1789 even a secure citizen like Delamain, in his expressed hostility to revenue inspections, reflected political alienation rather than economic uncertainty.

It was, moreover, the Paris credit crisis in 1787–8, deepened by the worsening fiscal one, not as in the late 1760s the collapse of rural demand, which caused the difficulties in the industrial centres which Young noted in 1789. The crisis, as one might expect of what was in its origins a credit crisis, was felt more in the industrial towns than in the countryside. Even Arthur Young writing on the eve of and during the crisis of 1789 can be seen as a source for a more nuanced and less pessimistic view of French social conditions: though knowledgeable about Irish social conditions, only once, passing through Peyrac, was he prompted to draw a parallel with Irish poverty.[23] His recording of the worst complaints relates very specifically to reports from the industrial towns. With failure which was less total than in 1767–73, rural trade remained at a high level, and rural conditions had elements of prosperity

[21] L. M. Cullen, 'History, economic crises and revolution', p. 654.
[22] HAJ, Delamain no. 1 letter book 1787–9, 13 November 1787, to MacCarthy frères.
[23] Arthur Young, *Tours in France and Italy during the years 1787, 1788 and 1789* (London, 1915), p. 25.

for grain growers and vineyard owners. In the late 1780s on the other hand, neither vintage nor harvest failures were as crushing. The failure was significantly less complete than in the earlier period, inland trade levels remained high, foreign trade did not fall, and demographic indica- tors – births and deaths – remained normal.[24]

The appearance of crisis was, however, heightened by the abrupt advent of singular weather in the winter of 1788 and spring of 1789 which first halted inland traffic on roads and rivers, and then kept them impass- able as melting snow produced flooding. With a remarkably cold summer in 1789 grain harvests proved poor again. Perhaps not enough thought has been given to the singularity of the weather in late 1788 and early 1789 which in a succession of snow falls, ice-blocked rivers and cata- strophic thaw created havoc for months. As can be seen in the letters of contemporaries, the events created in people's minds an overwhelming and hypnotic sense of foreboding which acquired a momentum of its own as an apparent physical parallel to the all too palpable political crisis.

Profits and political power

Merchants and the rich bourgeois distillers who could afford to distil to a high standard, and to either withhold brandy from the market if prices fell or simply to profit by selling it later as aged brandy, represented a new political force. Inevitably that was reflected in the process of profit trends and changing status over the century. What were the profits earned by the houses, and what place in society did they make possible? Details of profits are hard to come by. Early profits were modest enough. Augier hints at 15,000 livres in 1720. An oversanguine Martell got 'very near' 25,000 livres in 1720, though in the inflated paper money of that year, and seemed to regard an income of 10,000 livres a year as an attainable expectation.[25] In 1720 Augier claimed that he might have hoped to make 30,000 livres if he had not got involved in other business,[26] and in another letter seems to suggest that he made 25,000 to 30,000 livres in 1719. Of course 1719–20 profits, real or hoped-for, represented an exceptional situation; trade soared, and exports in 1720 were to remain the peak point of the century. Otherwise profits are modest and emphasise that the trade was not immensely lucrative. Augier's later calculations of profits in the mid-1760s are higher, appearing to represent something more than normal trading profits, though, at about or above 30,000 livres a year for

[24] J. P. Poussou, 'Le dynamisme de l'économie française sous Louis XV', *Revue Economique*, 40 (1989), pp. 967–8, 972–3, 978–9.
[25] MAC, letter book 1721–2, 16 July 1721, to Wm. Kastell.
[26] AAC, letter book June–December 1720, 1 June 1720, to Richard *l'aîné*.

the three years 1765–7, they hint very crudely at the figures which the more successful houses of Martell could have made in 1758–62 or Delamain in the mid-1760s.[27] In 1774 Martell's commission income, in other words his gross profits, should have been 14,000 livres.

Costs not recouped by commission agents were few, so that commission income is close to a clear profit. However, where we have figures for profits, they always seem larger than the gross commission income. Why this should be the case is not clear, even allowing for other income. Of course most merchants had sources of income which added to commission earnings on brandy and the full gamut of which embraced *métayer* income, some investment in *pacotilles* – small consignments – in the colonial trade, shares in Newfoundland fishing vessels in La Rochelle, other commodity dealings and some profit in exchange transactions. In Delamain's case there were very probably some profits as the comte de Chabot's man of business in Jarnac. There were also some profits from speculation in brandy stocks, bought at one price and sold at a higher one. The brandy houses denied to importers, who were deeply suspicious, that they made profits in this way. However, there was no way of knowing whether they were invoicing at market prices brandy which they had bought at a lower price. They did this but they had to be careful. If they all did it, that tended to put prices up, and could well result in resentment and loss of custom to other houses, as most foreign buyers took pains to be well informed by extensive correspondence with rival houses. The buyers deliberately chose to divide their commissions over several houses, and that was in a sense the price to pay for continuous intelligence. To these various sources of gain should be added some profit from the enhanced price of the spirit they rectified rather than purchased from mid-century to raise the strength of brandy. None of these sources can have been very large, at any rate before the 1780s, and speculation in brandy stocks occasioned losses as well as gains: hoping to hold customers, they were at times reduced to offering at market prices brandy which had been purchased at higher prices. Other commodities entered into trade; Augier dealt in flaxseed, and Delamain in both flaxseed and walnuts. Although they were mere *commissionaires*, they all speculated in some brandy buying and selling on foreign markets on their own account (and their foreign principals sometimes harboured dark and exaggerated suspicions over this conflict of interest). The activity was small enough, but Augier's *Etat de mes affaires* reveals business effects in Dunkirk in 1743, 1750 and more extensively in the 1760s. Delamain and Martell also speculated in this fashion in the late 1760s. French living costs were

---

[27] For Augier profits in the 1760s, see below ch. 7.

lower than Irish, possibly only half. Doubled to convey a sense of the
significantly lower French living costs, profits would therefore represent a
more substantial sum. In other words Martell's 14,000 livres in 1774
should, on this principle, signify not the simple £600 that a straightforward conversion into Irish money would yield but almost twice that
figure. Such a profit (and his commission income is probably an understatement of his profits) in 1774 would compare very favourably with the
profits of £876 going to each of the partners in the house of Courtenay
and Ridgway, the largest commission house in general trade in Waterford
city in 1792.[28] Neither the Martell nor the Courtenay and Ridgway
profits are princely ones. Moreover, they represent the upper range of
profits, and the profits of other houses were smaller. The existence of low
profits for others is hinted at in the steep peaks and deep troughs in the
graph of export trade, and in the abrupt and unexpected switches in the
fortunes even of houses such as Delamain, Martell and Augier, which
before the 1790s represented, despite vicissitudes, the success stories of
Cognac and Jarnac. The brandy houses in their fluctuating fortunes offer
a sharp contrast with the relative stability of the great wine houses,
German or Irish, in Bordeaux (the devastating war year of 1780 apart).

However, some houses had emerged as rich by the 1770s and both
dowries and bequests to children by the favoured few were high in the
1780s. The fortunes of the Martell and Delamain houses represented the
pinnacle of business success before the 1790s. Thus, whereas dowries had
been small (e.g. 6,000 livres for the Brunet and Lallemand marriages to
Jean Martell in 1726 and 1737, or for a Broussard daughter's marriage to
Philippe Augier in 1757), Martha Catherine Martell's dowry for her marriage to Etienne Augier in 1762, in the wake of the great brandy boom of
the late 1750s and early 1760s, was already 15,000 livres. Another daughter was married to a merchant in Pons in 1761 with 15,000 livres, and
Henriette-Jeanne's dowry in 1778 was 30,000 livres. The estate of the
Veuve Martell in 1788 was valued at 374,585 livres,[29] at the end of three
decades of growth of the business, and of having successfully seen off the
Irish challenge in the 1760s. Martell's envisaged dowries of
20,000–30,000 livres in the 1770s, and Delamain dowries a decade later,
were of the order of 20,000 livres. These would be small compared with
the resources of merchants and *parlementaires* (lawyers) in Bordeaux or
merchants and landowners in Dublin, but they represent dowry levels
which conferred an assured place in society. They would be akin to the
dowries among the smaller gentry in Ireland (large ones by French stan-

---

[28] L. M. Cullen, 'The overseas trade of Waterford as seen from a ledger of Courtenay and
Ridgway', *Journal of the Royal Society of Antiquaries of Ireland*, 88 (1958), p. 169.
[29] AAC, 1 February 1788, *partage de succession* (division of inheritance).

dards), and were, in fact, higher than the dowries of country and small-town nobility in France. Moreover, status was beginning to be reflected in houses, in the emergence of family portraits, and in marriage patterns.

In the period up to the 1780s we can conclude that only two houses really made a handsome living out of the brandy business. The Martell house certainly dominated Cognac in the 1770s and 1780s, and Delamain was the contemporary giant of Jarnac. He was probably on a par with Martell in the 1770s and was second in the 1780s. In the late 1780s the Martell commission income should have given them a gross income of 20,000 livres, or almost £1,000 Irish. It was, in Irish terms, of gentry proportions (doubling it to allow for the higher French purchasing power); in French terms, given less inegalitarian distribution of income and lower living costs, it was effectively even larger. It helps to account further for the divide between the Martells and the other houses in the 1780s.

By the late 1760s the greater weight of the region ensured that its political representations had to be listened to closely, even if the source of the first representations came not from the large hinterland, increasingly enriched by its wider markets and higher prices, but from the La Rochelle merchants, overwhelmed by Paris demand, soaking up supplies that in preceding years had reached the coast. These representations resulted in subsequent changes in taxation in 1771 which not only increased the taxation of inland trade but did so only at the point of arrival of brandy in Paris. In other words the changes were couched in a form which should have advantaged the coastal trade which supplied Normandy and Picardy, and also sent some brandy from the Seine ports to Paris at a lower strength. It may even be possible to see the hand of the town's patron, the great nobleman Montmorency, in this. Certainly, he was behind the town's representations on another matter at the time, which threatened further to challenge its place in the economic life of the region. With a growing demand for spirits in the colonies, Rochefort in 1772 sought the privileges of duty-free entrepot for colonial trade (eventually granted in 1775). La Rochelle's difficult circumstances made it easy for Rochefort to make uncomplimentary comments about La Rochelle's trade.[30] In turn, La Rochelle's memorandum defending itself revealed the town's insecurity as it leaned heavily on its past trading achievements.[31] Montmorency, who received this memorandum in Paris, promised that he would come to the town; in the meantime he assured the citizens that he would halt any adverse move against it.[32] He did come later in 1772,

[30] ACC, La Rochelle, no. 4211.   [31] *Ibid.*, no. 4213.
[32] *Ibid.*, no. 4216, Paris, 28 March 1772.

and welcomed the citizens at a great ball in the town. Saule, the young Irish merchant in La Rochelle, wrote a memorable few words on it, and on the easy mingling of townsmen and nobility.[33]

In the events of these years we have an interesting glimpse both into eighteenth-century lobbying and the sharpness of the internal conflict of interest between businesses in the port of La Rochelle itself and the new forces in its hinterland. While La Rochelle's lobbying was influenced by its opposition to the inland trade and its fear that Rochefort, close to Cognac, might carry off its colonial trade, both La Rochelle and the Cognac region at least found common cause in seeking to turn the decline in exports to their advantage in their appeals. In 1776, the London market apart, the European export trade had virtually vanished. While total exports had, despite the difficulties of the preceding years, recovered to 15,805 barriques, the colonies and the slave traffic accounted for 13,523 of the total. Thus, if we take the arguments of the now vigorous lobbyists seriously, as they dwelt on the problems facing them when the Atlantic world turned to peace again in and after 1782, we may believe that crisis ran far deeper than it did. Neither La Rochelle interests nor the export interest in Cognac and Jarnac, all variously inconvenienced by it, were in a mood, in defending their own immediate interests, to admit how prosperous the overland trade had become, or to take into account the prosperity of the coasting trade, control of which had passed from urban merchants to houses scattered along the coast.

Moreover, if La Rochelle carried weight in the early 1770s, Cognac merchants and the interest exporting through Tonnay-Charente had become the more powerful lobbyists in the 1780s. In 1782–4 Rohan-Chabot, comte de Jarnac and the duc de la Rochefoucauld carried the voice of Cognac to Paris, and the lobbying of the two men in 1782–4 was both insistent and successful. It was the representations proposed by Delamain in Jarnac and orchestrated by the comte de Jarnac and the duc de la Rochefoucauld which ensured that, when taxation of the spirit trade was made more effective in 1782, in the wake of the transfer of the collection of the *aides* to direct levying by a *régie* or state administration in place of the old-style tax-farming, the new principle, which quickly followed, of taxing brandy in proportion to strength was not extended to the main taxes on exports, which were much higher than the *aides*. Two years later, these export taxes were reduced by two-thirds in the interest of supporting the export trade. The memoirs which accumulated in a frenzy of representations in 1782 and 1784 are not to be taken at their face value in their description of the plight of the Charente: they were carefully pre-

---

[33] HAC, Saule, 27 August 1772.

pared in an orchestrated campaign to make the need for redress as compelling as possible. The *régie* which took over the management of the duties was still unpopular, partly because it entailed a significant rise in the taxation of goods in inland trade, partly because the new regime was made effective by inspections of the cellars of merchants and distillers, a power which revenue collectors already held but which had been a dead letter in the past, as there was only one level of duty. The new taxation itself was deeply resented, and the visits by the *régie* officials, rare in the past but now frequent and intended to flush out abuses, were seen as tyranny. Resentment over it helped to fan the embers of radicalism among the merchants in 1789.

3 Brandy: the distilling process, the product and the industry

The distilling process

The characteristics of brandy are a complicated mixture of wine, soil, skill and market. Before the advent of reliable hydrometers, control of production, rough and ready in its nature, required extensive empirical experience in making a beverage which in 1700 was still in its comparative infancy: the availability of the necessary skills was not to be taken for granted at the outset of the eighteenth century. As late as 1735 Régnier in Charente had a letter from his brother-in-law Vincent Bureau in La Rochelle lamenting the fact that brandy was losing strength and that he did not know how to make it 'merchantable'. Régnier wrote back that he had a distiller that did not know his business.[1]

Brandy is produced by distillation. As the alcohols contained in wine have a lower boiling-point than water, the volatile alcoholic elements separate easily from the liquid, leaving less volatile elements, some of them noxious, behind. In distillation the fire must be maintained evenly, since if the heat becomes excessive, the whole liquid boils over, and desired and undesired elements alike simultaneously ascend through the neck or head of the still and down through the cooling worm or serpentine into the basin intended to receive the alcohol. A single distillation of wine does not produce a palatable result, and a further distillation of the first distillate (sometimes even a third one) was necessary to obtain anything satisfactory: by the eighteenth century this was universal in spirit production. In the second distillation, today known as the *bonne chauffe*, the proportion of alcohol in the flow progressively declined to a point where the quantity of spirit in the flow fell short in volume of a watery and noxious residue. The first stage of the flow was known in the eighteenth century variously as *première* or *eau-de-vie bonne et forte* – the *coeur* of modern parlance. The later stage, down to the point where the aqueous residue began to exceed the alcohol in the flow in quantity, was known as *seconde*. The spirit as marketed in the seventeenth and eighteenth

[1] HAC, Régnier letter book 1735–6, 29 July 1735, to Bureau.

63

centuries contained both *première* and *seconde*, and the aim of the consci-
entious distiller was to admit no liquid beyond the stage of *seconde*. A
process, which was only beginning in the most advanced districts and
among the most skilful distillers, of culling only the *première* or *coeur* has
become universal in the modern distilling of cognac. In other words a
modern cognac is a finer and more palatable product than the typical
brandy of the eighteenth century. It was recognised even in the seventeenth century that recourse to further distillation (i.e. a third or fourth
distillation) would result in even stronger brandy. With the aim of producing a higher quality and strength, distillers developed a strategy of
carefully selecting the early flow from the still. No less important in preparing for the second distillation was to fill the still with brandy alone: an
older practice, and one that still survived in less advanced districts where
distillers operated under severe constraints of space or time, was to make
good any shortfall in brandy in the still as it was being got ready by
topping up generously with wine.

The distinction between different strengths of brandy had its first fiscal
recognition in a French declaration of 1687 which differentiated between
simple brandy at ordinary rates of taxation, *double* brandy at double rates of
taxation, and *rectified* brandy at treble rates on *esprit de vin* of greater
strength.[2] The decree itself was imprecise in technical detail, and its exact
purpose was a subject of confusion in later commentary. From later (i.e.
eighteenth-century) usage of the term *double* brandy, it meant the early
flow in a second distillation, either little tainted or untainted by *seconde* or
weaker brandy. Treble taxation would seem to have referred to the
product of a third distillation, and for imperfectly made brandies, i.e.
when the still had been topped up with wine rather than brandy, even
further distillations. The brandy in the early stages of the second distillation was itself designated as *esprit*, and the term 'rectification', while it
could and did refer to a selection in the second distillation, more commonly referred to the process of enhancing the spirit further by a third or
subsequent distillation. This was more particularly the case for the term
esprit de vin which signified the highest strength that was in cost terms economic. Thus the 1687 decree recognised the existence of three products:
simple brandy of relatively low strength as it had much *seconde*; double
brandy which had little if any *seconde* and which in consequence was
significantly stronger; and rectified brandy which by a third or further distillation carried the strength to an even higher degree of alcohol by
volume. The term 'rectification', used predominantly for a third or later

---

[2] Declaration of 9 December 1687, cited in letters patent of 13 February 1782, registered
at the *cour des aides*, 15 March 1782.

distillation but used also in the second distillation when it separated spirit from *seconde*, reflects an emphasis less on the distilling process itself than on delicate processes in the course of distilling which by separating liquids could greatly enhance the strength. Although all strong brandy resulting from the second flow was denominated as spirit or *esprit*, the term *esprit de vin* as a precise commercial term was confined in the eighteenth century to strong brandy (of above 80 degrees under optimum conditions) produced either in the first flow of a third distillation or in the return of a weaker spirit to the still for yet a further distillation. Savary des Bruslons' description of *esprit de vin* as a second distillation and *esprit de vin rectifié* as a third distillation is somewhat simplified and inaccurate: the logic of rectification strictly speaking meant either a very careful culling of a third distillation or an actual fourth distillation of the product of an inferior third distillation.

Some confusion has been caused by the terms 'single' and 'double' in English-language usage. Their use in auctions of brandy during the War of the Spanish Succession has led to the conclusion that some brandy had been shipped at the strength of a first distillation.[3] The suggestion is also made in the major work on the Irish whiskey trade that brandy spirits may have been imported of low strength after a single distillation.[4] However, *single* is simply a translation – or equivalent – of the term *simple* ('double' caused no comparable problem apart from its juxtaposition with 'single'). The language is clearer in the Irish regulations of 1662 which distinguished between imported spirits made from 'wine and spirits' taxed at 4d a gallon and 'spirits perfectly made' at 1s a gallon. It has been said that it is not clear what the distinction meant,[5] but in fact it was a sophisticated and realistic narrowing of the unenforceable triple range of single, double and treble spirits to two categories embracing basic and higher grades. In pitching the higher rate at treble the base rate, it revealed a perception of strength identical to the French one. Again the two-fold distinction was employed in a customs duty on imported spirits in 1717 which imposed a base rate and a higher rate on spirits above proof.[6]

At the time of the 1687 decree no precise measurement of alcoholic strength was possible. As a later memoir noted, 'on n'a jamais connu dans le commerce plus d'eau de vie double que de vin ou d'eau commune double: il n'y avoit de double réellement que le droit qu'on avait intention de percevoir'.[7] However, this observation reflected the new insights which

---

[3] R. Pijassou, 'Quelques aperçus sur le commerce des eaux-de-vie en Angleterre au début du XVIIIᵉ siècle', in A. Huetz de Lemps et Ph. Roudié, eds., *Eaux-de-vie et spiritueux*, p. 120.   [4] E. B. McGuire, *Irish whiskey* (Dublin, 1973), p. 97.
[5] *Ibid.*, p. 97.   [6] 4 George 1, c. 2 (McGuire, *Irish whiskey*, p. 104).
[7] ACC, La Rochelle, no. 3634, *Mémoire sur l'usage de l'aréomètre dans la perception de l'impost sur les eaux-de-vie*, p. 3. Me Lethinois, avocat, Paris 1772.

became possible when the strength of spirits could be measured accurately after the mid-eighteenth century and when instruments for this purpose had become widely accepted. A clear recognition of the parabolic curve in strength in the course of a single distillation followed. Equally, the progressive strengthening of brandy by successive distillations was recognised. In a later generation when measurement of the alcohol content of liquids was possible, one of the memoranda forwarded by the comte de Jarnac to the intendant of La Rochelle in 1782 noted that double and treble duties involved a much sharper increase in taxation than the actual increase in the strength of the alcohol.[8] An argument now advanced, when the thrust of representations was to oppose the revival of the 1687 principle of brandy taxation, was that the intent behind these increases had been prohibitive, i.e. to confine the trade to simple brandy, and hence by implication they stood to be condemned by the best and rational practice of a more enlightened age. This seems unlikely: the taxation levels merely reflected contemporary perceptions of alcoholic strength in an age when accurate measurement was impossible, and in which single, double and treble taxation corresponded to well-perceived, but unmeasurable insights into the changes wine underwent in distillation and rectification.

No mathematically precise measurement was possible in France as late as the 1750s. Neither Savary des Bruslons in the first edition in 1723 of his *Dictionnaire universel du commerce* nor the *Encyclopédie* in 1755, both very penetrating in their entries on brandy, have any reference to precise measurement. This is confirmed in the absence of any precise strength in the letter books of brandy merchants until the 1760s. At that stage, Lallemand, the presiding genius at Martell's, acknowledged in his letters to foreign correspondents the greater strength of the brandy of his rival Delamain who was newly established at Jarnac: on some occasions Delamain's brandy is described as being 2 to 5 per cent stronger. Lallemand in 1763 was familiar with Clark's London hydrometer. The London standard, as measured by Clark's hydrometer, was, according to Lallemand, 10 per cent (i.e. 10 per cent in terms of the readings on the hydrometer, not in alcoholic strength *per se*) above what was called in Cognac 'common proof'.[9] In 1763 he referred much to the question. He had seen the first Heath hydrometer which had arrived from Dublin, and at the end of the year he was awaiting the arrival of one he had ordered for himself.[10] One contemporary author, Munier, refers to Dutch instruments as well. However, as the bulk of the trade in Cognac itself was with

[8] ADC, Angouleme, 5C5, 20 June 1782, comte de Jarnac to intendant.
[9] MAC, letter book 1762–4, 5 December 1763, to Stritch.
[10] *Ibid.*, 14 November 1763, to McDermott.

London, English and Irish instruments were more relevant. Significantly, while Lallemand used the word 'standard' in referring to Dublin and London strength, he used the term 'proof' for commercial brandy in Cognac, which implies a contrast between the proof or *preuve* identified locally by the traditional empirical methods and strength or *force* measured abroad by instruments. Heath's hydrometer was already in use in Dublin in 1761, as Delamain, who actually arrived in Cognac the year before, recalled years later.[11]

By 1766 the hydrometer was in use in the Charente, and French models had appeared. Following the pioneering London instruments, both the Tessa instrument and the later Cartier instrument used the principle of measuring strength by notches on a device which sank more deeply in a strong alcohol because the specific density was lighter. True measuring of strength in terms of the precise content of alcohol came only with the Gay-Lussac instrument of the nineteenth century (whose measurement in terms of percentage alcohol content contrasted with the British revenue measurement of strength by reference to a cumbersomely defined standard or proof).

In 1766 the precocious Laurence Saule frequently gave the strength in degrees Tessa, and Lallemand did so in May 1767.[12] More slowly, strength in degrees Tessa was quoted by the Hennessy and Broussard houses in 1769. Lallemand, unconsciously exaggerating the length of time the new instruments were in vogue and their diffusion, observed in 1767 that 'since many years such is no more the case, hydrometers having been brought into fashion, our most dullsome people knowing the use of it as well as you and me'.[13] However, if known in the Charente, *éprouvettes* (provers or hydrometers) of any kind were slow to become known in Paris in commercial and scientific circles alike. Hennessy's relative, Pat Nagle, wrote to him in frustration in 1766 that:

I would have answered your letter long since had I not delayed in expectation of getting the eprouvette you mentioned but after all the enquiries I could make as well of grocers as brandy sellors [*sic*] and four members of the Academy of Sciences I could not succed, all [of] whom told me there was no such thing. Not content with that I waited for the return of Abbé Nollet, the royal proffessor of physicks who was att Versailles and who knows what belongs to them sort of things better than all others, He also assured me there was no such thing presented to the Academy. However Monseiur Belliew [*sic*] told me there was and that himself would get it which if he does you may depend it shall be sent without delay.[14]

---

[11] HAJ, Delamain no. 2 letter book 1781–3, 29 April 1783, to Hardin, Belfast.
[12] MAC, letter book 1766–7, 13 May 1767, to Gast Lallemand.
[13] *Ibid.*, 9 May 1767, to Pickworth, Hull.
[14] HAC, 24 April 1766, Pat Nagle, Paris, to Richard Hennessy.

Significantly, the only person familiar with the instrument proved to be Bellew, an Irish army officer planning to enter the brandy trade.

As a result of variations in the individual instruments or failure to allow for the fact that readings varied at different temperatures, differing strengths were quoted. In referring to the universal use of the new instruments, Lallemand lamented in 1767 that sellers, failing to have recourse to the thermometer as well, had unwarranted views of the strength of their brandy in warm weather. A lawyer in 1772 noted in regard to the appearance of the *aréomètre* or hydrometer that 'chaque négociant a le sien, qu'il se fait lui-meme à peu de frais, et sur lequel il compte autant que sur ceux dont on a fait tant d'étalage'.[15] Given unstandardised or individual construction, it was not an uncommon experience that instruments failed to agree.[16] As Saule noted in September 1766, in the case of a consignment 'there appears a ¼ of a degree difference between the sample bottle and the delivery to our prejudice by your three different provers. His prover must be of a very strong [i.e. insensitive] kind as the ¼ of degree difference makes no impression on it. We have such a one and therefore do not use it.'[17] The tract the lawyer wrote in 1772 had been prepared for pleadings against the use of the Cartier instrument which had been adopted by the revenue authorities in 1770. The belated and hasty recognition of instrument measurement in Paris would appear to have led to official sanctioning of an instrument different from the one which had already won favour in the brandy districts themselves. The first published account in France in 1770 gave the strength in degrees Tessa, thinking it unnecessary to identify the name, and the author noted that the change had occurred within the last twelve to fifteen years.[18] We can assume only that the Tessa instrument was the most satisfactory of several instruments that appeared locally. It had been objected against Cartier that other instruments already existed 'à-peu-près semblables aux siens'.[19] Up to 1800 at least, strength of brandy locally in Cognac was always estimated in degrees Tessa.

While the hydrometer quickly came to be used by the sellers of brandy and by merchants, the actual *bouilleurs*, sometimes peasant proprietors but mostly workmen employed by proprietors of vineyards designated as

---

[15] ACC, La Rochelle, no. 3634, *Mémoire sur l'usage de l'aréomètre*, p. 38.

[16] E. Munier, *Essai d'une méthode générale propre à étendre les connaissances des voyageurs ou recueil d'observations relatives à l'histoire, à la répartition des impots, aux arts, à la culture des terres, le tout appuyé sur des faits exacts et enrichi d'expériences utiles* (2 vols., Paris, 1779) in B. Sepulchre, *L'Angoumois à la fin de l'Ancien Régime* (Paris, 1981), p. 187.

[17] HAC, 25 September 1766, Laurence Saule, Charente, to Richard Hennessy.

[18] E. Munier, *Mémoire qui a concouru pour le prix proposé par la société royale d'agriculture de Limoges sur la manière de bruler ou de distiller les vins* (written 1766, published 1770); in B. Sepulchre, *L'Angoumois à la fin de l'Ancien Régime* (Paris, 1981), section x.

[19] ACC, La Rochelle, no. 3634, *Mémoire sur l'usage de l'aréomètre*, p. 7n.

bourgeois, may have been slower to use it. However, one should not exaggerate this. They were skilled workmen, and some or many of them may well have been conversant with the Tessa instrument. The case against them was made in documents in 1782 anxious to oppose revenue use of the Cartier instrument. Thus, one of the memoranda in 1782 claimed that 'il n'est pas douteux que beaucoup de bouilleurs ne sachant lire ni écrire, auraient de la peine à connaitre le pèze'liqueur de Cartier combiné avec le théomètre de Réaumur'.[20] The implication comes out also in a memorandum from the merchants of Cognac, Jarnac and Pons: 'veu qu'elle suppose la connaissance de l'usage de l'aréomètre et du thermomètre à des bouilleurs qui n'en ont aucune idée et qui la plupart ne savent ny lire, écrire ny connaitre les chiffres'.[21]

Before the appearance of instruments, the judgement of brandy strength depended variously on appreciation of taste and odour, and several practical tests. The most important one was the way in which the bubbles behaved when brandy was poured from a short distance or shaken in a partly filled small bottle or prover (in French *épreuve*, *épreuvette* or *prouvette*). According to Savary in 1723, 'il se forme alors une petite mousse blanche qui en diminuant fasse le circle, que les marchands d'eau de vie appellent le chapelet . . . n'y ayant que l'eau de vie bien déflegmée, et où il ne reste point trop d'humidité, à qui le chapelet se forme entièrement'. At spirit strength (*c.* 70 degrees by content), the bubbles disappear rapidly; at low strengths (below 57 degrees), a diffuse foam takes shape slowly and then disappears. In between these two stages the bubbles not only gather in a circle or chapelet but also hold their consistency for a time. The key moment in distillation, beyond which the alcoholic strength of the flow of liquid began to decline very fast, was the point at which, if a sample was subject to proving, the bubbles were found to reduce themselves to three, a large one and two adjoining small ones, the celebrated *trois perles* which is still described in modern manuals of distillation.[22] In modern distillation it marks the distinction between *coeur* and *seconde*. Cognac *négociants* sometimes advised London importers to use the same empirical methods to test the brandy sent to the London market (which should be above the *perle* in strength). Thus, Richard Hennessy, writing to a merchant in London in 1770, repeated the lore, in referring to 'glass proof that is to carry a good head when poured from some distance into a glass'.[23]

---

[20] ADC, Angouleme, 5C5, 'Mémoire ou observations'.
[21] *Ibid.*, memorandum by merchants of Cognac, Jarnac and Pons to intendant, signed by nine houses (not to be confused with another memorandum with the signatures of fourteen houses).
[22] R. Lafon, J. Lafon and P. Couillaud, *Le cognac: sa distillation* (4th edn, Paris, 1964), pp. 81–2.   [23] HAC, letter book 1769–71, 29 October 1770, to Ellis, London.

The *perle*, according to the article on 'eau-de-vie' in the 1755 edition of the *Encyclopédie*, is a corruption of *perte*, and relates to the point at which the spirit begins to weaken (*commence à se perdre*). Below that point, at which (as was later known) the strength was 58–60 degrees by content, agitation of the liquid resulted in a froth which did not crystallise into a small lingering cluster of bubbles before vanishing, or, as the *Encyclopédie* described it, 'une petite écume, qui est presque aussitot passée qu'apperçue'. Already in the 1720s the strength of the brandy of Nantes and Poitou, higher than that of neighbouring districts, was well known, according to Savary, because 'elles conservent plus longtemps l'épreuve du chapelet'. In the case of the *seconde*, the way to test it, according to the *Encyclopédie*, was to spill some on the *chapeau* or head of the still, light it, and if a blue flame appeared, it proved that spirit still existed. What the *Encyclopédie* meant, translated into more modern terms, is that down to 46 degrees brandy would ignite into a steady blue flame: beyond that point while there is still alcohol in the flow, the larger quantity of other substances quenched the flame: once a flame failed to maintain itself, brandy was deemed to be below proof. Slightly different methods existed to recognise *esprit*. In the case of spirit, according to Savary, no residue was left when some of the liquid was set alight when poured on to the warm copper of the still. An alternative was to set fire to a mix of brandy and gunpowder. If the gunpowder ignited, it proved the existence of spirit. If it failed to ignite it meant that aqueous substances were preventing the gunpowder from combusting and established that the substance was below spirit strength.

Measurement of alcoholic content and definitions of brandy

Simple brandy, depending on the amount of *seconde* in it, should range from a strength of 46–47 to 57–58 degrees. The latter strength was the *preuve de Hollande*, historically the strength at which brandy had been shipped to Holland. It was the product of the flow in a second distillation to the point at which the liquid could not sustain a blue flame and where on modern instruments the strength would read as 46–47 degrees. On the Cartier scale, at 15 degrees it reads from 18.5 to 21.5, or at cut-off point from 47 degrees by volume (corresponding to 18.5 degrees Cartier) to 58 degrees (corresponding to 21.5 degrees Cartier) for the entire accumulation of distillate. Fifty-eight degrees by volume corresponds to $3\frac{3}{8}$ degrees on the Tessa scale at a temperature of 15 degrees. *Eau-de-vie forte*, which was the *eau-de-vie bonne et forte* of *Encyclopédie* language in 1755, rated from above 22 degrees to just under 34 degrees. Reading in reverse, i.e. from the start of the distillation, output fell from a high of 33.5

degrees Cartier (14 degrees Tessa or approximately 87 degrees by volume) in the early stages of distillation down to 22 degrees Cartier (4 degrees Tessa or 60 degrees by volume) at cut-off point. In eighteenth-century revenue practice the accepted ambient temperature was lower than today: 10 degrees Centigrade in place of the 15 degrees in the present century (itself very recently raised to 20 degrees).[24] This would lower the cut-off point in degree of strength because lower temperatures depress strength, but lower temperatures could also radically redefine the brandy if it was close to critical points in measurement. The revenue tables of the 1780s and 1790s redefined brandy of below 22 degrees from *eau-de-vie forte* to *eau-de-vie simple* and below 18 degrees Cartier from *eau-de-vie simple* to *eau-de-vie sous preuve*. At 10 degrees of temperature, at the critical reading of 17.9 degrees on the Cartier scale, brandy would have hovered around zero on the Tessa scale, i.e. it would have rated as *eau-de-vie au dessous de preuve* and at 21.9 or approximately 3⅛ Tessa it would still have rated as *eau-de-vie simple* or *preuve de Hollande*. To summarise a complex situation, the basic commercial or traded brandy was an accumulation at a strength for the total mass of 3, 3⅛ or even 3¼ degrees Tessa, or, in order not to incur a higher rate of tax, 18 to not more than 21.9 degrees Cartier.[25]

While any brandy above 46–47 degrees by volume was within the *eau-de-vie simple* definition, the effective scope of the *preuve de Hollande* was

[24] ACC, La Rochelle, no. 3595, 'Table des enfoncements de l'aréomètre dans les eaux de vies et dans les esprits de vin'. There is an error in the tables. The column given as 10 degrees in the 'Combien la chaleur au dessus du 10 degrés augmente l'enfoncement de l'aréomètre' section should read 15 degrees. Without this adjustment part of the table is incomprehensible. The term 'esprit de vin' was reserved for spirit of 34 degrees Cartier, 14 Tessa or 86 degrees Gay-Lussac.

[25] Another document at the same time represented 3¼ degrees Tessa as equalling 22½ on the Cartier scale (ADC, Angouleme, 5C5, 'Mémoire ou observations'). The confusion may possibly arise out of the fact that the fiscal proof for simple brandy was set at up to 22 *exclusivement*, i.e. excluding 22 degrees, and hence unwittingly the author compared the top Tessa reading for ordinary brandy with the bottom reading for *eau de vie bonne*. The same problem arose in 1795 when Otard claimed that 4 degrees Tessa equalled 21 degrees Cartier in Paris, a reminder either of approximate readings on the margins or of inaccurate instruments. OAC, letter book 30 Vendémiaire an 4 to 4 April 1797, 14 Brumaire an 4 (5 November 1795), to Alleon. A reading of 3¼ on the Tessa scale, 'la seule connue dans cette province', according to the *hotel de ville* of the town of Saintes, was the equivalent of 21 on the Cartier scale. At first sight this might seem to be in contradiction with what has been said above. In fact this is not so, as a reading of 21 meant 21 including any fractions which did not raise the reading to 22. While superficially contradictory, it really means 21 as opposed to 22 (i.e. embracing not only 21 but 21 plus fractional additions not exceeding unity). Moreover, as the Tessa scale proceeded in eighths, 3¼ was the first reading above 3⅛ (ADC, Angouleme, 5C6, 'Extrait du registre des délibérations de l'hotel de ville de Saintes'). Readings of 3¼ or 3⅜ and even, on some instruments, a reading of 3 (because the first instruments were individualistic or imprecise) are the critical readings: at a temperature of 10 degrees a reading of 18 degrees Cartier brought brandy into the *eau de vie simple/preuve de Hollande* category and 22 degrees brought it into the category of *eau de vie forte* (see footnote 24 for source).

the entire flow from the outset of the second distillation until the *seconde* was exhausted. In practice, this could vary, depending on the intrinsic strength of the vintage (the number of barriques to make a barrique of brandy could vary from 5–6 in a good vintage to 10 in the really disastrous vintages of the century) and on the care with which the end of the *seconde* was identified. Hence, in practice, brandy fell below 3 to 3⅛ in wines of the Aunis, either because of their lower alcoholic strength or because the *seconde* was admitted overgenerously. In commercial terms the accepted proof, embracing both *eau-de-vie forte* and *seconde*, was about 57 degrees. This was designated as the *preuve de Hollande* or the *preuve marchande*, and when accurate (though still approximate) measurement first emerged in the 1760s the first two known quotations in the surviving correspondence give it as 3 and 3⅛ respectively on the Tessa scale.

To achieve a strength of 3 to 3¼ degrees Tessa for the mass, the amount of *seconde* had to be closely monitored; more precisely, *seconde* should not be taken into account at below a zero reading on a Tessa instrument, 18 degrees on a Cartier one, or 46 degrees on the later Gay-Lussac one (the first instrument to measure alcohol strength by volume and still the basic one).[26] The first known formal designation of brandy below 18 degrees Cartier (or 46 degrees Gay-Lussac) as *eau-de-vie au dessous de preuve* is a late eighteenth-century one, a copy of revenue tables of 1781 or 1782, but this is simply a confirmation in Cartier degrees of prevailing practice. The addition of brandy below 46 degrees was undesirable because it diluted the alcoholic strength of the batch, and also, as the brandy strength tapered off, the flow of liquid contained a progressively larger proportion of unwanted substances or 'phlegme' as contemporaries described it, which made the brandy unpleasant in taste or odour. On the Tessa instrument, which had emerged in the 1760s and which was the favourite instrument of the actual brandy makers, a point equivalent to 46 degrees was rated as zero.

If the decisive cut-off point between *seconde* and residue to produce a brandy at *preuve de Hollande* occurred at 46–47 degrees, in turn the distinguishing point between *eau-de-vie bonne et forte* and *seconde*, with its rapidly declining alcoholic strength, was deemed to take place at what was later recognised as the point where alcoholic strength fell to 57 degrees (at 10 degrees temperature). At that moment the accumulated flow in the basin at the outflow from the worm was in excess of 60 degrees. Its strength as the *coeur* in modern distilling in Cognac is 70 degrees; con-

---

[26] ACC, La Rochelle, no. 3595, 'Table des enfoncements de l'aréomètre dans les eaux-de-vie et dans les esprits'. A distillation which would result in 4 barriques of brandy *au quart* would yield only 3 barriques if distillation was interrupted by a *coupe à la serpentine*. ACC, La Rochelle, no. 3593.

temporary evidence giving at most a figure of 5 to 5.5 Tessa for the mass would suggest that the strength of such brandy was between 61 and 64 (or 63 and 66 at the 15 degrees temperature of twentieth-century practice). The contrast between eighteenth-century strength and modern strength could hardly arise simply from changes in basic techniques in distilling (as the best distillers were no less capable than those of today). A subtle change over time as the result of the systematic selection of grape strains which favour a higher alcoholic strength might contribute a little, though not decisively, to the result. Variation in the intrinsic strength of the brandy in the still for the second distillation was probably what explains most of the difference. This does not imply carelessness or lack of knowledge. In fact it arises from the actual methods of making brandy and the scale of the distiller's operation. Eighteenth-century distillers refilling the still for a second distillation traditionally added wine to make up losses in the first distillation. If, however, the content of the still for the second distillation was to consist exclusively of first distillate, then a higher strength would result from the second distillation. The addition of extra brandy to the still would be difficult for a small distiller with a single still in constant operation, and would be progressively easier for a distiller working several stills. The lower strength of brandy compared with today almost certainly reflects subtle variations in practice in refilling the still. The fact that distillers were larger and more prosperous around the towns of Segonzac, Cognac and Jarnac helps to explain why contemporaneously their brandy was held to be stronger, and why within the century they began progressively to market brandy at the strength of the *coupe à la serpentine*. For a small operator working intermittently or with a single still, such practice would greatly reduce his output, and as long as the basic commercial standard remained one which tolerated *seconde*, his practice made sense for his circumstances. Only when, around mid-century, specialist distillers began to buy brandy expressly for redistillation, did its merits come into doubt.

A third distillation today produces brandy of a strength of 77 degrees by volume; much stronger brandy (of about 87 degrees) would however be obtained either in the first flow of a third distillation or in a further or fourth distillation. Late eighteenth-century revenue tables identify *esprit de vin* at 34 degrees Cartier at 10 degrees temperature (or 34¾ at 15 degrees, the equivalent of 87 degrees Gay-Lussac). The tables show that the technical feasibility of achieving that strength was taken for granted. In practice, however, as in the case of more ordinary brandy, the actual degree of strength at which *esprit* was sold seems to have been somewhat lower than in modern times. Thus the strength of 'three-sixths' (i.e. 'one-half'), unambiguously differentiated in one Cognac source in 1800 from 'three-fifths' (and hence seen as a fourth distillation), was said to be 12 degrees Tessa, which would correspond to brandy of a strength of 83 degrees in modern times or to 81–82 degrees at the temperature common at the time. 'One-third', 'three-fifths' and 'one-half' did not refer to the precise strength so much as to the number of distillations: a second distillation above the *perle*, a third distillation and a fourth distillation respectively. To achieve the highest strength of spirit one-half (itself not the highest strength of spirit technically possible, but the highest grade regarded as commercially viable) would involve a sequence of four successive distillations, in the process making good losses from the addition of strong spirit already on hand, and not from weaker brandy. In practice, either considerations of time or cost ruled that standard out; weaker spirit (or even wine) was added and the outcome was less than the theoretical possible strength. This was more evident in Bordeaux port distilling than in Cognac. Cognac distilling to strengths above spirit 'one-third' was limited and some of it was specially commissioned. In Bordeaux distilling was highly commercial and speculative, often involving the fulfilment of large commissions at short notice for vessels about to sail and for customers less particular than the few who passed such commissions to Cognac. Brandy 'three-fifths' and 'one-half' in Bordeaux fell below the strength in Cognac. The Bordeaux distillers seem to have come from Cognac; a lack of distilling expertise cannot be seen as the root of the contrast between Bordeaux and Cognac.[27]

The 1687 decree was a tribute to the ambition of revenue collectors to make fine and revenue-yielding distinctions as well as an exposé of the limits of contemporary understanding of the nature of distilling. However, probably because little brandy entered into trade other than the relatively weak brandy combining *eau-de-vie bonne et forte* and *seconde*, the decree seems to have had no significance in the brandy producing regions for over fifty years after it had been devised. In the absence of measuring instruments, it would in any event have been unenforceable or a subject of endless litigation. In the earliest surviving letter book of the trade, the Augier letter book of 1681–6, there is no reference whatever to distinctions in grades of brandy. There is a mere assurance on a single occasion of brandy being of a 'good' proof. This is more amply confirmed by the later Augier letter books of which there is a complete run between 1717 and 1728. In contrast to the 1680s, *double*, meaning brandy above the basic proof, now entered into consignments overseas, though infrequently.[28] However, sophistication is revealed in the fact that the distinc-

---

[27] See OAC, Lettres à l'étranger, 17 June 1800–24 May 1802, 21 December 1800, to Da Rocha, Oporto. This letter shows how close the links between the two centres were.
[28] AAC, letter book 1717–19, 26 March 1718, Augier to Molinié, Hamburg.

tion existed in 1718 between both *esprit* 'one-third', the lowest grade, and higher grades. But despite the new-found sophistication, brandy above the simple Dutch proof was rare.

Conflicts of interest in brandy making

Commerce was built around a basic brandy, usually shipped out within the year after distillation, and containing *seconde* as well as brandy *bonne et forte*: in other words it was shipped at the *preuve marchande, preuve de Cognac,* or *preuve de Hollande,* all synonymous terms. Any liquid with a strength running from 46–47 degrees to 57 by volume fell within the definition of *preuve de Hollande,* and a second distillation, allowed to flow from the outset of distillation down to the point of 46 or 47 degrees, yielded an accumulated batch or mass whose general strength was of the order of 57 degrees. *Preuve de Hollande* is itself an ambiguous term, because it could be interpreted either as the minimum strength admitted to the batch, or the strength of the entire batch. This accounts for the glaring conflicts in modern accounts which profess to give the exact strength of the *preuve de Hollande.* It could be expressed either as the marginal cut-off point, i.e. *c.* 46 degrees (Gay-Lussac) by volume, or as the strength of the accumulation above that point, i.e. *c.* 57 degrees, which would be the strength at which a *négociant* bought a barrique of brandy at market. This strength read off the instrument just at or just above 3 degrees on the Tessa scale. On conversion tables, its maximum strength (at 10 degrees temperature) would read as 21.9 Cartier, 3⅛ Tessa or barely above 57 per cent. A further 5 degrees temperature would raise the reading to above 3¾ degrees Tessa or to above 59 Gay-Lussac. A merchant buying on the account of a customer had to be concerned both with the strength of the contents of the barrique, as it would damage his reputation or lose him a customer if it fell below the *preuve marchande,* and with the assumed strength of the final drops from the still into the barrique, because if brandy were admitted below the conventionally accepted minimum strength qualifying as *preuve de Hollande,* an excess of *seconde* could greatly damage the flavour. Given the complexity of brandy and the fact that a certain amount of *seconde* but no more was tolerated, the *preuve de Hollande* itself was quite subtle in its implications.

Much of the brandy shipped for Holland in the seventeenth century came from the Aunis, and in the eighteenth from Saint-Jean d'Angély. These regions, more particularly the Aunis, produced a weaker brandy than in Cognac, in part because their wine was held to result in a lower strength from the still and, more importantly, because of the different circumstances of the actual maker. Thus cognac from the vicinity of the town of Cognac was said to be 10 to 12 per cent stronger than other brandies from the region; in one letter Saint-Jean d'Angély was singled out as 10–15 per cent weaker than cognac.[29] Dissatisfaction occasioned by the low strength of the Aunis brandy, inferior even to Saint-Jean d'Angély, sparked the belief, not without reason, that the low strength reflected fraud by the presence of too much *seconde*. That from the Aunis in particular had already been the subject of local requirements (*règlement de police*) on 16 October 1700 and of a decree of the chamber of commerce on 31 May 1728 that it should be brought up to the strength of better thought-of brandies in the region. These measures, and more particularly reaffirmation in 1728, were prompted no doubt by the perception of the traders of La Rochelle that they were losing out to interests in the interior which benefited from the proximity of better brandy. The regulations were reflected more forcefully still in the decree of the council of state of 10 April 1753, itself the result of representations, which required brandy to be brought up to a 'preuve semblable à celle de Cognac, Aigre, Saint-Jean d'Angély et provinces voisines'. The decree sought to deal with the problem by giving new legal authority to a limitation of the amount of *seconde* to be admitted into the brandy, and to enforcement machinery by creating four posts of *agréeurs* to taste brandy in the markets, and even to do so a further time on the quays.[30] In the wake of this decree, as a later opinion in 1772 noted, 'les fabriquants sont astreints à ne meler dans leur eau de vie qu'un quart de seconde, c'est à dire, qu'un quart de ce fluide infirme, aqueux, flegmatique, qui reste dans l'alembic après la première distillation; l'eau-de-vie, affaiblie par ce mélange, est vraiment de l'eau-de-vie commercialle de la plus basse qualité'.[31] The receptacle for brandy was now marked in *pots*, and when 20 had been reached, only a further 5 *pots* of liquid should be admitted.

The problem with the *seconde* was that the yield or bulk of liquid passing through the worm or *serpentine* which was low during the first six hours in the second distillation up to the moment of the *perle*, increased dramatically during the 75 subsequent minutes which brought the brandy down from 57 degrees Gay-Lussac at the moment of the *perle* to a strength of 46 degrees, after which the flow was deemed to be below proof. While it was easy to separate *eau-de-vie bonne* from *seconde*, a cut-

---

[29] DAJ, letter book 1767–8, 12 July 1768, to Thomas Baildon, Helsingor; HAC, letter book 1765–9, Richard Hennessy to Bell and Rannie, Leith, 5 February 1767.

[30] ACC, La Rochelle, no. 3594 bis.

[31] *Ibid.*, no. 3634, *Mémoire sur l'usage de l'aréomètre*, p. 29. See also no. 3594 bis. The word 'première' is somewhat surprising, and would seem to result from error by the Paris lawyer: either a misunderstanding of the technique, or more probably simply a clumsy phrase to distinguish qualitatively the cut-off point between *coeur* and *seconde*.

off point in the *seconde* was much less easy. Either inattention or, where the alcoholic strength of the vintage was low, cupidity to maximise the amount of vendible liquid could result in a brandy which was both weak and nasty to the taste. The 1753 formula for the Aunis which limited the *seconde* to one quarter of the *coeur*, i.e. to one-fifth of the total volume of the brandy, was a convenient rule of thumb to limit abuse. As for the post of *agréeur*, itself an archaic way of responding to a real problem, the more obvious result was the creation of an extra venal office rather than an improvement in quality.

The *Encyclopédie* article suggests that the 1753 decree of the council of state applied to brandy in general. In fact it did not. It was confined to the Aunis (or more accurately to brandy coming to market within the Aunis), and corresponded to a local problem and to a conflict of interests between the merchants in the town and the brandy makers in the immediate hinterland. It was an ongoing saga in the Aunis, and tradition and a short-age of wood combined to encourage local producers to tolerate a high proportion of *seconde*. The regulation of 16 October 1700 had actually required brandy to be 'coupée au quart de perte seullement et non au tiers comme estait l'ancien usage'. More decisively, in this region of small and marginal distillers, the still when filled for the second distillation was commonly topped up with wine. In practice, a contrast persisted. Ordinary brandy in the Aunis was regarded as having a strength of barely 3 degrees Tessa, whereas in Cognac the basic brandy was a fraction higher, and an increasing proportion by mid-century was intentionally made to higher standards.

The politics of the change in 1753 seem to have revolved around the appointment in the preceding year of *commissaires* by the chamber of commerce to draft regulations to deal with a perceived crisis in the brandy trade of the port. The proposal grew out of criticism from northern France of the La Rochelle brandies, and it was feared by some that radical changes in regulations might be made in response to some of these crit-icisms. Thus, opposition was expressed at the time by a memoir to the chamber by ten signatories, though a later note in the margin of the memoir states tersely that 'on n'a eu aucun égard à ce mémoire, vu les articles arrestés par le règlement'.[32] In fact the draft regulations were in no way revolutionary, as the ten signatories had feared. When they in turn were converted into a draft decree sent down from Paris and passed on by the intendant, the draft became the subject of a long memorial on its pro-visions from the merchants of La Rochelle (including at least two of the signatories of the preceding petition), on the whole welcoming its provi-

[32] *Ibid.*, no. 3593, n.d.

sions as 'moyens pour rapeller l'étranger dans nos ports . . . des plus assurés et des plus efficaces'.[33]

The 1753 regulations themselves were backward-looking: they specifically prohibited purchases outside the market place, whereas much buying was direct from makers, and especially in the case of the stronger brandies. Legal definition of the amount of *seconde*, by further sanctioning an existing inferior practice, made an inferior brandy all the more inevitable, as in real-life distilling, given variations in the quality of the content of the still from batch to batch and year to year, the amount included should have been flexible. The new regulations themselves reflected the same lack of aliveness to change that those who petitioned against them had revealed in their own memorial. The ten petitioners had suggested that the merchants in Picardy and Flanders had demanded that all brandy be cut off *à la serpentine*. They went on to declare that 'il est inouy que dans toute la généralité de la Rochelle, Saintonge, Bordeaux et Nantes, il y aye jamais été fait des eaux de vie coupées à la serpentine mais bien au quart'. The conflict was more complex than is evident from their memoir. The merchants of Picardy and Flanders seem to have simply suggested that there would be large economies in sending out brandy *coupée à la serpentine*, in other words in the form of spirit. The petitioners, however, proceeded to misrepresent the northern merchants as intent simply on fraudulent practices: 'Mais ce n'est pas seulement sur tant de bénéfices qu'ils comptent. Ils ont d'autres vues plus considérables. C'est d'ajouter et mettre un quart d'eau dans ces eaux de vie, estant absolument impossible sans s'exposer à perdre la vie de les boire autrement. On scait parfaitement que cela se pratique de la sorte.' In other words they were unalive (or pretended to be) to what was already taking place on the fringe of the region: the growth of spirit making either for shipment to Paris or for adding to existing brandies. Indeed the petitioners revealed a staggering complacency about the brandy of the region: 'Ces memes eaux-de-vie au quart durent cinque ou six ans sans diminution de qualité.'

In this context the decree of 1753 furnished evidence of an antiquated outlook all round – on the part of the city which wanted to keep brandy buying in the market and to regulate the product by a panoply of regulations and *agréeurs*, and on the part of the merchants who did not see the point of spirit making. Ironically, within two decades the very *agréeurs* appointed under the decree plaintively listed an increase in the strength of

[33] *Ibid.*, no. 3592, 9 November 1752. The Presidial hearing of the case against the *courtiers*, set out in 169 pages of detailed testimony over the period 26 April–20 September 1749, plus detailed interrogations of eighteen individuals, survives in the intendance records. ADCM, La Rochelle, C186, no. 1.

brandy (their fees were based on the number of *pièces* inspected) as one of several reasons for the fall in their income.[34] It was precisely the spread of the *coupe à la serpentine*, especially from the 1740s onwards, which made makers and buyers more attentive to distilling practice and also in time created a fuller awareness of the qualities of brandy.

The dispute in the Aunis, culminating in the 1753 decree, seems to have originated in the 1740s. At the outset, it took the form of a quarrel between the *courtiers* or brokers and a small group of merchants who wanted to break through the archaic restrictions of markets and conventional strength. A memoir by twelve brokers in 1749 was a violent attack on the methods and business morality of the merchants, who were represented as the enemies of the producer and as boldly reselling 'en plein canton' brandy bought at lower prices before the producer was even aware of the change in price. In particular the brokers vented their ire on a preceding memoir as one prepared by 'six jeunes spéculateurs auteurs d'un mémoire, cherchant journellement à capter la confiance des bouilleurs et proprietaires, à fin de tirer l'eau de vie de leurs mains sans le ministère des courtiers'. While other issues were involved, one of them was the question of quality. The office of broker had not been a venal office for the preceding forty years: the solution proposed was the creation of the venal office of *agréeur*. The consequence was, the brokers pointed out, that the new officers 'exigéraient dans les eaux-de-vie du pays la meme preuve que dans celles de Cognac; ils les feroient toutes couper à la serpentine pour les pouvoir conserver plus longtemps sans diminution de qualité et faciliter ainsy les spéculations des commissionaires; en un mot la province seroit mise à contribution, et la denrée livrée à discrétion des acheteurs'.

Evident in this quotation is a rather loose hint at the extent of spirit making in Cognac. Indeed, the brokers recognised the existence further afield of brandies stronger than the basic strength. Reminding the *commissionaires* (buyers or factors) that 'les bouilleurs ne sont obligés qu'à livrer des eaux-de-vie marchandes', the brokers claimed that if deficient brandy was bought it was a result of the failure of the buyers to ensure that brandy was made 'au quart' (i.e. included not more than a quarter of *seconde*) and that as they were free to accept or reject brandy, 'ils doivent meme s'imputer si on ne les fait pas meilleurs dans la province'. The brokers claimed that if they paid more for quality they would get better: 'c'est eux qui authorisent sur cela le relachement des bouilleurs en ne faisant pas plus de cas des bonnes que des mauvaises, et ne voulant pas

---

[34] ACC, La Rochelle, no. 3522, n.d. The year 1766 is pencilled on the document, but it is clearly several years later.

augmenter le prix pour celles des maisons de Surgère, de Chatelaillon, de
Noyant, de Culant, de Saint-Georges, de Cramais etc, ne mettant aucune
différence entre les eaux-de-vie faites à Aigre, Villeneuve la Comtesse, et
celles faites par le paysan dans tous les autres villages; entre celles coupées
à la serpentine, et celles qui ne le sont pas'. This hints at a larger problem.
Quite clearly, with spirit being marketed at greater strength for Paris (by
the simple procedure of the *coupe à la serpentine*), variations in method
were emerging. The fact that the centres mentioned are all, apart from
Chatelaillon, inland (apparently running to Villeneuve-la-Comtesse in
the Bons Bois and to Aigre in the Fins Bois) is significant, because the
locations hint at inland markets in which a demand for spirit one-third
had emerged and in which rather specialised or innovating distillers
worked to that standard (or even above it).

The problems in La Rochelle have to be seen not simply in terms of the
lower strength of the brandies in the Aunis, but of La Rochelle's continued
retreat from a foothold in a much larger hinterland in which other buyers
had emerged. Not only was there a contrast between different villages
(and significantly the better villages were inland) but the question was one
of grade (spirit as opposed to brandy) rather than of consistency in a particular proof. In a declining market (i.e. the port itself as opposed to its
prospering hinterland), frictions inevitably emerged between broker and
factor: they had in any event existed as far back as 1729 and came to a
head in the 1740s when change was even more decisive. The fact that this
was not spelled out more clearly is itself a testimony to the archaic outlook
of the La Rochelle interests. What is interesting in the background,
however, is that some feared in 1752 that the response to the local debate
would be the radical one of making the *coupe à la serpentine* mandatory; the
outcome was the much less radical one of creating the venal office of
agréeur or taster to enforce the convention standard of brandy *au quart*.
The 1753 decree, in recognising the right of sellers to rectify brandy which
did not meet the market standard, was the admission of a new product and
a new market, which had in effect taken from La Rochelle the more
promising inland brandies and left its marginalised merchants with the
weaker and less attractive brandies of the coastal stretches of the Aunis.[35]

Changes in brandy strength

Because a brandy stronger than the *preuve marchande* could pass through
the Irish or English customs at no higher duty, and could be diluted subsequently, the brandy at *preuve marchande* strength after its purchase from

---

[35] See, on the background, *ibid.*, no. 3462, 'Mémoire pour réponse à celuy que les
commissionaires d'eau de vie ont présenté à Messieurs les directeurs et sindics de la
Chambre de Commerce', 23 January 1749.

the distillers came to be fortified by the shippers for the English market by
the addition of *esprit*. This was a novel standard in the 1720s, and
emerged as the trade with London passed from the hands of the
Guernsey merchants, who like the Dutch merchants were essentially
commodity handlers, into the hands of specialist brandy importers in
London, selling either to the retailers or to large customers who were
more worldly wise in the ways of brandy quality and strength. The
absence of a London proof, distinct from the regular proof, is evident
from the first Martell letter books. The earliest reference to a new standard is contemporaneous almost to the year with the emergence of direct
orders by the London brandy sellers. Augier, who was to enjoy much of
their custom over the next ten years, noted in September 1727 that:

> Some merchants of London have ordered here to put in every boot [puncheon] of
> brandy 7 or 8 virtels, who [*sic*] makes 14 or 16 gallons of spirits or double brandy
> which makes them very strong, and abel to carry the same quantity of clear water,
> when they are arrived, en [*sic*] yet to be of ordinary proof.[36]

Augier's English was imperfect, hence the employment of the term 'boot'
just as in the final line for 'and' he slipped into the Dutch usage, 'en'. This
is 3½ to 4 veltes (7–8 gallons) per hogshead. The term 'double brandy',
and this quotation is the earliest use of it by a merchant, is second distillation brandy undiluted by the *seconde*. It is the spirit 'one-third' which was
almost invariably the standard of the spirit added to commercial proof
brandy to bring it up to London standard in subsequent decades. The
Encyclopédie recognised in 1755 that 'quand on veut avoir de l'eau de vie
très forte, on lève le bassiot dès qu'elle perd ... on appelle cela couper à la
serpentine'. The *Encyclopédie* recognised that this spirit was not 'une eau
de vie de commerce', an observation which is confirmed in the letter
books of the first half of the century. This is spirits 'one-third', cheaper
and more convenient to make than higher grades of *esprit*, because it was
the product of a second distillation, and was first widely made for the
purpose of raising the strength of the basic commercial brandy sent to the
London trade in the 1720s. It corresponds to the *coupe à la serpentine*, the
coeur in modern distilling, and was (and is) empirically identified by the
perle. In modern analogy, its strength would be about 70 degrees; at the
strengths quoted for the period reading 5 to 5½ Tessa (62–64 degrees
Gay-Lussac), it was for reasons already mentioned somewhat weaker.

The emergence of a standard above the *preuve marchande* for London is
amply borne out in subsequent decades. Its emergence, moreover, is due
less to the shift to direct importation on the account of London houses,
than to the devising of a hydrometer by John Clarke, not the first but the
first workable one, in 1725. While assessment by Clarke's hydrometer did

---

[36] AAC, letter book 1727–8, 15 September 1727, to Holmes, London.

not acquire a statutory authority until 1787, it was used semi-officially from the outset.[37] As a basic standard the officers settled on a degree of strength corresponding to 4 degrees on the later Tessa scale of Cognac and which was therefore higher than the *preuve de Hollande*. In 1763 Lallemand noted that, measured by Clarke's hydrometer, the London standard was above the 'common proof' of Cognac.[38] In percentage he gave the difference as 10 per cent, though the percentage relates simply to the difference between divisions on the hydrometer, and not to the intrinsic strength in terms of volume of alcohol in the liquid.

In 1768 Delamain observed to a merchant that new brandy required 6 to 8 veltes of spirit per puncheon to bring it up to London standard.[39] Richard Hennessy generalised to a London merchant in 1770 that they added 9 to 12 veltes to a puncheon,[40] and indeed this observation is amply confirmed from the evidence of the Delamain, Martell, Augier and Hennessy invoice books which almost invariably reveal an addition of 4, 5 or 6 veltes of spirit 'one-third' per hogshead for the London market. The presence of 6 veltes of spirit 'one-third' in a barrel of 27 veltes in which the other 21 veltes were of 57 degrees strength capacity should have raised the alcohol content to 63 degrees. On the Tessa scale this is exactly 5, or (if expressed at 10 degrees in place of 15 degrees temperature) around 4¾: much of the brandy for London in the 1780s and 1790s seems to have been shipped at 4⅝ to 5 degrees Tessa, which suggests that even the watchful London revenue officers could be deceived.

Some brandy was allegedly higher, at 6 Tessa or 66 degrees Gay-Lussac which would approximate to brandy cut off at the *perle*, but the invoice books do not in fact bear out activity above 5 degrees Tessa. However, given ullage of brandy and the modest enough addition of spirit to brandy much of which was three or four years old, much of this brandy could have been between 5 and 6 degrees when it came from the still. In other words what had taken place in the case of some of the brandy for London, which was aged locally before shipment, was revolutionary. The inclusion of *seconde* had ceased; the basic strength of the brandy had in effect been raised to that of a *coupe à la serpentine* (spirits one-third), and the brandy was already recognisably modern. Such brandy was not universal, nor was all brandy for London cut *à la serpentine*. However, distilling (or some of it) had travelled a long way from the time when the quantity of *seconde* added to the *coeur* amounted to a further third in sheer volume, or from

---

[37] McGuire, *Irish whiskey*, pp. 51–2.
[38] MAC, letter book 1762–4, 5 December 1763, to Stritch.
[39] DAJ, letter book 1767–8, 6 February 1768 , to Robert Gillingham, Dunkirk.
[40] HAC, letter book 1769–71, 29 October 1770, to Ellis, London. In practice, a margin of tolerance in the instruments meant that brandy which was a little higher had to pay no extra duty.

the situation where in the region at large it was a fourth. The La Rochelle standard of one-fourth was, it must be remembered, in its origins simply a standardisation of an existing practice in the regions where brandy was perceived to be stronger than in the Aunis where the final product was permitted to contain a third in the form of *seconde*.

One of the problems in distilling was that the measurement of brandy was purely empirical until well into the eighteenth century. While recognition of the distinction between *première* or *eau-de-vie bonne et forte* (the modern *coeur*) and *seconde*, and between brandy and spirit was well established, fine distinctions of strength either within brandy or in spirit could only be approximate. In practice, apart from a challenge in Cognac in 1742, which will be referred to later, all commercial brandy passed under a uniform duty, and 'sous leur simple qualification d'eaux de vie'.[41] The same conditions seem to have applied in both Sète and Bordeaux at the time.[42]

For Dublin the brandy standard was the merchant or Cognac standard: 'our market standard is what we generally [ship?] for Dublin'.[43] Dublin brandy had rarely been topped up in the fashion of London. However, in and after the 1760s, largely because the advent of effective measuring instruments raised the sophistication of Dublin importers, brandy for Dublin tended to be raised to a higher strength. In 1770, Hennessy, in writing to a merchant in Dublin observed: 'we have here a market for the force of our brandy which is lower than that shipped for your market'.[44] The dispatch of brandy above the basic standard to Dublin was, as in London at an earlier date, promoted by the prospect of introducing a somewhat stronger brandy at no higher duty. In 1773 Hennessy wrote to the master of an Irish vessel that: 'I have made up yours and [Edward] Barret's brandy a ½ degree above our Dublin standard, which [brandy] I reckon equal to 4 per cent above the Dublin standard, which they will probably lower by the change of weather'.[45]

---

[41] ACC, La Rochelle, no. 3634. *Mémoire sur l'usage de l'aréomètre*, p. 5.
[42] ADC, Angouleme, 5C5, two-sheet document, unheaded and undated but apparently 1782, with details of duties in Angoumois and Saintonge, La Rochelle, Bordeaux and Sète, and Provence.
[43] HAC, letter book 1771–5, 22 January 1774, to Richard Cahill, Dublin.
[44] *Ibid.*, letter book 1769–71, 27 October 1770, to Jennings.
[45] *Ibid.*, letter book 1771–5 , 9 October 1773, to Capt. Silvester Sullivan. He set things out at much greater length in 1781:
   Dublin standard is but 3⅛ degrees of ours: our 4 degrees is 4 per cent above the Dublin standard. We reckon ¼ on our prover equal to 2 per cent. I tried brandy at 5¼: it goes 8 per cent on the Dublin prover
   do. 5½: it goes 10 per cent on the Dublin prover
(HAC, 23 July 1781, Richard Hennessy, Bordeaux, to John Saule, Cognac). One of the interesting things about this quotation is its matter-of-fact referring to strengths of 5¼ and 5½ Tessa.

Four and more commonly six veltes of spirit were now frequently added to a hogshead prior to dispatch to Dublin.[46] Sometimes brandy was strengthened to an even higher degree, as in the case of Luke Cassin, the most active of the regular specialist importers in the 1780s, who in 1783 requested 12 veltes to be added to a hogshead and 20 to a puncheon.[47] The standard of the brandy was monitored closely to see that it conformed to the expected strength: an exasperated Cassin complained to the Hennessys in 1789 that despite the addition of spirit to his brandy, the brandy supplied to a fellow importer, Crosthwaite, was 4 per cent higher. He then noted that: 'Had I given my order to Martell's house, I would not be served in like manner. Mr Saule served me in a like manner some years ago, for which reason I never wrote [i.e. ordered again from] him.'[48] In 1788 Delamain confirmed the universality of this higher standard in Dublin when he wrote that 'your hydrometer standard of 2 or 4 per cent over that is the strength our Dublin friends generally call for, from which we conclude it is most sealable [*sic*]'.[49] These two quotations harmonise perfectly with Hennessy's eighteen to nineteen years previously.

The strength for London (4 degrees Tessa standard) existed side by side with the local 3⅛ proof or standard in the 1760s and early 1770s.[50] With the rapid growth of overland trade to Paris in the 1760s sales to Paris at 4 degrees Tessa or even higher began to grow too, and the changes in strength were described in some detail in 1772.[51] The earliest explicit recognition within the region of this change came in 1769 when the Veuve Galwey from La Rochelle referred to a merchant in Saint-Jean d'Angély buying brandy in Cognac and raising it to 4 degrees for the Paris market.[52] Brandy was being shipped to Paris at even higher strength, i.e. in the form of 'three-fifths' (*c.* 77 degrees Gay-Lussac) or 'two-thirds' (*c.* 70 degrees Gay-Lussac): in 1767–8 the latter was the strength at which Delamain consigned it.[53] We can now identify, quite apart from *esprit*, brandies of several strengths, the Dutch (Cognac or Dublin proof) of 3⅛ Tessa (57 degrees Gay-Lussac), a London proof of 4 degrees (60 degrees

---

[46] HAJ, Delamain no. 2 letter book 1778–81, 1 July 1780, to Ally, Dublin; HAC, 2 February 1789, Luke Cassin to Hennessy.
[47] HAC, 18 October 1783, Luke Cassin to John Saule.
[48] HAC, 16 April 1789, Cassin to Hennessy and Co.
[49] HAJ, Delamain no. 1 letter book 1787–9, 12 January 1788, to Edward Byrne, Dublin.
[50] HAC, 23 July 1781, Richard Hennessy, Bordeaux, to John Saule, Cognac.
[51] ACC, La Rochelle, no. 3634, *Mémoire sur l'usage de l'aréomètre*.
[52] AAC , Broussard archives, 5 November 1769, to Broussard et fils.
[53] DAJ, letter book 1767–8, 25 August 1767, to Capran, Rouen. 'Les eaux-de vie ⅔ preuve de Cognac ou d'ici font ⅗ preuve de Paris, c'est de cette façon que nous l'envoyons dans cette capital du royaume'. The different notation suggests that in Paris a different basis of dilution with distilled water operated to compare standards. In this particular instance, whereas one-third water was added in Cognac, two-fifths were added in Paris.

Gay-Lussac), brandy variously at 5, 5½ and 6 degrees Tessa when it came from the still, and brandies, described as two-thirds or three-quarters, which were well in excess of 6 Tessa (a strength to which they were raised by a large addition of *esprit*). Even strong brandies at 5 degrees declined in strength by ageing to the point that three or four years later they invariably required fortification to ensure they met the London standard.

A strength of 5 to 6 is what the local merchants claimed in 1782 could be manufactured without the addition of spirit, and brandy at that strength (62 to 64 degrees or 23 to 24 Cartier) was said to be shipped to London to evade the duties.[54] There was some confusion among contemporaries. According to one account, it was said to be considered *simple* in England up to 5 degrees.[55] However, this misunderstands the position. There is no doubt about the London standard. Indeed in the wake of the Act of Union the Irish proof standard was brought up to the English level.[56] It is also confirmed in Cognac sources: according to one Otard letter the standard was 4 degrees and brandy was raised by a further five-eighths of a degree, as at that strength it could be slipped through. No invoices show brandy being shipped above 5 degrees at this time, which substantially bears out the accuracy of Otard's observation, and awareness of the strictness of the London customers' officers in applying their rules.

In the 1780s brandy *coupée à la serpentine* was available at the market in some quantity. Cut *à la serpentine*, it would be freer of imperfections, and quality and strength alike would give it a premium. The 1772 tract recognised that 'ils cessaient de faire voiturer à Paris du flegme ou de l'eau de Poitou et d'Aunis dans l'eau de vie. L'eau de vie arrivait pure', and dated the development in shipping *eau-de-vie forte* to Paris to 'généralement depuis dix ans'.[57] In Cognac, where the demand for London was prevalent, brandy at lower proof had declined. Significantly, Delamain in 1789 wrote in terms which imply that brandy of 3⅛ had *formerly* been common.[58] By 1800 it was possible to write that 'our brandy is market proof at 4 degrees which is equal to the London custom-house proof'.[59]

54 See ADC, Angouleme, 5C5, 'Extrait des registres du conseil d'état du roi', 9 May 1782; 'Memoire ou observations'.
55 *Ibid.*, 5C6, 'Remontrances en forme de mémoire adressé à Monseigneur le controleur général des finances, par le clergé, la noblesse, les maires, échevins et notables . . . de la ville de Saintes', 1784.
56 For equivalents on the Clarke and Sykes scales, see 58 George 3, c. 28, section 4; 40 George 3, c. 38. Irish spirits were to be charged a regular duty at 7 degrees over proof on the Sykes hydrometer and in proportion for higher strengths. McGuire, *Irish whiskey*, p. 190.   57 ACC, La Rochelle, no. 3634, *Mémoire sur l'usage de l'aréomètre*, pp. 4, 39.
58 HAJ, Delamain no. 2 letter book 1787–9, 27 April 1789, to Yeats and Brown, London.
59 OAC, foreign letter book 17 June 1800–24 May 1802, 21 December 1800, to Da Rocha, Porto. This letter has very explicit comments on the strength of brandy and spirit.

In other words, in Cognac the London market standard overshadowed the old Cognac proof.

Even well to the south of the Charente, George Boyd, who bought regularly at 4 degrees, and up to 5½ degrees, complained when brandy was 3 degrees Tessa. In fact the London standard now operated as the local standard. No compensation was paid for brandy above 3⅛ degree, the old standard of the region. However, 3 livres 10 sols to 4 livres was paid for every degree above 4 degrees, which was by implication in recognition of the London standard, despite the fact that Boyd was not buying for London. In Cognac in 1788 the standard for Paris was 7 degrees Tessa: in November Delamain was prepared to deliver brandy at 7 degrees (approximately 67 degrees at 10 degrees temperature, i.e. spirit 'one-third') but thought 8 degrees too expensive a strength to reach.[60] What he was saying in effect was that the saving in transport costs by raising brandy by a further degree was outweighed by the extra costs in spirit making to a higher strength.

Brandy for London was aged: usually, in post-1760s times, it was three or four years old, hence the generous addition of spirit reflected not a weak brandy but an older brandy and a greater need to make good losses in the ageing process. To an Irish customer in 1768 Delamain wrote that 'our old brandy is always 8 or 10 per cent under the new and indeed what we ship for the English market we strengthen with spirits to their standard. You dont mention any directions on this head and we shall therefore take a medium and raise to the strength of new brandy.'[61] As for the quantity, Delamain observed that 'we never yet met 10 year old brandy that 12 or 16 veltes spirit per puncheon would suffice'.[62] In another letter he put the figure as high as 12 to 20 veltes for brandy aged from three to ten years.[63] The merchants did not themselves age brandy. Even their large stocks in the late 1780s were not held for ageing but represented stocks purchased in the months preceding the seasonal upturn in foreign demand. At the time of purchase of a three- or four-year-old brandy – or of an older one – additions of spirit would be necessary to compensate for preceding losses in strength. In the interval the additions to make good ullage from the cask would not have made good the loss in strength.

Between 5 and 6 degrees Tessa, brandy was akin to modern brandy in

---

[60] HAJ, Delamain no. 1 letter book 1787–9, 8 November 1788, to Mérat, Orleans.
[61] DAJ, letter book 1767–8, 13 August 1768, to Bateson.
[62] *Ibid.*, 30 July 1768, to Berry and Sons, Hull.
[63] *Ibid.*, 6 February 1768, to Robert Gillingham. The addition was in 'spirits one-third'. The average ullage per annum in a puncheon of circa 60 veltes was ⅞ veltes. This is not far out in terms of contemporary estimates. Delamain observed that 'the best coopered cask in the world will want between ½ and 1 gallon per annum'. HAJ, Delamain no. 2 letter book 1783–5, 11 November 1783, to Alley and Darby.

nature, though somewhat below it in degrees Gay-Lussac. The 1753 decree arose from events in the Aunis, and both before and after 1753 the issue was less critical in Saintonge with its wine of higher alcoholic strength. In 1762, on the authority of Lallemand, Delamain was buying brandy at 2 to 5 per cent higher strength than Lallemand himself (in Lallemand's belief without adding spirit to it). A few years later in 1767 Lallemand, now as well equipped as Delamain with hydrometers, indicated that he bought no brandy at 3 degrees (except in the case of fifteen-to twenty-year-old).[64] However, when buying conditions were hectic, buyers had to make do with less good brandy, or to put it another way inferior brandies could be sold more easily. In 1764 Lallemand, embarrassed by complaints from London and eager to seize on a convenient excuse, claimed that '10 years ago brandy without augmentation was as strong as now raised 5 per cent and sometimes 10'.[65] Again, in 1787, Saule bought up much poor brandy by buying in a hurry, and Delamain himself, in 1789, faced with competition for brandy and resenting the higher duties after 1782, claimed that 'above three-quarters of what we receive since this regulation is lower than 4 degrees', and that the quality had deteriorated.[66] In fact that was not true, and the letter reflected his frustration in a season when brandy, however inferior, was put on the market.

Distilling in a conventional manner, the basic strength was significantly higher in Cognac than in La Rochelle and Saint-Jean d'Angély. Even as early as 1766, Laurence Saule seems to have made a distinction between a 'common proof' at Saint-Jean d'Angély and the various brandies he was buying at 4, 4¼ and 4½ elsewhere: he bought less readily at 3½ degrees, and offered some premium above 4 degrees. In fact, in 1767 the strength of one supplier's brandy in Saint-Jean, on Delamain's authority, was only 2¾ instead of 3, and one sample was as low as 2¼.[67] According to a memorandum of 28 September 1786 'la preuve des eaux de vie de l'Aunis qui d'après les règlements revient à 3 degrés est déjà bien faible, comparée à celles des eaux de vie de Saintonge et de Ré, la quelle va de trois degrés et demi à quatre degrés'.[68] The high standard in La Tremblade (in the Abonné de Marennes) and in Ré and Oléron is borne out in Boyd's correspondence in 1787 and 1788. In the Aunis itself the view was that brandy there even without the *seconde* only reached a strength of 4 degrees.[69]

[64] MAC, letter book, 1766–7, 16 May 1767, to Gast Lallemand.
[65] *Ibid.*, letter book 1762–4, 7 January 1764, to Steele.
[66] HAJ, Delamain no. 2 letter book 1787–9, 27 April 1789, to Yeats and Brown.
[67] DAJ, letter book 1767–8, 5 December 1767, to Chaigneau Senede, Saint-Jean d'Angély.
[68] ACC, La Rochelle, no. 3484, 28 September 1786.
[69] *Ibid.*, no. 3496, 'Observations sur le mémoire des cultivateurs et de celui d'un citoyen concernant le commerce d'eau-de-vie', 1 March 1790.

However, in the effort to compete, the standards at market were certainly rising: by 1783 brokers in La Rochelle were said to buy at 4 and 5 degrees.[70] Distillers were richer and larger in the Cognac region, and the fact that in the 1789 export returns more than half the brandy shipped from the Charente was *double*, i.e. at or above 'one-third' strength, emphasises how widely distillers, both richer and more enlightened than their counterparts elsewhere, worked to higher strengths.

Brandy taxation

The Tessa hydrometer was widely used by merchants, even if not necessarily by all *bouilleurs* and by very small sellers. With the Cartier hydrometer a further instrument was available. Introduced in 1770, its application was at first suspended by a decree of the Paris parliament, on this occasion as on others acting as the opponents of government and the supporters of an unchanging constitution. That decision in turn was overruled by a decree of the council on 27 September 1771, and in the wake of that decision use of the instrument was made effective by a decree of 21 August 1772. It was used exclusively for fiscal purposes, and solely by the revenue people. Even in the 1780s when the Cartier came to be used by the revenue outside Paris as well as in it, brandy continued to be measured locally on the Tessa scale. The hydrometer was a novelty in the 1760s in Cognac, and hydrometer quotations on the basis of any instrument became common only in the 1780s when the farmers-general at last began to effectively tax brandy outside Paris. The declaration of 1687 with a three-fold distinction between single duties for basic proof, double duties for rectified brandy and treble duties for spirit, had long remained in practice a dead letter: in Cognac the question of applying it to duties in general was first broached by the tax administration in 1742, and did not occur again in France at large apparently until 1770. In 1742 in the course of revenue visits to the premises of some or all of the merchants in the Cognac region, spirit was seized and confiscated. It was claimed by local interests that the extra taxation on spirit had been intended originally to be levied on brandy destined for final consumption and not on the production or intermediate sale of brandy.[71]

Significantly the declaration of 1687 seems to have contained reference to an earlier edict in 1686 which concerned the duty of *aides* 'dans les lieux de consommation'. In fact, when revenue authorities had proposed locally to apply the terms of the edict of 1687 in Saintonge and

[70] *Ibid.*, no. 3483, 28 August 1783.
[71] ADC, Angouleme, 5C5, memoir and covering letter of comte de Jarnac, 20 June 1782; also copy of letter of comte de Jarnac to *régisseur des aides* of same date.

Angoumois in 1742 to all duties levied on brandy for export, the result of instructions from Paris was that the point was not insisted on.[72] As a result, in the absence of further revenue challenge, all brandy within the region thereafter continued to pay only simple duties, and spirit or rectified brandy moved within the region was given a *congé gratuit* either for local removal or for dispatch to Paris. At the time the merchants claimed that their brandies 'ne sont pas extremement rectifiés, [et] qu'ils leur donnent souvent un peu plus de force'. This would suggest that rectification was still on a small scale, though the local collector had expressed some scepticism: 'je leur ferai bien connaitre que l'objet de leur fabrication est plus considérable'. The failure to make higher taxation stick encouraged specialist distillation, as the shipment to Paris of spirit in quantity, unpenalised by the tax system, economised on transport costs. In Paris in 1770 the issue of the edict requiring the levying of duties on brandy entering Paris on the basis of the 1687 edict was contested vigorously, but without ultimate success. As a result, taxation was now heavier for the Paris consumer, but it did not directly affect production within Cognac itself. Spirits moved within the region on the basis of taxation as simple brandy, and moving outwards they paid the *Traite de Charente* and other duties on shipment either overseas or to other provinces on the basis of simple brandy.

Cognac brandy became the subject of wider litigation by the taxation authorities only in 1781 when an effort was made to widen the taxation principles with new vigour, and in 1782 the administration sought to apply the terms unambiguously to all brandy in the districts subject to *aides*. This decision was conveyed by an edict of 29 May 1782: the net effect would be that both rectified brandy and spirit would *au premier enlèvement* (i.e. when sold off the property), pay double and treble duties, and exports would be subject likewise to double and treble rates of duty. This led to considerable lobbying from Cognac. In Paris the comte de Jarnac along with the prince de Lambert and the duc de la Rochefoucauld made representations, and the first two saw the controleur-général (the duc de la Rochefoucauld was not present because he was ill at the time). The representations proved successful on the main point. Exports both of brandy and spirits would not be subject to double or treble rates of duty. However, spirits destined for the regions of France in which *aides* were levied would be subject to duty on first movement within the province. Moreover, while rectified spirits intended for export were exempted from payment of double and treble rates for the *Traite de*

---

[72] See *ibid.*, letter from collector, Martin, in Cognac, 25 November and farmers-general, Paris, 10 December, quoted in 'Mémoire ou observations'.

Charente, they were not exempted from payment of double and treble rates of *aides*. The controleur-général turned down the case for relief for exports from the *aides* duty on the grounds that it was a minor duty and not of real consequence. Spirits for Paris, no longer enjoying the privilege of a *congé gratuit*, would be declared at an office in Ruffec where the duties would be paid. One of the objects sought by the merchants was freedom from revenue inspections on brandy on their premises. As long as a sole rate of duty existed, inspection was not of consequence, but if double and treble rates were enforced, then visits became vital to effective administration. The petitioners inevitably failed in their request for this concession, and revenue inspection, not a real feature since 1742, became for brandy distillers and merchants a harsh reality. It was bitterly resented, and in 1789 in a letter to Necker Delamain described it as a form of tyranny. However, if the merchants had lost their case, they had won on the main single issue – the concession that double and treble duties did not apply to exports, even if it meant that they would be subject to *aides* at double and treble rates and to the troublesome inspections.

Weakness in not standing up to the export interest inevitably encouraged further lobbying both of the controleur-général and of the intendant in La Rochelle with regard to existing duties on exports. A case, based on the difficulties of the brandy regions in 1782 and in 1783 and the evidence of brandy exports from other regions of Europe, for a reduction in the *Traite de Charente* was pursued in 1784 by the comte de Jarnac in association with James Delamain. On top of the concession already made in 1782 that duties would not be levied at double and treble rates, the *Traite de Charente* was reduced to one-third of its former level in 1784 as a support to the region's exports.

The increased duties, already significant in Paris for over a decade, were at first slow to take effect in Cognac, because of a delay in sending down the new hydrometer (itself an illuminating illustration as to how slowly the new approach to measuring brandy had spread from Paris to the premier brandy-producing provinces). Even as late as September 1784 Delamain advised Potter in Ireland that 'we have not been obliged to declare stronger but as we are informed the instruments of hydrometer and thermometer are come to our custom house we certainly soon shall'.[73] At this time the Cartier hydrometer acquired a practical significance. When the proposal to tax brandy according to strength using the Cartier instrument had first been put forward in 1782, one of the arguments of those opposing the heavier taxation was that it would result in a lower strength by the addition of more of the *seconde*, and thus the

[73] HAJ, Delamain no. 2 letter book, 1783–5, 5 September 1784, to Potter.

strength of brandy would be reduced from 22 degrees Cartier or 4 on the Tessa scale to 3¾ or 3⅞ on the Tessa scale to escape double duty. Delamain in 1789 in fact claimed that the increased taxation had precisely that result and that the strength of brandy had fallen.[74] There is a tone of exaggeration in the letter, and other letters reveal his animus against the new tax regime. Though a doubling of the duties would in fact be comparatively large, it may be doubted that it had quite the sweeping results attributed to it by merchants who were opposed to the duty in the first instance and were still, in 1788 and 1789, bitter about the inspections. The real situation is revealed in Delamain's 1793 observation that 'La force marchande de l'eau-de-vie à Cognac et tout ce département est 4 de l'aréomètre connu sous le nom de Tessa, ce qui est un peu supérieur à 22 degrés de Cartier'.[75]

In Britain with its high taxation, further raised in the 1750s, the effort to tax spirits in proportion to strength began early. That concern came only much later in Ireland. Indeed only in the wake of the political Union of 1800, and even then with a further time lag of twenty-three years, did Ireland adopt the full panoply of British spirit legislation and practice. In France, apart from some unenforced aspirations in 1687 and again in the 1740s, the taxing of brandy in proportion to strength first emerged in 1771 in the wake of the spread of an effective hydrometer, and became universal, at least for inland trade, in 1782. However, while the taxation of spirits in proportion to strength already existed in England, Clark's hydrometer was given legal authority only in 1787, and until 1800 that authority depended on annual renewals. Only from that date was it part of the permanent revenue legislation. In the uncertain world of spirits, that consideration both offers something of a parallel to French administrative hesitancies, and gives significance to French taxation regulations in 1771 and 1782. While they did not immediately affect spirits in all situations, they were ahead of British legislation by from sixteen to twenty-nine years (or fifty-two years if Ireland under the Union is taken into account) in giving permanent statutory authority to the readings of a measuring instrument. French legislation was even more in advance of that in Ireland. While Irish legislation had always made a distinction between brandy and spirits as far as import taxes were concerned, the distinction was a simple one of two levels of tax in contrast to the three-fold level in France, or the much more complex taxing in Britain (which had to be recognised in new legislation in the wake of the Act of Union providing for Irish spirits passing into Britain paying at British rates, but for British

---

[74] *Ibid.*, Delamain no. 2 letter book 1787–9, 27 April 1789, to Yeats and Brown.
[75] *Ibid.*, Delamain no. 2 letter book 1793–8, 30 November 1793, to Corneille. This is a very interesting letter on measurement.

spirits passing to Ireland paying the different and more lenient Irish taxation). Moreover, in the case of spirits made in Ireland, in contrast to the
taxation of imports, a single rate of taxation existed until the Irish tax
regime was absorbed into the British one in 1823. As long as this regime
lasted, it afforded a contrast with the regulations in England and also,
after 1771 and 1782, those in France.

The various standards of brandy

As markets expanded, the movement not only towards stronger brandy
but *esprit* increased in quantity, either to save transport costs or to lighten
the incidence of duties. The clearest survey of the variety of brandies in
foreign trade emerges in a letter which James Delamain wrote in August
1768 to Thomas Bateson, a customer in Belfast. Delamain sent him six
one-pint bottles, each a sample of a different grade of brandy:

No. 1 is what we call spirits ½ the strongest that can be drawn from the still. It
stands us double the price of brandy and £36 per 27 veltes manufacturing – of
this sort we have frequently sent to your neighbourhood, i.e. Londonderry.
No. 2 is an inferior sort of the same denomination and sells double the price of
brandy with £8 per 27 veltes manufacturing.
No. 3 is ⅔ [*sic*] our [i.e. made by Delamain] spirit a ⅗. [76]
No. 4 the old brandy to standard.
No. 5 the old natural.
No. 6 the hogshead of very old. [77]

Of the brandies in this list nos. 4 to 6 are more or less self-explanatory.
No. 4 was the regular brandy, aged and low in strength, but topped up to
standard. In the context this would have been the Cognac standard. No. 5
is the same brandy without the addition of spirit to bring it up to standard. Both are described as old. The term 'old' was virtually a technical
one. At any given time there were several grades of brandy of recent origin
on offer. The basic categories were brandy freshly distilled at various
dates from late October on, and brandy from the previous year, called
rassis, which was always, by definition, only a year or little more than a
year old. As the great bulk of brandy was shipped within the distilling
year, and indeed the shipping trade reached a peak of activity as early as
February, the supply of *rassis* itself was comparatively limited. Anything
other than these two basic categories was old, although much of it would

---

[76] Obscurely phrased but intended to state that they supplied spirit of their own manufacture ranging from spirit one-third to spirit three-fifths.
[77] The significance of the reference to hogshead lies in the fact that very old spirit was supplied in hogsheads not in puncheons. DAJ, letter book 1767–8, 30 August 1768,
Delamain to Bateson.

be just barely two years old. A significant amount of brandy was shipped at a greater age only for the London market. In 1768 Delamain intimated the age range of these brandies in advising a London importer that 'what we usually ship for said market is from 3 to 10 years old'.[78] The invoice books demonstrate that the bulk of brandy shipped for England was no more than three or four years old. No. 6 is described as very old; this was an elastic term, but in practice it would seem to apply to brandies of eight or more years.

Nos. 1 to 3 in the letter to Bateson are quite different: these are the product of a third distillation, or even of a fourth, hence sharply differentiated from ordinary brandy. They contrast also with spirit 'one-third', to which reference has already been made, which was brandy from the second distillation less *seconde* and which was used mainly to strengthen brandy above merchant proof. Spirit 'three-fifths' and spirit 'one-half' corresponded to the product of three or four distillations. Spirit 'three-fifths' was the product of a third distillation. Spirit 'one-half' represented a third or fourth distillation. Delamain made a distinction between two grades of spirit 'one-half': one – 'the strongest that can be drawn from the still' – had significantly higher manufacturing costs, and was clearly the product of a fourth distillation and probably also of a rigorous rectification process throughout the preceding distillations. Thus, as quoted by Delamain, while the manufacturing costs in 1768 of the basic grade of spirit 'one-half' were 8 livres, for the highest grade they were 36 livres. These are costs per barrique of 27 veltes. In the Boyd records for the late 1780s, costs on the northern shore of the Garonne per 50 veltes were 5 livres 10 sols for spirit 'one-third', 11 livres for 'three-fifths' and 22 livres for 'one-half' (described as *double*).[79] For like quantities these are fairly close, though lower.[80] The spirit 'one-half' was troublesome to make, and as Delamain noted 'it requires a certain space to be made properly'.[81] Quite apart from the direct manufacturing costs, the invoice costs of spirit had to be significantly higher than for ordinary brandy. In 1787, when the price of standard proof brandy was 108 livres, 54 livres were added to this figure in calculating the charge for spirit 'one-third', 72 livres in the case of

---

[78] *Ibid.*, 6 February 1768, to Robert Gillingham, London. Delamain added that such brandy required the addition of 12 to 20 veltes of spirit 'one-third' per puncheon.
[79] The term *double*, while technically applicable to all brandy of the strength of 'one-third' and upwards was, in practice, applied in the 1780s in Cognac and Bordeaux to brandy 'one-half'. This usage would seem to have arisen because its making involved twice the quantity of ordinary brandy. See HAJ, Delamain no. 1 letter book 1787–9, 21 July 1787, to Wm. Gunderson, Bordeaux.
[80] ADG, Bordeaux, 7B 1169–76, Boyd papers.
[81] HAJ, Delamain no. 1 letter book, 1787–9, 24 July 1787, to Kennedy; 21 July 1787, to William Gunderson, Bordeaux.

spirits 'three-fifths' and 108 livres for spirits 'one-half' to allow for the extra brandy that had to be purchased for the distilling operation.[82]

The price of spirit seems to have risen over time in relation to the price of brandy. Thus Augier, in 1718, when brandy was 50 livres, quoted spirits 'three-fifths 'at 79 livres, an increase of 58 per cent on the basic brandy price.[83] In 1787, however, when brandy cost 108 livres, spirit 'three-fifths' was charged at 185 livres, which suggested a percentage increase of 71 per cent on the basic brandy price. There was some increase in effective duty within the Charente in the interval, but this would account for perhaps only 2 per cent of the difference. In other words costs increased in a perceptible fashion.

The terms spirit 'one-third', 'three-fifths' and 'one-half'(or 'three-sixths') referred to the proportions of distilled water necessary to dilute the spirit to the common standard level of strength, i.e. the 46 degrees that qualified for the *preuve de Hollande*. Spirit 'one-third' means a spirit (rating about 70 degrees) which was in effect brought down to 46 degrees by the addition of one part of water to two parts of spirit. It is occasionally, though rarely, referred to more logically in contemporary sources as spirits 'two-thirds' on analogy with the methods of quoting spirit 'three-fifths' in which three parts of brandy had two parts of water added to them and in which the brandy rather than the water is the first number in the ratio.[84] Spirit 'three-fifths' meant a product in which three parts of brandy (at approximately 77 degrees) blended with two parts of water should produce a spirit with an alcoholic strength in volume of 46 per cent. Delamain in 1787 advised the Dublin merchant Edward Byrne how to dilute 'double brandy':

Double spirit may not be as saleable as standard proof brandy would be therefore by leave, saving your better judgement, to advise your having it reduced four parts of this spirit with three of good soft water (your Dublin pipe water very proper for this purpose) make stout seven of your hydrometer proof well blended together with the forcing rod. Let it stand on scantling for a fortnight, then racked off clear in the same manner you do wines will produce excellent brandy.[85]

Assuming that the strength was 77 per cent (as the proportions of four parts of spirits to three of water suggest a weaker double spirit), the mix would give a strength of about 44 degrees.

---

[82] *Ibid.*, 14 July 1787, to Andrew Kennedy, Dublin.
[83] AAC, letter book 1717–19, 26 March 1718, to Molinié.
[84] The charges for spirit were the subject of verbal confusion from time to time. For instance, in explaining the costs of spirit 'one-third' to Jennings on 27 October 1770, Hennessy stated that the cost was one-third higher. What he intended to say was that they were one-half higher (the brandy would have represented a third of the total cost).
[85] HAJ, Delamain no. 1 letter book, 1787–9, 8 December 1787, to Edward Byrne.

The quality of brandy

Standard brandy itself (i.e. the *preuve de Hollande*) was not consumed at the strength it was imported. Brandy importers diluted it. Hennessy made it clear to a London importer in 1770 that water should be added: one part of distilled water for five parts of brandy.[86] Incidentally, this proportion, one to five parts brandy, would indicate the addition of almost five veltes of water to 27 veltes of brandy. It would be much the same proportion as mentioned in the Augier letter of 1727 quoted earlier, and would suggest that this was a pretty standard practice. In supplying some twenty-year-old brandy to McCarthy of Bordeaux, apparently for an Irish connection of McCarthy's in 1785, Delamain advised that 'as it is for private use you will be well to acquaint your friend he can make it much mellower and more palatable by adding a gallon water to 7 or 8 but it must be the purest spring water boiled with much care and left to be perfectly cold before mixture'.[87] The advice he gave to a Paris merchant in 1793 is not in essence different.[88]

Customer sophistication existed. Even Martell, as a newcomer in the region, explained to one of his Guernsey associates in 1721 that 'il y a des cantons ici autour qui produisent des eaux-de-vies douces en gout, d'autres forte [*sic*] de preuve et un peu plus acre'.[89] Brandy was known to improve with age, and champagne was reputed to produce a distinctive quality in ageing. By 1780 Delamain could speak of 'champaign brandy, some of the finest growth in the world'.[90] By this time too its quality had led to the specific injunction absent in the early decades of the century: 'never mix champaign and other brandy'.[91] Cognac and Jarnac were where the injunction was carried out. Elsewhere it was less well grasped: even an essay published in 1770 by Munier in Angouleme could recommend that brandy of various strengths and ages could be mixed without harm to the product. Londoners' wealth, as much as the high British duties which discouraged the importation of cheaper brandies, made London the main market for quality brandy. As early as 1769 Richard Hennessy boasted of 'our champagne or choice brandy . . . The Londoners will have no other.'[92] More positively still, with the London trade at its peak for the century in 1788, Delamain spoke of 'the

[86] HAC, letter book 1769–71, 29 October 1770, to Ellis, London; 27 October 1770, to John Jennings.
[87] HAJ, Delamain no. 2 letter book 1783–5, 30 April 1785, to McCarthy frères.
[88] *Ibid.*, Delamain no. 2 letter book 1793–8, 23 September 1793, to Préau.
[89] MAC, letter book 1721–2, to Pierre Carey, 15 November 1721.
[90] HAJ, Delamain no. 2 letter book 1778–81, 13 May 1780, to Yeats and Brown.
[91] *Ibid.*, Delamain no. 1 letter book 1778–81, 18 May 1779, to Yeats and Brown.
[92] HAC, letter book 1769–71, 30 August 1769, to Capt. Walsh.

best judges in London as they cannot be rivalled in matter of taste by any other place whatever'.[93]

For much of the century there is no evidence of any clear price differential in the case of new brandy between champagne and other cognac (as opposed to the existence of a differential between cognac brandy at large and that of Saint-Jean d'Angély, Mortagne and other outlying districts). All young brandies of the Cognac district (at any rate in terms of the *canton* price which referred to a common strength) seem to have sold at the same price until quite late in the century when champagne brandies began to command a premium. The real difference in price seems to have arisen subsequently in the course of ageing. The cognac, other than champagne, was shipped out in the year of distilling to northern Europe and to Ireland. The champagne, on the other hand, was held by the producers for ageing, and entered the market only in its second or subsequent years. The absence of price differential can also be closely associated with the distinction made repeatedly by the merchants in Cognac between early sellers of new brandy at the outset of the distilling season, and others under no pressure to sell and who held back their brandy. These men, sellers of some substance and discrimination, had the option of either ageing their brandy or speculatively selling it while still young if prices rose sharply and they felt that the high prices would not hold. Holding brandy for several years required a substantial capital. The price of aged champagne rose significantly in comparison to young brandy from the same region. The practice of ageing emerged at much the same time as it had for wines and was fairly well developed by 1720. The earliest references to aged cognac are in two letters from 1718. In February 1718 Augier shipped two *pièces* of cognac, eight to ten years old, at 58 livres per barrique, and later the same year he dispatched on his own account 'des eaux de vie vieilles et des mieux choisies'.[94] To André Janssen in Amsterdam in 1725, Augier wrote of 'l'eau-de-vie vieille et bonne telle que je sais que vous la souhaitez'.[95] To another merchant in Amsterdam, Jacques Ranson, he wrote in September 1727 of old brandy 'telles que les délicats les aiment à Amsterdam . . . de champagne, vieilles et rousses'.[96] For Paris too the best quality was already appreciated. In 1729 Philippe Augier's sister, Madame Guérinet of Tonnay-Charente, asked her brother to purchase two *pièces* for the Paris market: 'que ce sont de la meilleure et plus douce'.[97]

---

[93] HAJ, Delamain no. 2 letter book, 1787–9, 6 September 1788, to James Hearn, London.
[94] AAC, letter book 1717–19, 12 February 1718, to La Roche père et fils; 3 September 1718, to Jean Cassaing.   [95] *Ibid.*, letter book 1724–6, 30 April 1725.
[96] *Ibid.*, letter book 1727–8, 8 September 1727.
[97] *Ibid.*, Guérinet letter book 1729, 5 May 1729, to Philippe Augier.

The price differential was not constant. In January 1728 Augier quoted new brandy at 77 and 78 livres per 27 veltes, and old at 81 and 82. Three years earlier, in 1725, Augier had stated as a principle that 'l'eau-de-vie vieille et bonne telle que je sais que vous le souhaitez s'achète toujours à 3 et 4 livres le 27 [barrique of 27 veltes] plus que la commune'.[98] In December 1735 Régnier quoted 63 and 64 livres for new brandy and 67 and 68 for brandy of the preceding year. However, in 1779, when new brandy was 75 and 80 livres, Delamain quoted an addition of 5 to 10 livres for one- or two-year-old brandy.[99] This suggests a significant rise in the differential in favour of old brandy. The same trend appears in the case of still older brandy. In December 1735 when new brandy was 63 and 64 livres, Régnier quoted 70 to 72 for five- and six-year-old brandy. Almost twenty years later the differential had widened perceptibly. In 1753, when new brandy was 76 and 77, three- or four-year-old brandy was quoted by Martell at 102 livres. In 1779, when the base price was 75 to 80 livres, Delamain quoted an addition of 40 to 50 livres for five- and six-year old brandy. The most detailed single quotation of prices is that by Lallemand in 1753:

New	76, 77
Last year	88, 90
2–3 year old	96
3–4 year old	102
7–10 year old	120[100]

In 1779 the highest price quoted by Delamain was 130 livres for five- to six-year-old brandy, but the following year, while new brandy had risen only by a single livre per 27 veltes, Fèbvre of Champagne sold seven- to eight-year-old brandy at 189 livres.[101] However, 1780 was a year of financial crisis and rising interest rates. That enhanced the premium commanded by the product.

Overall, aged brandy rose significantly in price relative to new brandy. One result of this was that rising costs tended to flatten out the range of ages available. In stating, in 1768, that 'what we usually ship for said market is from 3 to 10 years', Delamain may have been voicing the experience of the past rather than of the present and future.[102] Analysis of invoice books suggests that ages tended to bunch more typically toward the bottom of that range, frequently at three to four years, and merchants in their advice to correspondents were no longer in a position to quote a

[98] *Ibid.*, letter book 1724–6, 30 April 1725, to André Janssen, Amsterdam.
[99] HAJ, Delamain no. 2 letter book 1778–81, 19 October 1779, Delamain to Huntingdon.
[100] MAC, letter book 1753, 2 April 1753, to Hatch.
[101] HAJ, Delamain no. 1 letter book 1778–81, 1 July 1780.
[102] DAJ, letter book 1767–8, 6 February 1768, to Robert Gillingham.

wide range of prices as Martell had done in 1753. The narrowing age range occurred in the late 1760s when brandy prices soared. The temptation to reap a sure gain was hard to resist and sellers can hardly have anticipated the dramatic run of bad vintages that was to follow. High prices increased the costs of holding old brandy, if not for the sellers (who to some extent were distilling their own wine), then for the buyers. High prices for young wine inevitably resulted in a reduced amount of older brandy and in a reduction generally in the age of older brandy. In 1768 Delamain wrote to Berry that: 'your next party shall be 7 or 8 years old instead of 10 . . . You may easily vie with the Londoners in quality, and you must beat them hollow, for they within these few years have got little other than new brandy of most 2 or 3 years old. It seems the connoisseurs in that quarter are reduced to few in number.'[103] Hennessy had a remarkably similar tale in 1770: 'heretofore we used to ship a good deal of old brandy for your markets. Until within these three years, [it] was to be had by paying a certain price according to age and strength. We could get it then from two to 50 years old but it's now so scarce and dear it's no more called for'.[104] In 1768 Delamain still quoted prices for fifteen- and twenty-five-year-old brandy. A gentleman near Pons had fifty-eight-year-old brandy. In passing on this information he observed that:

As the quantity was occasionally diminished then constantly ullaged with new, they are infinitely below the opinion entertained of them, and by no means equal to the whymsical price they have . . . When our brandy here if of a primitive fine flavour has allowed twenty years it may be called any age.[105]

To a Londoner in the same year he observed that brandy had attained perfection at twenty years: 'overplus age in the denomination is a meer joke'.[106]

Another exacting requirement was the colour preference of both importer and consumer. For Hamburg what was required was 'une parfaite blancheur'.[107] So insistent were Hamburg importers on paleness that they would even settle for brandy which was *acre*, provided it was pale.[108] Young brandy was quite colourless: 'its quite pale on shipping', observed Delamain.[109] There were thus two distinct preferences: one for pale brandy, one for coloured brandy. For England, Ireland and

---

[103] *Ibid.*, *c.* 31 May 1768, to Berry.
[104] HAC, letter book, 1769–71, 27 October 1770, to Jennings.
[105] DAJ, letter book 1767–8, 2 August 1768, to Thos. Bateson and Co.
[106] *Ibid.*, 13 August 1768, to French and Hobson.
[107] AAC, letter book 1719–20, 25 November 1719, to Voigt.
[108] *Ibid.*, letter book 1717–19, 21 February 1718, to Molinié, Hamburg.
[109] HAJ, Delamain no. 2 letter book 1787–9, 23 September 1788, to Mark Butcher, Earshaw.

Amsterdam the preference was for coloured brandy. In other markets in northern Europe the preference was for pale brandy. Within Holland there was a contrast between Amsterdam and Zeeland, where the preference was for pale: 'Pour la Zélande comme pour toute la Flandre, il faut de l'eau-de-vie blanche à eau, nette de gout, et forte'.[110] Why there was such a sharp contrast is not easy to say. It is possible too that the preference reflected the existence or absence of a preference for a sweeter drink. Whiskey had been sweetened with various cordials in the seventeenth century, and in the case of the highly rectified spirits of Holland and Scandinavia there was a contrast between dry and sweetened products. Molasses or caramelised sugar, reduced in price by the influx of West Indian sugar after the mid-seventeenth century, offered a simple and now comparatively inexpensive method of sweetening brandy. The cost, while small enough in relation to the total cost of brandy sent overseas, was itself a tangible item: 'the colouring the spirit comes hellish dear', noted a merchant in 1783.[111] The basis of the colouring, which also imparted what was a consciously sought-after sweetening, was either molasses or caramelised or burnt sugar. The quantities of sugar for a puncheon seem to have been a pound of sugar, carefully blended in advance of admixture with a quart of brandy.[112] In the case of molasses, the proportion required by Galwey in La Rochelle in 1767 was 3 pints of molasses in a puncheon.[113] In 1784 Delamain used a half velte (the equivalent of 1 gallon) of what he described as brown sugar molasses.[114]

The detail of the operations, never set out in the correspondence because it was taken for granted by everyone on the Charente, comes to light by the accident of a long account from Delamain advising Edward Byrne, Dublin's greatest merchant whom Delamain was only too anxious to assist, as to how to convert spirit into a palatable brandy:

If you chuse it coloured, the method is very easy. Boil loaf sugar over a tolerable brisk fire in a pan till moderately burnt, constantly stirring it with a piece of stave and when by putting a few drops in an earthen plate, it appears black, perfectly transparent and brittle so that none of the glutinous part of the sugar remaint, [it is] to be taken off and carried at [a] distance of . . . the fire (for the steam would very easily inflame). Instantly add a small quantity of brandy, stirring very strong to prevent the sugar from hardening in the bottom of the pan which otherwise it would. The fermentation will be great at first but soon cease. Then you will add,

[110] AAC, letter book 1717–19, 19 November 1718, to Pierre Balguerie.
[111] HAJ, Delamain no. 2 letter book 1783–5, 28 June 1783. See also *ibid.*, no. 1 letter book 1787–9, 8 December 1787, to Edward Byrne, Dublin.
[112] *Ibid.*, 12 January 1788, to Edward Byrne.
[113] AAC, Broussard papers, 15 February, 12 March 1767, A. de Galwey to D. Broussard.
[114] HAC, 11 January 1784, James Delamain, Jarnac. See also HAJ, Delamain no. 1 letter book 1787–9, 8 December 1787, to Edward Byrne.

still stirring, sufficient quantity of brandy to bring the colour to a proper consistency for use.

The caramelised sugar, once poured into the brandy, should be mixed in well with a rod, then the contents of the cask racked off at the end of a substantial interval. Delamain's advice on this score was:

Lay the casks on scantling for 10 to 20 days as the weather prove. Then rack off clear with leathers and bellews, as wines are done. You will not have two quarts sediments in a cask of 130 to 140 gallons, and even that sediment with addition of as much water will pay the expense of running it through the still.

Distilled water would be added at this stage to bring the spirit – the instructions had been imparted to Byrne in the context of spirit 'one-half'– down to a palatable strength: 'The attention of letting stand to brighten is absolutely necessary for the putting in the water causes a fermentation and foulness which must have time to subside.'[115]

Sugar syrup was sometimes added to the brandy, which would add further to its sweetness. Delamain advised Byrne on an earlier occasion that 'a very great addition to the flavour would be when you mix the water to add to every 120 or 130 gallons brandy 2 quarts of best refined white syrop'.[116] Prune juice was sometimes used, though Delamain on another occasion held this to be unsatisfactory. The emphasis on flavour shows that the colouring of brandy stemmed not from an association of colour with age (a conceit of more recent tastes and of the commercial publicity that panders to it) but from the preference for a sweetened drink. It is worth recalling too in this context that the preferred upper-class way of drinking whiskey was in the form of punch, i.e. sweetened by an addition of water and sugar, itself a logical progression from the frequently sweetened spirits of the seventeenth century. Syrup had of course a further use, as the meticulous Turner observed to his partner James Hennessy in 1798: 'your house I think overloads them with syrop and I know that this will ever assist to cover a foul spirit'.[117]

Brandy as an industry

Brandy making developed quickly in the eighteenth century from a simple activity making an inferior and undifferentiated product into a more complex one, in which, beside the old-fashioned distiller, more sophisticated distillers worked consciously to a higher standard, and rectifiers also emerged to make spirit to add to ordinary brandy or to rectify existing brandy to much greater strengths. The transport econom-

[115] *Ibid.*, 12 January 1788, to Edward Byrne.
[116] *Ibid.*, 8 December 1787, to Edward Byrne.   [117] HAC, 30 November 1798, Turner.

ies to be gained as consignment overland to Paris grew was one catalyst. Another was the fact that brandy could be passed through the British customs at a higher strength without the customs observing it. The fact that in the 1790s brandy was consigned at the strength of 4⅝ in place of the statutory 4 degrees points to a margin of deception even in London. In the case of the north of England greater deception of the customs was possible, as Delamain noted in 1783, by the addition of 'a sufficient quantity of white sirrup [sic] so as to depress the strength to the eye', which 'we frequently do for some of the outports in England (not for London where they are too keen)'.[118] The *négociant*'s advice was that in testing brandy proof by agitation 'too great distance should be avoided in the fall as the fermentation which it caused raised the proof'. This advice would have been pointless in London as the customs there were alive to the practice and capable of detecting it by other means. In the north of England and in Ireland, the prospect of being able to avoid the telltale agitation of the brandy which would reveal a larger pearl or bubble caused by the presence of syrup, suggests either innocent or to say the least complacent customs officers.[119] Presumably as a result of these abuses in the English outports, the importation of spirit to England was totally prohibited in the 1780s.[120] Shipment of spirits, at a higher strength, even double spirits, however, still occurred to the north of Ireland, and Irish smugglers likewise often dealt in it.

The growth of a market for spirit, whether 'one-half', 'three-fifths' or 'one-third', meant the emergence of specialist distillers who provided spirit necessary to raise brandy above merchant proof. A later memoir in 1782 suggested that the emergence of specialist rectifiers, selling to the *négociants*, could be traced back to the 1740s or so:

les négociants trouvant autant d'économie et moins de risques ont cessé de rectifier l'eau de vie chez eux pour l'achetter de quelques bouilleurs répandus dans la campagne, la quelle eau de vie rectifiée estoit livrée chez les négociants sur des congés gratis, soit qu'ils mentionnaient eau de vie simple ou eau de vie rectifiée à quoy on ne faisait aucune attention non plus qu'à l'obligation de la part des bouilleurs de faire leurs déclarations aux Bureaux de leurs arrondissements avant de commencer leur operation, au terme des règlements. Quelques uns peuvent avoir négligé cette formalité, mais cela ne pouvait nuire aux règlements qui ont continué de faire l'usage permis de cette eau de vie rectifiée, à la connaissance de toute la province et des employés aux aides.[121]

In 1768 Delamain had eight stills, and in the 1780s he kept at least six stills in operation. Among the specialist distillers, La Grange had twelve

---

[118] HAJ,Delamain no. 2 letter book 1781–3, 29 April 1783, to Hardin.   [119] *Ibid.*
[120] *Ibid.*, Delamain no. 1 letter book, 1787–9, 18 September 1787, to Waddel Cunningham and Co., Belfast.   [121] ADC, Angouleme, 5C5, 'Mémoire ou observations'.

stills in 1769, mostly for brandy 'three-fifths'.[122] As a category these distillers did not exist in the 1720s but in the accounts of the 1750s they are
easily recognisable by the size of the bill business the Augiers did with
them. While the number of specialist distillers with a really large business
was small, the largest of them would have ranked with the *négociants* in
wealth and status.

Merchants had to buy the ordinary brandy in the form in which it was
on offer. While brandy could be rejected, it is not a point which merits
much attention in the correspondence, which suggests that while quality
was a point on merchants' minds, it was not an overriding one. Given the
speculative nature of the brandy trade, the buyer's problem as often as not
was one of getting any supplies at all: 'it has frequently happened us when
demand and scarcity combined against the purchaser to spend a whole
day in pursuit of five puncheons and not succeed at last'.[123] At such times
of hectic boom in the trade, the quality of brandy deteriorated. At the
beginning of 1779, when buying for the Paris trade was very active, the
buyer had little choice. As Delamain advised a Paris merchant in
February 1779, 'nous sommes obligés ici de recevoir de nos livreurs à la
force qu'il leur plait en leur payant le degré en sus de la preuve, telle est la
coutume du pays que l'on n'a pu jusqu'à présent trouver moyen de
réformer'.[124]

There were considerable contrasts in standards of care between the
bouilleurs or distillers, whether working on their own account or for
others, and the richer proprietors – clergy, noblemen, bourgeois, rich
farmers – who employed them. Moreover, some sold in haste in the
autumn to raise money to pay their taxes; others were in less of a hurry
and may have been able to offer a better product. Such *bouilleurs* brought
brandy up to the strength required for the English or Paris markets. This
was stated in a memorandum from the merchants of Pons, Cognac and
Jarnac to the intendant in 1782,[125] and re-echoed in another memorandum in the same season.[126]

Brandy above the minimum proof was thus readily available, a fact also
ascertainable from hints in the correspondence of Lallemand, Broussard
and Delamain in the 1760s. Its availability is confirmed in the 1789
export *états* in which Tonnay-Charente alone of French ports exported a
high proportion of its shipments (more than half) under the technical

---

[122] AAC, Broussard papers, 5 November 1769, Veuve Galwey, La Rochelle, to Broussard et
fils, Cognac.
[123] HAJ, Delamain no. 1 letter book, 1787–9, 8 August 1789, to Haworth and Bateman.
[124] *Ibid.*, Delamain no. 1 letter book 1778–81, 23 February 1779, to Arnoult, Paris.
[125] ADC, Angouleme, 5C5, Memorandum of *négociants* of Cognac, Jarnac and Pons,
addressed to the intendant in La Rochelle, 13 April 1782.
[126] *Ibid.*, 'Mémoire ou observations'.

classification of *double*.[127] *Double*, strictly speaking, meant brandy at or above a strength of one-third. Aunis brandy, at least at the *canton* (as opposed to private or direct transactions between buyers and sellers) with its statutory addition of a full dose of *seconde* which both depressed the strength and gave it a poor taste, contrasted with cognac. While there is some special pleading in the documentation directed against the increased duties in 1782, the quality of cognac was attributed to the absence of: 'une partie considérable du phlegme et de la partie acqueuse du vin appellé seconde, ce qui les rendraient acres et d'un mauvais gout'.[128] The description of brandy as *acre* is one of the few specific judgements on brandy which is re-echoed in the letter books across the century, and the comparative rarity of the comment is itself something of a commentary on standards. In 1782, faced with the imposition of higher duties on brandy above proof, several of the memorials of protest from the region argued that distillers would weaken the strength by including more of the *seconde*, thus reducing the quality and imperilling the export trade. Another memorial from the town of Saintes not only made this point with emphasis, but even argued that it was the higher cut-off which accounted for the difference between cognac and other brandies: 'l'abondance de phlegme les rendra égalles à celles des autres pays qui sont reconnues pour etre d'une qualité bien inférieure'.[129] The situation seems to be confirmed in a memorandum in the archives of the chamber of commerce in La Rochelle for 1790 which, intending to rebut the fears expressed by another writer, argued that to protect the repute of Aunis brandies:

il faut espérer que pour lors l'arret du conseil pour la fabrication des eau-de-vies [*sic*] sera aboli, qui ordonne le mélange de la seconde avec l'eau-de-vie, seul · moyen de la rendre de mauvais gout, que nous aurons assez de sagesse d'imiter nos voisins les Saintongeois, en portant la force de notre preuve à quatre degrés de l'éprouvette de comparaison, règlement qu'ils ont su faire sans aucun concours de pouvoir du gouvernement.

[127] AN, Paris, F¹² 1666. The only other case was Bordeaux where the bulk of brandy exported to *Angleterre* was *double*, reflecting the specialist activity of the port distillers. Sète exported some *double*, but not much, suggesting that this activity was largely confined to distilling for the domestic market when, on arrival at the Channel ports, it often had to be carried overland to its final destination in the towns of Picardy and Flanders.

[128] ADC, Angouleme, 5C6, 'Extraits du registre des délibérations de l'Hôtel de Ville', Saintes, 17 April 1782. See also memorial of merchants of Cognac, Jarnac and Pons to the intendant, 5C5, 13 April 1782. The latter memorial is not to be confused with another memorial, undated, and from a smaller number of merchants, from the same towns.

[129] *Ibid.*, 5C6, 'Remontrances en forme de mémoire adressé à monseigneur le controleur général'.

For the writer, this would be a better approach than 'la férule despotique d'un agréeur, qui juge du gout et meme de la force de l'eau de vie sans avoir aucune règle fixe'. In turn, such a standard would both eliminate the suspicion that La Rochelle brandy was mixed with inferior brandy, and leave the Aunis producer the choice of selling 'soit à Saint-Jean d'Angély, soit à La Rochelle, suivant que le prix ou le transport lui conviendra mieux'.[130]

The Bordeaux brandy trade had a poor image, and only the vine crisis of the late 1760s in the Cognac region gave it a fillip. At this point Bordeaux brandy began to make an appearance in Dublin together with Spanish brandy. A Dublin correspondent wrote to Hennessy on 2 June 1772 that: 'there is no cognac brandy now here but plenty of Bordeaux which sells from 6/4 to 6/6 per gallon. I am sorry to say the people here begin to relish it almost as well as the cognac'.[131] By the following year John Galwey in Bordeaux reflected a new optimism about the prospects in writing that 'we are certain your brandys are by a good deal superior in flavour to our brandys here, but we believe at same time our fortified or improved brandys are equal if not superior to a great part of yours.'[132] John Galwey's optimism seems to have been responsible for kindling his kinsman Richard Hennessy's interest in moving from Cognac to Bordeaux in 1776,[133] and in Dunkirk, the gateway to England for cognac, Thomas Blake, wishing Hennessy well on his plans to set up in distilling in Bordeaux, wrote that 'the trade of Cognac must certainly decrease, by the method they now follow of making up brandys at Bordeaux in the same manner. Several parcels came here lately from this latter place to be forwarded to England.'[134]

The Bordeaux trade offered a highly rectified spirit made from both indifferent and heterogeneous supplies of brandy often of low strength to start with. The spirit 'one-third' produced there – which should be comparable to the *coeur* of a second distilling – was weak, and it had to be distilled a third time. In other words Bordeaux 'three-fifths' was about as strong as Cognac 'one-third'. In 1787 Delamain, in some doubt as to what a letter by a correspondent meant, wrote that 'we presume he means spirit "one-third" which is 6 to 8 per cent stronger than the Bordeaux "three-fifths"'.[135] In Cognac brandy supplied to Dublin at 4 degrees

[130] ACC, La Rochelle, no. 3496, 'Observations sur le mémoire des cultivateurs et de celui d'un citoyen concernant le commerce d'eau-de-vie', 1 March 1790.
[131] HAC, 2 June 1772, Tom Egan to Richard Hennessy.
[132] *Ibid.*, 11 June 1773, John Galwey to Richard Hennessy.
[133] *Ibid.*, 2 April 1776, Gerard Galwey to Richard Hennessy, and letters from John Galwey in the first half of the year.
[134] *Ibid.*, 3 June 1776, Thomas Blake, Dunkirk, to Richard Hennessy.
[135] HAJ, Delamain no. 1 letter book 1787-9, 21 July 1787, to William Gunderson, Bordeaux.

Tessa was brought up to that strength by the inclusion of a mere 4 veltes of spirit 'one-third' in a barrel of 27 veltes; in Bordeaux to match that strength a barrel of 32 veltes of brandy involved not only the addition of 14 veltes of spirit but of the higher nominal grade of 'three-fifths'.[136]

Given the contraction in brandy distilling in the hinterland of Bordeaux, brandy for the stills was drawn in erratically from a variety of often marginal locations instead of being purchased from regular suppliers. These already heterogeneous supplies were then supplemented by erratic supplies from both Languedoc (via the Canal du Midi) and from Spain. In 1779 Delamain had noted that in normal years 'at Bordeaux they sent you only the produce of the country. It is at best but very indifferent, but when there is a demand you get Languedoc, Spanish, all sorts of trash'.[137] As late as March 1768 Augier could hold forth that 'people who advised that we receive Spanish spirits here have given false advices, the importation is not allowed and the bad quality and the charges would keep from ordering any if the law would permit it'.[138] However, the political policies of the Family Compact or political alliance of 1761 between France and Spain had already precluded the indefinite exclusion of Spanish brandy or any penal taxation of it, and hence it made its appearance both in Bordeaux and directly from Spain in the north of France. Richard Hennessy, who had the advantage of familiarity with the trade both in Cognac and Bordeaux, observed to a friend in 1785 that 'it's impossible you could find so bad as that which they get from hence, and yet they could find no fault but want of strength'.[139]

Only Armagnac, produced in a remote and poor region with varied agriculture in its fragmented topography, preserved or enhanced its reputation. Amid the shortages of 1789 Delamain wrote to a merchant in Bordeaux asking him to acquire 'du vrai Armagnac et de la meilleure qualité'.[140] Armagnac had already adopted one of the recognised brandy cépages from Cognac, the folle blanche,[141] a step which reflected its specialisation in the business as much as the suitability of the grape for brandy making. Even within Armagnac, the brandy district tended to be a compact region on the poorer ground, with substantial agriculture in addition to vine cultivation.[142] By 1825 in a nationwide survey of brandy, the greater strength of the cognac brandy was an established fact. The

---

[136] *Ibid.*, Delamain no. 1 letter book 1778–81, 30 January 1779 to Thomas Murphy, Dublin.   [137] *Ibid.*
[138] AAC, letter book of letters to English and Irish correspondents, 1768–82, 7 March 1768, to Harrison.
[139] HAC, Richard Hennessy to John Saule, 11 February 1785.
[140] HAJ, Delamain no. 1 letter book 1787–9, 27 October 1789, to Coppinger frères, Bordeaux.
[141] Serge Lerat, 'Introduction à la connaissance du vignoble d'Armagnac', in A. Huetz de Lemps and P. Roudié, eds., *Eaux-de-vie et spiritueux*, p. 124.   [142] *Ibid.*, pp. 122–3.

strength of brandy, measured on the Cartier hydrometer, shipped from the Charente was 22 degrees. Brandy from the Loire valley ran from 20 to 22 degrees. All others were decidedly lower. Armagnac and Languedoc were 20 degrees, the Gironde a mere 19 degrees.[143]

As early as 1725 there is evidence as to how seriously distillers took their work. In that year Augier advised a correspondent in Amsterdam that four stills or *chaudières* might be difficult to sell, as they did not have features sought in the region and which 'les particuliers [les] souhaitent à fin lorsqu'on brule de pouvoir faire un juste calcul de la qualité du vin'. Interestingly, too, the preference was for bigger stills on the grounds that 'il faut la meme quantité de bois pour une petite que pour une grande chaudière'.[144] However, though the stills varied, they remained small and in fact 40 veltes would seem to have been the upper end of the range. This was the size quoted by the *Encyclopédie* in 1755. The size was said by Munier in 1779 to be 30 to 40 veltes.[145] The cost of a still was then said to be 500 livres, and it would last for at least fifty years.[146] A sum of 500 livres would be the equivalent of almost two years' wages for an unskilled labourer. This comparison puts the cost of stills in proportion. Even small still owners would be far above the base of rural society. Some might indeed be peasant distillers; but most would be socially higher and many employed an artisan to conduct the actual distilling operations. Although some stills were imported, in the main they were made in the region. Their manufacture ensured a large demand for copper.[147]

Care in washing stills and utensils was also important; carelessness, especially in the use of the same – and sometimes scarce – water to wash equipment several times a day as the distillations ended, was known to give brandy a bitter taste: 'ce qui fait l'eau-de-vie acre' as Augier put it in 1718.[148] It took three days and six *chauffes* to make a barrique of brandy.[149] Over a distilling period of six months from November to April, it would be possible for a still to make roughly 48 barriques. In reality this is an optimum figure: labour demands in agriculture and seasonal water shortages could frequently affect output. In theory all should be sold at the weekly *canton*, which admitted the sale of produce of the preceding week or ten days. In the accounts of *négociants*, only a small number of large suppliers can be identified, some of whom were in reality rectifiers of

---

[143] Alain Huetz de Lemps, 'Les eaux de vie et liqueurs en France vers 1825 d'après Cavoleau', in *ibid.*, pp. 329–40.

[144] AAC, letter book, 1724–6, 6 January 1725, to Le Riget, Amsterdam.

[145] Munier, *Essai d'une méthode générale*, p. 191.   [146] *Ibid.*, p. 185.

[147] Valette letter book, 7 December 1773–29 April 1775 (in the possession of M. Alain Braastad, Jarnac), 26 February 1774, to Mathias Schleicher, Stolberg via Aix-la-Chapelle.   [148] AAC, letter book 1717–19, 21 February 1718, to Molinié, Hamburg.

[149] Munier, *Essai d'une méthode générale*, p. 191.

brandy made by others. In other words, most distillers would have been either small or intermittent producers, marketing the produce of one or two stills, sometimes owner-operated, sometimes conducted by a wage-earning distiller. If we assumed that the 100,000-plus barriques made in the Aunis and Saintonge were produced by full-time occupation for the six months, there would have been 2,000 stills at work. In practice as some worked at half-capacity, the true figure lies between 2,000 and 4,000 stills. On the other hand, as many owned several stills, the actual number of distilling proprietors is well short of the higher figure for stills. While brandy should be sold at the *cantons*, much was bought directly in the countryside, and even well ahead of manufacture by the allure of cash advances. Distilling was conducted by three types of individual: the recti-fying distillers, who are relatively easy to identify; the bigger brandy makers who are not easy to identify but who sometimes held perhaps several dozen puncheons of the market; and the smaller makers working one or two stills and selling only brandy distilled in the current season (perhaps even as little as 10 barriques in a year) but rather precipitately to enable them to meet tax demands. The distribution between the three categories varied from Segonzac with its large distillers to the Aunis with its predominance of small ones.

The development of skills depended on two things: first regularity of employment or, as part of that, the emergence of specialisation in spirit making; second, some degree not only of skill but enlightened self-inter-est in determining the decisive importance of a careful cut-off between the *coeur* and the *seconde*. The existence of recognised skills was reflected in the migration of distillers from Cognac to other regions. Bordeaux drew its skilled distillery workers from Cognac. In 1778 Richard Hennessy in Bordeaux, with orders for spirits 'three-fifths' in hand, wrote to his friend Saule in Cognac: 'pray see and find me a proper person for my stills etc'.[150] Significantly, he already had a Saintonge man in his employment. The rate of remuneration was 30 sols a day. Saule, however, offered 35 sols to a man named Pelluchon, though Hennessy did not want to go beyond 30 sols plus 'loging [*sic*],wines, fire and candele [*sic*] light'.[151] If the substantial allowance in kind is borne in mind, the payment is rather high: skilled distillers were at a premium, and simply were not available in Bordeaux. They moved abroad to the new brandy producing regions in Spain as well. In 1782 it was claimed that foreign houses, English, Irish, Danish and even French, had set up in Catalonia and Valencia and that 'ces commerçants se sont associés des fabricants de

---

[150] HAC, 5 December 1778, Richard Hennessy, Bordeaux.
[151] *Ibid.*, 29 December 1778.

la Saintonge. On a attiré nos propres ouvriers et jusqu'à des tonneliers'. The comte de Jarnac, who sent this document to the intendant, in adding his own notes on the margins claimed that 'un homme de Cognac, où la fabrication de l'eau de vie est le plus renommé, et dont je connais le nom et la famille, est présentement associé de la Maison Wumbevells [*sic*] Arabet et Compagnie de Barcelone, il leur fournit les détails les plus suivis et les plus utiles sur les meilleurs procédés dans la fabrication de l'eau de vie'. In addition, according to the count, 'un espagnol nommé Ischerdos est établi à Paris depuis trois ans, et sous la protection de son ambassadeur, il prend toutes les notures les plus utiles au commerce, et plus particulièrement à celui de l'eau-de-vie'.[152]

---

[152] ADC, Angouleme, 5C5, Memoir dated Jarnac 20 June 1782, forwarded under cover of letter of comte de Jarnac on same day to the intendant in La Rochelle. The earliest reference to such a movement is in ACC, La Rochelle, no. 3474, memoir to the chamber of commerce of La Rochelle, 21 February 1761.

4 Brandy production and internal trade in France

Brandy production in the Charente

Until the end of the seventeenth century, brandy, while distilled in a broad hinterland of the Charente, was an undifferentiated product. It was also for the most part shipped from a single port, La Rochelle, though subsidiary activities, such as salt production along the coast and on the islands, sustained lesser centres of brandy supply as well. With subsequent growth, differentiation gradually emerged between different qualities, and the best brandy began to be shipped from Charente, a location which also served to distinguish it from inferior rivals.[1] At first a mere gathering point of brandy for La Rochelle, Tonnay-Charente acquired in and after the 1710s a merchant community shipping directly overseas. The members of the chamber of commerce of La Rochelle dated the decisive change in the declining brandy fortunes of their port to the 1710s. In 1731, in setting out its grievances against the farmers-general, the chamber of commerce claimed that formerly La Rochelle houses used to employ factors in Cognac, Pons and Saintes to buy and hold for them brandy which was then sent down river as required. In all 8,000 to 10,000 *pièces* were allegedly purchased and stored in this fashion (though this total included buying by Bordeaux and Paris houses). As late as 1716, 1717 and 1718 there were three individuals in La Rochelle who bought each year up to 800 pipes.[2]

The bypassing of the port of La Rochelle by reliance on factors and new houses in Tonnay-Charente inevitably speeded up the growth of Tonnay-Charente as a port of dispatch. Moreover, as it was within

---

[1] René Pijassou, 'Quelques aperçus sur le commerce des eaux-de-vie en Angleterre au début du xviiie siècle', pp. 119–20. The change can be recognised in the fact that nineteen out of ninety mentions of brandy in the sale of prize wine in London newspapers during the War of the Spanish Succession distinguished cognac from Bordeaux, Entre-deux-mers, Rochefort, Oléron and Nantes brandy. The price of cognac was, moreover, the highest in a hierarchy of French and Spanish brandies. One sole mention specified Charente itself, which suggests that while the qualities of cognac were already recognised as pre-eminent, the port of Charente was still subsidiary to other centres in the region.
[2] ACC, La Rochelle, no. 4245, 2 May 1731.

Saintonge, shipment there made it possible to avoid the extra duties involved in passing from the Provinces réputées étrangères of which Saintonge was part, into the Aunis, which was in the Cinq grosses fermes. The number of houses increased rapidly: at least as far back as 1717 the Augier family had a house in Charente as well as in Cognac. The house of Régnier, which settled in Charente around 1719, had become an important one by the 1730s, taking most of the surviving bulk orders for Holland. While some orders were those of Dutch houses in La Rochelle and were passed on to Régnier to execute and to ship direct from Charente, the house equally received large commissions direct from Holland. By 1731 La Rochelle was on the defensive. The great days of the port's brandy business, as the chamber of commerce's memoir of that year suggests, were already well and truly in the past. On the Charente itself, with a small and defective port and a rapidly growing but competitive and jealous group of new merchants, success created its own problems. By the late 1720s as many as twenty or thirty vessels could be loading simultaneously at the peak of the distilling season. In 1730 the merchants of Amsterdam collectively complained of the delays, and alleged that they were even reduced to sending goods to La Rochelle or overland to Mortagne. They contrasted the prompt dispatch when there had been few commission agents with the breakdown, as the number of vessels grew, in the good order and management of loading.[3]

In 1718 Philippe Augier in Cognac claimed that he did most of his buying within 2 leagues (8 kilometres) of the town of Cognac.[4] However, in 1725, when the trade was at a greater pitch than in 1718, his purchases, he said, took place within a radius of 3 or 4 leagues (12 or 16 kilometres) of the town. Territory within such a radius would in fact embrace the modern regions of the Champagnes, Borderies and Fins Bois: 'Je vais à 3 et 4 lieues à la campagne, j'achète pièce à pièce une partie d'eau de vie, je la jauge, je la goutte, et fournis des magasins pour la recevoir.'[5] Martell in April 1721 had said that he purchased brandy in a radius of 7 to 8 leagues (28 to 32 kilometres),[6] but this was within the hectic period 1720–1 when brandy exports from the Charente reached an unprecedented level.

Some purchasing books (*livres de paye*) for both the Delamain and Martell houses provide evidence of the buying patterns of the second half of the century. For the house of Augier, we can go back as far as the 1720s, not from *livres de paye*, but from small volumes with details of the

---

[3] *Ibid.*, no. 4241, Amsterdam, 30 October 1730.
[4] AAC, letter book 1717–19, 12 March 1718, to Gatebois.
[5] *Ibid.*, letter book 1724–6, 1 January 1725, to Voigt, Hamburg.
[6] MAC, letter book 1720–1, 19 April 1721. In the peak time of frenzied buying in mid-1720, Augier even referred to a circumference of 10 leagues.

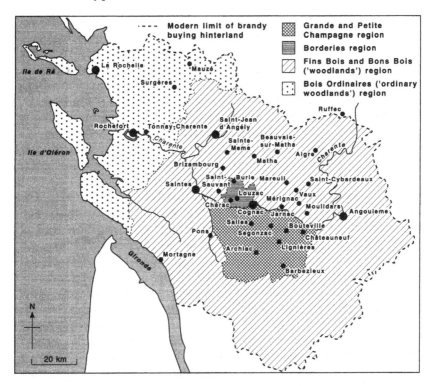

Map 2 The brandy-buying hinterland of the town of Cognac.

acquits issued on the basis of *soumissions* to the *aides* administration. From these books we can work out with some precision the buying pattern in the late 1720s and 1730s when Augier's buying was conducted within a region whose perimeter corresponded loosely to his definition of 3 to 4 leagues. The outer frontier ran from Saint-Cybardeaux, Moulidars and Chateauneuf in the east to Barbezieux and Archiac to the south, Saint-Sauvant, Brizambourg and Sainte-Meme to the west, and Matha to the north. Ignoring purchases in Cognac (which at its Saturday *canton* sold a variety of brandy), the main buying was clearly in the Grande Champagne region (with Segonzac, Lignières and Salles, and to a much smaller extent Bouteville, predominating) and in the Borderies (Chérac especially, Burie and Louzac). Archiac and, rarely, Barbezieux and Chateauneuf represented the only buying in the Petite Champagne, as defined in modern times. Jarnac was an important source of supply for Augier also, though from its place on the frontier between the later Petite Champagne and Fins Bois, the buying regions cannot be distinguished with precision, as the town drew both on Champagne and Fins Bois alike. In Augier's purchases in Cognac, itself like Jarnac on a frontier, buying in the Fins Bois region, though much less so than brandy from the Borderies–Grande Champagne axis, was extensive, especially at Moulidars, Mérignac and Saint-Cybardeaux (near Rouillac). Other Bons Bois districts to recur were Mareuil, Sainte-Meme, Saint-Sauvant, Mérignac, Vaux, Matha, Beauvais-sur-Matha and even Aigre. By the 1750s the pattern had changed considerably, concentrating on the Grande Champagne (Segonzac, Lignières and Salles), with support buying more at Chérac and some other locations in the Borderies than at Archiac in the Petite Champagne.

The general pattern is striking in its marketing implications. The absence of buying eastwards of Moulidars, Saint-Cybardeaux and Chateauneuf-sur-Charente points to the countervailing hinterland of Angouleme. To the north, the fact that buying never occurred beyond a Matha–Saint-Cybardeaux line with the exception of some occasional purchases in Aigre, points to a frontier beyond which Paris purchases predominated. As early as the 1720s in a year of vintage failure along the Loire, the buying activities of the Aigre houses even made themselves felt in the immediate hinterland of Cognac. Apart from regular purchases at Archiac, there was little buying by Cognac men in the Petite Champagne, which suggests that Pons merchants bought there and that the Petite Champagne was responsible for the prestige of the best brandy from Pons. To the west, a clear frontier suggests that the transition was made quickly to the buying hinterlands of Saintes and Saint-Jean d'Angély.

The picture is complicated a little by the fact that the revenue *acquits* granted in Cognac excluded by definition brandy that did not pass through Cognac, and hence brandy purchased elsewhere on the account of the Augiers, especially at Saint-Jean d'Angély, and sent down the Boutonne. However, the evidence does provide a clear definition of Cognac's own immediate hinterland, and makes the distinction between the Champagne brandy and others. It also hints at the sharpening differentiation between that brandy and others in a much greater Augier dependence on Champagne (together with some Archiac and Chérac brandy) in the 1750s. From the late 1720s Augier was increasingly reliant on the London market; Delamain in Jarnac depended more on the Irish and Paris markets, though Jarnac's location made it convenient to draw on both Champagne and Fins Bois for different market requirements. Thus Delamain in the 1760s was a buyer of 'woodlands' as well as Champagne brandy, in contrast to Augier's concentration even a decade earlier largely on the Champagne for the London market. From as early as the 1720s there was an explicit contrast between Champagne brandy, designated as such in the invoices, and the brandy for the large but less demanding Irish market, merely designated as 'best cognac', mainly though not exclusively Fins Bois in origin.

There is not a great deal of contemporary information on the vines which produced the wines destined for the still. While in the hinterland of Sète in the Languedoc and in the Angoumois red wine went to the still, in the Cognac region white wine exclusively was distilled. Indeed, at a time of shortage in 1727, a merchant made it clear that while red wine was less in short supply than white, that did not ease the problem of the distillers: 'il y a plus de rouge propre pour la consommation du pays, mais qui ne va pas à la chaudière'.[7] Nor did the pattern change later. In late 1766, when the Dutch, in the wake of a poor vintage, made unexpectedly large purchases of the *petits vins rouges* of the region, it was feared that the local inhabitants would consume their own white wine with serious consequences for the distiller: 'ce qui fera un vuide pour les chaudières, puisque il faudra prendre sur les blancs les consommations ordinaires'.[8] The red wines of the region were of poor quality, and commanded little respect: 'nos vins rouges ne sont pas d'une qualité à pouvoir etre envoyés au loin'.[9] Only quite exceptionally, as in the autumn of 1766, did foreign demand arise for them. As a result, the market for red wine was normally limited to local consumption, and, local needs apart (and there were few large towns), most of the region could be devoted to the grape varieties suitable for white wine and for what was already recognised as the classic cognac.

Not all white vines were suitable for distilling purposes. If distillation was to expand, it meant substituting a vine yielding a weak acidic wine which distilled into a strong brandy for the vines which made the palatable and internationally recognised white drinking wine of the region. The area had long had a reputation for these wines. In 1726 Augier furnished a Paris house with a description of the local wines in terms which a Parisian could understand. Apart from ordinary red wines which he compared to Orleans wines, the wines were in the main white. The most sought-after variety was the Grandes Borderies, which was suitable for long voyages. This was a sweet strong wine with exceptional keeping qualities made from grapes plucked late in the season ('pourriture noble') and said to have a slight *gout de terroir*. The next variety was a middle-grade Borderies which Augier likened to the best white wine available in Paris, and the third quality was an ordinary white wine.[10] By 1720 many of the vineyard districts which had produced these white wines must already

---

[7] AAC, letter book 1727–8, 3 November 1727, to L'Eglise et Chaille, London.
[8] MAC, letter book 1766–7, 29 November 1766, Lallemand to Perié, Montpellier.
[9] AAC, letter book 1727–8, 21 May 1727, to Kastell.
[10] *Ibid.*, letter book 1726–7, 21 October 1726, to Espraud, Paris.

have switched over to the *folle blanche*, the vine variety which produced the grape favoured for brandy distillation. The only district which offered any resistance was the Borderies, now the last district producing any of the region's prestigious white wines. The change from wine to brandy was made more quickly and more completely in the Champagne than in the Borderies. Though Champagne wine was shipped overseas as late as the 1680s, there is no evidence of such a traffic a generation later. It was speeded by the fact that, as in 1648–65, Champagne wines sold for a third less than Borderies. The Borderies district held out longest against the complete substitution of the brandy vine, and some of the vineyards remained planted with the old vines.[11] The most important customer was the French East India Company: 'la Compagnie des Indes en font charger tous les ans assez considérablement'.[12] The reputation of these wines remained high, and in October 1719 Augier wrote to a firm in Bordeaux that 'nos vins de Borderies sont surement meilleurs qu'ils n'avaient été depuis 1708'.[13]

But though less complete than in the Champagne the conversion was nonetheless far advanced. In 1718 Augier stated that the region produced 1,500 *pièces* of brandy a year, and that its normal export of wine was 1,000 tons.[14] A figure of 1,500 *pièces* would amount to 4,500 barriques of brandy. In normal conditions up to 8,000 tons of wine would be required to produce this quantity at the still. These calculations would suggest that of the total quantity of wine produced with the still or the export customer in mind, only one-ninth actually left the region as wine. This output, moreover, was no longer sought by a large number of northern European customers as in the past: its main taker was the East India Company. That custom apart, only a handful of other customers remained, mainly in Holland, formerly the main market for the Charente white wines. While the new perceptions of brandy were one factor in promoting the change, one may speculate too that there was a switch in demand from sweet wines to others. A measure of comparative profits in Borderies wine and brandy and a portent of future trends was the fact that in the wake of frost damage to the vines in 1717, even Borderies wine seems to have been distilled in the following year to meet demand.[15]

The changeover within the region to brandy vine stocks from stocks more suitable for drinking wine was almost complete by the 1720s. The

---

[11] *Ibid.*, 26 August 1726 to Boué *le jeune*. For the relative prices of Champagne and Borderie wine in 1648–65, see J. George, *Mercuriales d'Angouleme, de Cognac et de Jarnac* (Mémoire de la société archéologique et historique de la Charente, Angouleme, 1921), p. 67.
[12] AAC letter book 1724–6, 23 November 1725, to Floch, Paris.
[13] *Ibid.*, letter book 1719–20, 25 October 1719, to Petit frères, Bordeaux.
[14] *Ibid.*, letter book 1717–19, 21 February 1718, to Ryswick.
[15] *Ibid.* See also a letter of 21 May 1718.

Champagne districts were probably already far advanced in changeover in the first decade and were exclusively brandy-producing in the 1710s, in marked contrast to forty years earlier when both the Borderies and the Champagne districts provided wines for export. This left the Borderies in the 1720s as the residual legatee of the great tradition in sweet white wine which had, apart from salt, made the reputation of the region in early modern Europe. The prestige of the champagne brandy is reflected in the constant reference in the 1720s and 1730s to *la vraie champagne* or *meilleure champagne*. In 1727 Augier described some old brandy as 'telles que les délicats les aiment à Amsterdam . . . de champagne, vieilles et rousses'.[16] The champagne brandy and the region which benefited from its reputation reached on the south side almost to Pons as it does in its modern appellation. Augier described a consignment of brandy in 1718: 'ce sont des marchandises de la bonne Champagne de Ponts [*sic*]'.[17] Beyond Pons, the reputation of the brandy fell off, and even as late as the 1780s none of the brandy around Mortagne, the Garonne-side port for a hinterland to the south of the town of Pons, was aged, reflecting its lower esteem. Even as new brandy, it commanded several livres per barrique less than brandy from the Champagne district. Only in the exceptional wartime circumstances of the outset of the 1780s was this relationship reversed.

By the 1720s clear distinctions existed between different qualities of brandy. Thus in 1721 Martell, a newcomer, wrote to one of his fellow Channel Islanders that 'il y a des cantons ici autour qui produisent des eaux-de-vie douces en gout, d'autres forte de preuve et un peu plus acre'.[18] In the Champagne district, now explicitly recognised, much of the brandy in the invoices was described as champagne, especially for the London market. Other brandy was merely described as 'cognac' or 'best cognac'.The brandy from Saint-Jean d'Angély was shipped in quantity both from Charente and La Rochelle. It was said to be 'inferior to cognac 10 to 15 per cent in strength and flavour'.[19] Dardillouze, one of the largest shippers in Charente in 1730, said that the brandy coming down the river Boutonne, in other words from Saint-Jean d'Angély, amounted to 3,000 to 6,000 *pièces* a year.[20] In crude terms this would, if we ignore the complicating presence of a coastal market, amount to a half or more of total shipments from Charente.

Given Saint Jean d'Angély's location close to the frontier between the modern Bons Bois and Fins Bois regions, purchases represented two con-

16 *Ibid.*, letter book 1727–8, 8 September 1727, to Jacques Ranson, Amsterdam.
17 *Ibid.*, letter book 1717–19, 23 February 1718, to Gatebois.
18 MAC, letter book 1721–2, 15 November 1721, to Pierre Carey.
19 DAJ, letter book,1767–8, 12 July 1768, to Thomas Baildon, Helsingor (Elsinore).
20 ACC, La Rochelle, no. 4241, Dardillouze, December 1730 (precise day left blank).

trasting categories: brandy purchased to the west of the town which was positively not cognac, and brandy to the east of the town which passed under the name of cognac. Thus the town, using its good river communications down the Boutonne to Tonnay-Charente, supplied brandy shipped under the name of Saint-Jean d'Angély, and at the same time was the main subsidiary centre of brandy distilling and buying for Cognac houses. Large bulk consignments from Tonnay-Charente to Holland in the Régnier invoices were not given the prestigious term cognac: they were also several livres lower in prices than cognac. In the case of brandy from Saint-Jean d'Angély, in the 1760s Delamain drew a sharp distinction between Saint-Jean brandy and cognac, and assumed brandy for Elsinore to be the former.[21]

Thus in a broad sense a four-fold distinction existed in the 1720s. The first three categories included brandy from a radius of 3 or 4 leagues around the town, much though not all of which was designated as champagne brandy; other brandy designated as cognac from the fringes of this region corresponding to the Fins Bois of modern designation (and as new brandy selling for the same price as champagne); and a further category from beyond this again, some shipped under the name of Saint-Jean d'Angély or, on the far side of the Charente to the west and south of a line from Saintes to Pons, the Bons Bois of modern definition. While the cognac brandies including champagne sold at the same price when new, the brandy in Saint-Jean d'Angély sold for less than cognac (as did Mortagne brandy when Mortagne became an important source of supply for Ireland) even in the 1730s. For the Dutch, its main takers in the 1730s, Saint-Jean d'Angély brandy was invoiced under the name Saint-Jean. However, with the growing prestige of the term cognac, these brandies passed under the name cognac in the second half of the century. In the 1780s, although overland costs excluded brandy from Cognac itself, the brandy shipped from Mortagne to Bordeaux was described as cognac, though it was regarded as a distinctly inferior product, to be sharply differentiated from cognac proper.[22] To these three categories (champagne, cognac, 'best cognac'), including at a lower grade both Saint-Jean d'Angély and Mortagne cognac, should be added a fourth

[21] DAJ, letter book, 1767–8, 12 July 1768, to Thomas Baildon. A further distinction arises in the case of barrel staves. Barrel staves for cognac came down the Charente from the Angoumois (drawn from the oak forests of Limousin), while in Saint-Jean barrel staves from ash and chestnut had also been used. See passing references in correspondence 1729–43 preceding the 1743 decree on brandy barrels in ADCM, La Rochelle, C186, intendance, nos. 1, 2, 3, 4, 7, 8, 11, 16, 17, 18. The origin of barrel staves, compared with later times, never crops up as an issue in merchant letters, though the trade in barrel staves is routinely illustrated in the inland correspondence of the brandy houses.

[22] See HAJ, no. 1 letter book 1787–9, 7 July 1787, to Surtees, Johnston et Cie.

product – brandy produced in the maritime districts, from the northern parts of the Aunis and from the Abonné de Marennes (Marennes and La Tremblade) beyond the La Rochelle and Rochefort marshlands, or from the two islands, Ré and Oléron. In the eighteenth century this brandy was shipped direct from source or through La Rochelle, almost exclusively for the French market. It never entered into purchases by houses domiciled in Cognac, except possibly in a crisis year like 1769 when such purchases are hinted at in the panic buying of the autumn. It would approximate to the Bois Ordinaires of modern definition, and by analogy with the known existence of the term Fins Bois (in the English-language usage by merchants of the term 'best woodlands') may have already passed under a designation of this sort. However, in the eighteenth century the term 'cognac' was never applied to this brandy.

Given the heavy emphasis on champagne brandy, Fins Bois brandy existed as the residual element in the pattern of single-price intensive buying around Cognac. The term Fins Bois was never used in the early letter books, but it does occur as early as 1767–8 in Delamain's reference on occasion to 'best woodland brandy', itself an almost literal translation of Fins Bois. The emergence of a clear recognition of Fins Bois, which certainly existed in the 1760s, may be detected in a change in the pattern of buying of the Augier house in the 1750s, where their purchases concentrated on brandy from the Grande Champagne and the Borderies. The virtual exclusion of brandy from the area corresponding to the modern Fins Bois region, from which they had purchased a good deal in previous decades, suggests a conscious decision in buying, which is perfectly consistent with Delamain's use of the term a decade later. In the 1780s the distinction was more positive as it was now consecrated by a price differential: when champagne was 75 livres the 'best woodlands' was 72.

By the 1760s the basis of the main legal designations of later times already existed in a loose sense. We are lacking only a designation for Borderies brandy and a distinction between Petite and Grande Champagne; in contrast to 'best woodlands', the terms Borderies and Petite Champagne never occur in the eighteenth century in designating brandy. Indeed the very term 'woodlands' in its origins probably derived from a distinction made in the seventeenth century – or earlier – between the intensive cultivation of the Champagne and Borderies for their sweet white wines, and a more variegated economy of white wine, brandy and cereal and pastoral agriculture in the surrounding regions.

The term 'cognac' seems to have been limited originally to brandy from within a close radius of the town of Cognac, and in a very loose sense the original definition corresponded to the parameters of a region in which the producers were likely to accompany some or much of their brandy to the Saturday *cantons*. With the growth in volume of business, the term later embraced brandy shipped through Tonnay-Charente: that included both brandy coming down the Charente from Jarnac and Cognac and brandy from Saint-Jean d'Angély carried down the Boutonne or from Pons down the Seugne. The overland carriage of brandy was deemed to be expensive. For instance, when shipment from Mortagne soared in the 1770s and 1780s, the costs were deemed to prohibit brandy from the central districts around Cognac being sent there. In 1781 Delamain advised a Dublin house that 'land carriage is too expensive at any time. Therefore we are forced to buy in such places as lay contiguous to Bordeaux river'.[23]

The Charente flowing westwards through Angouleme, Jarnac, Cognac and Saintes, and two tributaries, the Boutonne (serving Saint-Jean d'Angély) and Seugne (serving Pons), were the vital links in making Tonnay-Charente the main focal point for the brandy of Saintonge. Barge traffic on the waterways was slow. In summer there was often too little water for the barges; in the winter, if the rivers were swollen, they waited eight or fifteen days to pass under the bridges, and the delays were a subject of conflict with the farmers-general whose suspicious clerks wished to levy duties for local consumption on goods held up unduly in their slow progress downstream.[24] The river was termed 'rivière de patience' in a memoir from the chamber of commerce,[25] an expression that already existed at a much earlier date in exasperated merchants' letters.

The French internal market

The story of brandy has concerned itself with foreign demand. Yet a large and expanding domestic market is a key aspect of the brandy trade. A market for brandy had emerged in the non-wine-producing regions of northern France, and especially in Paris, itself on the limit of the wine-producing regions. When did this consumption pattern emerge? It is impossible to say with precision. It already existed in the 1720s, when the evidence first becomes sufficient for serious study.

To the west of the Saint-Jean d'Angély–Tonnay–Pons axis the greater Cognac region was drawn towards La Rochelle which served a declining foreign clientèle and a burgeoning coastal traffic for northern France. The eastern side of the greater Cognac region and some of the northern

[23] HAJ, Delamain no. 2 letter book 1781–3, 18 September 1781, to Alley, Dublin.
[24] ACC, La Rochelle, no. 4239, 1 November 1730, reply of chamber of commerce. See also no. 4245, reply from the chamber of commerce to objections by the tax farmers and deputy tax farmers, 2 May 1731.   [25] *Ibid.*, no. 4239, 1 November 1730.

fringe which was more remote from water transport hence turned towards the expensive overland route to Paris. Aigre and Angouleme were the business centres of these districts. The painfully slow navigation of the Charente limited Angouleme's interest in the maritime brandy trade, but as inland lines of communication with Paris multiplied in the eighteenth century, Angouleme acquired a new-found economic importance. The frontier for this market was Jarnac, which both directed brandy westwards towards Tonnay-Charente and at the same time was at the western limit of a region supplying Angouleme and Paris. Overland traffic to Paris traditionally wended its way north through Aigre, though with a new road opened in 1772 Ruffec replaced Aigre as the nerve centre of the carting services within the brandy region. The selection of the town by the tax administration as the place where traders paid the excess duty on rectified or double spirits (*double*) after 1782 seems to have reflected this role.

In normal years, in the purchasing zone within 3 or 4 leagues (12 or 16 kilometres) of Cognac, merchants in the inland trade played no role of any consequence, and the surviving letter books are remarkably free of reference to them. Only in years of poor vintage, when shortage of brandy and an inrush of buying commissions from Orleans and Paris led merchants to purchase further afield, do they come to light. Entering in a big way in bad years when all merchants were less price-sensitive, their reputation, at least among the established merchants, who had to face competition from grain-based and Spanish spirits in their overseas markets, was one of paying over the odds. This reputation went back to the 1720s and was already sufficiently well defined to suggest that it had been earned in earlier decades. Hectic buying for the Paris market prompted Augier, writing to Touze of Orleans in 1727, to contrast them with 'l'étranger qui est lent et extremement circonspect dans ses entreprises'.[26] Delamain, who had a regular trade with the Paris region, observing the buying by Angouleme merchants in 1788, made the comment that 'ils ont des moyens pour se tirer d'affaires que nous ignorons et nous ne cherchons jamais à etre en concurrence avec eux pour les prix'.[27] The story was no different in another hectic autumn season in 1769 when the Irish house of Galwey and Guérin in La Rochelle observed to a Cognac house that 'nous sommes comme vous d'opinion que messieurs les spéculateurs de Saint Jean et de Jarnac ne peuvent guère réussir dans leurs entreprises qu'ils ont faites dans votre voisinage où on dit qu'ils continuent d'acheter'.[28]

[26] AAC, letter book 1726–7, 1 February 1727, to Touze, Orleans.
[27] HAJ, Delamain no. 1 letter book 1788–90, 22 November 1788, to Dassy, Meaux.
[28] ACC, Broussard papers, 12 November 1769, A. de Galwey and Guérin, La Rochelle, to Broussard et fils, Cognac.

Merchants in the central cognac region, who were accustomed in most years to a market devoid of serious competition from domestic buyers, did not usually think in overall terms of the demand for the product. But the house of Galwey was quite untypical in the 1760s, since it drew on Cognac for its supplies for its overseas customers, though it was based on La Rochelle. Hence it was much more acutely aware than the physically more isolated houses within Cognac itself of the aggregate level of demand. In consequence, in 1769, it broached the question of aggregate demand in terms which no other house did at any time in the century: it observed an uncommon invasion of the Aunis by purchasers from Jarnac and Saint-Jean. It thought that, in response, 10,000 *pièces* more brandy than usual would be made in the province of Aunis and in the offshore islands. Galwey and Guérin anticipated that buyers from the Saintonge would make aggregate purchases of 20,000 to 25,000 *pièces* with the result that merchants in La Rochelle would not make up their normal complement: if so much brandy had not already been sent out in the form of 'three-fifths' by land, there would have been, in their opinion, ten extra cargoes to ship from La Rochelle. This observation at the very outset of the new distilling season (actual rectification on any serious scale at this stage, as opposed to mere commissioning, would have to be largely of the previous season's brandy) points to the strength of the inland demand funnelled through commissions given to merchants in Saint-Jean or in Jarnac. (Mention of the latter town probably serves as a form of short-hand for commissions sub-contracted from Angouleme houses.) In other words, in 1769 there would seem to have been some shift both from the coastal and foreign trades to the overland trade, with brandy passing through Saint-Jean to move directly north to Chatellerault and Orleans or through Jarnac on its way, as a first stage, to Angouleme or Aigre. Not only was export trade annihilated by this competition but the coastal trade for northern France was likewise greatly reduced: Galwey and Guérin, at the time of writing, noted only 'de petits besoins pour la Picardie'.[29]

If we take Galwey and Guérin's crude estimate for the forthcoming season of 25,000 *pièces* as a measure of the overland trade from the Aunis and Saintonge, this would give a total of 75,000 barriques, to which should be added figures for exports and for coastal trade to arrive at the total trade. Exports present little problem: an average of 6,565 barriques (struck from 5,944 barrels shipped in 1769 and 7,135 in 1770) would represent them accurately. An estimate for the reduced coastal trade of Tonnay-Charente, La Rochelle and the islands is more problematic.

---

[29] *Ibid.*, 5 November 1769, Galwey and Guérin, La Rochelle, to Broussard et fils, Cognac.

Perhaps a halving to a figure of 25,000 barriques might represent a not indefensible estimate for the reduced coastal traffic. This would result in a total trade of around 105,000 barriques. While vintages were poor, they were very far from being as disastrous as the decline in coastal traffic or the collapse in exports suggested (exports fell to 2,549 barriques in the nadir year of 1772). While the bad vintages automatically reduced supplies, their real effect was the replacement of price-resistant buyers on foreign or northern French accounts by buyers acting on commissions pouring in from Orleans and Paris. In 1769, as in other crisis years, exceptional commissions for the Paris region not only pushed the exporting merchants out of business but also those buying for the brandy market in Picardy and Normandy.[30]

This estimate for 1769 has some crude but effective corroboration from figures in the long entry on the commerce of La Rochelle in the 1742 edition of Savary's *Dictionnaire universel* as set out in table 4:

Table 4. *Brandy output in barriques*

Cognac	40,200
Saint-Jean d'Angély	24,000
Saintes	4,000
Aigre	1,833
La Rochelle	14,500
Ile de Ré	10,000
Ile d'Oléron	4,000
Total	98,533

Source: Savary des Bruslons, *Dictionnaire universel*, vol. I, pt. 2, cols. 137, 138, 149, 150, 151, 152. A figure of 40,000 barriques elsewhere for Ré (col. 119) is ignored. The Aigre figure is calculated from the estimate of wine production, assuming that half was white and that 6 barriques of wine made 1 barrique of brandy.

These figures omit any estimate for the Abonné de Marennes, and do not include the output of the Angoumois, estimated at 5,600 barriques. The figures for Cognac compare with an estimate for exports of 35,000 barriques. This figure compared with Cognac output of 40,200 barriques might suggest that the difference – 5,200 barriques – was drawn into overland traffic, which would be augmented by the 1,833 barriques from Aigre and the 5,600 barriques from the Angoumois. Savary based most of

[30] Export data from the La Rochelle chamber of commerce *états de la balance du commerce* figures as reproduced in Bibliothèque municipale, La Rochelle, MS 2703, Claude Claveau, 'Le monde rochelais de l'Ancien Régime', p. 767.

the figures on a memorandum by the Sieur Edmé in 1727 and they seem plausible enough for a decade as early as the 1720s. If exports overseas from Charente were not above 25,000 barriques (approximately two-thirds of the known total foreign shipments from the *généralité*), shipments coastwise from Tonnay-Charente should have been of the order of 10,000 barriques.

The crisis overland traffic of up to 75,000 barriques in 1769–70, if sustained in part from a long-term fall in exports of up to 20,000 barriques and a shortfall of 25,000 barriques in coastal shipments, implies a more normal – or pre-crisis – level of 30,000 barriques. It could then have jumped – using the Galwey and Guérin figure as the basis of the calculation – from the normal level of 30,000 barriques to as high as 75,000 barriques in the harshest vintages of the late 1760s and 1770s. In the individual years of major failure of the vines on the Loire, overland trade from the Charente may conceivably have been even larger and coastal shipments correspondingly reduced. The inflated level of overland trade, caused by the poor northern vintages in the late 1760s and in the 1770s was perpetuated for a little longer by war at the end of the 1770s: as a result the beneficial effects of better vintages on the coastal trade were not seen until the early 1780s. At that stage foreign exports began to run at 30,000 barriques; coastal traffic as measured by the La Rochelle *octrois* (municipal duties) was up to 30,000 barriques and even above. The size of the overland trade and of Tonnay-Charente coastal shipments are unknown: competing with a recovered export trade and with a continuing overland demand, coastal traffic at Tonnay probably fared less well than the traffic measured by the La Rochelle *octrois* (as that brandy was not normally important either in foreign trade or in the Paris overland trade). A figure of 20,000 barriques almost certainly does not overstate the coastal trade from Tonnay-Charente (over 7,000 barriques were recorded coastwise in 1789 to the free port of Dunkirk, to which should be added shipments of unknown size to other ports in the north of France). A round 30,000 barriques is probably an underestimate of the base level in the overland trade, especially if the Angoumois traffic is also borne in mind. These figures, though on a flimsy basis, point to a total traffic of not less than, and probably more than, 110,000 barriques, and hence to an overall rise compared with the 1760s and 1770s: better vintages and a multiplication of non-quantitative evidence of simultaneous steady foreign, coastal and overland traffic warrant the same conclusion.

These estimates, for what they are worth, cover the Aunis and Saintonge. They do not include the Angoumois, which to start with had a smaller and more backward brandy industry. Its market was almost exclusively the Paris one, and little brandy passed between Angoumois and Saintonge. In the infancy of the inland trade, when the question of buying further afield arose, there was a reluctance to incur the transit duties on passage between Angoumois and Saintonge: in times of abundance, it was sometimes possible to do business by exchanging a parcel of brandy in Saintonge for one in Angoumois.[31] Thus, at the beginning of the century, the Angoumois stood aside almost totally from the currents of brandy business in the Aunis and Saintonge. As time passed the divide became less clear-cut, but the take-off of brandy distillation in the Angoumois depended entirely on the Paris market. The great growth of Paris business in the 1760s, combined with the high level of foreign demand in Saintonge, which made any exchange of parcels purely marginal and inflated the price of goods even before transit duties were added, gave business in the Angoumois a new fillip. It was there, with its more backward distilling, not in Saintonge, that the first printed account directed to improving distilling techniques appeared: the memoir by Munier, a member of the Société d'Agriculture d'Angouleme, written in 1766 but not published until 1770 in the wake of the commercially sensitive 1769 vintage.[32] This memorandum obliquely illustrates the dependence on Saintonge, and the author somewhat grandiosely saw the brandy of the Angoumois sharing the reputation of Saintonge brandy 'dans toute l'Europe'. As an internal trade for Paris grew, moreover, more brandy passed from Saintonge into Angoumois than in the past. Angouleme buyers were emerging in the busy or bad years, as had happened as early as 1718, and this became much more evident in the 1760s when serious buying by Angouleme merchants for the Paris market began. Very little, if any, passed in the other direction. A sign of the very different production conditions is the fact that red wine was distilled in the Angoumois. Munier expressed surprise that the white grape was not more prevalent there: 'on doit etre étonné après cela, de ce qu'on ne cherche pas davantage à le multiplier en Angoumois surtout, où les vins rouges ne sont guère propres qu'à faire de l'eau-de-vie'. However, conditions had changed by the late 1780s. When foreign demand outstripped local supplies, a house like Delamain's purchased in Angouleme, and some Angoumois brandy was even making its appearance in Bordeaux.

There is no hope of firm estimates for aggregate domestic trade (inland and coastal trade combined) even for the longer-established Aunis and Saintonge trades, and the calculations set out above are probably as good

---

[31] AAC, letter book 1717–19, 12 March 1718, to Gatebois, Saintonge.
[32] E. Munier, *Mémoire qui a concouru pour le prix proposé par la société royale d'agriculture de Limoges*.

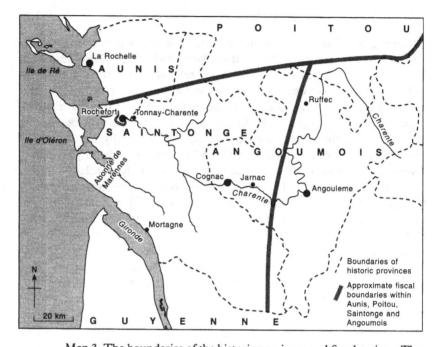

Map 3 The boundaries of the historic provinces and fiscal regions. The boundaries indicated are those of the historic provinces of Aunis, Saintonge and Angoumois. For fiscal purposes, however, the boundaries varied at several points: for example, the boundary between the Aunis and Saintonge, which also marked one of the frontiers between the Cinq grosses fermes and the Provinces réputées étrangères, was drawn to the north of Rochefort, as indicated approximately (on the basis of the sketchy information in Necker's *Compte rendu au roi*, 1781) by the continuous black line. Similarly, the frontier between Angoumois and Saintonge (serving also as the boundary between the *généralités* of La Rochelle and Limoges) was drawn to the east of the historic provincial boundaries and included within the fiscal province of Saintonge a salient of the province of Angoumois, in which were located Cognac, Jarnac and Chateauneuf (-sur-Charente). Thus, the inhabitants of Cognac and Jarnac sometimes described themselves as Angoumois, though fiscally they were in Saintonge. While the islands of Ré and Oléron were in the Aunis, and the Abonné de Marennes was in Saintonge, they had a distinctive fiscal character (Ré and Oléron were even outside the Cinq grosses fermes) and goods exiting from them were free of all duty. It will be noted that the *généralité* of La Rochelle had the uncommon distinction that the land-based section of the Aunis was within the customs union of the Cinq grosses fermes, while Saintonge and the islands were outside it. The historic Angoumois was divided both fiscally and administratively with the easternmost section, including its 'capital' of Angouleme, in the *généralité* of Limoges. To the south the province of Guyenne was part of the huge *généralité* of Guyenne (Bordeaux).

as can be hoped for. However, for the coastal trade on its own, some statistical elements exist. For La Rochelle itself, there are figures (in barriques) for shipments to 'divers ports du royaume' in four years:[33]

1749	13,672
1750	12,050
1751	9,626
1752	7,268

These figures are unduly depressed by the poor vintages of the period, and shipments would have been higher in more normal years. The figures may also conceivably be limited to brandy declared within La Rochelle as opposed to brandy transhipped in the port, or loaded elsewhere in the Aunis for direct shipment to coastal destinations in the north of the kingdom. Hence they fall below the real level of shipments for the Aunis and the islands at large. A later account in 1781 recalled that, according to 'l'estimable auteur de l'histoire de la Rochelle', in 1757 up to 40,000 barriques were shipped from the Aunis 'pour la Picardie, la Normandie et autres pays de consommation'.[34] In 1745 a memorial from the merchants of La Rochelle to the chamber of commerce claimed that 60,000 to 70,000 barriques of brandy were shipped from the port of La Rochelle, 'année commune'.[35] This figure could not possibly be correct if it applies to La Rochelle. On the other hand there seems to be some confusion in the calculation. Perhaps as the document was intended to deal with the total shipment of brandy from the province to all destinations, the gross figure was arrived at by adding the exports from the généralité of La Rochelle (the états for which did not distinguish between the different provinces) to coastal shipments.[36] If the exports, running at 25,000 barriques, were deducted, the resulting figure would be close to other calculations.

The octrois for the town of La Rochelle provide an estimate of the coastal traffic in the 1780s. As there was no significant consumption within the town, and the figures would need to be reduced by not more than 4,000 barriques to account for shipments from the town directly overseas, they provide a reliable estimate of the coastal traffic.

---

[33] ACC, La Rochelle, no. 3710.
[34] Ibid., no. 3648, 'Vérités démontrées ou nouveaux calculs relatifs à la culture des vignes dans le pays d'Aunis', Maitre Croizelière, avocat, La Rochelle 1781; and no. 3649, letter from d'Aligre to Croizelière, Paris, 21 January 1781.
[35] Ibid., no. 3709, 20 January 1745.
[36] The first document which distinguishes between the component 'bureaux' or creeks in the généralité is for 1783 and no comparable document has been found at an earlier date in the surviving états in the chamber of commerce.

Table 5. Octrois *of the towns of*
La Rochelle (in barriques)

1779	18,373
1781	30,220
1782	28,220
1783	22,253
1784	28,689
1785	48,394
1786	43,976
1787	29,583
1788	25,632
1789	23,866
1790	2,651

Source: Bibliothèque municipale, La
Rochelle, MS 2703, Claude Claveau,
'Le monde rochelais de l'Ancien
Regime', p. 767.

The accuracy of the *octrois* figures seems to be confirmed in the fact
that another source published at the beginning of 1781 put the coastal
shipments from the Aunis at 30,000 barriques,[37] and that the exaggera-
tion-prone chamber of commerce itself claimed that 20,000 barriques of
brandy were shipped from La Rochelle to Normandy and Picardy.[38] The
rising trend in the *octrois* seems to be confirmed in another estimate in
1786 which assumed that 12,000 *pièces* (36,000 barriques) were shipped
annually from the Aunis.[39]

The *octrois* did not originally include goods which had originated elsewhere in the Aunis, or in the Abonné de Marennes and the islands of Ré
and Oléron, and which either remained on board the vessel or were trans-
ferred in the harbour from one vessel to another. However, in 1775 an
attempt was made to levy the *octrois* on such shipments, and contestation
arose over the *octrois* being levied for 'une destination directe pour la
Normandie par expéditions prises à la Tremblade'.[40] The rise in exports
in the 1780s, compared with past levels, was less a function of recovery
than of a successful levying of the *octrois* on trade that did not enter La
Rochelle. Significantly, shipments in the 1780s, on the basis of the *octrois*,

[37] ACC, La Rochelle, no. 3648, 'Vérités démontrées ou nouveaux calculs', and no. 3649,
letter from d'Aligre to Croizelière.
[38] ADC, Angouleme, 5C6, Representations from the chamber of commerce of La Rochelle,
13 February 1784; ACC, La Rochelle, no. 3663.
[39] *Ibid.*, no. 3484, 28 September 1786.
[40] *Ibid.*, no. 3635, 12 August 1775, petition of forty houses to chamber of commerce. See
also ADCM, C188, no. 152, letters of 12 August, 22 August and 19 September.

are considerably higher than the *agréeurs'* figures for the same years, which do not go above 23,586 futs (apparently the equivalent of bar-riques) in any year: roughly twice as high.[41] If this is the case, they give us a convenient mechanism to estimate the difference between total coastal shipments and the proportion actually put on board vessels at La Rochelle: roughly half commissioned in direct orders to other coastal centres and to the islands, and the remainder for the most part commis-sioned from the town itself to a hinterland that did not go very far beyond the port.

With a contracting hinterland, and given the invasion by buyers for Paris, the coastal districts became increasingly important in the buying activities of La Rochelle merchants. In October 1771 the intendant referred to the chamber of commerce memoir by 'différents particuliers tant de La Rochelle que de plusieurs paroisses des environs . . . pour se plaindre de ce que certain négociants mélangent des eaux de vie de Marenne ou de Oléron avec celles de La Rochelle et les font ensuite passer pour eaux-de-vie de La Rochelle'.[42] However, even in these condi-tions the trade was said to be small. This also seems to be borne out in the few statistics available and which, because they cover these years alone, were inspired no doubt by concern about the traffic.[43] In any event two-thirds of this brandy was for Guinea and the colonies.[44] Figures for coastal shipping coming to La Rochelle in 1773 seem to give no evidence of a brandy trade.[45] What the small quantity of brandy actually entering La Rochelle suggests is not only how little involved the town was in the physical handling of the product, but the likelihood that an increasing proportion of the trade was handled by direct orders from the north of France to merchants in the coastal regions themselves.

The brandy trade from the Aunis at large was quite substantial, if we choose to disregard accounts like that of the chamber of commerce which represented the coastal traffic in a secular decline from 40,000 barriques to 30,000 and finally to 20,000 in the 1780s. The progressive decline in La Rochelle's effective hinterland, and even the switch of brandy in the Aunis to an inland route to Paris in place of a coastal route, left the towns-men with the picture of a mythical past. In 1784 the chamber of com-

[41] *Ibid.*, no. 3713, 'Etat des eaux-de-vie agrées et embarquées au port de la Rochelle 1780–7'.   [42] *Ibid.*, no. 3478, 5 October 1771.
[43] The quantity of brandy from La Tremblade, Marennes, and the islands of Oléron and Ré, mainly Oléron, from 1 October 1769 to 30 September 1771 amounted to 943 *pièces*, 1 barrique and 13 ancres. *Ibid.*, no. 3711, 'Etat des eaux-de-vie'. See also *ibid.*, no. 3712, for a smaller total for the same period.
[44] *Ibid.*, no. 3470, letter from chamber of commerce to the intendant, 12 December 1771, which further reduces the size of the true coastal trade into La Rochelle.
[45] *Ibid.*, no. 4025.

merce seemed to hint at a past state of grace in which a very fanciful figure of 20,000 to 30,000 *pièces* of brandy were exported from the Aunis to Picardy and Normandy.[46] The trade at large did not decline. What happened was that a higher proportion of the brandy handled in La Rochelle and its vicinity came from the coast and islands, and less from La Rochelle's immediate hinterland which was once the monopoly of the port's merchants. Within the hinterland, the brandy which was too weak for the export trade was drawn off by the Paris trade (and in the process made more palatable by a higher degree of rectification before departure). In the case of brandy consigned along the coast, more of it originated in response to northern commissions coming direct to coastal and island merchants than to sub-contracts from agents in La Rochelle itself. In this way La Rochelle was pushed out of an active role in the brandy trade. The prime trade – the export trade – had become almost exclusively a business of Tonnay-Charente. Inland merchants dominated the overland route to Paris, and much of the brandy passing through La Rochelle did so only physically. The trade was not directed by La Rochelle houses, and rested on direct ties between northern France and the coastal and island merchants. Far from this trade being small, in the 1780s it was at least as large as the foreign trade of the entire *généralité*, and in boom years twice that size. Despite its large scale, the coastal traffic receives little recognition in the surviving letter books in Cognac or Jarnac. They refer, insofar as domestic trade is concerned, almost exclusively to the Paris trade, and to the overland carriage of brandy for the capital. In other words, the coastal region was in economic terms a distinct market zone.

Thus La Rochelle had lost out in the coastal trade. It had lost out too in its own inland market region. In the past inland trade orders from Orleans did not go beyond Aigre and Jarnac, and there was therefore into the 1760s some degree of stability in La Rochelle's hinterland. When the four offices of *agréeur* had been created in 1753 to certify brandy at a fee of 7 sols per *pièce*, they handled brandy coming from Saint-Jean, Mauzé and Surgère, and even Aigre as well as from places within 3 leagues of La Rochelle. Their revenue implied a turnover of 48,000 barriques a year: after 1766 this fell to 18,342 barriques. It then fell to an even lower figure, and within a few years of 1766 they lamented that 'depuis bien des années ces memes eaux de vie d'Aigre, de Saint-Jean d'Angély, de Mauzé, de Surgère etc prennent la route d'Orléans et par conséquent ne viennent plus ici'. In the bad years it was traders from Mauzé who were blamed for buying the brandy close to La Rochelle: 'des particuliers établis à Mauzé

[46] *Ibid.*, no. 3663, 13 February 1784.

venus jusqu'à demie lieue de cette ville en enlèvent les eaux de vie et leur font prendre la route de Paris'. The brandy handled by the *agréeurs* now came only from within 2 or 3 leagues of the town.[47]

As a result of the weakening role of the port, the number of merchants involved in signing petitions in relation to the brandy trade declined. When the port had close ties with the brandy districts, almost all merchants in La Rochelle had some interest in the trade. A petition in 1752 was signed by sixty-five merchants, and as late as 1775 another bore forty names.[48] Two petitions on the brandy trade in 1783 and 1786 had a mere nine and eighteen signatories respectively.[49] In the petitions of 1788 from the *négociants* of the Aunis, Saintonge et Angoumois against the *régie des aides* only seventeen out of forty-nine signatories were from La Rochelle. In essence the petitions reflected the domination of the trade by powerful inland groups, seventeen from the Champagne districts (four from Cognac, four from Charente, five from Jarnac and four from Pons) and fifteen from other districts (five from Angouleme, five from Saint-Jean d'Angély, three from Surgère, two from Saintes). The shift inland of the centre of economic power in the region seems striking.[50] Buying by people in Mauzé, hitherto an undistinguished town in the business activity of the region but singled out by the *agréeurs* in their bitterness around 1770, pointed to new business initiatives in the hinterland. Details of the certificates of the unloading of brandy in the northern provinces which had to be returned to the port of shipment survive for 1783 and 1786. A total of nineteen houses were involved in La Rochelle, of whom only five did a large volume of business.[51] This hints at the decline in La Rochelle's control of the coastal traffic, and at a shift in directing the operations to other centres in the province. This is also borne out in the statistical evidence of the 1780s which could be interpreted as showing that half the brandy paying *octrois* was coastal. The town's real brandy trade would effectively have been limited to buying in a narrow hinterland in its immediate environs, itself subject to invasion from a rising class of inland merchant. There is evidence from other sources of direct buying from the islands and the Abonné de Marennes and of the emergence of substantial traders there. In the 1780s when the Bordeaux merchant George Boyd did extensive business in the south-western fringe of Saintonge he variously made or planned large purchases from them. La Rochelle's decline

---

[47] *Ibid.*, no. 3522, petition from four *agréeurs* to chamber of commerce, n.d. A pencil note indicates a date of 1766 but from the internal evidence it appears to be several years later.
[48] *Ibid.*, no. 3592, 9 November 1752; no. 3635, 12 August 1775, petition of forty houses to chamber of commerce.   [49] *Ibid.*, nos. 3483, 3484.
[50] *Ibid.*, no. 4008, nine petitions at various dates in April 1788.
[51] *Ibid.*, nos. 3946, 3950.

in coastal traffic can be paralleled in foreign shipments from the Aunis, the adjacent islands and the Abonné de Marennes, which can be documented statistically for 1783 and 1789. By 1789, in a dramatic fall from the already modest level of little more than 1,000 barriques in 1783, a mere 73 barriques were declared physically in La Rochelle. Though Marennes and the island of Ré, the main export 'bureaux', were technically distinct provinces, all the Ré exports and most of the Marennes exports in 1789 were described as Aunis, which illustrates how the name of Aunis remained widely used as a trade name, as in the past when La Rochelle physically handled most of the coastal brandy, in disregard of the fiscal realities of provincial jurisdictions.[52]

Some coastal traffic in the 1720s and 1730s, via shipment to Rouen or Elbeuf, had been destined for Paris. However, the expansion of the Paris trade from the 1740s rested on the conversion of ordinary brandy into the stronger categories of spirit 'one-third' and spirit 'three-fifths' (with the further advantage of effectively lightening the fiscal burden which did not distinguish in practice between brandy and spirit), and which made the inland route competitive with the coastal route. Significantly the decree of the council of state in 1753 which appointed the *agréeurs* of brandy specifically recognised the rights of the sellers of brandy to 'fortifier et rebouillir' brandy.[53] It was the continued growth of this overland trade which aggravated La Rochelle's problems in the 1760s. The absence of reference in the letter books can be accounted for by the fact that the purchases for Normandy and Picardy were largely carried out in Aunis and in the islands. This brandy was itself markedly inferior to brandy in the region running from Saint-Jean to Chateauneuf-sur-Charente. This fact also tends to confirm that the brandy shipped coastwise was in the main for consumption within the northern provinces of France, and not for shipment up the Seine to Paris. Comments in 1769 suggest a tension between Paris demand and other demands, either coastal or foreign. In other words the coastal traffic after mid-century corresponds almost wholly to demand in the coastal provinces of the north-east of France. When coastal demands recovered from the late 1770s, with better vintages, it was exclusively in response to consumption within the coastal provinces themselves.

Normandy and Picardy were the key centres of coastal consumption. The traffic dates from the very end of the seventeenth century. In Alençon

---

[52] Marennes also exported a sizeable amount of Saintonge brandy. In the 1780s the two-way traffic between the Abonné de Marennes and the western reaches of the Saintonge, which reflects the marked increase in internal circulation within the region, is itself a parallel to a new two-way movement of brandy, as speculation warranted, between Saintonge and the Angoumois.   [53] Versailles, 10 April 1753. *Ibid.*, no. 3594 bis.

in 1699 and Caen in 1703 the farmers-general allowed the importation of brandy, a permission that was all the more easily granted as it seemed a small traffic compared with the consumption of pear and apple wines. The trade in brandy in Dieppe was 1,600–1,700 barriques a year and even up to 2,000 barriques. While much was for consumption in the town, there was also importation for the countryside. In 1734 it was alleged that in the course of two years 1,016 barriques were imported on the account of the deputy tax farmer of the *aides* in Dieppe 'pour obliger les seigneurs, curés et gros fermiers de la campagne qui font des provisions d'eau de vie.'[54] As early as 1718 local merchants had established roles as agents of merchants in Picardy, Normandy and other places.[55] In the wake of the abundant 1743 vintage, Picardy was represented as the sole market for brandy from Poitou and the Aunis,[56] and in 1763 Normandy was said to take 'des quantités prodigieuses de nos eaux de vie qui se chargent par mer pour Rouen, Le Havre et Dieppe'.[57] The growth in the trade is also reflected in the fact that the pattern of a single importer reselling brandy to numerous retailers was giving way to a multiplicity of direct orders from customers in the hinterland of the ports of Saint-Valerie, Calais and so on.[58] While the change was seen as successful by importers anxious to minimise demands on their working capital and to shift the burden of the growing tax liability to the final importer, the concern of the chamber of commerce in La Rochelle was the paperwork it created for the exporting brandy merchants in the Aunis. The reality was the dynamic emergence of a retail sector in depth for brandy and the increasing ease of handling small consignments intended for obscure retailers. A consignment of 200 *pièces* of brandy dispatched to Saint-Valerie in the 1780s might involve 100 separate *soumissions* on behalf of customers, 'la majeure partie de ces particuliers, livrés à un petit commerce de détail'.[59]

The sheer scale of the consumption in the coastal provinces of northern France can be seen from the fact that, as inland carriage of brandy to Paris developed from the 1740s and replaced shipments up the Seine, the growing coastal trade became predominantly one serving markets within the coastal provinces. So important was the trade to the two main importing provinces, Normandy and Picardy, that a memorial in 1782 claimed

---

[54] *Ibid.*, no. 3708, year 1734. Dieppe, the chamber of commerce of La Rochelle, and merchants and syndics of commerce of Rouen versus Rosot, deputy tax farmer of *aides* for the *généralité* of Rouen. Similar complaints arose in relation to Picardy more generally in 1745. See *ibid.*, nos. 3705, 3706, 3708, 3709.
[55] *Ibid.*, no. 3612, 3 December 1718, petitions of judge and consuls of La Rochelle.
[56] *Ibid.*, no. 3709, *négociants* of La Rochelle to chamber of commerce, 20 January 1745.
[57] *Ibid.*, no. 3553, chamber of commerce, La Rochelle, 7 October 1763.
[58] *Ibid.*, no. 3719 n.d., no. 3727, n.d., no. 4007.   [59] *Ibid.*, no. 3944.

that the two provinces were said to have formerly had 'un commissionaire en titre dans Cognac'.[60] The growing lobbying power of interests in the trade is seen in 1781 in the concession by Joly de Fleury, the controleur-général, for permission for La Rochelle to accept fictitious declarations to foreign destinations from vessels loading brandy for ports within the kingdom in wartime.[61] The coastal traffic to Rouen and other Channel ports was already the main business in the letter books of the Veuve Guérinet at Charente in the 1720s. The minutes of the notary Cherpantier, the most active Tonnay notary in trade circles, also point to the regularity of the traffic.

While Picardy and Normandy were the main focus of the trade, other provinces imported as well. Thus Calais, Boulogne and behind it the *pays boulonnais* were important centres as early as 1730.[62] Dunkirk had been a centre for Flanders, although in 1747 it was refused an exemption from local duties levied on shipments which Calais had enjoyed since 1730 and the centre of the trade for Flanders shifted from Dunkirk to Calais.[63] Because of its exemption, Calais supplied brandy to Saint-Omer (the distribution centre for inland Flanders), Artois and Hainault. In 1780 the farmers-general sought to remove the privilege which Calais enjoyed.[64]

In 1784, in the depth of difficulties, one of the memorials, no doubt harking back to the crisis of the late 1760s, claimed that shipments to Normandy and Picardy had ceased since 1767.[65] However, whatever the problems of the La Rochelle merchants themselves, and their difficulties in the late 1760s and early 1770s were real, the trade reasserted itself, as the trends in the *octrois* in the 1780s show. In 1787 Delamain made one of the rare *négociant* references to the traffic, writing of the 'many who have commissions for the coast of France'.[66] This was a time of hectic upsurge in the trade, and Delamain's uncommon reference to the traffic implies that houses in Charente with coastal commissions were buying further inland than usual. A figure of 29,583 barriques of brandy paying *octrois* in La Rochelle in 1787 suggests that the strong demand also existed in the

---

[60] ADC, Angouleme, 5C5, letter of comte de Jarnac and accompanying memorial, 20 June 1782.   [61] ACC La Rochelle, no. 3720, 23 May 1781.
[62] *Ibid.*, no. 3498, 8 December 1730, letter of controleur-général to the intendant of La Rochelle.   [63] *Ibid.*, no. 3499 bis, and no. 3501.
[64] *Ibid.*, no. 3502, 1780. More information on the question is contained in *ibid.* no. 3508, memoir by chamber of commerce, La Rochelle, 4 January 1782. However, despite Calais' advantage, Dunkirk enjoyed substantial local trade. Approximately one-third of the 18,000 barriques said to be shipped to Dunkirk in 1778 were supposedly to be sold in the town and surrounding provinces (AAE, CPA, vol. DXIV, ff. 274–5).
[65] ADC, Angouleme, 5C6, memoir 1784, untitled, first line reading 'Le commerce des eaux-de-vie de Saintonge et d'Angoumois . . .', six signatories.
[66] HAJ, Delamain no. 1 letter book 1787–9, 8 December 1787, to Thos. Cullen and Co., Ostend.

Aunis. There is no evidence that transit by inland carriage fell: quite the reverse is indicated. Export trade which had plummeted in the 1770s, in part because of the rise in inland traffic, recovered in the 1780s: in 1783, it was over 30,000 barriques. While continuous figures do not exist, brandy exports were high again in 1787, 1788 and 1789, probably maintaining a 30,000 barriques level, and soaring well above it in 1789. The likelihood is that aggregate trade rose, perhaps even more sharply than these tentative estimates suggest: the fact that all the competing branches of the trade, overseas, coastal and inland, seem to have fared well, and that price levels and price trends were moderate in the 1780s, suggest as much.

Regional markets and prices in the south-west

Prices had varied considerably within the south-west at the outset, and a general market as such did not exist. That could not continue. External demand, concentrated on favoured ports, was supplemented by a strong coasting demand for northern France and from within the hinterland for the overland route to Paris. That meant more competition and inevitably a combination of steadier prices overall and, on occasion, when conditions caused prices to soar, a ripple across the entire brandy economy of the region. As late as the 1720s a wide gap existed between brandy prices in La Rochelle and Cognac and between both of them and Bordeaux. In the Charente region – Aunis, Saintonge, Angoumois – the main international market was originally in the port of La Rochelle, which was not directly served by a river opening up the interior. The only good waterway, although still difficult to navigate, was the Charente well to the south. In addition, relatively small though the region was, it was broken up by internal tariff barriers: that between Saintonge and Aunis and between the Angoumois and Saintonge and Aunis. With the shift from La Rochelle to Tonnay-Charente as an export centre, it was possible to load brandy into vessels on the river for direct transport to foreign markets; and if it had been purchased within Saintonge it was subject only to local duties – in other words a sole set of inland duties. In La Rochelle, unless the brandy was the coastal or Aunis brandy, it would have had to pay duties three times over: brandy paid duties when it first left Saintonge, it paid a second duty when it entered the Aunis and a third duty when it was exported from the Aunis.

La Rochelle was in the customs union known as the Cinq grosses fermes whereas Saintonge, Angoumois and Bordeaux were all in the Provinces réputées étrangères, and hence paid duties either in transit into the Cinq grosses fermes or into each other. Duties could of course be avoided by entrepot procedures which ensured that, if declared for export via entrepot in approved ports, brandy avoided the payment of further duties in the entrepot centre. However, even this decisively favoured Tonnay-Charente as a direct centre of dispatch for foreign destinations: entrepot facilities elsewhere entailed two loadings – one on a coastal craft from Tonnay and a later one on the vessel for abroad. Entrepot facilities, moreover, were jealously limited by the revenue authorities. Although extensively available in Bordeaux, the most important port in France, in La Rochelle they were limited to goods destined for the French colonies.

Significantly, though the general run of brandy was poorer in La Rochelle than in Cognac, the price in the early decades was 3 to 11 livres higher. As cognac already sold for the highest price of any brandy overseas, its lower prime cost enhanced the attractions for foreign customers of making direct contact with houses in Cognac. The price differential provided the impetus for Cognac merchants to take the brandy trade into their own hands: with direct access to the Charente as a waterway, with fewer duties to pay if the point of shipment for overseas was within Saintonge itself, and avoiding a second commission (i.e. the commission to a buyer sub-contracted to act for a La Rochelle house), they could either offer brandy at lower prices, or capture some of the profits of other intermediaries after the early decades. Even reference to La Rochelle prices became very rare in letters.[67]

In contrast, Bordeaux quotations, never mentioned in the sole letter book of the 1680s, were frequent in the letters of the late 1710s and 1720s. At this stage Bordeaux prices were much higher than La Rochelle and higher again than Charente/Cognac prices. Between 1719 and 1727 prices in Cognac ranged from a nadir of 55 livres in 1719 to a high point of 85. Converted into the same-sized barrel as in Bordeaux (32 veltes as compared with 27 veltes), the price range was 65 to 95 livres. In Bordeaux the range was 80 to 120 livres. Even in the brandy season of 1726–7 the gap not only persisted but widened to a peak between November 1726 and February 1727 (80 livres in Cognac, 118 to 120 livres in Bordeaux). In other words, despite all the evidence of Aigre demand for the inland route, it was difficult to turn circumstances to advantage. Bordeaux, on the other hand, though it was already beginning to move to a secondary position in the trade, was able, because of its better shipping opportunities, to profit in price terms out of a sudden upturn in demand.

The rapid development of Cognac, however, led to a substantial closing of the gap between prices in Bordeaux and Cognac. In November 1766, the price in Bordeaux was 140 livres; in Cognac, when converted

[67] A later memorandum noted with some emphasis or surprise that the price of brandy in La Rochelle was much higher in October 1787 than in Cognac (ACC, La Rochelle, no. 3496). Only such an unusual situation led to a now uncommon comparison of prices in the two centres.

into Bordeaux barrels, the local price was 133 livres (112 livres in Cognac barrels). In the immediately subsequent years the old relationship was finally and dramatically reversed. The bad vintages – less failures in themselves than a speculative anticipation of shortage combined with the enhanced Paris demand for brandy from Cognac – sent prices sky-high. In early December 1768, Delamain, quoting 140 livres in Bordeaux and 192–200 livres in Cognac, observed that 'a great disproportion has for some time past subsisted between that place and this which must undoubted be the effect of plenty with them and scarcity with us.'[68] Throughout the 1770s, expressed in Bordeaux equivalents, Cognac prices were equal to or above Bordeaux prices, and at times significantly so. In January 1776, prices in Bordeaux were 125 livres, but 145 and 160 in Cognac. By January 1779 the pattern reversed itself, however (130 livres in Bordeaux and 125 in Cognac), reflecting the presence of masked vessels in Bordeaux concealing their origins under a neutral flag, and opportunities in wartime foreign trade that small centres like Charente lacked, and which lasted into the early peace years because of a freak high demand in Bordeaux from Irish smugglers. From the vintage of 1784 onwards, however, Cognac prices edged ahead, and the gap in Cognac's favour became more marked still when Paris demand was fevered: in April 1789 when Bordeaux prices were 140 livres, Cognac prices for the local (Cognac) barrique were 135 livres. Thus a complete revolution had taken place in prices.

One of the factors which helped to arbitrage prices was movement in brandy within the region, not from the Aunis, but from Saintonge (Tonnay-Charente, Rochefort or Mortagne) to Bordeaux. If the ultimate destination, by process of reshipment, was not France but overseas, it was economic in part because brandy declared on the invoice for export did not attract further duties, provided it was held in entrepot on its arrival in the second French port for transfer to a vessel for the declared final destination. This depended on agreement by the farmers-general to entrepot procedures. While it was an established option in Bordeaux, it was not one in La Rochelle (except for the colonies, in which case it was free of all duties),[69] one suspects from pressure to preserve Aunis brandy from competition from Saintonge brandy. The position was unchanged in 1773, as Saule in La Rochelle explained to Richard Hennessy, in the case of brandy sent from Cognac to La Rochelle:

the droits de sortie must be first paid at Charente comme pour province étrangère and when the same brandy be arrived here, it must pay a droit d'entrée and moreover when reship'd or discharged on board another vessell, *a new duty must be paid*

[68] DAJ, Delamain letter book 1767–8, to Berry, 8 December 1768.
[69] See ACC, La Rochelle, no. 3615, 26 September 1736. See also no. 3621.

therefor, just as if you had paid nothing before, notwithstanding the bureau de Charente accounts with ours.[70]

The problems were illustrated in a different way in 1768 when Cognac prices were high and when the idea of shipping Bordeaux brandy from Tonnay-Charente seemed at least to a customer in Ireland attractive. Richard Hennessy explained that in such circumstances not only would the brandy have to pay the 19 livres per barrique when finally shipped for Ireland but it would accumulate exit and entry duties amounting to a further 34 livres.[71] Delamain purchased brandy in Bordeaux from Baudry in late 1767, with the needs of the Irish market in mind, and was hopeful at that time of devising a way of avoiding the 'heavy' duties at Rochefort or Charente.[72] As Hennessy and Delamain were in regular contact, the categorical tone of Hennessy's advice to his Irish correspondent a few months later probably reflects advice from Delamain, in the wake of his fruitless exploration, that there was revenue resistance to creating an entrepot for such consignments.[73]

The infrequent opportunities for Ireland on the Charente (except in the great boom of the 1750s and 1760s) and the hundred or so sailings a year from Bordeaux to Ireland ensured that brandy moved to Bordeaux via Rochefort and Tonnay-Charente, or via Mortagne, which was within Saintonge but on the Gironde itself and offered a cheaper brandy and a shorter sailing to Bordeaux. Hennessy remarked in 1766 that merchants in Dublin and Waterford had had their cognac via Bordeaux until eight or ten years previously (meaning by transport from Mortagne), at which time they switched to direct importation from Rochefort.[74] When a combination of recession in Dublin brandy demand and soaring Cognac prices resulted in a virtual collapse of direct sailings in 1767, Dublin merchants in need of cognac found that consignment through Bordeaux was the only opportunity unless they were to incur a long and indefinite wait for infrequent and unpredictable direct sailings from Dublin. The consequence was that within the year, from the autumn of 1767, Mortagne became a serious option again.[75] Mortagne had no fiscal advantages over Rochefort. As far as customs procedures were concerned, they were in essence identical in Tonnay-Charente, Rochefort and Mortagne. All three were in the Saintonge, and the only entrepot facilities they had access to for the European market were in Bordeaux. Duty would be avoided at the point of final shipment provided that the goods were, at the

---

[70] HAC, 4 February 1773, to Richard Hennessy.
[71] *Ibid.*, letter book 1765–9, 4 April 1768, to Cassin.
[72] DAJ, letter book 1767–8, Delamain to Laurence Saule and Co., 15 December 1767.
[73] See also HAC, letter book 1765–9, 4 June 1766, to Phil Stackpole.   [74] *Ibid.*
[75] *Ibid.*, 26 March 1768, to Gernon, Bordeaux.

outset, declared for the foreign market and a certificate returned later of their having been 'chargé pour l'étranger'.[76] Bordeaux exports as recorded in the port's *états de la balance du commerce* to *Angleterre* in the 1770s amounted to roughly 1,000 Bordeaux barriques a year, and the comparative absence of reference to Mortagne business in the Cognac letter books before 1778 confirms that the entrepot of Mortagne or Cognac brandy in Bordeaux, which would need to be added to these figures to arrive at the real amount of goods actually loaded aboard vessels in Bordeaux, was likewise modest. However, with the advent of war and the prospect of Bordeaux as the sole route of transit for Ireland, Delamain acquired a warehouse in Mortagne reinforcing a new level of competition for brandy at Mortagne. Brandy purchased in Mortagne, which had usually been cheaper than in Cognac, now came up to Cognac price levels, and even exceeded them, especially in the winter months. In January 1782, when prices were 68 and 70 livres in Cognac, in Mortagne 'proprietors insist on 81, and its with utmost difficulty we can get any at about 75 livres'.[77] It was wartime which had created such a monopoly situation, and Delamain expressed the wish that they could revert to the old practice of sending vessels to the Charente to bring brandy to Bordeaux. In 1781 or 1782 a possible 150,000 veltes for Ireland shipped at Mortagne (and almost exclusively consigned through Bordeaux) may be hypothesised. This would have been the equivalent of almost 5,000 Bordeaux barriques. In 1783, entries at Mortagne for *Angleterre* were down to 64,920 veltes, or around 2,500 barriques. This figure was larger than the 1770s level of entries for Mortagne, Rochefort and Bordeaux combined. The return of peace effectively broke the monopoly that Mortagne had enjoyed during the war years: from 1783 there is no reference to a premium in Mortagne prices, and with a brisk demand in Ireland in 1784 there were regular shipments round from the Charente to Bordeaux.[78]

The not insignificant quantities of brandy shipped at Mortagne for Bordeaux under invoice for a foreign customer were, for fiscal and statistical purposes, included in the statistics for the *généralité* of La Rochelle. On the other hand, brandy shipped to Bordeaux for rectification there would not qualify for exemption from duty and, as a rectified product, it would technically be a product originating at the point of redistillation and hence invoiced from there. This means that export figures for Bordeaux (including both brandy which originated in the *généralité* of La Rochelle

[76] HAJ, Delamain no. 2 letter book 1783–5, 30 April 1785, to MacCarthy frères; same date, to Forster Brothers.
[77] Ibid., Delamain no. 2 letter book 1781–3, 22 January 1782, to Alley, Dublin.
[78] Ibid., Delamain no. 2 letter book 1783–5, 24 August 1784, to Bateson, Belfast.

and some Mediterranean and Spanish brandy) give an unduly favourable impression of the ready availability of brandy in the immediate hinterland of the port, and at the same time, as they do not contain figures for the brandy held in entrepot in Bordeaux for the arrival of Irish vessels but which for statistical purposes were recorded in the ports of Saintonge, underestimate the actual volume of brandy loaded aboard vessels in Bordeaux. The detailed breakdown of the shipment of brandy from the *généralité* of La Rochelle in 1783 is the first firm measure we have of the scale of the Mortagne trade.[79] In 1783, with the recent end-of-war return to Rochefort still incomplete, entries at Rochefort – 70,231 veltes – just exceeded those at Mortagne.

Between 1783 and 1785 custom house entries in Bordeaux, i.e. brandy or spirits which had to be declared in Bordeaux itself because they were not covered by entrepot entries elsewhere, must have been as high as or even higher than the entrepot traffic: it corresponded to new business in holding Mortagne brandy speculatively in Bordeaux and in rectifying brandies of various provenance in Bordeaux to the requirement of shippers. Rectifying activity even extended to the larger cognac brandy region, as Hennessy's partner Boyd set up a distillery at Royan, and the warehouse at Mortagne (ceded by Delamain to the two men) was an adjunct to the new Royan business. In the 1780s buying in both Mortagne and Royan was increasingly dominated by speculative Irish houses in Bordeaux which replaced Cognac houses like Delamain's as purchasers there. In the figures for 1789, the exports of Rochefort were a modest 2,213 barriques (of Angoumois provenance, however). An *état* for Mortagne does not even appear to exist, and the most recent activity, that by Hennessy and Boyd, had been mainly, some rare English orders apart, geared to a fluctuating Irish market. Their business had in any event collapsed by 1789. In that year, even Angoumois brandy, a lower grade from an inferior brandy-producing province, entered into the export trade of Bordeaux: 2,453 muids were entered outwards as Angoumois. Also recorded were 1829 muids of *double*, almost exclusively for *Angleterre* and Russia. The fact that none of this *double* was recorded as Saintongeais, marked the final demise of the Hennessy–Boyd rectifying enterprise at Mortagne and Royan on the Saintonge coast of the Gironde.[80]

The main distillers and rectifiers in Bordeaux and along the Gironde were Irishmen closely linked to other Irish houses either in Bordeaux or Cognac. The Irishman, Geoghegan, partner to Theodore Martell of Bordeaux, bought for the partnership in the Saintonge in the mid-1770s;

[79] ADC, Angouleme, 5C5, 'Eau de vie envoyée à l'étranger', 1783.
[80] AN, Paris, F12 1666.

another Irishman, one of the Bordeaux Gernons, had an association with the Broussards of Pons at the end of the same decade; and the sojourn of Richard Hennessy, Irishman and erstwhile Cognac resident, in Bordeaux from 1776 to 1788 was a long saga. All these events showed how the Bordeaux–Cognac hinterlands had integrated and how specialisation had altered the brandy trade beyond recognition. Individuals at all levels from that of the *négociant* down to the artisan-distiller moved between the regions with ease. Brandy from Rochefort or Mortagne met the needs of Bordeaux houses when foreign customers sought the best product; and Bordeaux rectifying, a specialist activity providing a lower quality of product, drew on brandy, personnel and even foreign custom supplied by the Cognac houses. The elimination of a large price differential between Cognac and Bordeaux reflected all this, and could not have occurred without it.

Competition from rival spirits on the French market

With consumption increasing rapidly both in Paris and in the coastal provinces of northern France, the brandy business more than held its own. While Paris drew off more of the brandy in the 1760s and 1770s, consumption did not actually fall in the northern coastal provinces. If coastal consignments from La Rochelle seemed to dip, the effects of the shortfall were eased by the entry of Spanish brandy. This first became a subject of comment in 1760 when the north, which formerly got all its brandy in the Aunis, was said to have imported massively from other places, and especially from Catalonia, in the wake of a poor season in 1759.[81] The chamber of commerce claimed in early 1761 that in the last two years prices had doubled, and in consequence imports from Spain soared. In the preceding year (1760 or – in the context – more probably 1759) 15,000 gross *futailles* (presumably of 32 veltes each) were said to have been imported by Calais, Dunkirk and Boulogne for the consumption of Flanders, Hainault and Artois, another 5,000 by Saint-Valerie, Dieppe, Le Havre and Rouen for Picardy and Normandy.[82] The admission of Spanish wine and brandy was now permitted under the Family Pact. In a letter on 20 December 1764, in relation to the even more sensitive grain trade, Choiseul went so far as to see France and Spain 'ne faisant qu'une seule nation'.[83] In 1772 the Chevalier Ruthledge of

---

[81] ACC, La Rochelle, no. 3472, 15 February 1760, 'Mémoire tendant à faire maintenir la bonne qualité des eaux de vie à La Rochelle et dans la province d'Aunis'.
[82] *Ibid.*, no. 3474, 21 February 1761, 'Mémoire à Messieurs les directeurs et syndics de la Chambre de Commerce pour servir de suite à celui qui leur sera présenté'.
[83] *Ibid.*, no. 6305.

Dunkirk, commenting on the advance of Barcelona brandy, noted that it was already beginning to be marketed 'sans répugnance' under its own name.[84] In the same year the first suggestion arose that Spanish brandy was reaching Paris: 'de gros marchands de Paris meme tirent de ce dernier royaume une grande quantité d'eau-de-vie qu'ils tiraient ci-devant de l'Aunis et de la Saintonge, et disent qu'elles leur deviennent moins couteuses'.[85] The complaint was a still more explicit and frequent one in the various memoirs of 1782.

Complaints about the disadvantage that Aunis brandy faced because of allegedly lower duties on Spanish brandy at its export than on Aunis brandy leaving La Rochelle began to abound.[86] In the local shortages occasioned by the poor 1788 vintage and soaring Paris demand, Spanish brandy made its appearance in La Rochelle, and was apparently placed in entrepot for the trade with the colonies and Guinea. One author of a draft pamphlet, surviving in the chamber of commerce papers and obviously inspired by the chamber itself, feared that if it was not sold for its original purpose, it could be exported to northern France, and would, to the detriment of the reputation of French brandy, nourish fears there that La Rochelle brandy was mixed with Spanish. The author felt that steps should be taken both to quarantine the brandy and to keep the chambers of commerce of northern France abreast of the steps 'pour prémunir les commettants contre les insinuations insidieuses que quelques écrivains pourraient imputer à nos eaux-de-vie, en voulant les taxer d'etre amalgamées aux eaux-de-vie de Barcelone'.[87] In addition to Spanish competition, Languedoc brandy was a formidable rival. The French East India company purchased from Marseilles as well as from the Atlantic coast, and some of the Bordeaux brandy itself came from the Agenais.[88] More ominously a memorial of the chamber of commerce asserted in 1784 that 'c'est depuis peu d'années que l'on a vu sortir de Sète des chargements d'eau de vie complets pour venir dans la Manche'. The complaints were still being voiced in 1786.[89]

[84] AAE, CPA, vol. XDIX, f. 221, memoir, 4 April 1772. Comments begin to multiply at this time. For striking examples see MAC, letter book 1774–5, 25 April 1774, to Stritch, Dublin; Archives du port, Lorient, East India Company, IP286, liasse 145, 14 May 1768.

[85] ACC La Rochelle, no. 4211, 'Très humbles et très respectueuses représentations de la ville de Rochefort au Roi', Paris 1772.   [86] *Ibid.*, no. 3502, 1780.

[87] *Ibid.*, no. 3495. undated, but obviously written in the aftermath of the 1788 vintage, either in 1789 or even 1790.

[88] See Archives du port, Lorient, East India Company, IP283, liasse 100, no. 46; IP286, liasse 145, no. 14; liasse 146, nos. 39, 45; IP286a, liasse 152, no. 65.

[89] ACC, La Rochelle, no. 3666, 'Nouvelles et très respectueuses représentations de la Chambre de Commerce de La Rochelle', 13 February 1784; no. 3726, chamber of commerce to king and council, 22 November 1786.

Thus the overall pattern was a complex one, but on balance one in which the strengthening of demand for spirits in northern France and in northern Europe more than outweighed the effects of increased competition. The change was paralleled by a rise in consumption and output of cider brandy, though the interests in the Aunis, with their extensive involvement in the coastal trade, preferred to see that development as a threat. Distillation of cider existed as far back as 1700 and beyond. It was tolerated in its traditional centres, but its dispatch to Paris was prohibited by a decree of 13 March 1699.[90] In a royal declaration of 24 January 1713 the use of cider and cider brandy, and their manufacture and commerce, were prohibited in the kingdom with the exception of Normandy and part of Brittany. Foreign trade equally was prohibited, and consumption by the crews of vessels was confined to the coastal trade.[91] In practice the use of cider brandy was wider, as was suggested by a petition from Bermont, a merchant in Honfleur, who in 1764 wanted to load 25 tons of cider brandy on his vessels for the slave trade. He referred to its use by slaves on the slaving vessels, and by crews on vessels trading with the colonies. He even asserted that 'les matelots qui sont partis pour la peche du grand banc n'en ont jamais embarqué d'autre'. According to the words attributed to Bermont, 'les fermiers généraux qui en font, dit-il, un commerce exclusif n'en ont jamais refusé pour ces sortes de voyages'. The official reply was that his claims were incorrect and that until a new statute was issued, the use of cider brandy was permitted only in slaving voyages.[92] A wider flexibility, at least in time of scarcity, is shown by the fact that when another Honfleur merchant, Morlange, requested permission to load 12,000 to 15,000 *pots* of cider brandy for a voyage to the Ile de France and the Ile de Bourbon, the permission was granted in the knowledge that it conflicted with the prohibition of 24 January 1713.[93]

The question of granting wider permission for the export of cider brandy was much in the air in the 1760s, even before the crisis in the vintages, which suggests that, as in the case of wine brandy, cider brandy had expanded rapidly in output. A Rouen merchant, Simon, sought permission in 1765 to export 10,000 *pots* of cider brandy to New Orleans, complaining that the duty on cider brandy in the 1664 tariff was the same as that on wine brandy, although cider brandy was only half the price. In this case the response to the applicant was a firm refusal.[94] However, these were normal years with no critical shortages. Moreover, the question was at the time a delicate one, as the freeing of the cider trade was already being claimed, raised in the first instance by the provinces of Normandy

[90]   Savary, *Dictionnaire universel* (1723 edn), entry on 'eaux-de-vie'.
[91]   ACC, La Rochelle, no. 3630, 28 January 1764.   [92]   *Ibid.*, no. 3630.
[93]   *Ibid.*, no. 3633, 5 November 1770.   [94]   *Ibid.*, no. 3629, 11 November 1765.

and Brittany. The opinion of the wine-producing provinces was sought on this request. The chamber of commerce of Guyenne opposed it, objecting that cider had 'aucun frais de culture', and that, if mixed with brandy, it would have a detrimental effect on the brandy business.[95] The chamber of commerce of La Rochelle opposed the request in even more hysterical terms. It felt that the competition of cider brandy would be more detrimental than the trade in grain spirits which existed abroad. That affected only the prices of brandy, whereas if trade in cider brandy was permitted, it would destroy the brandy trade itself by the doubts it created about the authenticity of brandy shipped overseas. Cider brandy itself was a virtually undrinkable product, it claimed, and the chamber professed to see the large shipments of brandy from the Charente as destined for mixing with what it claimed to be 'une liqueur dangereuse et malsaine . . . n'y ayant jamais été trouvées agréables'.[96] The issue was still in the air in 1765 as the intendant's office consulted the chamber about the proper level of duties which should be levied if the export of cider and pear brandy were permitted. However, the terms of the letter itself hinted at an expectation that the proposal would not take effect.[97]

The debate over cider brandy paralleled an even longer-standing one over rum and derivatives of sugar. The making of rum was permitted in the British colonies, and the export and re-export trade was widespread throughout the king's dominions: rum consumption spread rapidly, directly or indirectly, through shipment to continental ports (including the free port of Dunkirk). In the 1760s its re-export was making it an important rival, in an ever more mixed international trade in spirits, to the more traditional Spanish and French brandies. In France conversion of sugar molasses into rum in the islands or its import were both prohibited. As far back as 1752 the chambers of commerce of Montpellier and La Rochelle were in agreement about retaining this prohibition.[98] In this case too the question of liberalisation was strongly in the air in the 1760s. In 1763 the intendant referred a proposal to the chamber of commerce in La Rochelle to allow the introduction of taffia or rum in entrepot for re-export.[99] While the limited concessions to Normandy and Brittany in the matter of cider brandy reflected the pressure of provincial interests, the concern about rum was inspired by the rapidly expanding trade in British rum. The proposal met with predictable opposition in wine- or brandy-producing provinces, and in its opposition the chamber of commerce in La Rochelle enjoyed the support of the judge and consul of Orleans and

[95] *Ibid.*, no. 3554, Observations on intendant's letter of 6 August 1763.
[96] *Ibid.*, nos. 3553, 7 October 1763.   [97] *Ibid.*, no. 3561, 2 October 1765.
[98] *Ibid.*, no. 4632, 8 August 1752.   [99] *Ibid.*, no. 3718, 22 October 1763.

of the chambers of commerce of Toulouse and Montpellier.[100] The opposition was thus powerful, and long deferred any progress. It was only in 1769, in a new and highly politicised wave of liberalisation and an acute shortage of spirits, that permission on a very restricted basis to put taffia from the Isles in entrepot was given.[101] Thomas Sutton, the great gentleman shipowner, became a purchaser, if supplies were available in the French ports, regarding it as 'plus saine et meilleur à tous égards que l'eau-de-vie'.[102]

Equally disturbing for the brandy lobby was the expansion of gin as a spirit in international trade. Gin, a highly refined and neutral spirit, made either from grain or sugar derivatives, was long established in Holland and Britain. Its trade had advanced in the seventeenth century as part of the general precocity of Dutch manufacturing: rather as in the case of other Dutch industries, trade was later choked off in the eighteenth century by a combination of spirit production in consuming countries, and soaring trade in both brandy and rum. In an expanding and increasingly heterogeneous trade in spirits, it found a place once more and imported gin was prominent in Dunkirk, which as a free port was emerging as the best barometer of the international spirit trade. The question then arose of the detrimental effect of existing prohibitions which prevented French entry into a new and apparently lucrative activity. In November 1775 two houses, Corpeau and Stival, were permitted to distil gin in Dunkirk on the condition that it was not sold in the kingdom.[103] The original purpose was to supply gin to the smugglers in the port, but rumours spread about the gin interest being permitted to supply it for consumption in neighbouring provinces: four individuals were said to have this design, and a tax receveur was even alleged to have a one-quarter interest in one of the distilleries.[104] Assurances were forthcoming from the controleur-général, Necker, on this score.[105]

One of the distilling interests was the house of Stival, an important house in the port's cognac trade. In such circumstances it is easy to see how considerations of policy were said to prevent the chamber of commerce in Dunkirk from opposing gin distilling.[106] Rumours were abroad

---

[100] *Ibid.*, nos. 4632, 4633, 4635, 8 August, 22 November, 22 November, 1763.
[101] *Ibid.*, nos. 5428, 5429. See also J. Tarrade, *Le commerce colonial de la France à la fin de l'Ancien Régime*, vol. I (Paris, 1972), p. 331. The concession related solely to rum consignments to Roscoff for smugglers.
[102] Archives départementales du Morbihan, Vannes, Lamaignère and Delaye papers, E2375, Paris, 2 December 1778, to Antoine Delaye, Lorient.
[103] See ACC, La Rochelle, no. 3565, Dunkirk, 1 October 1777.
[104] *Ibid.*, no. 3563, no. 3564, two letters of 23 August 1777.
[105] *Ibid.*, no. 3566, 24 September 1777.   [106] *Ibid.*, no. 3567, Dunkirk, 19 April 1780.

in 1777 of permission being conceded for establishing gin distilleries in Flanders itself, and for the import of gin into neighbouring provinces. In the resulting concern in La Rochelle, a memorial with many signatures was presented to the chamber of commerce.[107] Later permission was granted for some of the locally made gin in Dunkirk to be supplied to Flanders and Artois.[108] This seems to have been the permission granted to the gin distillers in 1784 to introduce 100,000 *pots* of gin into the kingdom each year. The Dunkirk chamber of commerce (with a powerful vested interest in the wider spirit trade conducted through the port) seems to have been less wholehearted on this issue, and something of a seesaw in policy existed: although after representations permission was suspended, a second decision then confirmed it for a year.[109] The spread of gin distilling into Dunkirk and some extension of trade from the port into France itself provides a commentary, given the jealous object of protecting the politically powerful vine regions, on the strength of demand for spirits in the 1780s.

---

[107] *Ibid.*, no. 3562, no. 3562 bis.   [108] *Ibid.*, no. 3572 undated draft memoir.
[109] *Ibid.*, nos. 3573, 3574, January 1785, 11 June 1785.

5 Competing markets: Parisian and foreign demand

The rise of the Paris market

The Paris market was, the relatively firm London demand for champagne brandy apart, the most stable feature of the trade. It was also the most important market, taking roughly a third to a half of the total output of the Charente. This was first graphically testified to in the comments in the original edition of Savary, and the Loire, given its proximity to Paris, was the first brandy region to profit by the growth of the second largest of western Europe's cities. The expansion of the Paris market in turn accounted for the steady decline in exports from Nantes to external markets: they fell quite sharply from a peak of 18,636 barriques in 1728, to two-thirds or even half that level from the beginning of the 1730s. As the vintages around 1730 were good and prices in 1732 plunged to the lowest of the century, the reasons for the fall in exports lay outside the export market. Subsequent exports from Nantes were sizeable only in three years: 1744, 1761 and 1762.[1] These were years of exceptionally high exports in La Rochelle as well. As prices did not rise in 1744 – they were, on the contrary, the second lowest of the entire period 1718–80 – this points to an abundant vintage. As exports tended to peak in the first half of the calendar year, high exports should logically reflect abundant vintages in the preceding calendar year, in other words in the autumns of 1743, 1760 and 1761. To take one illustration, the merchants of La Rochelle as late as January 1745 were preoccupied by problems of prices and marketing in the wake of the vintage of 1743.[2]

Paris demand had overflowed into the Charente region as early as 1718, and in January of that year Augier noted that 'cette marchandise est

[1] Export figures exist in the chamber of commerce archives in the Archives départemen-tales de la Loire Atlantique. Some of the figures have been published in Jeulin, *Evolution du port de Nantes* (Nantes, 1929).

[2] ADC, La Rochelle, no. 3709, petition, 20 January 1745. Evidence of brandy prices is slight for these years. However, wine prices were very low in 1741–4, 1760 and 1761: B. Bézaud, *Vignes, vins et eaux-de-vie* (Cognac, 1883), p. 92.

demandée pour Paris à 50 et 51'.[3] Severe frost in 1717 had damaged the vines – Augier had estimated that as many as one-quarter of the vines had been destroyed – and in 1718 even the precious Borderies wine seems to have been distilled to meet the demand.[4] The vines had suffered neither in Bordeaux nor along the Loire to the same degree. In the wake of the bad vintage of 1717 Paris demand, already evident on the northern borders of the Charente, acquired significance in Cognac itself, and even after the following and better vintage of 1718 its existence was recognised in Augier's observation in January 1719 that 'des gens de Bordeaux, d'Orléans et de Paris achètent par spéculation'.[5] The high costs of inland transit ensured that Paris was normally supplied either from the maritime regions close to La Rochelle, or overland from around or near Aigre, well to the north of the Charente and its navigable tributaries. Paris purchases further afield soared in an even more unprecedented fashion in the wake of the 1725 vintage, which was extremely bad in northern France and poor in Charente. Only a third of the amount of brandy produced the previous year came from the stills, and of the reduced quantity of wine going to the stills, in contrast to the four or five parts of wine necessary in Augier's highly optimistic view to produce one part of brandy in 1724, eight and even ten parts were required.[6]

One of the consequences was that, whereas brandy had fallen in price from 58 livres per barrique in late 1724 to 41 livres by June 1725, it soared to 81 livres in December 1725. Despite the reduction in the coinage which should reduce prices, the price of brandy held up. Another bad vintage occurred in 1726. In August, Augier expected a vintage of a half or a third of the norm: in September he noted that a famine in brandy at Saumur and on the Loire generally was compelling Paris merchants to draw from Chatellerault, and the price had reached 88 and 90 livres in September.[7] Augier himself, with the prospect of a good trade to Paris the

[3] AAC, letter book 1717–19, 3 January 1718, to Theodore Ryswick, Amsterdam. The letter was inadvertently dated in the letter book as 3 January 1717. The price per barrique was the standard quotation in the trade and prices in this chapter refer to the price per barrique unless a distinction is expressly made.

[4] *Ibid.*, 21 February 1718, to Ryswick. See also a letter of 21 May 1718.

[5] *Ibid.*, 14 January 1719, to Pierre Balguerie.

[6] *Ibid.*, letter book 1724–6, 1 December 1725, to Burlier, Orleans; 3 November 1725, to Mundt, Hamburg; 12 December 1725, to Le Riget des Rouchères. Augier's suggestion of as little as four parts of wine to one of brandy in a good vintage seems highly optimistic. In 1726 six parts of wine made one part of brandy, and the following year was almost legendary, five parts making one of brandy. *Ibid.*, Veuve Guérinet letter book, 1726–8, 25 November 1727, Veuve Guérinet to Bonnaller, Paris.

[7] *Ibid.*, letter book 1726–7, 28 August 1726, to Laurencin, Nantes; circular letter of 21 September 1726.

following spring in brandy and even in wine, was prompted to write seeking the names of good merchants from a merchant in Orleans.[8] Moreover, a regular coastal traffic in brandy to Rouen and the north of France already existed. A passing reference in a letter to a Rouen merchant in the spring of 1725, when prices were very low and falling, noted that 'nous avons presque toujours des barques en charge pour chez vous'.[9] This demand was already reaching Tonnay-Charente on a regular basis, and the known coastal trade was for Augier a less suspect outlet than the overland route. His sister-in-law, the Veuve Guérinet, conducted a business shipping brandy from Tonnay-Charente to Yvetot and Rouen, much of it intended for Paris.[10] Augier thought the business by sea greater than the overland business, observing, in a comparison of the final stage of the coastal traffic with the last one in the overland route, that traffic was 'plus considérable de Rouen à Paris, qu'elle ne l'est de Chatellerault à Paris'.[11] Moreover, the coastal route remained active in the more normal conditions of the distilling season of 1727–8, and a season later, in the busy spring of 1729, there were vessels in the Charente for Rouen in addition to others for the port of Dunkirk (for the London market) and for foreign destinations.[12]

Despite quite large-scale business in Tonnay-Charente for the coasting trade by the 1720s, overland business was a novelty in Cognac. It was in the hands of merchants from Aigre, often referred to simply as 'les Aigriers' – small buyers or jobbers with commissions from Orleans and Paris. Sent overland from the Charente region, the brandy was loaded at Chatellerault on barges for Orleans by agents in the pay of the Aigriers.[13] In Cognac itself the reputation of the Aigriers preceded their appearance. According to Augier, 'ils avaient la louable habitude autre fois d'acheter en pièces fidèles et de transvaser en d'autres qui ne l'estoient point'.

In October 1725 Augier, purchasing 10 *pièces* of brandy in store in Chatellerault on behalf of an Orleans merchant, found that they had already been sold at a higher price than originally quoted by the Aigriers to the merchants there. Of this *fait accompli*, Augier observed: 'à quoy patience. Nous sommes moins apportés que messieurs d'Aigre de faire voiturer à Chatellerault et mettre à prix pour etre pris au gibet, quand la

[8] *Ibid.*, 2 September 1726, Augier to Touze, Orleans.
[9] *Ibid.*, 2 April 1725, to Boulard and Bottereau, Rouen.
[10] Two of her letter books survive to illustrate the coastal traffic to Paris. *Ibid.*, 1726–8, 1729.
[11] *Ibid.*, letter book 1726–7, 29 July 1726, Augier to Brouet, Paris.
[12] *Ibid.* Veuve Guérinet letter book, 1726–8, 25 November 1727, to Pommier, Paris; letter book February–September 1729, 20 February 1729, Guérinet to Richard, La Rochelle.
[13] *Ibid.*, letter book 1724–6, 8 September 1725, Augier to Guérinet, Charente.

marchandise augmente. On [presumably the Cognaçais] refuse, quant il [presumably referring to the conditions of trade] en est autrement. Il ne parait pas un commerce égal d'icy en dehors'.[14] A year later, with more Cognac experience of the land route, Augier observed that: 'j'aime moins la route de Paris que celle de Rouen. Les eaux-de-vie passent par tant de mains allant par terre. Quelque bonnes qu'on les fournisse icy, elles deviennent marchandise commune avant de vous parvenir'.[15]

The Aigriers themselves pushed further afield in months of hectic speculation in search of goods for Paris: the cost of transport had almost doubled in the three months preceding September 1725.[16] An equally telling measure of the novelty of the overland trade in Cognac was the fact that the comparative costs of the sea and overland routes were not self-evident: Augier, with prospects of servicing overland commissions, had to inform himself of them. The matter had become a pressing one. In March 1726 'messieurs d'Aigre offrent 65 et achèttent autant qu'ils donnent d'argent.'[17] In May he estimated that there had been sales of 600 *pièces* of brandy to the 'fougeux Orléanais'. These were purchased at 90 livres a barrique in Cognac, and sold at Chatellerault for 112 livres.[18]

Nor did the demand cease. It remained strong and maintained the level of prices: 'c'est la route de Paris qui soutient ce prix et qui en apparence en tirera toute l'année prochaine. Il est à craindre que l'étranger tirera par préférence de Bordeaux et autres ports de France, où les Orléanais ne peuvent aller'.[19] In July 1726 brandy at Chatellerault cost 110 livres per barrique; free on board in the Charente for the sea route it cost 100. In late September, when brandy cost 88 and 90 livres in Cognac, Augier quoted the charge free on board as 110 livres in Charente for the sea voyage and 119 on board in Chatellerault for the river voyage.[20] In March 1726 Augier was encouraging a Paris merchant to order brandy by sea, observing that 'Messieurs les Aigriers sont mieux postés que ceux de Cognac quand ce commerce se fait par terre'.[21] He quoted the freight to Rouen as 30 livres per ton of 2 *grosses pièces*, plus insurance at 4 per cent. This would work out at as little as 5 livres per barrique to be added to the price on board in Charente of 120 livres. Such an addition to the price

---

[14] *Ibid.*, 13 October 1725, to Jacques Barbier, Orleans.
[15] *Ibid.*, letter book 1726–7, 7 September 1726, to Luzarde, Paris.
[16] *Ibid.*, letter book 1724–6, 8 September 1725, to Guérinet, Charente. Costs rose from 25 to 45 livres. It is not perfectly clear to what unit of transport the price of carriage relates.
[17] *Ibid.*, 9 March 1726, to Augier, Charente.
[18] *Ibid.*, letter book 1726–7, 27 May 1726, to Le Riget des Rouchers, Charente.
[19] *Ibid.*, 26 August 1726, to Balguerie, Middelbourg.
[20] *Ibid.*, 21 September 1726, to Dunet, Paris, and circular letter of the same date.
[21] *Ibid.*, letter book 1724–6, 2 March 1726, to Hazon frères, Paris.

would ensure that the price of the brandy landed at Rouen was more or less the same as the price put on board a barge at Chatellerault: 'tout au plus les eaux-de-vie couteront-elles rendues à Rouen ce qu'elles vallent rendues à Chatellerault. Reste à savoir s'il en coutte autant de Rouen à Paris que de Chatellerault à Paris'.[22]

The vintage of 1725 created an exceptional crisis, with failure along the Loire pushing brandy buying into the heart of the Cognac region. In better years, when the custom of Paris retreated to the coasts and inland to Aigre, the disruptive presence of Paris bidding no longer provided occasion for comment. A good vintage in 1727 ushered in a plateau of abundant vintages in 1728–33, matched only in 1760–2, and of low prices rivalled – and then only fleetingly – in 1744. The year 1732 was the last year of the century in which prices fell as low as 42 livres.[23] In these seasons of abundance or low prices, exports failed to pass the peaks of the 1720s: the inference has to be, unless one assumes a decline in the cultivation of the vine or a rise in local consumption of brandy – and both have to be excluded – that in normal years Paris, supplied either by coast or by land, had become a bigger draw on the production in the region. The abrupt fall in the export figures for the *généralité* of La Rochelle from the high level of 34,105 barriques in 1725 to the comparatively low level of 13,582 barriques in 1726 is a crude reflection of the scale of the novel Paris demand that year. The return to more normal trade was reflected in exports of 23,680 barriques in 1727 and 28,845 in 1728.

While the Cognac house of the Augier family acquired no permanent Paris business, despite the great flurry of letters with Paris and Orleans houses in 1726, the Paris market strengthened its position on the fringes of the region. To the already established maritime route for Paris via the Seine was now added the inland route for the capital, upgraded from a doubtful affair in the hands of obscure figures, the Aigriers of Augier's obsession, and prompting distillers to systematically strengthen their brandies to a higher proof to economise on transport costs. The key decade in the change is the 1740s. In years of inadequate vintage the Paris demands made major inroads into Charente supply. That is the explanation for the abrupt downturn in exports from the La Rochelle *généralité* in 1736 and 1737, 1739–41, 1748 and 1750–2.

---

[22] *Ibid.*, letter book 1726–7, 17 August 1726, to Boesmer, Blois.
[23] Forty-two livres is the price in the *états de la balance du commerce* for 1732. The same price is recorded for 1732 in the Cognac prices set out in Bézaud, *Vignes, vins et eaux-de-vie*, p. 92. In a fleeting dip in June 1725 market prices had fallen to 41 livres. Such a low level had not been registered in any source – either *états* or merchants' quotations – from 1717 onwards.

The fall in exports in 1736 and 1737 was the least sharp. Though prices in July 1735, with the promise of an abundant vintage, came down to 44 livres, they rose later the same month because of reports of bad weather in Orleans, Blois and Nantes. As a result, 'Paris a donné des ordres considérables pour en faire acheter à Cognac et à Saint-Jean'.[24] The gamble proved right: in the autumn there was said to be one-third less wine than the preceding year, and prices of brandy, as low as 45 livres in June 1735, were 66 and 67 livres at the outset of the new season and held firmly at 58–60 livres the following spring.[25] The relatively poor 1735 vintage, then, is the explanation for the fall in exports in the calendar year 1736. Exports rose again in 1738: this reflected a good vintage in 1737 because in January 1738 prices were as low as 43 and 45 livres. The 1738 vintage itself, however, was less good and the prices in the La Rochelle *états de la balance du commerce* rose from 55 livres in 1738 to 83 livres per barrique in 1739 and to the very high levels of 122 and 120 livres in 1740 and 1741 respectively.[26]

Abundant years followed the crisis period of 1739–41, remarkably so after the 1743 vintage, to be interrupted once more in the second half of the 1740s. The 1742–3 Martell letter book, which documents the

---

[24] HAC, Régnier letter book 1735–6, 26 July 1735, to Michael Hatton.

[25] *Ibid.*, 6 November 1735.

[26] Prices in Tonnay-Charente, from the Régnier invoice book, bear out the trends: prices were 79 livres in February 1739, and never fell below 65 livres later in the year. By May 1740, in the wake of the bad 1739 vintage, Régnier's prices peaked at 88 livres. They were as high again in the spring of 1741 and yet again in the early spring of 1742, reflecting the aftermath of another two difficult vintages. The *états* for the *généralité* suggest still higher prices – 122 livres for 1740, 120 for 1741. If La Rochelle prices were on an f.o.b. basis, the difference might be accounted for in part by the fact that the Régnier quotations were market prices, in other words buying prices before additional costs in getting the brandy ready and aboard vessels were incurred. This is not, however, the likely reason for the divergence, because, despite the f.o.b. basis of La Rochelle calculations, a few years earlier and later alike they had a reassuring closeness to the market prices. The prices in the Régnier invoice book, lower than in the *états*, suggest that brandy prices in 1738–42 almost doubled. The vagaries of coastal and inland routes may reflect some of the intermittent differences between La Rochelle and inland prices. High coastal prices around 1740 may have been caused by coastal shipping for the north of France, and could have been one of the catalysts of the rapid development at this time of overland trade at a higher proof. Reverse swings, i.e. higher inland prices, could also occur: thus, in 1745, when prices were 52 livres in La Rochelle, they were said to be 75 or 80 livres in the inland districts (or Provinces réputées étrangères). ADC, La Rochelle, no. 3709, Representations of the chambre of commerce. It was a near-permanent condition in the closing decades of the century. There are no good runs of brandy prices available in other sources. The December price in the *mercuriales* runs only from 1695 to 1729 (J. George, *Mercuriales d'Angoulême, de Cognac et de Jarnac*, p. 69); another run, on a monthly basis from 1766 to 1815, is in Ravaz and Vivier, *Le pays du cognac*, p. 258. The *mercuriale* figures are very close to prices from merchant letter books where they can be matched; in the later figures the peaks fall short of those quoted by merchants, and thus hint in some obscure way at the emerging problem in price quotations in the *états*.

outcome of the 1742 vintage, shows prices as low as 45 livres in December 1742, and rising no higher than 50 livres by September 1743. In both 1747 and 1748 the prices in the La Rochelle *états* were 105 and 103 livres respectively. In the Régnier invoices a rise occurred as early as the spring of 1746, which may hint at an indifferent vintage in 1745. A bad 1746 vintage is more certain given that prices were 107 livres in March 1747. The 1747 vintage must have promised badly as prices were still higher at 112 livres in August. That the outcome corresponded to the poor expectations is amply borne out in the data: exports for the calendar year 1748 (export season for the 1747 vintage) were down to a staggeringly low 3,952 barriques, a level lower even than in 1741 and second only to the export season of 1772 (in the aftermath of the terrible vintage of 1771). In August 1748 prices were still around 110 livres. A bad vintage outcome in 1748 is borne out in prices as high as 80 as late as May 1749; they were still around that mark in the spring of 1750. The official prices also rose sharply to 105 and 103 livres for 1747 and 1748 respectively. After easing somewhat they then soared to 135 and 122 livres for 1751 and 1752 respectively: levels which point to discordance between strong demand and limited supply after the vintages of 1750 and 1751. The whole run of seasons from 1746 to 1751 seems to have proved disappointing, if not to the jobbers at least to the exporting merchants. Exports from the Charente region (i.e. from the *généralité* of La Rochelle) were chronically depressed in the years 1746–54 with low points in 1748 and 1750–2. The low exports were accompanied by high prices which reflect more the countervailing force of the Paris market than the outcome of the Charente vintage itself. The plateau of high prices in the *états de la balance du commerce* corresponds also to the sharp reversal in Régnier's invoice book for 1746–50 from the low prices of the immediately preceding years. Moreover the market prices in Régnier, available for 1746–50, are close to the *état* figures. What that means is that, given extra costs still to be added, the *état* prices are themselves probably an understatement of real f.o.b. prices.

A run of high exports from 1756 to 1765 emerges less as a resumption of the export activity of the pre-1739 period than abnormal conditions in which war and novel demand for spirits in general combined to provide an exceptional and temporary boost to foreign demand for cognac. Quite apart from a less stable rum supply, disastrous harvests in northern Europe in 1755 and 1756 reduced the supply of barley for distilling and boosted the demand for brandy; after the war bad harvests in 1765 and 1766 had precisely the same result. For once, the emerging pattern of Parisians pricing exporters out of the brandy market was reversed, as foreigners, faced with a rising home demand and spirit shortages, persisted in buying large amounts at soaring prices. The fact that good vintages were not reflected in more dramatic price falls – prices even in the *états* never went below 70 livres in the years between 1760 and 1762 – pointed to a deepening of demand all around.

The change is all the more striking if deficiencies in the prices in the *états* are taken into account. Market prices in the late 1760s very significantly exceeded them. The prices in the *états*, though in the past close to market prices or in 1739–41 above them, were now to fall below them. Why this was the case it is not possible to say, as the prices given for brandy (in contrast to other commodities)[27] had been hitherto close to market prices. It may well reflect some emerging inadequacy in collecting prices and striking a balance (such defects on an even more glaring scale were evident in Irish and English trade figures).[28] The *état* price of brandy, down to 65 livres per barrique in 1757, had increased by almost 50 per cent to 90 and 92 livres in 1758 and 1759 respectively. For the next three years, 1760–2, it was back to 70–75 livres, and exports soared. The year 1759 was one of high prices: the *état* level of 92 livres is supported by Ranson's rather large purchases for Cognac houses in July 1759 at 100 livres per barrique, more than the official average but not wildly so. Exports were also down in volume in 1759 compared with preceding or following years. But as firm foreign buying even at the higher prices existed, the underlying strength of foreign demand meant that when vintages were exceptionally good, exports climbed to near record levels as they did in 1760–2 (1761 itself was the third highest export total of the century). A year later in the autumn of 1762, Martell's were buying actively and at prices for new brandy of 68 to 70 livres which were very close to the *état* figure of 70 livres for 1762.

A very significant change for whatever reason did take place in the mid-1760s: the *états* from that time consistently understated market prices, very markedly so in the real crisis years. Whatever the reason for the divergence, the *état* prices, now very misleading, understate the upsurge in demand and its strength. Market prices, already high by historic standards, virtually doubled in 1768, and even the good vintage of 1769 was

---

[27] On these prices, see P. Butel, *L'économie française au XVIIIᵉ siècle* (Paris, 1993), p. 78.

[28] However, some contradictions from other sources of the *état* prices have to be set aside. Thus the sweeping claim in February 1761 that brandy in October 1760 had been 190 to 200 livres per 27 veltes in Cognac, and in La Rochelle 165 livres per 27 veltes, has to be ignored (ACC, La Rochelle, no. 3474, 21 February 1761) as it does not accord with what we know of prices from other sources. The same document's other assertion that in two years prices had doubled, though not borne out to the same extent in the *état* prices, is supported more loosely in the sense that brandy rose in 1758 and 1759 from a low level in 1757. Wine prices were very low in 1757 but higher in 1758 and 1759 (Bézoud, *Vignes, vins et eaux-de-vie*, p. 92).

not reflected in a sharp fall. The years 1771 and 1772 were to be the peak years with prices of 170 livres and 160 livres respectively according to the *états*, but with much higher prices on the market culminating in levels of 255 livres in the spring of 1772. These were the highest prices of pre-revolutionary times, far exceeding the peaks of the 1709 and later rises.

The evolution of inland demand remains obscure, partly because evidence of the brandy trade is scarce for the 1750s. The Martell letter book for 1753 is particularly unhelpful for an attempt to tease out the impact of the Paris trade. This is in part because Martell's had suffered, like their rivals the Augiers, in the penury of supply for the foreign trade in the late 1740s and early 1750s, in part because the letter book relates to the aftermath of the vintage of 1752 in which with low brandy prices (in the *états* they had sunk from the preceding year's high of 122 livres to 70 livres) there was no occasion for an export merchant in Cognac to worry about competition with inland merchants. However, reflecting a strengthened Paris market, the permanent inland traffic for Paris had already extended beyond Aigre on the fringe of the region to Jarnac, where at the end of the 1750s the house of Ranson, regularly and without reliance on intermediaries, did a substantial business with Paris.

The changes in Jarnac, moreover, were a parallel to an even larger scale development of Angouleme as a centre of commissions for Paris. The growth of the Paris, and also of the Normandy and Picardy, markets made itself felt throughout the 1760s, and the needs of Paris especially repeated themselves in the 1770s. In the upsurge of the autumn of 1774, even on the banks of the Charente it was Angouleme and Jarnac buyers who were active.[29] Delamain was an example of the new type of buyer for the Paris market in Jarnac. For Angouleme we know much less, but it is easy to identify quite a substantial business group there from the 1760s onwards. Angouleme's regional role as a business centre now overshadowed La Rochelle's, and buying by La Rochelle houses virtually disappeared. In this context the bill trade of Cognac houses shifted quite dramatically from a La Rochelle axis to an Angouleme one. The growing economic strength of Angouleme, which made it possible for export merchants to use its services, was part and parcel of the move of brandy buying further south and of the upgrading of the jobbing merchants of the early decades in the interior into substantial figures in regular commerce. In Delamain's letter book for 1767–8, it was buying by Antoine Marchais of Angouleme, offering 5 or 6 livres per barrique more than others, that started the price spiral from August 1767, and by January 1768 even Delamain was purchasing for him.

---

[29] HAC, letter book 1771–5, 7 November 1774.

Impact of the Paris market

A further sign of the growth of the market, indeed a condition of its continued expansion, was a change in the nature of the product carried overland. In the 1720s the brandy was dispatched at its Dutch or market
proof; in later times much of the brandy was in the form of spirit. This
practice accelerated in the late 1730s and early 1740s when inland business waxed in face of a waning export trade: the dispute with the revenue
authorities in 1742 shows that they were fully alive to what was happen-
ing. They could not but do so as the business was in the hands of a few
houses: Martell observed in December 1742 to a Paris correspondent
that two or three houses had monopolised all the *charrettes*. The business
surged again almost a generation later when bad vintages and the readiness of Parisians to outbid the export houses led, in 1768–72, to a repetition of the earlier collapse of export business. As in the case of the
abortive attempt in 1741 to tax spirit more effectively, decisive change in
the scale of the business was reflected in the edict of 1771 which switched
taxation of brandy arriving in Paris from a single low and undis-
criminating charge to three rates corresponding to the strength of the
brandy.

Export merchants in their casual reference to their rivals in the inland
trade now recognised it as one in spirits: In 1767 Hennessy referred to 'a
very great call from Paris for our *spirits*' (italics mine).[30] In November
1769, according to a letter from a merchant house in La Rochelle, much
brandy had been sent overland in the form of spirit three-fifths at the
expense of the coastal traffic. The writer even suggested that the practice
might not persist as it had caused dissatisfaction both to the chamber of
commerce in La Rochelle and to the farmers-general.[31] In this context
the 1771 decree seems to have been the outcome. Lobbying by La
Rochelle business interests was a potent feature. The memorandum
which they were preparing in 1771 was said to highlight the damage to the
province, the prejudice caused to the wine trade by excessive distilling,
and the loss of occupation for sailors as the coastal brandy traffic was
undermined by inland spirit traffic to Paris.

In France, as elsewhere, the 1760s and early 1770s are a key phase in
the growth of the spirit trade: bad vintages in 1766 and 1767 had resulted
in a sharp rise in demand for brandy in the Charente region. Moreover,
the 1765 vintage itself may not have been a good one: in April 1767, by
referring to two preceding bad vintages, Hennessy implied that 1765 as

[30] *Ibid.*, letter book 1765–9, 18 July 1767.
[31] AAC, Broussard papers, 5 November 1769, Veuve S. de Galwey to Broussard et fils,
Cognac.

well as 1766 had been below par.[32] The probability of a bad season in 1765 is borne out in the fact that exports fell in 1766 while prices were high in the autumn of 1765 at 110 and 112 livres, and did not fall below 100 livres in the course of 1766. Nevertheless, 1765 itself was only a moderately adverse vintage, as Delamain's more authoritative recollection of the 1768 vintage being the third successive bad vintage excludes by definition the 1765 one.[33] That 1766 was the first memorably bad vintage of the decade seems to be borne out in a greater rise in prices in 1767 than in 1766. Only in the autumn of 1767 with a second really bad vintage did prices reach catastrophic levels. The 1768 vintage was then to be even worse, preceded in August by 'the heaviest rain and hail ever remembered here'. The Charente rose seven feet in an hour, entire villages were swept away, both grapes and vine stocks were ruined and Delamain thought it would take two or three years for vintages to recover.[34] Though prices fell in 1769 and 1770 they did not come down to the levels, already regarded as high, of the hectic 1765 and 1766 brandy-selling seasons. In mid-1770 prices soared again, reaching 170 livres at the outset of August in anticipation of a bad season: in November 1770 Hennessy repeatedly referred to the vintage, somewhat subjectively, as the worst ever experienced. By December prices had reached 185 livres. A bad vintage in 1771 pushed prices to new heights, the highest of the century so far. The consequences were dramatic, involving the deflection to Paris not only of what would otherwise have supplied the foreign market but of what in the past had been carried by coastal vessels for Normandy and Picardy: the contraction in exports from the Charente in 1768–72 was even sharper than in 1748–52, and prices at their peak twice what they were in the earlier crisis. The recorded exports of the *généralité* of La Rochelle sank to their lowest point of the century in 1772. Even in the preceding year, under less disastrous conditions, in December 1770, normally the time approaching the peak season for foreign purchases, Augier noted that 'we have no ships at all in our river which is a wonder in this season'.[35] The following year the story repeated itself, with Augier noting in November that in the preceding month only a sole ship to freight for Dunkirk had entered the river and that it would take a long time to make up her cargo.[36] The Paris competition was all the keener, because as prices soared, the relative cost of overland transport as an addition to final price fell dramatically. Despite overland costs from

[32] HAC, letter book 1765–9, 4 April 1767, to Derham, Dublin.
[33] DAJ, letter book 1767–8, 4 October 1768, to Berry, Hull.
[34] *Ibid.*, 20 August 1768, to Thomas Murphy; 23 August 1768, to Derham.
[35] AAC, copy letters to English correspondents, 1768–82, 17 December 1770, to Harrison.
[36] *Ibid.*, 11 November 1771, to Harrison, London.

the region to Paris jumping from 20–24 livres to 57 livres at peak periods
of movement, they were relatively lower on brandy prices of 160–250
livres in crisis years than on 40–60 livres after abundant seasons.

It was less the scale of the failure (the vintages, though bad, were far
from a complete disaster) than the upsurge in Paris demand which
accounted for the sharpest rises in prices, and the letter books of *négociants*, in contrast to the past, referred frequently to the trade with Paris.
Even the newcomer Hennessy had noted the Paris demand in July
1767.[37] A more established merchant like Delamain provided a similar
commentary on the Paris market. In August 1767 he noted that 'the
demand for Paris continues pretty brisk'.[38] More significantly, there was
no let-up even with the new vintage later that year: in October he reported
extensive orders for Paris, and in December observed to one of the Irish
captains that 'Paris consumes a great deal of our brandies'.[39] For Augier,
the primacy of Paris orders and the bad vintages went hand in hand. He
noted in October 1767 that 'as Paris order [*sic*] large parcels of our spirits
it occasioned the augmentation. The bad success of the vintage contrib-
utes very much to it'.[40] Later in the same month, he noted that 'we never
had such a scarcity since 60 years ago'.[41] Prices, which were 138–140
livres per barrique in September, had soared to 203 by the end of the
December.

As early as 1766 and 1767 the rise in Paris demand was the key factor
in maintaining the level of activity as both foreign buyers and buyers in
Normandy and Picardy, faced with high prices and the competition of
Paris, turned increasingly to the cheaper brandies of southern regions,
Mont de Marsan (the market for brandy from Armagnac) and more
importantly the Mediterranean (both Languedoc and Spain). In Cognac
itself, in 1767 Saule and Delamain cooperated in a joint speculation in
brandy purchased in Mont de Marsan, shipped from Bayonne in the
spring of 1768 to Rouen and destined for Paris. In 1767 Martell speculatively purchased brandy in Spain for the Dunkirk market. In 1767–8 only
the recklessness of Laurence Saule, imprudently expanding his purchases
to outdo his rivals, prevented the decline in the foreign trade from being
even sharper. By contrast, Delamain's export business declined compared with the halcyon early years of the decade, and Hennessy struggled
to survive at all. In February 1771 Augier noted that brandy was 'much
cheaper in Spain, everyone gives their orders there'.[42] With the virtual

---

[37] HAC, letter book 1765–9, 18 July 1767.
[38] DAJ, letter book 1767–8, 22 August 1767, to Walsh.
[39] *Ibid.*, 10 October 1767, to Richard Coppinger, Dublin; 12 December 1767, to Walsh.
[40] AAC, copy letters to English correspondents, 5 October 1767, to Harrison.
[41] *Ibid.*, 19 October 1767, to Harrison.
[42] *Ibid.*, 11 February 1771, to Harrison, London.

absence of foreign custom, the inland trade alone kept business going: in January 1770, normally a very busy time, Hennessy noted that 'it is our jobbers rather than our shippers who are buying at present'.[43] Given the virtual absence of effective foreign demand, prices remained surprisingly firm. Even when in an interlude between two periods of high or soaring prices in 1767–8 and 1770–2, prices eased somewhat in 1769 and in the first half of 1770, speculative buying by jobbers was a factor keeping prices up. In July 1769 the jobbers, offering 5 livres more than the shippers, pushed prices up to 145 livres after they had slipped by 20 livres in the preceding months: the new buying was triggered by reports that the vines in Orleans were all 'distressed'.[44]

The vintage of 1768 in the Charente had an element of purely local character – the freak rains of August 1768. The fact that, although it had been a wet and cold summer, vintage conditions were not quite as bad in other regions is shown in a decisive downturn in the spring of 1769 from the high prices of late 1768. In the autumn of 1768 Bordeaux brandy prices, for instance, were dramatically more favourable than Cognac prices.[45] The bad vintages of 1770 and 1771, however, were part of a wider weather cycle. Even in Bordeaux brandy rose in December 1770 to 190 livres per barrique: 'it was never so high'.[46] The cereal harvest failed as well, resulting in appalling conditions of general misery as the cash supports of the region – wine and brandy – alike faltered. The pattern repeated itself in the 1771 vintage, and even in Languedoc and Spain, though better than elsewhere, the vintage was down on the preceding year.[47] Inevitably there was not only a sustained rise in brandy prices in early 1772, but market quotations surged to 225 and 240 in November 1771 and to a peak of 240 and 255 in April 1772. Many of these quotations, moreover, were simply prices offered, i.e. prices which failed to secure supplies. These were far higher prices than those of 1709. In Bordeaux the highest buying prices were 196 in May and 266 in June 1709 per *pièce* of 50 veltes.[48] Converted into La Rochelle barriques, such prices would be 106 and 144 livres.[49]

In 1772 exports from the Charente virtually folded up. This explains why the merchants dealing in the foreign trade emphasised the upset so

---

[43] HAC, letter book 1769–71, 15 January 1770, to Steele, London.
[44] *Ibid.*, various letters, especially 10 and 17 July 1769; AAC, copy letters to English and Irish correspondents 1767–82, various letters July 1769.
[45] DAJ, letter book 1767–8, 8 December 1768, to Berry, Hull.
[46] AAC, copy letters to English correspondents, 3 December 1770, to Harrison.
[47] *Ibid.*, 14 October 1771, to Harrison.
[48] Huetz de Lemps, *Géographie du commerce*, p. 237.
[49] Even in the *états* of the *généralité* of La Rochelle, which in the later decades of the century understate price peaks, the price level reached 170 livres in 1771 and 160 livres in 1772, the highest calculations in the *états* for the entire period 1718–80.

heavily in their correspondence, and why they harked back to 1709 rather than to 1748–52 for a parallel. In 1748–52 even if they did not sell as much in the kingdom or out of it as normal, both the merchants and the commissions they received from abroad were at least an indispensable part of the market equation. In 1768–72 this was no longer the case with brandy from Languedoc and Spain and rum flooding on to the international market. In a crude comparison with immediately preceding good years, prices doubled in 1748–52; in 1768–72 a prolonged doubling really occurred only in one year – 1772 (the sharp rise in 1768 had proved rather short-lived) – and given the universally bad vintage in 1771 it is perhaps surprising that prices did not go even higher. In other words the price plateau was less marked than in 1748–52. The change in the equation was that, in addition to a growing trade in Languedoc brandy, for the first time Spanish supplies were entering the French market and had actually begun to reach Paris from 1768. Even the coastal demand could draw on other supplies, either Spanish or from Languedoc: that explains why the buyers for Normandy and Picardy as early as 1769 when prices were high but sustainable were not prepared to compete with the Paris buyers, and why coastal shipments from La Rochelle, like foreign shipments from Tonnay-Charente, virtually collapsed as Paris buyers, buying further afield especially in overland commissions, pushed up prices.

The phenomenon of Paris demand now obtruded even on the better intervening years. In the years 1773–6 exports failed to revert to anything like their pre-1767 peaks. They were roughly halved, and this would reflect in all probability an upturn in the level of overland exports to Paris (and a recovery of the coastwise trade in which at lower prices the merchants of Picardy and Normandy could survive in competition with the Paris houses). In October 1774 when a bad outcome to the vintage further north was certain, at the very outset of the distilling season all brandy ready was bought up for the Paris market at 150 livres.[50] The strength of the market is also testified to in the fact that higher effective duties in Paris on brandy from 1771 do not seem to have discouraged the development of the market. By this stage, a large number of commissions were regularly placed in the region directly by the Paris houses, bypassing the Aigriers or the Orleans houses which in the past had mediated much of the demand.

While shipments of coastal brandy from the Aunis to northern France recovered after the crisis, the coastal trade in Tonnay-Charente suffered, given a more persistent encroachment by Paris on the inland fringes. In

[50] HAC, letter book 1771–5, 31 October 1774, to Cassin.

mid-century evidence of the trade cropped up frequently in the minutes of the Tonnay-Charente notary Cherpantier. However, in 1784, one of the memorials about the brandy trade recalled that up to 1767 brandy for Picardy and Normandy had been loaded at Charente,[51] and a memorandum forwarded by the comte de Jarnac in 1782 recalled that the two regions had formerly 'un commissionaire en titre dans Cognac'.[52] In the autumn of 1767 Delamain already had a firm preference for the land route, observing that 'les coulages sont si considérables par eau que nous croyons que vous feriez mieux de tirer par terre'.[53] This was in sharp contrast with Augier's preference forty years previously for the coastal route. The cost of land carriage soared: already 30 sols per velte in October it reached 35 in December, and was down to a more normal 24 sols per velte in June 1768. Faced with these charges, despite his preference for the land route, in January Delamain envisaged sending 500 barriques to Paris via Rouen.[54]

In general coastal shipments for the northern maritime regions of France concentrated more on the port of La Rochelle, the heart of the Aunis, on the islands of Ré and Oléron and on the Abonné de Marennes (all three were independent provinces in the Provinces réputées étrangères, unlike the Aunis which was in the Cinq grosses fermes, and untypically Ré, Oléron and the Abonné had no exit duties on brandy). Admittedly in the fatal years 1769–72 even these markets collapsed, as Paris demand put brandy at a level which both foreign buyers and Normandy/Picardy customers, who had alternative sources of supply, were not prepared to pay. Coastal brandy now enjoyed a less secure place than in the past, and in the crisis of 1782–4 the chamber of commerce of La Rochelle in its special pleading was ready to claim that shipments of brandy coastwise from the Aunis had fallen dramatically from past levels.[55] The chamber claimed that: 'de nombreuses cargaisons de vins distillés par les Catalans arrivent tous les jours dans les ports de ce royaume'. In the case of Spanish brandy destined for the Paris market, it was said to be fortified to 32 degrees on the Cartier scale (which would mean that it was supplied at the strength of spirits three-fifths), which would greatly reduce the costs of the carriage from the coast to Paris. Since 1768, 50,000 muids of Spanish brandy were said to have entered

---

[51] ADC, Angouleme, 5C6, Memoir 1784 about brandy commerce of Saintonge and Angoumois, untitled (first line reading 'Le commerce des eaux-de-vie de Saintonge et d'Angoumois . . .'), six signatories.
[52] *Ibid.*, 5C5, under cover of comte de Jarnac's letter of 20 June 1782.
[53] DAJ, letter book 1767–8, 10 October 1767, to Dunoutier, Paris.
[54] *Ibid.*, 23 January 1768, to Douard, Paris.
[55] ADC, Angouleme, 5C6, Representations of the chamber of commerce, 13 February 1784.

Paris. This would amount to an average of almost 4,000 muids (or 5,333 barriques) a year.[56]

One of the memoranda from the Charente claimed that shipments loaded in Charente fell from 50,000 muids (66,667 barriques) in 1765 to 25,000 muids (33,333 barriques) at the outset of the 1780s.[57] As foreign exports from the *généralité* of La Rochelle (predominantly from Charente) were 25,000 barriques in 1765 and 20,000 barriques in 1780, coastal shipments from Tonnay-Charente should have fallen from 42,000 barriques in 1765 to 13,333 barriques in 1780.[58] The difference might plausibly be taken as representing the minimum level of increase in over-land shipments from the Cognac region over the 1770s. Actual shipments would, however, vary a good deal, falling sharply in the wake of poor vin-tages further north when Paris overland commissions multiplied, and recovering a good deal in intervening years when the costs of overland transport would favour a resumption of buying along the Loire. In the 1780s with a run of good vintages coastal trade fared well, and steadier demand seems also to have resulted in a preparedness to bid against the Parisian interest when prices were rising.

The strength of the Paris market can be seen in its importance during the war years from 1778 to 1781 when foreign trade presented its cus-tomary wartime problems. The years 1778–81 were years of good to remarkably good vintages. The previous calendar years of 1776 and 1777 had already been active years. There was a sharp recovery in exports in 1776 and despite a good vintage in 1775 prices had remained stable. The 1776 vintage and the following 1777 vintage were both followed by high prices with peak points in both years of around or above 200 livres. These were abnormally high prices, and contrasted with prices which after the

---

[56] *Ibid.*, 5C5, memorial dated Jarnac 20 June 1782, under cover of letter of comte de Jarnac of same date. In his marginal comments on the memorandum the count gave a figure of 40,000 muids of Spanish brandy entering the capital from 1768 to 1780. The figure of 50,000 may be a slight confusion caused by the fact that elsewhere in the memorandum the figure of 50,000 muids was given as the total shipment of brandy from Charente in 1765. In the text above exports are taken as amounting to 40,000 muids from 1768 to 1780.   [57] *Ibid.*

[58] The muid is a confusing measure, used for solids as well as liquids. In commerce it would seem to be a measure of 144 *pots mesure de Paris* (see ADC, La Rochelle, nos. 3520, 3627, 3636) or of 36 veltes (e.g. *ibid.*, nos. 3609, 3666). The muid would thus be a third larger than the standard 27-velte barrique of La Rochelle. Four *pots* seem to have equalled a velte. The figures in AN Paris, F[12] 1666 confirm also that the officials of the office for the *balance du commerce* employed a muid of 144 *pots*. See also George T. Matthews, *The Royal General Farms in eighteenth-century France* (New York, 1958), pp. 156–7. On the muid see also Savary des Bruslons, *Dictionnaire universel* (1742 edn), vol. III, col. 1454, and AN Paris, F[12] 208, 'Nomenclature de différentes mesures applicables à plusieurs espèces de marchandise', undated from period of Revolution, useful but not always correct or sufficient.

vintage of 1772 and 1773 went as low as 140 livres per barrique and which only fleetingly exceeded 150 after the 1774 and 1775 vintages. A high level of demand from Paris appears to have been the explanation for the 1776 prices. The 1777 vintage was a particularly poor one. In November 1777 Augier quoted brandy at 220 livres, and as late as March 1778 Hennessy quoted 210 livres. In July 1778 prices were still holding up at 185 and 189 livres.[59] There was inevitably a virtual collapse in export markets: in 1778 brandy exports from the La Rochelle *généralité* were a mere 6,850 barriques.[60] High prices, strong Paris demand and a collapse of shipments overseas did not represent of itself a permanent threat to foreign trade. Even the outbreak of war did not do so and a good vintage in 1778 held out expectations of recovery which were fulfilled in 1779. In November 1778 Delamain commented on expectations that 'our trade in a more flourishing state than for some years past'.[61]

More intriguing than the predictable Paris demand in the aftermath of the poor 1777 vintage was the strength of the overland route after the apparently satisfactory 1778 vintage. In his letters to foreign correspondents, Augier, who had been silent for several years (even in early 1778) on the Paris market, wrote on 7 December 1778 that 'it come [*sic*] daily large orders from Paris where the brandy is sent from here there by land'.[62] Delamain in Jarnac, which was closer to the inland route, had multiple references to the Paris trade in his letter books of 1778 and 1779. Moreover, the Paris trade was active without the not uncommon concomitant of rising prices: prices fell sharply to 130 and 125 livres by November 1778. In late November 1778 purchasing was so active that Delamain observed that 'l'on achète dans les campagnes pour expédier à Paris à 130 livres. Si cela continue une augmentation est infaillible'.[63] On several occasions the situation in Paris was described as a brandy famine, and the sudden rise in demand outran the transport facilities. Many letters at this stage refer to the abruptness of the rise and to high rates for carts for Paris. In January 1779 Delamain noted that 'la demande est très bornée par la rareté des voitures et navires'.[64] This want was itself but a temporary obstacle: the facilities expanded in response to needs and in February he noted 'the exportation to Paris being immense'.[65] The rise in

---

[59] The *états* give only a price of 150 livres, thus considerably understating the rise in 1778.
[60] The downturn revealed by the *états de la balance du commerce* was not a freak for a year in which war broke out. While no figures survive for 1777, the 1776 total was boosted to a respectable level only by abnormally large exports to Guinea (i.e. for the slave trade).
[61] HAJ, Delamain no. 1 letter book 1778–81, 7 November 1778, to Falk and Lovelace.
[62] AAC, copy letters to English correspondents 1768–82, 7 December 1778, to Harrison.
[63] HAJ, Delamain no. 2 letter book 1778–81, 24 November 1778, to Dassy, Meaux.
[64] *Ibid.*, Delamain no. 1 letter book 1778–81, 5 January 1779.
[65] *Ibid.*, 2 February 1779, to Yeats and Brown.

the overland market resulted from a switch from coastal shipping to over-land carriage consequent on reports of the seizure of neutral vessels by enemy privateers.[66] Neutral ships had already entered into the export trade. It is not perfectly clear whether Augier was suggesting that they also carried the coastal traffic for Rouen or simply that in the aftermath of the seizure of the vessels all traffic was halted for the time being, put off by fear of the risks occasioned by increased enemy privateering. The real interest of the Augier reference lies in the fact that it illustrates that, though coastal trade had receded in the early 1770s, it was again a sizeable component of the domestic brandy consignments from the greater Charente region in 1778, and by implication from Tonnay-Charente itself.

The 1779 vintage was exceptionally good. Prices plummeted to 75 livres even in mid-October 1779, and as Augier observed: 'our brandy which have [*sic*] been very dear since 1766 is now at a low rate'.[67] This good vintage was the basis, through entrepot in Ostend, Holland and later Hamburg, for the high level of exports in 1780. It was also the first of several remarkably favourable vintages. The low prices of 1779 and 1780 cannot be attributed to depressed wartime demand, as Labrousse and others have argued. Conducted largely on neutral vessels, export trade got on its feet quite quickly after the disruption of 1778: exports in 1779 were up to the level of the mid-1770s and in 1780, at 19,740 barriques, were the highest since 1765. Large exports to Holland which had virtually ceased to be a market for cognac, and some to Ostend suggest how, under neutral flags and shifting entrepots, trade for the British market was largely uninterrupted.

Whatever the general depression of foreign trade in the south-west as the economic effects of the war bore in on the economy in 1780, exports of brandy from the *généralité* of La Rochelle in 1780 were reassuring, and the sharp upswing in exports to Hamburg and the north simply reflected a further switch to Hamburg as an entrepot when Holland seemed likely to lose its status as a neutral. The use of neutral vessels for the trade helped to maintain the volume of turnover, and occasional slackness reflected a shortage of vessels rather than a fall-off in demand. Paris demand was also a reflection of the attraction of Cognac's low prices, but more significantly of the ever-growing importance of the inland route. In December 1780, Delamain reported 'brandy particularly demanded for Paris'.[68] It was abundance which concealed the functioning of the regular trade currents. With general abundance in supply, Paris custom did not

[66] AAC, copy letters to English correspondents, 1768–82, 7 December 1778, to Harrison.
[67] *Ibid.*, 16 October 1779, letters to Harrison and to Prettyman.
[68] HAJ, Delamain no. 2 letter book 1778–81, 2 December 1780, to Richard Hennessy, Bordeaux.

overflow into the prime Cognac–Jarnac region in quite the manner it had in 1778 or 1779. When Delamain quoted prices in December 1780, he also quoted prices given in Angouleme, which points to the existence of an independent market as Angouleme buying receded to its normal channels.[69] Despite the Paris demand, there was no general upsurge in prices: in July 1781 they were under 70 livres. The 1781 vintage once more was good, and in January 1782 prices in Cognac were as low as 68 and 70 livres per barrique. Only the 1782 vintage brought to an end the sequence of four good vintages, and prices turned upwards, reaching 95 livres in March 1783.

Despite his large Paris trade, Delamain was sparing in comment on it in the course of the rest of the 1780s, suggesting little encroachment into the prime Cognac districts by houses not regularly engaged in buying there. The signs of a disastrous vintage in the autumn of 1788 changed things, however, and sent the Angouleme merchants buying further afield again. The first reports of brisk buying for Paris emerged in August, and as early as 13 September Delamain reported that 'cette semaine des personnes d'Angouleme ont acheté une assez forte quantité d'eau de vie'.[70] In such conditions it was the consequent rise in the number of buyers for Paris which appeared to push prices up.[71] A measure of the concentrated demand is that the cost of carriage or *voitures* rose sharply. Eighteen years previously, in 1770, itself a hectic season, the rates were 18 sols per velte to Orleans and 23 and 24 sols per velte to Paris. In the second half of 1787, when business was at a normal level, the rates to Orleans were still 18 and 19 sols. However, with a sharp rise in Paris business, Delamain reported in October the rate for Paris as 30 sols, and for Orleans as over 22 sols. Even these rates were soon thought reasonable 'vu la cherté des vivres'.[72] The scale of the demand is all the more impressive as at the same time the *octrois* show a remarkably high level of coastal shipments from La Rochelle. Even as early as 4 October Delamain claimed that he executed an order for a Paris house only out of friendship: 'nous avons pour ainsi dire renoncé à toutes liaisons avec Paris en cet article'.[73] Yet even if an established merchant like Delamain had begun to withdraw from buying for Paris, others did not and the demand was said to continue to rise 'surtout pour la route de terre'.[74]

---

[69] *Ibid.*
[70] *Ibid.*, no 1 letter book 1787–9, 25 August 1788, to Brown and Webster, Knaresborough; 13 September 1788, to Jos. Merat, Orleans.
[71] Delamain observed to a Saumur house in September that 'les ordres étant en plusieurs mains cela ne contribuera pas peu à en faire soutenir le prix'. *Ibid.*, 2 September 1788, to Maupassant frères, Saumur.   [72] *Ibid.*, 25 April 1789, to D'Assy, Meaux.
[73] *Ibid.*, no. 1 letter book 1787–9, 4 October 1788, to Merat *l'aîné*, Paris.
[74] *Ibid.*, 18 November 1788, to Dassy, Meaux.

The bad winter conditions which set in in December held back trade, but after a resumption of business in February prices soared to 150, *voitures* for Paris were unobtainable at 30 sols per velte, and charges in May reached 34 and 36 livres. The extent of the overland supply for the Paris market was all the more impressive, as buying in anticipation of British demand had already reduced stocks in cellars in the region,[75] and the Paris market was now the main driving force in prices in the repeated view of Delamain. With London importers holding back in the hope of imposing a price fall on the Charente houses, only Paris prevented prices from tumbling. It was Paris demand, too, quick to realise that the bad vintage of 1788 would mean shortages, that first set prices on the path to recovery. London buyers joined in later, and an estimate by Delamain in August 1789 indicated that exports were running at 5,000 puncheons (10,000 barriques):[76] such a figure for the tail end of the 1788 vintage would suggest for the year exports of twice or three times that level. Martell's exports, measured by his invoices for 1789, were exceptionally high (16,165 barriques), and the pattern was of a brisk London trade. Given strong Paris demand, the London needs were met partly out of the swollen stocks in merchants' warehouses in 1788, partly by the abandonment of other overseas markets: the Irish one, for instance, folded up.

The 1789 vintage was disastrous, and a repeated pattern, now on a heightened scale, of Paris buyers paying over the odds and foreigners turning to other sources underlined the enhanced importance of the Paris market. As early as September 1789, with the certainty of a disastrous vintage and recent destocking, prices had soared to 240 livres. The scale of internal shortage and the consequent high level of prices was the prime factor in accounting for the sharp decline in foreign activity from its still high level in 1789 to a low level in the following year. This was all the more inevitable as the vintage in Saintonge was said to have suffered more than that in the Aunis, and it was anticipated by March 1790 that the Saintonge would be buying in the Aunis.[77] Significant in Jarnac at least from mid-century, Paris demand was now for the first time a regular feature in Cognac. In consequence, the role of Paris demand in the 1790s can be seen within the business pattern of an increased number of Cognac houses, something which was in part a consequence of war but also of an intensification of internal demand from northern France.

[75] *Ibid.*, 13 September 1788, to Thomas Gordon, London.
[76] *Ibid.*, 8 August 1789, to Haworth and Bateman, Hull.
[77] ACC, La Rochelle, no. 3496, 'Observations sur le mémoire des cultivateurs et de celui d'un citoyen concernant le commerce d'eau-de-vie', 1 March 1790.

The Paris brandy buyers

The Paris customers, where they can be identified, are usually designated as grocers. Some ordered over long years, but comparatively few did so in large quantities. There was a contrast between Paris and London in that London had its specialist brandy merchants, some of them on a very substantial scale, offering in payment what were arguably the most sought-after bills in Anglo-French trade. Paris, in contrast, seems to have generated a much larger number of individual orders emanating from traders who were not specialist brandy merchants. The fact that they were not specialists or on a large scale meant that they did not exert pressure in Cognac comparable to that created by the London houses, whose switches in custom between houses packed a punch and whose moods the exporting houses went a long way to placate. The London houses exerted pressure on the Cognac shippers not to supply retailers, and small orders from non-established houses – which could be seen as an attempt by retailers to enter into the import business – were sufficient to arouse their ire. As a result the London buyers remained a relatively small group of large buyers who effectively kept newcomers out of the trade. In contrast the Paris houses were very numerous. When Paris buying expanded, not only did commissions to the region rise, but their distribution over many houses at many points within the region greatly increased competition. In contrast to the London commissions, their buying commissions crossed the customary internal boundaries in the region. Without exception, when prices in Cognac soared beyond conventional limits, the cause was unrestrained buying on Paris accounts.

In addition to Paris orders, there were outside Paris a number of direct orders from customers, especially from curés, monastic houses, officials and noblemen, for brandy. The absence of such orders from Paris suggests that in the capital comparable customers acquired their supplies from the city's grocers. These orders were usually for a barrique or even less: significantly they were often for old brandy. Our only direct evidence of Paris custom is from the Delamain business. As it was an established house in the central core, the business would be weighted towards the quality end, and would not represent the pattern of houses which did not buy regularly in Cognac or Jarnac and which, hence, were less oriented towards quality. This would not be surprising when it is borne in mind that the mainstay of the Paris trade was not the core Cognac district but the eastern, northern and coastal fringes of the region, and that in times of shortage the buyers for Paris bought indiscriminately in a wider hinterland.

6   The merchants of the brandy regions

Family connections among Cognac merchants

The house of Augier has the reputation of having being founded in 1643, and of being the oldest house in the region. The earliest surviving letter book for Augier – indeed for any Cognac house – is for 1681–6. All that can be said with certainty is that Augier was already in the brandy business in the 1680s. The distinction of being the oldest surviving brandy family in the region belonged to the Ransons: they were among the merchants mentioned in the monopoly dispute in 1604; they were Augier's closest business connections in the course of the 1680s; and through the marriage of a daughter of Isaac Ranson of Jarnac in 1762 to James Delamain the partnership of Ranson and Delamain, for a time in the 1760s probably the largest house in Cognac/Jarnac, came into existence.

In 1681–6, in addition to the Ransons, other merchant families who were to prove of consequence in the eighteenth century – Broussards, Lallemands, Brunets and Richards – were all active. Apart from the Ransons, none of these names had occurred in the first decade of the century. No Augier is mentioned in 1604: the family seem to have originated in Angouleme, and to have later migrated to Cognac. There is a marriage contract in Angouleme of a Philippe Augier as far back as 1571. In 1643 the family was still living in Angouleme, when another Philippe married Elizabeth, daughter of Diresh Jansin [*sic*]. Given the family tradition that the business was founded in 1643 the balance of probability is that it was this Augier who later moved to Cognac, and tradition within the family somehow or other transformed the date of the marriage contract into that of his move to Cognac. The surviving letter book of 1681–6 should thus be either his or that of his son Pierre, father in turn of the Philippe whose letter books between 1717 and 1728 all survive, and make him the first member of the family who can be studied in detail.

The marriage of Philippe in 1643 into the Janssens connected the Augiers with one of the Dutch paper-manufacturing families who had settled in the region. In France as in Ireland, outside the ports, the Dutch were significant as manufacturers bringing in advanced techniques, not primarily as traders.[1] The Janssens had already married into local families, as Elizabeth's mother was an Elizabeth Barraud. Nor were the Janssens the sole Dutch family in paper manufacturing in Angouleme. Another family to have a long career there were the Vantongerens who relied even as late as the 1730s on a French brandy merchant in Charente, to whom they were connected by marriage, to handle their paper for export.[2] The Janssens retained ties with Holland: one was a merchant there as late as the 1720s, another member of the family, the Chevalier Janssen, made an appearance in London, and André Janssen married a third daughter to Antoine Vareille, a Huguenot in Dublin in 1720.[3]

In the 1680s the Augiers had commodity business with Theodore Tersmitten in La Rochelle and a brother of Theodore's in Amsterdam, and bill dealings with another Tersmitten, Tersmitten *père*, either their father or uncle, in Paris. Tersmitten is not a local name, and as the young men of La Rochelle and Amsterdam are addressed by Augier as cousins, the connection may well have first come through the Janssen marriage. In the 1680s one of the regular correspondents of the Augiers in La Rochelle – Theodore Paget – is also described as a cousin. Despite their new-found activity, the Augier family were not yet established in direct overseas trade. Their only shipments overseas were to their Amsterdam cousin, and most of their business was with La Rochelle alone. Indeed, their commodity business outside Cognac and its inner hinterland was conducted in its entirety with cousins – Tersmitten and Paget in La Rochelle and another Tersmitten in Amsterdam. The only evidence of any new business was their Amsterdam dealings through their cousin: as La Rochelle effectively dominated the commodity trade of a large interior, direct communication reaching beyond that city, even if with a cousin, was something of a novelty in Cognac.

The Ransons recur in the letter book as suppliers of brandy to Augier. The balance of probability is that the Augiers were at that time the most important family in business in general. However, it is conceivable, as the Augiers handled wine more than brandy, that there was some balance of function between the two families: the Augiers more important in general trade, the Ransons, who supplied the Augiers with brandy directly, conceivably in touch with a greater number of distillers. Indeed, given the importance of wine, the more easterly location of the Ransons at Jarnac

---

[1] L. M. Cullen, 'The Huguenots from the perspective of the merchant networks of western Europe (1680–1720)', in C. J. Caldicott, H. Gough and J. P. Pittion, eds., *The Huguenots and Ireland: anatomy of an emigration* (Dublin, 1987), pp. 129–49.
[2] HAC, Régnier letter book 1735–6.
[3] AAC, letter book 1724–6, letter on or immediately after 5 January 1726.

may have conferred some advantage on them as buyers of brandy. The relative precocity of both families is shown in the fact that they were among the first local families whose members later settled abroad. Philippe Augier spent five years in Amsterdam at the beginning of the eighteenth century, and a Jacques Ranson was a merchant in Amsterdam in the 1720s and 1730s.[4] Another local family in Amsterdam were cousins, the Richards: Jacques Richard was in Amsterdam in 1718,[5] and another brother, Pierre Richard, seems to have either visited or resided in Amsterdam at an earlier date.[6] Other Cognac associates, the Le Rigets, had a brother established in Amsterdam throughout the 1720s. Philippe Augier's sister, married to a Guérinet, had a son apprenticed in Amsterdam by 1725.[7] A further local family, the Brunets, had a member in Dublin in the 1720s, ordering brandy from his relatives in Cognac and wine from Bordeaux.

The pattern of young men going abroad to learn trade or more permanently to settle as merchants was quite common in the south-west of France at the end of the seventeenth century and in the early decades of the following one.[8] It points in one sense to the enhanced importance of the region's commodities and to the ambitions whetted by that change. It also helps to identify a small group of families who were closely connected, and had already intermarried or were soon to do so: Augiers, Richards, Guérinets, Brunets. To this circle should be added in business terms the Rigets and Ransons. With Amsterdam and La Rochelle ties, it was this group which effectively broke the dependence on La Rochelle houses and created the direct link between houses in Cognac and Jarnac and foreign ports.

Marriage ties linked houses together, something made easier by the dominance of Huguenot houses. When Augier married a Brunet in 1726 it brought him a Lallemand mother-in-law. It was also a Brunet marriage in 1726 which effectively integrated an outsider, Jean Martell, into the region. When his wife died, he took as second wife a member of the Lallemand family, and when she was widowed, it was her brother, already helping the house before his brother-in-law's death, who really turned the

---

[4] *Ibid.*, letter book 1727–8, 6 September 1727, to Pierre Néau. In fact Augier seems to have returned in 1706, as he said in 1718 to Janssen that twelve years had elapsed since he had set up at Charente (*ibid.*, letter book 1717–19, 5 February 1718, to Janssen). This seems to be confirmed more or less in what is said in a letter of Augier's on 28 August 1725 (*ibid.*, letter book 1724–6, to Guérinet).
[5] *Ibid.*, letter book 1717–19, 7 March 1718, to Jacques Richard.
[6] *Ibid.*, letter book 1724–6, 18 February 1726. The date referred to appears to be 1716, but this has been taken to be a difficult reading for 1706, when Augier himself was in Amsterdam.   [7] *Ibid.*, 28 August 1725, to Guérinet.
[8] ADG, Bordeaux, 6B 47–50, passports 1727–50. See also Cullen, 'The Huguenots', p. 142. Huetz de Lemps, *Géographie du commerce*, p. 496, has passport figures for 1712–18.

Martell house, which was a spent force in trade, into a business to be reckoned with. The continuing local family interests can be detected in the pattern of the marriages of Philippe's sons: one of them, another Philippe, married Anne Marie Broussard in 1757 and Etienne married Martha Catherine Martell, daughter of a Lallemand mother, in 1762.

The only outsiders to enjoy real as opposed to transient success before the 1780s were the Martells from Jersey (but arriving via Guernsey), who were integrated into the region by two successive marriages, and James Delamain from Dublin, who became successful through his Ranson marriage of 1762. Other outsiders appeared, equally drawn by prospects in the brandy trade, but like several Germans who were shippers in Tonnay (though not buyers in its hinterland), or many of the Irish in the 1760s, they made no permanent impact. The temporary success of the latter in the 1760s was a function of the extraordinary demand conditions in their home market at that time. Not until the 1780s did the only other survivor of the new group, all of them Irish and with one exception Catholic, John Saule, seem to succeed in expanding the turnover of the ailing house which Richard Hennessy left him on his own departure for Bordeaux in 1776, and which he took over again at the end of 1788 after Saule's death. A small circle of native Huguenots (or *convertis*) and their allies by marriage controlled the trade. The basis for this ascendancy itself was created by the shift of trade from La Rochelle to Tonnay-Charente. The only other houses to rise to prominence were the Arbouins in Pons, the Otards and Dupuys in the last two decades, and Roullet in the same years, though much more modestly. Their control of business was enhanced by a supporting circle of Gasts, Lallemands, Augiers and Dardillouzes as shipping agents in Tonnay-Charente for their Cognac friends and connections. The prime trade in brandy, mainly for London by the 1780s, was effectively in the hands of around ten houses in Cognac, Jarnac and Pons, of which one alone, that of Saule, was unconnected by marriage to the local merchant milieu. Even Saule owed some of his success to his integration into the region to marrying, against family opposition, into a local *notable* office-holding family in 1778 (André Bernard, *entrepreneur des travaux du roi*, and *conseilleur et procureur du roi à l'hotel de ville*). His rise was marked by tension between him and the Martell/Lallemand interest, and earlier in the 1760s Lallemand had displayed considerable animosity to the invading Irish. Likewise Samuel Turner, a nephew of Delamain's who had a meteoric rise from 1789, owed something to a local marriage in 1787 as well as to his uncle's local family associations.

The prominence of this circle – local Huguenot with some intermarriage from the outside – can of course be overstressed. Its ascendancy was confined to the central Borderies and Champagne districts; it did not reach the outer regions of the brandy trade in which a large number of firms inland or on the coast competed. Within their limited or well-defined region, the Cognac/Jarnac/Pons houses faced competition from buyers in the outer districts when brandy prices rose. The rise of this outer group can be crudely identified in the growth in the number of houses beyond La Rochelle with a brandy interest and in the concurrent fall in the number of houses within the port of La Rochelle itself.

The pattern of the merchant community at large over the century can be easily summarised. First was a local coterie of five or six long-standing families in the central districts which absorbed the two foreign arrivals, Martell and Delamain. Lallemand, brother-in-law of the first Martell, was the presiding genius of the Martell house in mid-century, and the house dominated the export trade in the 1780s; Ranson gave Delamain his inland or Paris trade which made it possible for him to avoid the collapse or near collapse, faced by the Irish houses within a few years of their arrival, in the boom of the early 1760s in an unexpectedly difficult internal and foreign *conjoncture*. Second, a small number of other indigenous houses can be recognised as coming to the fore at various times such as Régnier with ties in La Rochelle and marrying locally (into the influential Dardillouzes); the Arbouins of Pons; Roullet; or latterly the Otards and Dupuys who advanced from the role of buyers to that of *négociant*. Third, Martell and Delamain apart, other foreigners entered the region, of which the Englishman John Baker was the first. He was in fact the last in the once pronounced pattern of Scottish and English settlement in La Rochelle (although two Irishmen, the last Irish immigrants in the port, appeared later). His own migration to Cognac at the beginning of the 1730s reflected the collapse of the port of La Rochelle in the brandy trade, and his example was followed after an interval by the Irishman Daniel Galwey, who chose to settle in Cognac rather than La Rochelle. Apart from Delamain, four Irish merchants along the Charente followed in the 1760s, plus one who settled in La Rochelle but who operated on the basis of his commissions being executed by agents on the Charente.

Trade patterns and inland merchants

As it deepened, the trade developed a neat pattern of specialisation. First, the export trade centred on Cognac, Saint-Jean d'Angély and Pons: as the London market grew and the Dutch and German business fell, Cognac's business was in the main of Champagne and Borderies brandy, supplemented by Fins Bois and in boom years or for the Irish market by Bons Bois. Second, Aigre, Ruffec and Angouleme were the transit points for supplies for the Paris market, and the territorial frontier of normal business can be traced by the fact that, except in the 1760s, Jarnac's largest house, Delamain, did more business with Paris than with the export market. Third, the coastal districts supplied the maritime provinces of northern France: their former traffic in brandy to Paris via the Seine contracted dramatically except for short periods in which Paris demand outran capacity on the inland *charrettes*. Tonnay-Charente, as the Dutch market fell, expanded its business in coasting craft for northern France. It had the advantage of being within Saintonge where brandy could be shipped without incurring duties in transit to the Aunis. As it became an effective port, it both deprived La Rochelle almost entirely of the export business (apart from the colonies), and built up a large coastal trade which rivalled that of the Aunis. La Rochelle, which had already long lost its trade in cognac for the foreign market, experienced further losses in the home market as inland buyers for Paris appeared more regularly on the fringes of the hinterland, and as the development of Tonnay as a shipping centre was followed by the emergence of independent merchant houses in La Tremblade and on the islands of Ré and Oléron which received orders directly rather than through the hands of La Rochelle intermediaries. Thus a petition from Rochefort in 1772 seeking entrepot privileges in the colonial trade stressed that foreigners looking for brandy got it in the islands or on the Seudre (the river serving La Tremblade and the port of Marennes).[9] This claim is substantially borne out by a breakdown in the export statistics for 1783, almost a decade later, which showed that Marennes and the two islands shipped 82,768 veltes of brandy overseas, more than twice the exports of La Rochelle, a mere 32,399 veltes (excluding exports to the colonies).[10] When the Bordeaux merchant George Boyd opened his distilling business in Royan later in the 1780s, his correspondence with these districts revealed the existence within them of brandy buyers on a large scale.[11] La Rochelle's decay has to be seen not as a consequence of the decline of its hinterland, but of the rise of new trade circuits and more substantial and more independent merchants in a prospering hinterland.

The buyers at large are difficult to study because we only have details of the exporting houses, which covered a comparatively small segment of the total trade. The rise of houses catering for the French market is related both to the growth of Paris consumption and to the increased importance of subsidiary centres like Pons and Angouleme. As early as 1720 some

---

[9] ACC, La Rochelle. no. 4211, p. 25, 'Très humbles et très respectueuses représentations de la ville de Rochefort au roi', Paris, 1772.   [10] ADC, Angouleme, 5C5.
[11] ADG, Bordeaux, 7B 1171, letter book of George Boyd and Co. of Royan, 1785–8, and of Bordeaux 1788–9.

houses, like Belesme's in Saint-Jean d'Angély, were quite substantial. Buying on a large scale, they received much of their funding from the *négociants* in the form of bills of exchange. The bills were of use to them only because they could readily sell them: that in turn created a link between them and the revenue receivers. This turned them into important businessmen both as suppliers of bills to revenue receivers and purveyors of specie to the brandy districts. They were already or became substantial houses. They were also in some cases landowners: they distilled *esprit*, bought brandy for the bigger houses, and were embryonic merchants in their own right. Significantly, the largest among them were already using the term *négociant* in the 1750s. The exporting houses depended heavily on them for much of their brandy. Thus Belesme at Saint-Jean d'Angély in the 1720s, Marchais de la Chapelle *fils aîné* at Jauc en Angoumois in the 1750s, or from the same period Otard at Brive are examples of the rise of such houses in two key periods of change in the brandy trade.[12] Salignac is one of the merchants on whom Laurence Saule relied heavily in 1766. Marchais was very evident in the business in the late 1760s, when he seems to have been the pre-eminent Angouleme house in buying further afield; Nouel of Angouleme was buying as well. The Otards are an even more interesting instance; they were in the Hennessy circle in the 1760s.[13] Brandy buyers to start with, though not exceptionally prominent, they eventually made the step into foreign trade in the 1790s in partnership with another new house.

After the mid-eighteenth century, centres like Pons and Angouleme had acquired a new-found importance. This is very striking in the case of Angouleme, which was becoming a large market for the sale of bills on Paris. The centre of gravity of the region was shifting eastwards, and by the 1780s when its turnover was substantial the Cognac house of Saule often settled accounts with brandy sellers in bills on Angouleme. This contrasted with earlier times when La Rochelle and Saintes represented the business centres of the region. As early as 1769–70, a legal dispute, which prompted the famous treatise on interest rates by Turgot, intendant in Limoges, had arisen out of an ingenious but unscrupulous attempt by some Angouleme houses to turn the usury laws against their creditors during an acute credit crisis.[14]

---

[12] Belesme is well documented in the Augier letter books in the 1720s, the others in the bills of exchange and other accounting records of the 1750s and 1760s for several houses.

[13] References to them are, however, rare and they were not part of the otherwise closely integrated group.

[14] See 'Mémoire sur les prêts d'argent', in G. Schelle, *Oeuvres de Turgot*, vol. III (Paris, 1919), pp. 154–202.

The deepening of the merchant network

While two houses emerged in time as outstanding, the trade at large, unlike the export trade, was never dominated by a handful of houses. While the Martell house represented a unique presence in the export business in the 1780s, the export trade was a smaller proportion of total production than earlier in the century. It had effectively narrowed to England (if we disregard a now smaller and fluctuating Irish business), and within the English trade the Martells preserved their dominance in the 1770s and enhanced it greatly in the 1780s. While *négociant* houses did not increase in number – in the town of Cognac itself, specialising in quality brandy for the external market, their number was static – the number of buying houses of all sorts, spread out over the region, increased quite sharply. In other words, overall there was no tendency towards monopoly, and the benefits of expanding trade were ultimately diffused over several thousand distillers in the *généralité*.

If the number of *négociants* remained small, it was in part because a large number of merchants buying for the inland trade emerged. In boom years the invasion of the Cognac hinterland by brandy buyers beyond the fringe was very evident, and it was this process of high prices for Paris which intermittently annihilated exports. The trade, in aggregate terms three or even four times the size of the export market in good years, grew over the century. The growth of this market is also linked dynamically to the increase in the number of towns involved in the brandy trade beyond La Rochelle itself and equally beyond Cognac, seat of the single largest Saturday brandy market or *canton*. In the 1720s Saint-Jean d'Angély was the only other buying centre of consequence for the export trade, though further inland Aigre and Angouleme had begun to serve a similar purpose for the Paris trade by the overland route. Moreover, Tonnay-Charente's role as port of shipment was closely linked with the growth of Pons: as the Paris market absorbed part of Cognac's hinterland and intermittently bought brandy at the Cognac *canton*, Pons acquired importance as a new centre which could conveniently supply brandy to shippers at Tonnay-Charente. Tonnay's emergence can be seen in its ceasing to be a mere point of shipment and becoming a buying centre in its own right: Régnier, opening his house there in 1719 without the back-up of a commissioning link in La Rochelle or existing ties in Cognac itself, like the Augiers had, is a convenient marker. Right up to the 1760s some houses, as they opened, were content to be shippers at Charente, loading vessels at the direction of merchants in Cognac rather than buyers in their own right.

Tonnay-Charente's importance both as a shipping point for brandy

from Cognac–Jarnac and, in a separate nexus, from Pons was quite
considerable. Thus Régnier set up his house there in 1719, as did
Laurence Saule in 1763 before moving to Cognac. Pons was increasingly
important, and in the 1760s several houses formed links with Pons interests. The Irishman Geoghegan bought there for a Bordeaux partner from
1775 and the Gernon house in Bordeaux had a partnership with the Pons
Arbouins in the early 1780s. Delamain maintained a warehouse at
Mortagne just beyond it as a shipping point for brandy. Tonnay's own
importance rested on its coastal as well as on its foreign traffic. In the
1720s a sister of Augier, married to a Guérinet and by 1724 a widow, had
a business entirely with Paris or Rouen. The house did a substantial business with Paris, buying at Saint-Jean or Cognac, and shipping to Yvetot at
the mouth of the Seine. The two houses reinforced one another, and this
was an example of a frequent pattern in the region: when one house had
commissions to fulfil in a hurry, friendly houses provided them with
brandy, and in the case of business with Paris houses which sometimes
wanted champagne brandy, Guérinet acquired it through her brother
Philippe in Cognac.[15] Dardillouze, one of the Tonnay-Charente shippers,
seems to have been a nephew of the widow Guérinet. While the
Dardillouzes acted as agents for several Cognac houses shipping to
foreign markets, they appear even as late as the 1750s to have been particularly prominent in loading vessels for Caen and Rouen.[16]

Thus Tonnay was peopled with shippers, either acting for merchants in
the interior, or working on their own account. The two activities were not
incompatible, and all the Tonnay houses described themselves as *négociants*. Moreover, some of the Tonnay families were related to or intermarried with Cognac families. Four agents were particularly important:
Lallemand and Gast, Gourg, Dardillouze and the Augiers. Two stand out
above the others. The first is Jean Gast, Lallemand et Cie who shipped for
Martell.[17] In 1756 this house, the key Gast partnership, also had connections with Jean Gast in La Rochelle. The other main shippers were the
Dardillouzes, who shipped for many, including Baker and Bryhan in the
1750s, and the Pons houses.[18] They shipped for Hennessy and for
Delamain as well. The divide between the houses of Gast Lallemand and

[15] AAC, letter books, Veuve Guérinet et Cie, 1726–8, 1729; Augier letter book 1726–7, 19
February 1727, to Etienne Augier (concerning Guérinet affairs); letter book 1724–6, 28
August 1725, to Guérinet, Amsterdam; letter book 1726–7, 8 February 1727 to Daniel
Martheile, Amsterdam (concerning Guérinet son).

[16] ADC, Angouleme, *étude* Cherpantier. See summations 13 November 1749, 9 December
1752, 18 July, 17 December 1753.

[17] He was a brother of Isaac Gast, *négociant* of Tonnay-Charente, who died in January 1756.
Ibid., 15 March 1756, *inventaire après décès*.

[18] *Ibid.* See in particular the protest of 30 September 1758.

Dardillouze in some measure corresponded to a divide between the Lallemands and others in Cognac itself. In the second half of the century a contrast can be detected between the closed Lallemand circle, and the Augier–Broussard–Dardillouze group who formed links with newcomer interests in the region on several occasions. As the Augier family had members in Charente it did not need Dardillouze's services to load for them, but significantly the Dardillouzes became shipping agents for the newcomers and for rivals of Martell's in the region, such as Delamain and Hennessy, in the 1760s.

Etienne Augier, as shipping agent for Philippe Augier, handled the business of the Cognac house and was succeeded by his son Daniel. Along with Dardillouze, Augier seems to have been the loader of vessels for northern Europe in the 1750s, together with another house, Gourg. These houses intermarried. Thus in 1747 Jacques Gourg, *négociant* at Tonnay, married a daughter of Charles Dardillouze.[19] Her brother Charles Jacques in turn married a daughter of Léon Régnier, one of the early outside interests, in 1759.[20] One of Léon Régnier's letter books and an invoice book survive in Hennessy's archives today. The reason that they lie among the Hennessy papers is probably because they came through the Dardillouzes who did so much business for the rising Hennessy house.

Other merchant houses

Foreign settlement in the brandy business had first occurred at a time of buoyant trade at the end of the 1710s, when the Channel Islanders Le Mesurier and Martell made their appearance, followed after a short interval by the Londoner John Baker. Baker's orders can be traced as early as 1724. He later moved to Cognac and became a partner of Pierre Bryhan, apparently a German. The business of the house (which survived until the death of the second partner in 1758) centred on northern Europe and on the Isle of Man. One of the new businessmen in the region, Régnier, who appeared in Charente in 1719, was French and well connected: one brother-in-law was Vincent Bureau in La Rochelle, who was, as he put it in 1736, 'en relation avec Monsieur Paris de Montmartel et messieurs de la route de Pons qui font un gros commerce avec Amsterdam, Rotterdam, Hambourg, Bremen et Londres'.[21] He was probably one of the two main beneficiaries of Augier's loss of the northern business in the 1720s. When space was needed on a vessel for paper, he boasted to another brother-in-

---

[19] *Ibid.*, 8 April 1747.   [20] *Ibid.*, 13 February 1759.
[21] HAC, Régnier letter book, 1735–6, 7 February 1736, to Bureau.

law, the paper-manufacturer Vantongeren, that 'tous les capitaines sont fort de mes amis, il n'y a point qui ose me refuser quand ils le peuvent'.[22] The Dutch trade remained important until 1735, and the Hamburg trade until 1737. The competition of new houses, whether a Frenchman, Régnier, who was well connected to the waning Dutch interest in La Rochelle, or foreigners like Baker and Bryhan, made it impossible for Augier to recover a place in traffic to these destinations.

For Augier the precaution by buyers of spreading commissions over several houses heralded an unwanted challenge in buying for established markets, which had recovered progressively in the good seasons of the late 1720s and early 1730s, and he never really re-established himself as a central figure in supplying them. In the altered trade of 1735–6 even Régnier was reduced to seeking the support of Bureau in La Rochelle to widen his custom, especially in Pons, a favoured centre for Dutch commissions.[23] This plea must not have gone unheard because from 1737 his most regular orders, though not the largest, came from Videau et More of Pons. His total business in 1738 came to 30,032 veltes, or just above 1,000 barriques. It was only a third of Augier's business at the time, and illustrates rather well how the decline of the Dutch trade in the late 1730s created problems, and how an individual house could be so badly affected by the change of fortunes in the Dutch trade. Dependence on the London trade, which in some ways was a weakness, protected Augier in the short term. The evidence of Régnier's letter book is also instructive on the uncertainties of trade. In 1735 the Dutch themselves were shifting their orders from La Rochelle to direct commissions, a trend which buoyed up Régnier's expectations in mid-year. In reality the change reflected wider problems within Dutch dealings in cognac. It was not, as Régnier expected, a prelude to more direct Dutch commissions; it was a prelude to the virtual termination of a more than century-old tradition of Dutch buying in the greater Charente region.

Régnier, even more than Augier or Martell, both of whom had experienced dramatic reversals in fortune in their best markets in the 1720s, is a good example of the challenge volatile brandy markets posed for all merchants. He was on the face of it a highly successful merchant at least up to 1735: in addition he was in partnership with a brother in Marennes, he shipped much paper for his brother-in-law Vantongeren, and he seems to have marketed Irish butter in conjunction with him. All sorts of misfortune hit him in 1736: fever carried away both his youngest son and his clerk in March of that year.[24]

[22] *Ibid.*, letter between 21 and 26 July 1735.
[23] *Ibid.*, 21 July 1735, to Rasteau; 7 February 1736, to Bureau.
[24] *Ibid.*, 15 March 1736, to Rasteau.

While he lost out on the Dutch and Hamburg trades, Augier could at least congratulate himself on the success of his English trade. That state of affairs was, however, not to endure. For Augier the real problem was, as he had conceded to a relative, Crommelin, in 1747, the many new agents who had appeared in the region. This referred to internal traders busily extending their purchasing as the Paris trade soared. The problem their presence created for the small circle of established exporting houses was to be compounded by the appearance of some new external buyers as strong growth in the international spirit trade and good vintages from 1752 led to sharp recovery in the almost decimated foreign brandy trade of the La Rochelle region. At one level, the new demand came not from well-defined centres of consumption overseas but from a more cosmopolitan market in which European houses speculated in brandy consignments for new buyers, such as the rising contraband trade driven from the Isle of Man. Baker and Bryhan's business profited from the rise of this contraband market for brandy in the Isle of Man (which, as far as Cognac was concerned, they had pioneered). After the second of the two partners, Pierre Bryan, had died in 1758, brandy for Jan Topman in Douglas was loaded in 1761 by Etienne Augier as agents of Lutter and Ferhold of the island of Ré.[25] In particular the town of Pons, with access both to champagne brandy and, to the south of the town, to inferior brandies, became important as Cognac switched to brandy for the London market at a premium price, and as Paris either by overland or sea routes increasingly mopped up the combined surpluses both of the coastal districts and of the inland districts to the north of the Charente. The importance of Pons was already evident to Régnier in 1736, and he corresponded with a house there, Bertin and Colinau.[26] The Pons house of Arbouin was already in existence in 1727, and from mid-century a London house of the same name suggests that they had entered directly into foreign trade. The growing importance of Pons can be seen in the fact that by 1747 at the latest northern merchants had begun to enter into association with the merchants there. In that year Videau of Pons was in partnership with a northern merchant, Schallback.[27] In the 1780s the Pons house of Arbouin, now sporting a northern partner Zimmermann, was the last house in the region to keep alive the Dutch and German associations. In the German trade, which was still active in the 1750s, Germans can be identified as shippers or clerks in Tonnay-Charente. The

---

[25] ADC, Angouleme, *étude* Cherpantier, 31 January 1761.
[26] HAC, Régnier letter book, 1735–6, to Bertin and Colinau, 7 February 1736.
[27] ADC, Angouleme, *étude* Cherpantier, summations 12 May 1747, 21 February 1750. In 1757 Annibal Broussard of Pons had as a partner a man named Basset (summation 9 March 1757). His signature reads like a foreign-sounding Hassel, both here and elsewhere, but should not be so read.

La Rochelle merchant John Gast employed a German clerk, Jean-Jacques Wiertz, as 'l'un de ses commis dans son comptoir du présent lieu de Tonnay'.[28] As late as 1765 a German, Jean Creatier Blosfeldt, was a shipper in Tonnay-Charente.[29]

Just as La Rochelle had once been the centre of Dutch and German interests, the Irish brandy interest in the region first emerged in the port, before expanding beyond it. By 1748 Walter Geoghegan, who came to France in 1739, was already an established Irish house there,[30] and the family was later to have a more direct interest in brandy buying within the hinterland (though it is not clear that the Stephen Geoghegan of the 1770s was an immediate relative). The first Irish house to appear in Cognac itself was that of Daniel Galwey.[31] It started at a bad time, in or before the early 1750s, and it is hardly surprising that in the wake of the virtual collapse of the export trade it went bankrupt by 1753. Irish houses did not reappear until the brandy boom at the end of the 1750s began to alter prospects. The accidents of death – four in 1766–8 – were less decisive than the instability of Irish demand in reducing an influx. No others came, except Andoe as a distiller in 1774 to Bordeaux, and Samuel Turner in the early 1780s prompted by kinship to Delamain, and Exshaw, and who married into the Dublin branch of the Bordeaux Nairac family, at or just after the end of the century. To this list, however, should be added Thomas Hine, an Englishman who had been a clerk at Delamain's and who, though he left France during the Revolution, was invited back by Delamain, because of his dispute with his own sons, to a partnership and to marriage in 1796 to a Delamain daughter.

The Martells' dominance in 1789 was unprecedented. Had they relied complacently on their commissions, the vicissitudes of commerce and the deep distrust of the Charente merchants that difficult times stirred in the breasts of brandy importers, could easily have turned the Martell story into a parallel to that of Augier: leadership followed by genteel decline. While the accident of business acumen in a family is inevitably a factor in continued success, structural changes, transforming a house from the role of mere passive commission agents, were essential. An extremely wide range of customers in London in the 1770s steadied their trade, and

---

[28] *Ibid.*, 24 January 1756.   [29] *Ibid.*, 21 June 1765.

[30] AN Paris, Oi 231, f. 47, *lettres de naturalité*, 1755. He was a signatory with other La Rochelle merchants of a petition to the chamber of commerce on 9 November 1752. ACC, La Rochelle, no. 3592. He is also mentioned as a creditor of Daniel Galwey of Tonnay in a *procès-verbal* (interrogatory) about brandy in Tonnay. ADC, Angouleme, *étude* Cherpantier, 20 January 1753. Geoghegan's account books appear to have dated from 1739 and ended in 1755, when he went bankrupt. See ADCM, La Rochelle, B398, Jurisdiction consulaire de La Rochelle, 16 April 1755.

[31] *Ibid.*, *procès-verbal* on bankruptcy, 20 January, 19 March 1753.

a growing network of financial ties with both Paris and Bordeaux resulted in an efficient disposal of bills and the conversion of the proceeds into cash and local paper. A key factor in making this possible was Theodore Martell's emergence in Bordeaux as a general merchant in the 1770s which created the first real transformation of the external relations of a local house in the Cognac business milieu. Though the aspiration to set up outside the region was not new (the idea haunted Augier in 1720 and again in 1747, and Jean Martell had temporarily set up in Bordeaux in 1723 as the junior partner in a Bordeaux house), Theodore Martell was the first Cognaçais who made a real success of such a venture. The bill business of the Cognac house gave him considerable standing in Paris. The Martell paper on London was one of the largest single blocks of paper on London on the Paris market, and probably the surest, drawn as it was on the singularly stable and solvent London brandy importers: an ability to dispose of it in either Paris or Bordeaux made Martell's singularly independent of any individual banking house. Theodore Martell's standing is reflected in close ties with the house of Boyd, Benfield and Co., a banking curiosity established in 1785 and which in essence grew out of the re-established French East India Company's need for London paper. Benfield remained a correspondent of its successor house in 1793,[32] and by his friendship with Girardot, Necker's banking successor and an associate of Boyd, he illustrates the importance that London bill custom had given the house.[33]

The Irish merchant, Richard Hennessy, followed the path to Bordeaux more modestly as a distiller in 1776, and, while the Hennessys returned to Cognac in late 1788, Richard himself continued to maintain close ties with Bordeaux. These ties were of considerable benefit in the 1790s, and Otard, rising to merchant ranks in the mid-1790s, repeated the pattern in a brandy partnership which embraced Cognac and Bordeaux. Theodore Martell's standing in Bordeaux and its usefulness, even to a thrusting house like Hennessy and Turner, created a business alliance between the two houses and resulted in the Hennessy–Martell marriage of 1795. Martell was no respecter of the old conventions. A contemporary noted him as lively and brilliant with a conversation 'remplie de sarcasmes mordants':[34] indeed the latter characteristic stands out in his letters to James Hennessy. He left Bordeaux for good some time after 1803 for Paris. In

---

[32] Jean Bouchary, *Les manieurs d'argent à Paris à la fin du xviiiᵉ siècle*, vol. II (Paris, 1940), p. 149.

[33] Some more general, but useful, information is available in R. Firino-Martell, *La famille Martell* (Paris, 1923), pp. 47–62. He did not have access to the Hennessy archives and only lightly used the firm's accounting records. However, his own researches on documents of the Revolution from outside the firm are invaluable.   [34] *Ibid.*, p. 62.

1816 another Hennessy–Martell marriage occurred and in the 1810s a
Martell resident in London for a time marketed Hennessy brandy there.

The emergence of new houses

The rise of new houses was helped by ties with Bordeaux, the centre of
new wealth, new faces and easily got material prosperity. One Cognaçais,
Theodore Martell, was an early example of their significance, and his
marriage alliance to the Bordeaux house of Arneaud in 1777 set the
pattern for the marriage of a daughter of Jean Martell to a Beyerman in
1778 and of a granddaughter to a Martini in 1796. Others were attracted
to Bordeaux, such as Daniel Augier who opened a commission house in
1785.[35] Another Cognaçais who opened a shop there was one of the
Otards. They had long been successful as local brandy merchants in the
Cognac region, buying on a large scale for the export houses since at least
the 1750s. One of the Otards, Pierre, appeared as a merchant in Bordeaux
by 1795, and rose during the decade to the position of magistrate in the
city. A circular by its sister house in Cognac in revolutionary year 8 stated
that 'La maison de M. Otard à Bordeaux par ses moyens et son crédit
peut exécuter tous les ordres et en général se charge de toutes affaires que
vous auriez à leur confier'.[36] The rise of an Otard house in Bordeaux was
accompanied by the appearance of a brandy house in Cognac in the
hands of a younger brother, Otard *jeune* or Jean-Baptiste Antoine, which
was already in existence when the first of the surviving letter books commence on 30 Vendémiaire, revolutionary year 4. Otard *jeune*'s letters are
characterised by indifferent spelling and handwriting, and in the first
letters even by the author's declared bad health. The business, as an
offshoot of the boom in brandy, seems to have involved an 'association'
with Dubergier and L'Isle Ferme, a house in Bordeaux, and then or
earlier, another Bordeaux house, that of Fauars. Otard *jeune* himself had
married a L'Isle Ferme in 1792. Correspondence was addressed to L'Isle
Ferme *l'aîné* in Bordeaux regarding shipment of brandy to Altona.[37]
Otard's elder brother seems to have been a partner in the brandy venture
as well. For the elder brother, who was engaged in more general trade, the
brandy house was a convenience in securing brandy. However the house
in Cognac quickly became one of the three largest houses on the banks of
the Charente.

---

[35] Daniel Augier circular on 18 May 1785 in both the Hennessy and Martell archives.
[36] OAC, letter book, 26 Floréal, an 7–18 Pluviose, an 8, circular of 12 Frimaire, an 8.
[37] *Ibid.*, letter book, 30 Vendémiaire, an 4– 4 April 1797, 12 May 1796 (23 Floréal, an 4), to
L'Isle Ferme, Bordeaux.

More modestly, other houses emerged. Thus the house of Salignac and Babin had made an appearance by revolutionary year 7. Otard, Dupuy et Cie referred to them as a small partnership in which Babin 'est un propriétaire assez aisé qui est d'un certain age. Il a toujours fait quelques petites affaires.'[38] The Salignacs had long been brandy buyers in the regions. In 1789 Babin was buying for Turner[39] and by 1799 Salignac and Babin were shipping to Hamburg in their own right. They also extended their business to speculation in grain.[40] Likewise, the house of Marchais de la Berge, prominent in the past simply in supplying brandy to *négociants* in the region, was shipping direct to Hamburg, without an intermediate link of established brandy houses being interposed, in 1798. If some houses rose, others inevitably languished. Delamain is one instance. So for most of the 1790s was the house of Broussard: 'Monsieur Broussard depuis 10 ans ne faisait rien à disposer de ses fonds et se trouvait sans argent et sans une goutte d'eau de vie nouvelle'.[41] Broussard's, however, made a recovery in 1799.

The prestigious term *négociant* was virtually limited to houses who dispensed with commissions from local wholesalers and who, cultivating direct liaison with principals in northern France or abroad, bought and sold paper claims on external centres. The essential characteristic of a *négociant* was his commercial standing: he could not conduct trade unless his reputation was such that bills drawn by him on houses outside the region were readily accepted locally. *Négociants* with foreign commissions had always been comparatively few in relation to the total network of intermediaries (and in financial terms were readily identified by the fact that they drew on banking houses in Paris and not merely on provincial commercial houses); other merchants, handling brandy in a wholesale way and hence meriting the title *négociant*, were not numerous, though their numbers increased in the second half of the century especially in the towns. These houses themselves grew out of a milieu of *propriétaires* who did the distilling of their own vintage and extended their business by buying the brandy of smaller producers. There was also always a substantial trade in brandy between the exporting *négociants* themselves. The rising class of buyers/distillers or *propriétaires*/sellers supplying the shipping houses represented a response to the larger scale of brandy production and trade in the region as the century progressed. Even as far back as

---

[38] *Ibid.*, letter book, 13 Nivose, an 7–20 Thermidor, an 7, 4 Floréal, an 7, to Jn. Bois et Cie, Paris.   [39] HAC, 3 June 1789, James Hennesy to Turner.
[40] *Ibid.*, copy letter book to partners, 9 December 1799–29 Ventose, an 8, 17 Pluviose, an 8 to Otard, Bordeaux.
[41] OAC, copie des lettres aux associés, 1 Germinal an 8–9 Prairial an 9, 1 Germinal an 8, to Otard, Bordeaux.

1720, Augier's depended very heavily on the house of Belesme at Saint-Jean d'Angély buying for them in the competitive trade of that year. Some of the buyers were on a large scale like Marchais de la Berge, and as the trade became more commercialised they were to be found further inland. Thus in the very competitive 1780s the Angouleme house of Nouel were buying on a large scale for Saule and Co. Some of the houses of this sort, like Otard, already enjoyed the name of *négociant* in the 1750s. In all in the 1790s there were about fifty buyers of brandy at the Cognac *cantons*. Before 1793 only ten or so would have been export houses, and many of the others would have been simply executing buying commissions from other houses in the region. In the 1790s both the number holding commissions from northern France (in other words acting in their own right as *négociants*), and the number executing commissions received from abroad increased.

A clear distinction has also to be made between the *négociants* of all sorts and small distillers, whose production was large enough to raise them above the level of farmer distillers, and who could also on occasion speculatively buy and sell small quantities of brandy. It is important not to date the foundation of *négociant* houses simply from the evidence of operators in the region whose descendants may later have become *négociants*. Thus, a date of 1724 for the foundation of the firm of Rémy Martin is debatable because no one of that name features among the recognised *négociants* of the century. A Rémy Martin had a licence to plant vines in 1731, and an excise inspection in 1744 listed 1545 veltes of his own distillation in his cellars.[42] However, this is simply an indication of a distiller on a scale larger than a peasant distiller. The world of the brandy business was an intimate and only slowly changing one despite expansion. It required the upheavals of the 1780s and 1790s to speed up the process of change. By the end of the decade the house of Otard and Dupuy, itself a new export house, was buying quantities of brandy from names like Bisquit or Camus, which were insignificant before this but which were to become important in later times. The name Bisquit as a local seller of brandy goes back at least to the 1750s, but several generations were to elapse before it emerged as a *négociant* house.

There were also the jobbers. These were in competition with the *négociants* and in times of speculative rises, in particular for Paris, they tended to enter the market in a big way, and to be the vehicle which ensured that prices rose, so incurring the wrath of the *négociants*. To the *négociants* they were a nuisance, but they were in fact an indispensable link in the chain of converting rising demand into higher prices to the actual brandy maker in

---

[42] *The Wine and Spirit Journal* (Toronto), 7, no. 3 (March 1905), pp. 53–4.

what would otherwise have been the monopoly position of the *négociants* and larger buyers.

The changing status of brandy merchants

From the 1770s merchant families were visibly beginning to make clear their high status. The houses of the Martell and Delamain families are the finest eighteenth-century mercantile residences in the towns of Cognac and Jarnac respectively, with a style that speaks of a self-conscious imitation of fashionable building and its pretensions. The Augier mansion, a sixteenth-century house restructured in the eighteenth century, is comfortable but more modest, and reflects a different story: one of success which aborted. Richard Hennessy lived modestly in rented accommodation and only during the Revolution did he and his son become property buyers. The purchase of the country house of La Billarderie in the 1790s was, however, more than that; it was an expression of status. Lacking land on the waterfront, they could not house themselves grandly, as Delamain did in Jarnac, on land at the water's edge or like the Martells at the end of the built-up waterfront in Cognac. A house on the rue Saulnier, purchased in 1760, was enlarged in 1788 into the elegant house of Jean Martell the younger.[43] On lands acquired in 1769, between the place de la Salle Verte and the old walls, the other and even more elegant house of Frédéric Martell took shape.

The Martell Lallemand house had passed into the hands of the two sons, Jean and Frédéric-Gabriel, in 1776 and legally so in 1786 with the death of the widow, Rachel Martell (née Lallemand). Jean made a prestigious marriage with a Rasteau of La Rochelle in 1787. Frédéric who had married a Broussard in 1774 seems, however, to have been the directing genius of the Cognac business in the 1780s: Saule's tensions were with Frédéric. The marriages of his daughters which created ties with the Hennessys in 1795 and with Martini of Bordeaux in 1796 are as central to the business and social ascent of the house as Theodore's settling in Bordeaux and marriage there. The family portraits start with Jean and Frédéric-Gabriel and those of their wives; the rehousing of the families with such éclat also starts with them. The Martells also profited under the Revolution, as did many others, from the purchase of confiscated church property.

With success a new obsession, that of gentrification, was overtaking merchants. Richard Hennessy was already worried about his son's Irish brogue in the 1780s. Hennessy's acquisition of a rural seat was the

---

[43] Firino-Martell, *La famille Martell*, p. 79n.

declaration of a new social elevation. No doubt there was some lingering thought of the gentry background they sprang from in Ireland and of a return to rural surroundings in keeping with gentry status. Not only was Richard worried about his son's brogue, but the son, James Hennessy, the most prosaic and hard-headed of men, referred to the family genealogy on one occasion, and speculated on the family's relatives in London. Occurring in the 1790s and at the time when Hennessy and Turner was the most prosperous house, the acquisition of La Billarderie represented in masonry the Hennessy aspiration to higher status: if business required James Hennessy's constant presence in Cognac, the father, who was now only lightly involved in the business, had it as his residence. No successful merchant could afford to remain away from the counting house for long. However, with Martell and Delamain they began to house themselves in more princely dwellings, and later residences were, if sometimes within easy reach of the quays, firmly out of sight of them, and the allurements of public office, first mayoralty (for Turner and then Otard) and later parliamentary seats (for James Hennessy in 1824) beckoned as well.

The building of substantial houses as in the case of Delamain and Martell or the acquisition of a country residence in La Billarderie which gave such pleasure to Richard Hennessy, and a further house, Bagnolet, acquired *c.* 1830 by James Hennessy, reflected a new-found sense of social prestige as the standing and wealth of the families increased. Most dramatic of all in its rapidity was the business success of Otard and Dupuy, which within a decade from 1796 put them on a par with the Martells and the Hennessys. Somewhat more slowly than for other families, though more splendidly, their status was reflected in stone as well as in other ways. Thus Jean Dupuy, brother of Léon, built a magnificent house around 1840 which is now the municipal museum, while around the same date Léon Otard, son of Jean-Baptiste Antoine, built a house in a large park, today the Hotel de Ville.[44]

Rising status seems to have been accompanied, in the case of the Otards, by a new emphasis on their origins. Their background presents an intriguing intellectual challenge. Otard or la Grange was already a seller of brandy in the 1750s (to the Augiers and in the 1760s to the Hennessys as well as to others). Prominent in the social life of the town and its hinterland, an Otard was secretary of the Cognac masonic lodge in both 1747 and 1761: it may have been the masonic association rather than either Jacobite or British ties that brought them into the circle of the Hennessys.[45] Their foreign business emerged only in the 1790s, and apart

---

[44] *Grands notables du premier empire* (Paris, 1986), pp. 46, 81.
[45] J. Royr, *Histoire de la franc-maçonnerie en Charente* (Paris, 1994), p. 215.

from a concern in brandy distilling and selling, their first ties in business
emerged in Bordeaux through their Bruneaud relatives from Libourne
who had set up business there at a fairly early date. By 1788, however, an
Otard already had property in Bordeaux, as Hennessy was apparently
renting a warehouse from him for a second year at that time.[46]

The Otards regarded their background as noble, something suggested
by Guillaume Otard's comments as early as 1757 when his pursuit of a
bride ran into difficulties: 'je vois avec douleur qu'on cherche à me perdre
à vos yeux; ma fortune est, en effet, peu importante, mais on ne pourrait
sans injustice contester la force et la hauteur de ma naissance' (sentiments
re-echoed in the 1790s).[47] Yet despite an elaborate genealogy drawn up
by De Valls, the son-in-law of D'Hozier, and hence probably in the early
nineteenth century, concrete evidence of a Scottish ancestry is slight, and
they certainly did not form an intimate part of the small English-speaking
– or Irish – coterie. Their business success, however, was startling in the
1790s and in the early nineteenth century; they became the business
equals of the older-established houses, and Jean-Baptiste Antoine Otard
was mayor of Cognac from 1804 to 1824. The De Valls commission
represents a claim with some substance probably prompted by the
family's launch into social life post-1804. The ambiguities in the genealogy, however, point to some problem glossed over or gilded by the genealogist, and it is difficult to avoid concluding that a wider aristocratic
background was manufactured for them by the embroidery of a dormant
Scottish connection (perhaps either a collateral or illegitimate one). Late
in the nineteenth century, perhaps at the same time as the printing of the
earlier De Valls genealogy in 1882, the name was rendered as an even
more improbable O'Tard. The question also remains whether the portrait
of James II in the modern *comptoir* is simply a later acquisition or a copy of
a portrait of the monarch to embellish the Scottish link.

It seems to play much the same role as the nineteenth-century portrait
of Richard Hennessy. The Hennessys also seem to have engaged in some
embroidery, not of their genealogy but of their army service. James
Hennessy, though a practical man, displayed an interest in the family
genealogy in 1789, and the military career of his father was later embell-

---

[46] HAC, letter book, 1787–8, 16 July, 27 August 1788, to Otard.
[47] OAC, text of a letter as given in 'Généalogie de la famille O'Tard de la Grange précédée
d'une notice historique et chronologique sur le Jarl Norvégien Ottard et ses descendants
Barons de Gournay de Dunnottard et de la Grange par le Comte de Valls, gendre du
généalogiste D'Hozier', p. 12. The letter, quoted by the comte de Valls, does not seem to
survive. I am greatly indebted to Monsieur Gérard De Ramefort, at the time managing
director of Otard's, for a copy of this document, and for showing me the evidence and dis-
cussing the uncertainties in the Otard genealogy documented by his painstaking
researches into a fascinating question.

ished. Though his father Richard never discharged even for a day the duties of the officer commission which finally came his way in February 1753 (he can be traced as entering as an *homme de troupe*, awaiting a commission, from 1748), a portrait of him in officer uniform was painted at some stage in the nineteenth century, emphasising the family's commitment to France which had been challenged opportunistically by political rivals in 1824. James Hennessy, who had become a Restoration parliamentarian for the Charente, faced accusations by his opponents in that he was a mere foreigner, which might have deprived him of his seat. It was in this context that the certification of Richard's ten years' military service (which conferred citizenship) became relevant. It referred to ten years dating from 1757 (which was a generous concession in an official capacity by an Irishman, the comte de Thomond, to a member of a family with distinguished Irish Brigade associations, and was prompted by the need of such a certificate to give Richard immunity as a resident when the French overran Ostend in 1757), but either by accident or design the ten years were later interpreted as running from 1753 when the records show that Richard's connection with the army had been decisively severed rather than from the date of service certified in 1757.

The local world had changed with a vengeance in the closing years of the century. The brandy trade was now dominated by two very large houses to which were added for the first half of the nineteenth century the house of Dupuy and Otard. In 1809 Jean Martell had an estate worth 500,000 francs; in 1818 his brother Frédéric had one which was almost as large. In 1824 Jean-Baptiste Otard's estate was worth almost 426,000 francs, and Léon Dupuy's was to be 590,900.[48] These were large sums, far in excess of the fortunes of the eighteenth century. Turnover, fortunes, houses and status, however, were now to mark the emergence of the legendary cognac merchants, a by-word in the nineteenth and early twentieth centuries for their place in French society and business.

---

[48] *Grands notables du premier empire*, pp. 48, 70–1, 81.

7   The Cognac brandy trade: 1720s–1760s

Speculation and a changing brandy trade

There is a world of difference between Philippe or Pierre Augier's environment in the 1680s and that of a son or possibly a grandson, thirty years later, which can be seen in the first surviving eighteenth-century letter book running from 22 November 1717 to 21 August 1719. Brandy business was much more important than at the time of the earliest book of 1681–6, and the collapse of La Rochelle as the dominant focus for incoming orders for Cognac had already occurred. The acute speculation of 1719–20 accelerated existing trends at an uncommon pace: the scope for commodity speculation and for credit and foreign exchange facilities in La Rochelle was small; Cognac houses acquired speculative ties in commodities and credit with both Bordeaux and Paris houses. The limitations of La Rochelle were expressed for the first time in the communications of Cognac merchants in slighting comments on La Rochelle and its narrow market for both bills and commodities.

The brandy business benefited at least as far back as the close of 1717 from a Guernsey clientèle, the bulk of whose custom at Cognac came to Augier. Export business in Cognac had benefited from the initial impact of Law's famous or notorious system of banking and of managing the national finances which was being set in place in France from 1718. In a decidedly downward trend, the exchanges fell by 45 per cent between January 1718 and November 1719, the downward turn being particularly marked in June 1718. This helped to boost trade by cheapening brandy to purchasers converting foreign currency into French money: brandy prices were at a high level of 75 livres per barrique in June 1719. In that month a huge order from Guernsey for 50 tons of brandy was in process of execution. Philippe had already shipped 300 *pièces* of brandy in the first two months of 1718, probably as much as or more than his father shipped in an entire season.[1] He was to observe in 1720 that 'dans les moindres années jusqu'à présent j'ai eu icy 100,000 livres de commission'. This

---

[1] AAC, letter book 1717–19, 22 February 1718, to Sureau, Saint-Jean d'Angély.

would suggest around 2,000 barriques of brandy a year in the late 1710s. It was at this stage that whirlwind changes began in the story of Cognac and the Augiers. Brandy exports from Cognac reached their peak for the century in the calendar year 1720. From the *généralité* of La Rochelle they were larger than exports from Bordeaux had been in 1699–1700, the other benchmark in brandy exports from France before 1720. Even when the Cognac merchants' abortive commodity speculation in other products became unstuck in 1720, the brandy business at first went along merrily.

Augier's activities from December 1719 had also widened from commission trade in brandy and wine to speculative non-commodity business. This involved a new and separate partnership, though the full implications of this were not comprehended at the outset: Augier at first kept copies of some key letters about the great speculative affair either on loose sheets or entered in his commission letter book. A feature of the Augier interest at this time was an alliance with Jean Martell from the Channel Islands who had been brought to Cognac in 1718 by the upsurge in the Guernsey business. Martell, freshly arrived in Cognac in the hope of finding a place in business, handled the recent and booming demand from Guernsey in 1720, while Augier had a growing volume of business with Holland and Hamburg, the two staple markets for Cognac brandy.

While the partnership established at the end of 1719 between Augier and his cousins the Richards (with the eldest of them, Richard *l'aîné*, hastening to Paris) was in name distinct from their separate brandy businesses, the two activities were interlinked in several ways. The established brandy business provided a framework for the bill operations which were intended to raise the initial capital to finance investment in Law's paper. In turn the monetisation involved in French speculation at large, by depressing the exchanges more rapidly than commodity prices, cheapened brandy dramatically to foreigner purchasers and, as Augier noted as early as February 1720, 'le relais extraordinaire des changes étrangers anime tous les chargeurs; il y a au cours en ville de très gros ordres'.[2] The foreign obligations created by the bills drawn on Amsterdam or London by the bankers or *banquiers* in Paris as compensation for the cash put at the disposal of the partners would, it was expected, be met by commodity sales overseas, and, in a reversal of the existing downward trend, by a strengthening of the French livre, which would through overseas sales of bills on Paris provide much of the necessary funds painlessly to meet the commitments that arose when payment of the bills drawn from Paris became due.

[2] *Ibid.*, letter book 1719–20, 19 February 1720, to Jogue, Orleans. The exchange effect was already seen at work very clearly in November (*ibid.*, 13 November 1719, to Desguères, Paris).

With the favourable uplift of business in the late 1710s, the young brandy merchants in the Augier circle set their sights on greater things and rather headily on Paris itself. As the exchanges reduced prices to foreigners and inflation in the supply of paper seemed to guarantee rising internal commodity prices, Paris bankers were not only ready to lend them cash for commodity buying and speculation in paper claims but, with some time lag, to speculate on their own account in commodities: thus, they began to employ Cognac houses to buy brandy in speculations for the foreign market on their own or joint account. Without this link with Paris bankers and without the credibility provided by the extraordinary business in brandy, bankers, however reckless, would have been less accommodating to people who in their private correspondence actually referred to themselves unflatteringly as provincials. The idea even developed of Augier eventually going to Paris to conduct a brandy agency there. Paris ties and the optimism of the times were both vital in the process of terminating the waning dependence on La Rochelle, and in these years it effectively ended (though the importance of La Rochelle as a social centre was to continue).

An outsider like Martell, arriving in a small market with finite outlets, would be distrusted in other circumstances. With business booming in all markets, however, the original idea of a common interest in providing brandy for the Guernsey business group was quickly departed from. Martell's role at the outset had been intended to be secondary. While he ordered brandy, it did not preclude island commissions to Augier, and the management of his own account itself was conducted in consultation with Augier. Even as late as 1 June 1720 the idea of a partnership in which Martell would be appointed agent in Guernsey for a Cognac brandy circle was broached.[3] However, there appeared to be more business than any one man could handle. The boom altered things, with Augier concentrating amicably as far as commodity trade was concerned on Holland and Hamburg, and Martell on the British Isles, including the soaring Guernsey business. When Martell's first surviving letter book from the mid-1720s takes up the story, it bears testimony retrospectively to a large business already in course of execution. A large proportion, a third or more of the record exports of 9,842 barriques from the La Rochelle *généralité* to *Angleterre*, was probably in his hands.

Augier's concentration on the Dutch and Hamburg business rather than on extending his resources competitively to cater for Guernsey business seemed a rational decision and allocation of resources. Not only was Holland the largest single market for brandy but it was also very active. Moreover, Augier's established connection with Holland in the brandy

[3] *Ibid.*, letter book 1 June–18 December 1720, 1 June 1720, to Richard *l'aîné*, Paris.

trade provided the nexus to justify bankers providing cash in return for the right to draw on Amsterdam, counting on the fact that the partners would soon have cash there. By the outset of 1720, apart from Augier's executing in February the balance of the large order from the preceding October, the conduct of the Guernsey business at the Cognac end was now firmly in the hands of Martell. There was thus sufficient common ground for both Martell and Augier to get involved in a common speculation in foreign exchange operations, with Martell helping to provide foreign bills and becoming a partner for a small share in the complex cooperative financing of the foreign bills necessary to finance the Paris speculations.

The overall scheme was a complex one linking speculation in *actions* with the proceeds of speculation in commodities and the movement of the foreign exchanges. However, it rapidly came unstuck. Losses on speculation in Paris, a sharper rise in commodity prices than had been anticipated, and a failure of the livre to strengthen as had been expected meant that the plan had begun to fall apart even before May 1720. At the end of that month it was totally undermined by the writing down of the value of shares and notes by Law, and a consequent weakening instead of the expected strengthening of the French currency on the foreign exchanges. In the short term the speculators were only saved by the fact that, as their bankers had drawn the bills on Amsterdam as recoupment of cash advanced to the speculators, the bankers' credit was so involved that the Paris bankers did not dare bring them down and negotiations dragged on into 1721.

As long as a trade in brandy could be conducted, some prospects of future settlement could be held out. However, a decline in business confidence and, amid the confusion generated by the many changes in Law's monetary arrangements, the growing problems of getting means of payment acceptable to brandy sellers meant that by the autumn of 1720 the problems of the brandy business were acute. As Augier remarked, paper was so unwanted that with settlement in paper at 180 livres per barrique, the price was 40 livres in specie, 'le plus bas qu'on l'a jamais vue'.[4] This meant in effect an enormous premium for specie. A price of 40 livres was artificially low, as at the end of October even small notes, the notes most sought after as the larger denominations were too big for most brandy purchases on the local markets, passed from their nominal value to a discount. But prices remained in the doldrums, even as things settled somewhat. The rate of 60 livres per barrique in mid-November declined to 52 and 53 livres in early December. The gloomiest phrases so far occurring cropped up in correspondence at this time: the words 'triste

---

[4] *Ibid.*, letter book, 1720–4, 2 November 1720, to Morel, Amiens.

temps' and 'triste commerce' became a refrain. The brandy trade was 'presque à terre' by the end of November.[5] Although the par rate of the London exchange was 16¼ pence to the écu, the actual exchange quoted in November was 26½.[6] However, Augier, quoting the par on London as 16¾ to 17, observed that an offer of 25 pence would not tempt buyers.[7] This does not imply at all that transactions did not take place – quite the reverse. While buyers of bills were few, would-be sellers were numerous, and in the absence of local buyers, a Paris banker or merchant could make a very large profit taking bills at the high sterling premium that desperate sellers were prepared to offer; the proceeds then financed bills drawn for a smaller sterling premium in deficit-plagued Paris. Martell came to an arrangement in December with Gibert to buy foreign bills for him for a 1 per cent commission: he observed that 'sur le pied où est le change il ne peut y avoir un commerce plus avantageux que celui de prendre des lettres sur l'étranger aujourdhui'.[8] Foreigners had more choice than merchants resident in France. Given the difficulty of appraising the effective exchange, they were less likely to deal in or quote for the livre at all. No quotations were made in England on France for the last three months of the year: that itself underlined the monopoly position of the few buyers of bills in France on the Anglo-French exchange market. They bought cheaply from the few active commercial houses in the provinces, and sold dear to the few remitters to London, mainly in Paris, who were made desperate by the absence of a normal foreign exchange market. The vagaries of the bill market and the prospects of large profits by buying bills cheaply from provincials in acute need of cash, however, reinforced a financial nexus between Paris and Cognac; the fact that Cognac houses had the alternative of selling bills to Paris speculators meant that they were not under any compulsion to sell on the glutted Bordeaux bill market on which even smaller sums of cash would have been realised: the events thus foreshadowed Cognac's future circumstances of becoming, to the advantage of its *négociants*, a small but vital component in arbitraging the quotations in the foreign exchange markets of both Paris and Bordeaux.

Depression and recovery in brandy business 1721–1723

In the difficult season of 1721, things fell apart even for Augier's commodity business in Cognac, which had so far survived. News of his problems soon led to difficulties. He wrote on 25 January that 'il n'est pas

---

[5] MAC, letter book 1720–1, 25 November 1720, to Dobrée.
[6] AAC, letter book 1720–4, 23 November 1720, to Gibert.
[7] *Ibid.*, 23 November 1720, to Voigt.
[8] MAC, letter book 1720–1, 21 December 1720, to Gibert.

fallu de beaucoup que je n'aye vu vendre mes meubles'.[9] He was to spend much of 1721 in two long visits to Paris, and the letter book testifies to the near total halt of routine commodity business. Between 25 January and 3 March and again for a short spell within the period March to 11 August, gaps appeared, accounted for by Augier's absences. He kept a separate book while in Paris with the first letter dated 7 February: the book itself was styled in Dutch *Copie boek van brieven begonnen tot Paris den 7 February 1721*. The book even contains laundry accounts from March to June, which emphasises the tentative nature of his sojourn. The last Paris entry was dated 25 July 1721. These stays were not simply occasions for attempting to settle the partnership's affairs, but also for fulfilling an old intention of going to Paris, though in altered circumstances, in which the discredited Richard *l'aîné*, now back in Cognac, no longer played a role. The letters mostly relate to the conduct of a brandy business with Holland and Hamburg, a fact highlighted by the styling of the book in Dutch. The business was not large, and the correspondence had more gaps as time went by. The negotiations for an arrangement with his creditors were ongoing in Paris but came to nothing. We may speculate that his brandy problems removed the residual credibility of the proposal to pay off creditors over a number of years from the profits of the brandy trade: one of the legal problems of keeping up the business was the liability of the brandy house to pay its creditors in specie, a key factor in determining the precise scale of its insolvency.

A small number of loose letters to Richard *l'aîné* in Cognac describes the problems more graphically. On 15 February Augier wrote that 'je suis icy dans la plus triste situation du monde, jamais un quart d'heure sans voir un créancier pressant'. By 4 March he had come to the conclusion that 'entre nous il y auroit de la folie de s'engager à payer 8 années d'interests; et en prenant cet engagment nous serions certains de ne le point remplir'. The last letter in the Paris book was on 25 July, and Augier returned to Cognac. This meant not only that the arrangement with creditors, so hard fought for in 1720, did not come about, but that the hope of a Paris brandy business had collapsed.[10]

In essence Augier's task in 1721 was that of dealing with two groups of creditors: the Parisian bankers who had provided funds in 1720, and the more miscellaneous group, largely mercantile, which was affected by the plight of the brandy house in Cognac. Far from the brandy business admitting of funds to pay off Paris liabilities, its liabilities in its own right were formidable. On 22 March 1721 Augier grimly observed that 'notre

[9] AAC, letter book, 1720–4 , 25 January 1721, to Le Gendre, Saint-Jean d'Angély.
[10] *Ibid.*, 1 September 1721, to Dirkel.

charge sera des plus pezantes à Paris, mais celle de province le sera au moins autant'. This was a consequence of purchases on their own account, and of their accountability for funds put into their hands for purchases on behalf of others or on joint account. Their economic situation was becoming steadily worse, and in 1721 they were losing their custom in brandy: 'les avis de quelques jaloux nous ont fait perdre beaucoup de nos correspondances'.[11] In August, on his way back to Cognac, he heard of three Orleans merchants with large buying commissions: he wrote to a merchant in Paris proposing a joint speculation.[12] However, Augier's poor credit was now well known. Martell was approached by Bosselman of Lille, who had an unpaid promissory note of Augier's for 15,000 to 20,000 livres: Martell in his reply made it clear in confidence that liquidation of their affairs was inevitable and that that would determine the real worth of their paper.[13] Augier's only hope of staving off nemesis was their appeal against settlement of old liabilities in specie. As that was doomed to failure, bankruptcy inevitably followed in 1722.

The trade took some time to recover from the problems of 1720. Gloom was unrelieved to the end of the year. But optimism first reappeared with an observation by Martell on 4 January 1721 that 'il est à croire que le commerce se rétablira un peu et que l'on négotiera avec un peu plus de facilité que l'on ne fait depuis quelque temps'.[14] Martell's trade recovered in the first half of 1721 from its plunge in late 1720. By March vessels from Guernsey were reappearing in some numbers, and his trade had reacquired the momentum of the first half of the preceding year. Prices too began to pick up in March from the depressed level of just above 50 livres. At the end of the month they were at 60 livres. One way of dealing with the problem created by discredited paper and a shortage of specie had been a requirement in December for all payments above 500 livres to be made in *écritures de banque* (transfer by bank entries).[15] This requirement, amid the monetary problems, may have helped to bring about some recovery in trade, but at the price of generating its own problems in time. In July 1721 Martell observed that: 'il m'est resté des sommes affreuses en banque qui me mettent hors d'état de faire ce que j'aime si cela eut été converti en argent'.[16] Despite difficulties, trade benefited from a stable exchange through 1721 and more or less without interruption until April 1724. As the exchange was a low, stable one for the livre, brandy was not only cheap to foreign purchasers, but exception-

[11] *Ibid.*, 4 March 1721, to Richard *l'aîné* from Paris.
[12] *Ibid.*, 11 August 1721, to Hibon le Comte et Cie, Paris.
[13] MAC, letter book 1721–2, 20 October 1721.
[14] *Ibid.*, letter book 1720–1, 4 January 1721, to J. Le Mesurier, Auregney.
[15] *Ibid.*, 4 December, to Mauger.   [16] *Ibid.*, letter book 1721–2, 16 July 1721, to Kastell.

ally so: if its price of 75 livres in September 1721 was translated into foreign money at the current exchange, it was at a historic low point, the same price as in 1706, 1707 and 1708 when the price in Cognac had been 28 and 30 livres.[17]

Martell built up a large and stable business with Guernsey. Perhaps Augier might have had some hope of making a recovery if the Dutch had not so obviously withdrawn from the unstable French market and if the 1721 vintage had been a good one. A poor vintage in France in 1721 inevitably increased demand from the worse affected northern districts of France, and the rise in prices also slowed the return of the Dutch, who had their own and now booming grain-based spirit industry. Prices on a floor of 52 and 53 livres in the first five months of 1721 had climbed to 75 livres in September 1721 and to 95 and 96 in January 1722. While the price-insensitive English market held up well in all the vicissitudes of 1721 and 1722, the Dutch market, after halving in 1721, halved again in 1722, to a very modest total. In the early weeks of 1722 a few letters were still being written from Augier in Cognac suggesting that he had hoped to continue business. However, his business was for all practical purposes inoperative, and the regular correspondence came to an end on 23 February. The Augiers seem to have finally conceded bankruptcy in the same month: this presumably came in the wake of the frustration of their last hope – a favourable outcome to their legal proceedings. Martell reported on 21 March 1722 to their old acquaintance Gibert that 'il ne leur parait pas que peu d'effets icy et un seul petit bien de campagne. L'on fait monter leur faillite à une forte somme. Aussi il est à craindre pour les intéressés qu'il n'y ait gros à perdre.' He added that: 'il est vrai qu'ils sont jeunes et entendus dans le commerce de sorte que si leurs affaires s'accommodent ils pourraient avec le temps faire quelque chose'. The second Augier house at Charente and Richard *l'aîné* also went bankrupt.[18] *Bilans* were lodged in both Saintes and Angouleme and the statutory contract with the minimum three-quarters of their creditors was signed on 22 June 1722. As one of their creditors was Lutkins in Bordeaux, it was registered there on 23 August,[19] and with the judges of the consular jurisdiction of Paris on 7 October 1722. All this related solely to the brandy business, though added complications arose from demands of the Paris banker creditors of the speculators. No evidence of an arrangement with them

---

[17] AAC, letter book 1720–4, 4 September 1721, to [name indecipherable]. This observation is substantially correct. The *mercuriale* for Cognac gave the December price as low as 26 livres for December 1707 and 32 to 36 livres for December 1706. A rise to 66 livres was recorded for December 1708. George, *Mercuriales d'Angouleme, de Cognac et de Jarnac*, pp. 68–9.   [18] MAC, letter book 1721–2, 23 March 1722, to Girault, Rouen.
[19] AAC, letter book 1724–6, Paris, 25 May 1725, to Martin des Fontenelles. This letter is a succinct retrospective account of events.

exists, and the debts seem to have remained unpaid. In other words, given the insolvency of the brandy business, the bankers finally had to cut their losses.[20] There is silence for the rest of 1722 and for all of 1723 until the very end of the year.

Perhaps the recovery of the Dutch and Hamburg trade in 1723 and more strongly still in 1724 encouraged Augier, once the leading agent for these regions in Cognac, to return to business. Perhaps an end in 1722 to the legal problems, consequent on their failures, may have been another reason. With the opening of a new brandy season in late 1723, a small account book has various letters from 6 December 1723 to 26 February 1724. This was obviously a prelude to a real comeback. By the spring Philippe Augier had need of a regular letter book, and on 4 March 1724 he appended to a volume which had contained the letters of the dying trade of the end months of 1720 a notice that 'ce livre de copie de lettres ayant esté deux ans sans servir – nous avons continué à en faire usage ce 4 Mars 1724'. As he advised Voigt in 6 May 1724, 'j'ay commencé à faire quelque commerce icy sous mon nom particulier'.

The dynamic long-term consequences of the Law years

The speculation of 1720, and the place brandy held in it, were both in a sense an oddity – part of the involvement of a small circle in Cognac in the world turned upside down. However, while the speculation lasted, it emphasised brandy as a commodity, and, in the record shipments of 1720, put Tonnay-Charente firmly on the map. From another point of view the period marked a crisis in the affairs of La Rochelle. While this was at the time wedded to a misplaced belief in Cognac's niche in a Parisian world, more meaningfully it saw Cognac business becoming closely linked to Bordeaux for specie and paper on a permanent basis. The fruits of this were somewhat concealed in the economic crisis of 1721–3, but they were already apparent in the Martell–Fiott partnership based on Bordeaux from 1723 to 1725.

Moreover, at a time when spirit production was growing in England and Holland, the low foreign exchanges launched cognac decisively into foreign markets. In the short term that created a recovery in demand for cognac among the Dutch, despite the fact that they were already beginning to turn elsewhere, and in more stable fashion created a London market. It led to a great decade of expansion in 1725–35 and, in the wake

---

[20] *Ibid.*, 'Mémoire instructif des raisons de la veuve Augier et fils que M. Jean Poisalotte, l'un des procureurs aux consuls de Paris, est prié d'employer en comparaissant pour eux', 2 August 1723. It consists of two sheets (four pages) inserted in a small soft-covered volume. This volume has a large number of calculations by the Augier family about their affairs.

of the Guernseymen's speculative debut, to a new pattern of whole ship-loads of brandy. The demand in 1720 had accelerated the existing use of Paris as a financial centre, and speculative dealings in Bordeaux in turn created a similar and geographically more convenient function for Bordeaux. Thus in 1720 Cognac changed from a small centre in which its activities were financed by a small bill nexus with both La Rochelle and Paris into an enhanced circuit within which Paris and Bordeaux inter-acted. Indeed Bordeaux grew relative to Paris, and an outlet for bills on Amsterdam or London in two French centres prevented Cognac houses from being held to ransom by their correspondents in Paris or Bordeaux. The closeness of the movement in the exchanges in the two cities empha-sised how effectively the exchange later worked.

As for the immediate results as far as the brandy trade was concerned, they were two-fold. First, after their withdrawal in 1721–3, the Dutch returned in force for several years, and the English importers, imitating their Guernsey suppliers, stole a leaf out of their book and supplanted them by ordering direct on their own account. The consequences of all this can be seen in Tonnay-Charente where Régnier and others catered to new direct Dutch orders, and in the role of Martell and Augier succes-sively in catering for the London market. Martell survived misfortune in Bordeaux in 1726 by the resumption of a modest brandy trade in Cognac, and Augier, getting on his feet again, handled the bulk of English orders for the next two decades. Second, Cognac no longer operated as an appendage of La Rochelle on commissions sent out from the city's varie-gated colony. Few new foreign faces were to appear in the merchant com-munity of the port of La Rochelle itself. Outsiders now settled in Charente or Cognac: the transferral of Baker from La Rochelle to Cognac illustrated the change of fortune, and the few who settled in La Rochelle relied heavily on a Cognac network. La Rochelle became a backwater: it generated little paper in European trade, and Cognac needs for specie and local paper fitted into a Bordeaux–Paris nexus. Even by mid-century Martell's sold as many foreign bills in Bordeaux as in Paris, and in the second half of the century even more. Tellingly, the foreign letters of Cognac houses ceased quoting either exchange rates or brandy prices in La Rochelle in the 1720s.

The trade changed greatly in the early 1720s. The Paris trade, an alter-native outlet for brandy, had already become established on the fringes of the area, its buyers invading even the central districts of the Cognac region in the vintage crisis years of the mid-1720s, the early and late 1740s, and the late 1760s. For the export trade such competition could be countered only by houses firmly anchored in the region, and the story of the export trade up until the late 1750s is woven around two houses,

Augier and Martell. The Augier business, on its feet once more, was active during 1724. There was correspondence with the Le Rigets in Charente and Amsterdam, much with Martell in Bordeaux and on 14 October 1724 they opened correspondence with the Paris banker Schmidlin. There was also correspondence with Crommelin de la Villette in Paris, the old family friend. The pattern of an associated house in Charente also re-emerged: Etienne Augier opened a business there.[21] The directing genius of the house which resumed the style of Veuve Augier was Philippe Augier. Much of the correspondence was in Dutch, but the business was big enough to occupy several individuals and letters were entered in the letter books in several hands. Pierre Richard's business continued in La Rochelle. Jacques Richard seems to have set up in trade in Paris, but hardly with success, as in February 1726 he was thinking of giving up and going to Germany.[22] However, the Richard house in La Rochelle, though surviving into the 1730s at least, was not of great consequence. In other words, the Richards' speculative interests in the early 1720s were disastrous.

The Guernsey circuit in Cognac and Bordeaux: success and crisis 1720–1726

Augier's speculative problems, the jaundiced Dutch perception of French currency experimentation and the bad 1721 vintage had all combined to bring down the Augier house in 1722. Martell's simultaneous rise was fortuitous in some ways. He had first appeared as a minor figure representing a new outside circle of young men – members or associates of families who had prospered in Guernsey's recent wartime boom – who were attracted into the brandy trade. When he arrived in France his knowledge of French was far from perfect: even as late as 27 October 1721 he admitted to Cluzeau in Paris that: 'mon dessein est de me fortifier dans la language française (qui ne m'est pas encore trop familière)'. In their plans of mid-1720 the Augier circle even saw him returning to the Channel Islands as a partner in a large brandy venture.

In the first half of 1720 Martell took over all the business for Guernsey. By the end of the year, with the Augiers now in dire trouble, and with Paris bankers faced with the deteriorating balance of payments in competition with one another to buy foreign bills in the provinces, he had replaced the Augiers as local correspondent for the Paris house of Etienne Gibert.[23] Martell's prospering business with Guernsey, which generated

[21] *Ibid.*, letter book 1724–6, December 1724 (day not noted), to Rocquier, Rotterdam.
[22] *Ibid.*, 18 February 1726, to Jacques Richard.
[23] MAC, letter book 1720–1, 7 and 21 December 1720, to Etienne Gibert.

the bills he had to sell, was behind this transformation. In December, looking back over the preceding twelve months he observed that 'j'ai d'assez bonnes commissions à Guernsey dans l'année dernière',[24] a view expressed even more confidently in September 1721: 'je me suis attiré la majeure partie des affaires de Guernsey'.[25] At the end of 1720, in estimating the trade with Guernsey, he put the quantity variously at 1,200 to 1,400 *pièces*, and at more than 1,500 *pièces*.[26] His estimate of his turnover (which suggests a rough 5,000 barriques) implies that he handled virtually all the business for Guernsey in 1720,[27] and in October 1721 he stated that he was the only person loading for Guernsey and Jersey.[28]

Throughout 1721 English trade remained at a high level, benefiting from the growing taste for spirits which was running ahead of domestic output in the short term, in contrast to the Dutch trade which had to compete with the most advanced indigenous spirit industry in northern Europe. The exports of brandy to Holland from the La Rochelle *généralité* were more than halved from a huge 26,151 barriques in 1720 to 11,780 barriques in 1721. In contrast exports to *Angleterre* fell only slightly from 9,842 barriques to 7,105. This explains why the Guernsey trade was the catalyst for demand, and by May Martell boasted that 'j'ai présentement les plus belles affaires du pays'.[29] In September he estimated his business since January at 'mille et quelques pieces' (i.e. more than 3,000 barriques) for a value of 250,000 livres.[30] The season of 1722 must have been even better: whereas exports to Holland were halved again, from 11,780 barriques to 5,376 barriques, exports to *Angleterre* rose to 7,204 barriques and were to climb even further in 1723 to 8,557 barriques. Next to the record exports of 1720, they must have been the highest exports in a single year for that market until the late 1780s when, after the Commercial Treaty of 1786, exports to England and Wales probably reached a new peak in the exceptional year of 1789.

While low prices and a favourable exchange were part of the reason for the high demand in 1720 and 1721, the strength of Guernsey demand was such that even when prices in the second half of 1721, with a poor vintage, doubled from the low spring level of 50 and 52 livres, it not only maintained itself but rose further. The Guernsey trade in 1721 is especially impressive because it had been for a time at the end of 1720 totally disrupted by quarantine regulations in England (there were no vessels from Guernsey in December). Ways round them were soon found, and

---

[24] *Ibid.*, 25 December 1720, to Drake.   [25] *Ibid.*, 29 September 1721, to Seale.
[26] *Ibid.*, 25 December, to Drake; to Derigson, Calais (same date).
[27] *Ibid.*, 11 January 1721, to Forty, Saint-Malo.
[28] *Ibid.*, letter book 1721–2, 6 October 1721, to Schmidlin.   [29] *Ibid.*, 14 May, to Kastell.
[30] *Ibid.*, 24 September 1721, to Forty.

with their relaxation by March trade was on a regular course again, with Martell observing that 'l'arrivée de tous les vaisseaux de Guernsey a mis un feu sans égal aux eaux de vie'.[31] Martell's figure of 250,000 livres for his turnover to September 1721 would, for less than a whole year at the lower prices of 1721, imply a turnover as large as that of 1720. Martell must have accounted for about half the total exports to *Angleterre*: in other words for the entire Guernsey component in the total shipments from the entire *généralité*. He was in a state of near euphoria in mid-1721, thinking that if he knew Dutch he could capture 'un grand tiers du commerce de cette ville [Cognac]'.[32] Martell's interest in the Dutch market was prompted by the fact that because of the plague the Dutch could no longer get brandy from Provence and Languedoc.[33] With prospects for an enlarged trade, Martell had already suggested to his cousin William Kastell in Jersey that he should join him 'here [for] a few years. I doubt not but that with some application it should be more advantageous to you than to stay at Jersey, for it should not be a hard matter to get every year 12,000–15,000 livres.' On another occasion, he held out prospects of 10,000 livres a year, and said that he had himself got near 25,000 livres in 1720.[34]

Martell's interest in the Dutch market had no outcome, beyond a small speculation on his own account at the end of the year. The Dutch market was disappointing in 1721, and still more so in 1722. Martell noted an easing-off of trade in September 1721 which he attributed to an abundance of grain-based spirits because of a plentiful Dutch harvest.[35] Brandy prices did not rise in Holland in the autumn: 'cette marchandise ne hausse point en Hollande qui est le lieu le plus considérable pour la consommation'.[36]

In September he was optimistic about diversifying his business, claiming that 'les affaires me viennent de divers endroits de sorte que je puis me flatter de former un bon établissement ici'. His hopes were boosted by a poor vintage in France, which would compensate for adverse effects on the Charente of cheap grain in Holland.[37] Paris buying resulted in prices rising from 80 to 100 livres over the month of October. Martell was sanguine about benefiting from the rising inland market. He corresponded with Rouen and Abbeville in 1721, and in the spring solicited business in

---

[31] *Ibid.*, letter book 1720–1, 24 March 1721, to Dobrée.
[32] *Ibid.*, letter book 1721–2, 16 July 1721, to William Kastell.
[33] *Ibid.*, 22 September 1721, to Falla, Guernsey.
[34] *Ibid.*, letter book, 1720–1, 14 May 1721, to Kastell; letter book 1721–2, 16 July 1721, to Kastell. Multiplied by fifty, as commission was 2 per cent, this figure suggests a crude ceiling of 750,000 livres for gross turnover.   [35] *Ibid.*, 1 November 1721, to Schmidlin.
[36] *Ibid.*, 5 November, 1721, to Testard, Rouen.
[37] *Ibid.*, 24 September 1721, to Forty; 19 November 1721, to Hoogwerk.

Orleans and Amiens also. However, despite the favourable circumstance, his only real success was in buying for two Paris customers, both bankers, Cluzeau and Schmidlin. Moreover, this was less a break into the Paris market, which was dominated by Orleans and other Loire merchants, than a case of speculation on a rising market by bankers who had offered commissions on joint account. In other words he failed to get any buying commissions from the Paris grocers, who alone were likely to prove durable customers.

The buoyancy of the Guernsey market, combined with the uncommon weakness of Dutch demand, turned Martell for a time into the most important house on the banks of the Charente. This comes out still more strongly in the bill trade, the real arbiter of standing. With Augier in dire trouble, the former major house had virtually ceased to count in the second half of 1720. As France's balance of payments was in trouble, Paris houses desperately wanted foreign bills of exchange. For instance, throughout 1721 the house of Cottin was buying up such bills in La Rochelle with the result that the usual gap between the two exchanges had vanished. From the end of 1720 Martell had an arrangement to buy bills on Gibert's account for a commission.[38] In the knowledge that his own bills on Paris were backed by a foreign trade, Martell enjoyed a preference over other sellers of inland paper,[39] and sold his bills readily to local tax collectors anxious to remit the proceeds to Paris.

Martell's optimism concealed the fact (probably even from himself) that his success did not rest on solid foundations. Despite the soaring inland business, he established no foothold in the trade with northern France, and he failed to find a solid brandy market in Paris. Though he enjoyed a monopoly of the Guernsey market in 1721–2, the best single market that Cognac had in a depressed time, that outlet depended on the ability of a small group of young Guernsey merchants to keep brandy merchants in London happy enough not to switch to direct ordering in France. His survival was not due to any special astuteness. His involvement in the foreign exchange speculation in 1720 reveals that he was party to the collective bad judgement of the Augier–Richard circle. So close had he been to the partners that when they failed, for fear of the 'divers mauvais raisonnements sur mon compte' it could cause, he asked his La Rochelle correspondents, ironically the brothers of Richard *l'ainé*, not to put his paper on London into circulation, and instead to draw on a Paris account.[40]

Martell only had orders coming from or through Guernsey and his

---

[38] *Ibid.*, 7 December, 21 December 1720, to Gibert.
[39] *Ibid.*, 22 December 1720, to Cluzeau.
[40] *Ibid.*, letter book 1721–2, 18 March 1722, to Pierre and Jacques Richard.

business was based on a single commodity. That may have prompted his move to Bordeaux in 1723, which was not to a business on his own account but to a partnership with Jean Fiott from Guernsey.[41] The Guernsey houses were big buyers of wine as well as brandy. Established British houses dealing with France had been decimated in the long period of war for almost a quarter century from 1689 to 1713, and by 1713, apart from the Irish houses in London, no business group existed in England with first-hand knowledge of the French trade. Only the Guernsey houses, with an extensive business in prize wine and brandy from their successful privateering and its consequent newly created financial business base in London, maintained an interest in French wine and brandy. When the wars were over, they sought to turn their wartime interest into a durable peacetime trade. This accounted for their heavy buying of brandy for the London market, which they pioneered as little French brandy came to London from other sources in the 1710s. Guernsey carried on a large business in wine in the 1710s, and the London interest of the islandmen is revealed in their buying the fashionable and expensive wines as well as the lesser Bordeaux wines which entered into a more diffuse and sometimes unorthodox market in the British Isles.

If the Guernsey merchants had encouraged Martell to go to Cognac, it was equally logical that they encouraged him to go to Bordeaux. That hope did not quite work out because the business prospects suggested by growing recognition of Bordeaux wine were severely restrained by the high duties. However, the reputation and volume of the new French clarets on the London market were in the ascendant in the 1720s. In moving to Bordeaux, Martell did not surrender his brandy trade in Cognac. Day-to-day management there was left to Antoine Le Mesurier, who was answerable to Fiott and Martell in Bordeaux: as Martell put it, 'nous y avons raison qui travaille sous le nom d'Anthoine Le Mesurier'.[42]

---

[41] As there is a gap in the Martell records between 1722 and 1724, the date cannot be fixed with accuracy. However, in the second surviving letter book, that for 1721–2, a note was appended reading 'Journal appartenant à Martell, Fiott et Cie, Bordeaux le 17 Aout 1723'. Firino-Martell, regarding the date as doubtful, added a sic (p. 64). He took him to be acting there on account of an existing partnership (La famille Martell, p. 65). It seems, however, in reality the opening date of the new venture. The exact date of Martell's departure to Bordeaux cannot be pinned down, as his surviving letter book only began in August 1724. However, from letters in Augier's books, it is clear that Martell was already established there by May 1723.

[42] Ibid., letter book 1724–5, 26 August 1724, to L. Cocq. Le Mesurier was already in Cognac, though his presence there is poorly documented. Forty years later the Le Mesurier family was described by Lallemand, presiding genius of the Martell house at the time, as the first Channel Island family to have settled in Cognac: 'our house is the eldest next to his in the brandy trade'. Ibid., letter book 1766–7, 27 December 1766, to Salisbury, Lancaster.

The evidence in the 1724–5 letter book suggests a business mainly in wine and an enlarged correspondence with at least ten Guernsey houses. Fiott and Martell were buying Margaux wine at 350 livres: in other words they had dealings at the top end of the London market (Haut Brion and Margaux). Wine was consigned directly to Elisha Dobrée in London. The house was big enough to have two clerks; and having two they had to decline to employ a son of one of the Le Febvres in 1725.[43] They also had an ongoing association with Augier's resurrected business in Cognac: they negotiated bills in Bordeaux for them, and dispatched specie to Cognac.

Martell was too junior to be the head of a house with the diverse contacts and activities which Fiott, Martell and Co. enjoyed in 1724. When Le Mesurier was given instructions in December 1724, in the course of a visit by Martell to Cognac for brandy buying, the tone of the letter reveals that Jean Fiott was the effective director of the enterprise, in other words the senior partner.[44] The business in Bordeaux was an active one: the house handled imported wheat throughout 1724, some of it from Pierre Carey, a leading merchant in Guernsey. Moreover, their wine business brought them into relations with Ireland: they were buying for Jean Brunet of Dublin at the beginning of 1725.[45] Brunet had a brother Henry in Cognac (who also did a small trade in brandy with his Dublin brother), and some of the funds for the wine purchases in Bordeaux came through Cognac.[46] These links may explain why Martell was drawn into the Brunet circuit. Again, as Philippe Augier married a Brunet, one can sense that the goodwill between Martell and Augier which had survived the debacle of 1720 was a factor in effecting the introduction. On 1 January 1726 Martell married Jeanne Brunet. This marriage became the first stage towards integrating him into the region, and his wife's mother was a Lallemand. The marriage also made his return to Cognac easier after the Bordeaux business, which he continued after the dissolution of the partnership with Fiott later in 1726; it also led, after his wife's death, to his second marriage in 1737 to Rachel Lallemand, his wife's first cousin.[47] The dowry was not large but it brought his second wife's powerful and domineering brother, Louis-Gabriel, at the time described as a student, into the ambit of the house, making its later success possible. The consequences of the dominant Lallemand presence went further, their overbearing and narrow influence converting house and family alike

---

[43] *Ibid.*, letter book 1724–5, 28 February 1725, to Samuel and Daniel Le Febvre, Guernsey.
[44] *Ibid.*, 27 December 1724, to Le Mesurier.
[45] *Ibid.*, 13 January 1725, to Jean Brunet.   [46] *Ibid.*, 3 March 1725, to Le Mesurier.
[47] For the marriage contracts of 1726 and 1737 see Firino-Martell, *La famille Martell*, pp. 17–21. The date of death of Jeanne Brunet is unknown.

from an expatriate into a thoroughly indigenous presence, steeped in local values and, beyond business, deaf to the external world and ideas. Business conditions were difficult in the first half of the 1720s. Prospects of a reduction in the value of specie (with its deflationary results and a rise in the exchanges) lurked in the background. In July 1721, for instance, Martell, seeing a reduction as imminent, advised his Guernsey customers to buy as the rise in exchange rate would be immediate, whereas the fall in prices would operate more slowly.[48] However, nothing happened at this stage. But the comparative, if fragile, stability of the exchanges was interrupted with a reduction in the currency in April 1724 and again in September, which caused the exchange to rise. The vintage in the autumn of 1724 seems to have been remarkably good: exports in 1725 were a near-record 34,105 barriques. The consequence was that a firming of prices expressed in external currency compounded the effects of a good vintage in leading to a fall in internal prices: prices in French currency drifted down from 58 livres in December 1724 to 41 livres in June 1725.

Reductions in the value of specie entailed monetary losses for merchants who held cash. In September 1724, Martell, referring to a 20 per cent reduction in specie, observed that by anticipating the change (in other words having got into commodities quickly) he had avoided losses.[49] A climate of uncertainty, however, was hardly good for business. Failures were numerous in Bordeaux in the autumn of 1724.[50] The Paris business world was in crisis too: 'on dit qu'il n'y a que très peu de banquiers qui payent à Paris'.[51] It is not surprising that if bills on Paris houses were insecure, the revenue receivers chose to send the government's revenues in specie to Paris. There was, in the opinion of observers, another and more sinister motive for this: if the state sought specie at its existing low valuations as its preferred means of tax settlements, it could imply an imminent revaluation of the precious metals and a short-term painless profit for its treasury. Such a specie-gathering operation by the revenue receivers with its implications of yet more tinkering with the currency injected a further element of uncertainty into business. Revenue demand for specie made it even harder to sell paper on Paris, both because the revenue receivers themselves were the main takers of bills and because the dispatch of specie drained the region of cash.[52] According to Schmidlin, 'la misère règne toujours à Paris et la confiance y est entièrement

---

[48] MAC, letter book 1721–2, 31 July 1721, to Nicholas Dobrée.
[49] Ibid., letter book 1724–5, 25 September 1724.
[50] Ibid., 23 October 1724, to Pierre Richard. See also letters of 27 November, 2 and 6 December 1724.   [51] Ibid., 27 January 1725, to Broussard père et fils.
[52] Ibid., 27 January 1725, to Etienne Augier.

perdue'.[53] Funds were now being sent in specie from Guernsey. Schmidlin was in difficulty, asking Fiott and Martell not to draw on him in March, and Martell wrote: 'nous craignons que Mr Schmidlin a perdu du brillant crédit qu'il avait cy devant'.[54] In Bordeaux 'l'argent est d'une rareté inexprimable, et ceuz à qui l'on doit, ne donne pas le moindre répit'.[55] In such a situation the Martell and Fiott house too had its problems.

The full story cannot be told, as the surviving Bordeaux letter book does not run beyond 21 March 1725. Some of the story can be taken up from the Augier letter books. By August 1725 the partnership had dissolved. A letter from Augier to Fiott suggests that external circumstances were more decisive than local ones, as he posed the question of who would compensate them for the separation: 'je vois la dissolution de votre société. Je souhaite que chacun en votre particulier fassiez des avantages; qui vous dédommage de la perte réciproque que vous faites en séparant deux hommes d'une probité peu commune'.[56] The separation did not envisage the termination of trade itself: it seems that Fiott in Guernsey would represent both men, and his intended journey home lay through Cognac where the former partnership had a large buying interest in brandy. While there he took ill, and an alarmed Augier wrote to Martell that 'cela est facheux pour vous parce que sa présence vous aurait été utile à Guernsey'.[57] The change was apparently prompted by some jealousy at the Guernsey end: Augier, choosing to put some of his words in English, referred to silence from there: 'ils n'écrivent vous réfuser a certain estime, but I dont beleave that there be for you a natural cordiality'.[58] Fiott's interrupted journey was to deal with a crisis in relationships, as Augier emphasised the importance of writing to Guernsey: if Fiott could write, it would at least be a substitute for his presence there.[59]

In the wake of a major economic crisis in France, Martell's Guernsey support, the basis of his business, collapsed. Why the differences occurred we cannot say with confidence. They could have arisen from personal jealousies at the Guernsey end (Martell was from Jersey, and Fiott was also from a family of Jersey origin). More probably they were prompted by erosion of support for the Guernsey intermediaries by London houses, and consequent recrimination between Guernsey and Bordeaux about responsibility for occasioning London grievances. While the issue involved wine, it also involved brandy and for similar reasons. The idea of Dunkirk replacing Guernsey as the staging point for supplies

[53] *Ibid.*, 17 February 1725, to Schmidlin, repeating what Schmidlin had said in a letter.
[54] *Ibid.*, 21 March 1725, to Philippe Augier.   [55] *Ibid.*, 21 March 1725, to Le Mesurier.
[56] AAC, letter book 1724–6, 4 August 1725, to Fiott.   [57] *Ibid.*, 18 August 1725.
[58] *Ibid.*, 8 September 1725.   [59] *Ibid.*, 12 September 1725.

to England, and of the transfer of the conduct of the trade from Guernsey houses in London into the hands of English brandy importers was certainly abroad. In February 1725 Bucknell of Portsmouth had been in touch with Augier: significantly he inquired benevolently about Martell, which implied that the blame was placed on the Guernsey circuit itself rather than on Martell.[60] In that case the fear in Guernsey may have been that Fiott and Martell might opt for a direct liaison with London and betray their old principals in Guernsey. Real difficulties in supply in the autumn of 1725 – a bad vintage – can only have accelerated problems. Exports to England, which had been large and stable between 1720 and 1725, fell in 1726. Objectively the circuit did rather well in the crisis of 1725–6: exports to *Angleterre* fell less than to Holland and they accounted in that year for one-third of all exports from the *généralité* of La Rochelle. In the summer and early autumn of 1726 the export branches of the brandy trade had virtually folded up. With another bad vintage Augier represented the Paris trade as 'le plus courant',[61] and little foreign business was done in the autumn of 1726. The reduction in the value of specie in France in June 1726 had the immediate effect of raising prices by almost 30 per cent to foreigners. However, as in another crisis in the 1760s, importers made few allowances for difficulties overseas and blamed their suppliers for problems of price, supply and regularity of dispatch. Crisis can only have encouraged brandy merchants to switch from a passive role as buyers in London into the active one of importers on their own account.

Fear of such a change could have caused a rift in the interests of the London–Guernsey–Cognac circuit. That something akin to this was the case is suggested in a letter from Augier to Martell referring to 'la manière dont Monsieur Dobrée dépeint le commerce de liqueurs de Guernsey en Angleterre, je crains fort qu'il y aura une interruption dans celui de Guernsey chez vous'.[62] There was a visible crisis in the brandy trade to *Angleterre* with a sharp fall in 1726 (the crisis year of the trade), a low point in 1727 and little recovery in 1728. By way of contrast Dutch custom, falling sharply only in 1726, bounced back in the subsequent years. Something was clearly amiss. The break-up between Fiott and Martell on the one side and their Guernsey principals on the other magnified the short-term interruption of trade and speeded up the interposition of new faces and new routes. Martell's own bankruptcy in 1726 can only have confirmed doubts about the value of the old route. Augier already had an order from Bucknell of Portsmouth in the spring of 1726,

---

[60] *Ibid.*, 26 February 1725, to Bucknell, Portsmouth.
[61] *Ibid.*, 17 August 1726, to Lees and Co.   [62] *Ibid.*, 5 December 1725, to Martell.

which he described as his first [i.e. meaning English] order for a long time,[63] and he was in correspondence with Elisha Dobrée of London on the subject of trade through Dunkirk in August 1727.[64] He engaged in a flurry of correspondence with London in the autumn of 1727. He made contact with James Hatch in London at this time and his invoices in 1728 show a respectable volume of business with Hatch and with other London houses. Another house in Charente, Alleret and Moynet, had an English business in the same years: thirty-five of their sixty-five consignments between 31 March 1728 and 31 March 1731 were for Dunkirk, and the total for the British Isles amounted to 530 *pièces* and 93 barriques out of total overseas consignments of 941 *pièces* and 104 barriques.[65] In the absence of Martell's letter books for the period we know little of his failure, beyond the fact that he had gone bankrupt in 1726 and that a year later 'par là son billet n'est pas d'un grand prix'.[66] Martell had to seek a composition or an arrangement with his creditors: creditors for 58,000 livres had already signed, and others for 10,000 to 11,000 had still to do so. Augier saw Martell as 'un homme droit quoique malheureux et peut-etre imprudent'.[67]

French business difficulties in 1725–1726

Schmidlin, Martell's Paris banker, had failed earlier in July 1726. From the second half of 1725, rumours of monetary experiments abounded, even of Law returning: this suggested the possibility of abandoning the policy pursued in 1725 of reducing the value of specie and even raised the prospect of the reintroduction of paper money.[68] The result was that bills on Paris and commodities alike became difficult to sell, as people were anxious to hold on to specie in the belief that, if they turned it prematurely into goods, they would lose the profits of its expected upward revaluation. At the end of 1725 these expectations were confounded once more: specie was again reduced and further reductions were expected in January. Indeed the reduction was a stepped one in which the value of silver was to be reduced from 40 livres per mark to 30 in three stages. In

---

[63] *Ibid.*, 3 April 1726.
[64] *Ibid.*, letter book 1727–8, 25, 27 August 1727, to Elisha Dobrée, London.
[65] Figures as given by R. Kléber, 'Le trafic des eaux-de-vie charentaises 1660–1750' (Travail d'étude et de recherche, University of Bordeaux, 1971), pp. 149–50.
[66] AAC, letter book, 1727–8, 15 December 1727, to Crommelin de Villette.
[67] Martell's brother-in-law John Seale was one of the creditors, and Augier advised another brother-in-law creditor, Alexandre Sheabe, to sign. There is a reference to a Seale as godparent to Jean Martell.
[68] See AAC, letter book 1724–6, especially 15 September 1725, to Schmidlin.

consequence the pressure on holders of specie was enormous to pass it on in discharge of obligations to other individuals or to the state before it fell further in value. However, such a sequence of reductions was a pre-liminary – and seen as such – to a reminting operation in which the state would put currency into circulation in February at a value still to be determined, but on the basis of a higher value of the precious metals in money of account and windfall profits in the reminting. In such a climate of uncertainty about the timing of changing valuations, the only firm fact was the short-term one that debtors were eager to pay off debts before specie lost some of its value: 'dans la crise d'aujourdhui chacun songe uniquement à payer ses dettes'. This contributed to a sharp rise in prices by the end of 1725: brandy prices, as low as 41 livres per barrique in June 1725, were 81 livres in December. However, doubts which set in about the direction of future monetary policy injected uncertainty into commodity markets. Five hundred *pièces* were unsold for want of buyers at a *canton* at the end of December.[69] In January Augier reported 'tout en inaction, ainsi nos marchandises n'ont point de prix fixe',[70] and, despite shortage, brandy slipped back to 58 livres. Augier did not fully take up his credit with the house of Schmidlin: buying had halted as a general reluc-tance to sell for an uncertain means of payment meant that holders of commodities were not keen to part with them.[71] Government policy and the uncertainty which it engendered was bitterly resented by merchants, Augier even believing that war alone, though it was 'un terrible fléau', was the only hope of redressing the situation.[72] He designated government operations with sarcasm: 'La nécessité me fait vendre mes meubles; le meme motif m'oblige à en racheter un peu. Qui voudrait un tour de lit avec la courte pointe de rencontre presque neuf? Cela se doit souvent trouver à Paris dans un temps de misère comme aujourdhui.'[73]

In the end, the expectations of January were confirmed in a reissue of coin announced on 1 February at 41 livres the mark, and prices which had remained low in the uncertainty of January recovered on the news to 70 livres: 'miracle' as Augier sarcastically observed.[74]

The fact that despite the bad 1725 vintage prices did not rise very sharply in 1726 is a reflection of the depressed economic conditions. Augier noted that it was the worst wine for thirty years and 12 barriques

[69] *Ibid.*, 19 December 1725, to Bellesme, Saint-Jean d'Angély.
[70] *Ibid.*, 5 January 1726, to John Seale.   [71] *Ibid.*, 7 January 1726, to Schmidlin.
[72] *Ibid.*, 19 January 1726, to Boué *le jeune*, Hamburg; 23 January 1726, to Martell et Cie.
[73] *Ibid.*, 26 January 1726, to Jacques Richard.
[74] *Ibid.*, 9 February 1726, to Balguerie frères, Middelbourg. See also letters to Martell, 23 January; to Jacques Richard, 23 January; and to Jean du Peyron *le jeune*, Amsterdam, 11 February 1726.

were said to make only 1 barrique of brandy.[75] With exaggeration he claimed to a merchant in Hamburg that only one-eighth of the last year's brandy would be distilled.[76] Brandy which would have gone abroad was drawn to Paris at 75 livres per barrique. Damage caused by the preceding uncertainty would have been reduced if the revaluing operation on 1 February had not been bungled: the new coin made a slow appearance and, as foreseen by Augier, it would make a still slower appearance in the provinces. The delays compounded all other problems: in Augier's words in late February operations of this sort 'peu à peu sape[nt] les fondements du commerce'.

The balance of payments crisis, currency problems, and a disastrous vintage all reinforced one another. A wide gap emerged between the exchange quotations in Amsterdam and Paris: this signalled the depth of the business crisis. In effect sellers of foreign exchange had to offer a large premium in foreign money to entice anyone to take bills at all. This corresponded to an alarming rise in the discount on inland bills as well. In March and April, in contrast to the usual rate of 0.5 per cent per usance, it had widened to as much as 2 or 2.5 per cent. Brandy prices fell to 63 livres by 16 March, and to a mere 50 livres on 8 May. The accumulation of disasters and the general lack of confidence may have prompted yet another reversal of policy in June, when the value of silver was again reduced. This revaluation, however, was to stand the test of time until the Revolution, with one technical adjustment in the 1780s. Inevitably, whatever the beneficial long-term benefits, the short-term effects were merely another turn of the screw. As a result of the revaluation in June, brandy prices would have seemed 30 per cent dearer to foreigners. The economic difficulties in the short term became even more painful. Martell failed in 1726 and in July Schmidlin, his banker in Paris, did the same.

As if all this was not bad enough, in August 1726 a vintage of only a half to a third of the normal was expected.[77] Prices held up in the second half of 1726 and even rose somewhat to 84 livres by March 1727. Trade was still limited, and the Paris crisis of 1726 left a bitter legacy: 'la confiance de Paris icy est sy reserrée que peu de personnes tirent'.[78] Objectively, the crisis in 1726–7 was less disturbing than the preceding one. Some of its features corresponded to a widespread economic crisis in other countries: in 1726 it was very clear that foreign demand itself was weak. Dutch demand recovered in 1727, and the external market at large followed in 1728.

---

[75] *Ibid.*, 12 January 1726, to Mundt.   [76] *Ibid.*, 19 January 1726, to Boué *le jeune*.
[77] *Ibid.*, 28 August 1726, to Laurencin, Nantes.
[78] *Ibid.*, letter book 1726–7, 1 February 1727, to Deprès de Bussy, Orleans.

The brandy business in Cognac 1728–1746

Martell's failure put him out of business temporarily, and his effective absence from business is reflected in the prominence of the Augiers in the English trade in 1728 when its recovery began, although somewhat more slowly than in the Dutch trade: Philippe Augier had a correspondence with the major new importers. He had written to Elisha Dobrée in August 1727 and to Holmes the following month. Augier referred to a boom in brandy in November 1727.[79] His bill circuit in the autumn was extended to include the banking house of Mallet, with whom he established contact because of differences with Cottin. Even if he still spoke in deprecating terms of his business[80] and even though his English custom was just emerging, he was becoming more self-confident: in May 1727 he wrote to Kastell that 'je sais assez d'anglais pour bien entendre ce qu'on m'écrit en cette langue, mais non pour m'exprimer aussy facillement qu'en Français'.[81] From 1729 his English trade became important, and it was the mainstay of the house in the 1730s. It was easy for Augier to hold it because as Dutch demand declined decisively from the mid-1730s, and English interest did not falter, a well-defined pattern emerged in which the Dutch drew a small number of bulk consignments of cheaper and younger brandy from the fringe of the region, and the English buyers increasingly took all or nearly all the dearer and older brandy from the Cognac heartland. The English trade recovered very rapidly in 1729: exports of 6,902 barriques were almost double the 1728 level and rose to 8,438 barriques in 1731, a level not exceeded until the 1760s when the figures incorporated a large trade with Ireland. In the 1730s the trade was to prove static. After 1733, apart from a high level in 1735 (7,714 barriques), the highest figure of the decade was to be 4,466 barriques in 1738. The long-term market was to prove stagnant in volume terms. At the peak of the early 1750s, in 1754, it was a mere 3,479 barriques, and the 1770s' peak was 4,404 barriques in 1774. However, this was largely champagne brandy, little of it shipped for the shifting channels of the illegal trade, and consigned to a quality market buying at crushing rates of import tax. Within the total for *Angleterre*, the proportion taken by London almost certainly grew. Hence, while the total for the heterogeneous entity of *Angleterre* changed little or even fell, trade with London grew: that gave the town of Cognac itself, champagne brandy as its

---

[79] *Ibid.*, letter book 1727–8, 17 November 1727, to Piet de la Dechidire, Chateauneuf.
[80] *Ibid.*, letter book 1726–7, 15 June 1726, to Schmidlin; letter book 1727–8, 29 November 1727, to Isaac Mallet.   [81] *Ibid.*, 21 May 1727.

product and its shippers a dynamic role which is concealed in the crude measure of gross statistics.

Given this specialised trend, a house like Alleret and Moynet[82] with a varied trade was unable to establish a hold in the business whereas Augier seems to have succeeded in doing so very effectively. On the evidence of a very untidily kept ledger for 1724–41, we can form a picture of the Augiers' business: regular commissions from northern Europe were for a mere two Amsterdam houses, one Middelbourg house and three Hamburg houses. The absence of a large connection with Holland and Hamburg suggests that the house, or at least its manager Philippe, had not been forgiven for the inglorious speculation of 1720. However, his eleven regular London correspondents included the largest houses, Holmes, Mahew and Hatch. His individual accounts in the early 1730s were very large. For instance, he supplied 290 pipes to Holmes in 1731, and his total English orders on the basis of a crude tot would have been of the order of 1,161 pipes plus 30 tierçons in 1731. If the pipe is the equivalent of a *pièce*, this means a total of just over 3,500 barriques in 1731.[83] His ledger seems to have gaps for the second half of the decade, but the invoices which survive for that period bring out the existence of large orders to James Hatch. His business between 1736 and 1740 was running at a level of 2,500–3,000 barriques: this would have made up the bulk of all shipments from the La Rochelle *généralité* for England. Others, like Régnier, became the dominant houses in the weakening Dutch trade of the mid-1730s. Significantly, the houses that did well in the London market – Augier in the 1730s and 1740s, Martell in the 1750s and later – were or became increasingly dependent on a single market.

Despite restarting business in a year of extreme difficulty, 1724, Augier's old connections and his family ties may have helped to put him quickly on his feet again. His turnover with the Paris house of Schmidlin from December 1724 to May 1725 amounted to 58,347 livres. Doubled to give an annual figure, it would, at the prevailing prices, suggest at an f.o.b. price of 80–100 livres a turnover of roughly 1,450 barriques. Of course Augier also ran accounts at the time with Fiott, Martell and Co. in Bordeaux and with Pierre Richard in La Rochelle: these accounts did not represent further funds so much as the proceeds of inland bills on Schmidlin which were disposed of locally to raise the funds for brandy buying. This seems, given his failure and the problems of the time, a quick recovery. Attracting the custom of the English trade in the crisis that took

---

[82] See Kléber, 'Le trafic des eaux-de-vie', pp. 149–50.
[83] The term 'pipe' was not in regular use in the trade. It probably reflects confusion on either his customers' part or his in the use of *pièce* and pipe.

place in the mid-1720s in the roundabout channels from London to Cognac via Guernsey, he became in the 1730s and 1740s the largest house in Cognac, dominating the English trade in particular. The switch from reliance on a Guernsey circuit was reinforced by Martell's business failure in 1726 turning business in Augier's direction.

Table 6. *Augier's exports compared to the total brandy exports from the La Rochelle* généralité *(in barriques)*

Date	Augier	La Rochelle total
1736	2,335	18,464
1737	2,538	18,944
1738	3,296	25,144
1739	2,909	11,504
1740	2,409	13,048
1741	2,029	8,365
1742	3,271	n.a.
1743	4,814	n.a.
1744	3,030	34,394
1745	2,122	n.a.
1746	1,430	16,574
1747	1,564	18,101

Source: Kleber, 'Le trafic des eaux-de-vie', p. 157; AAC, invoices 21 January 1736–29 January 1748 inserted into end of volume entitled 'Comptes coursants 1826–7, Etienne Augier et fils, Charente'. For La Rochelle exports, see *états de la balance du commerce*, ACC, La Rochelle. Augier's exports given in veltes have been converted into barriques of 27 veltes.

The fact that in the crisis years of 1739 to 1741 his exports remained as high as they did testifies to his indispensable role, just as the better following years pointed to good fortunes in 1742, 1743 and 1744. The valley periods represent a combination of shortfalls in vintage and a switch to the Paris market. In good years and bad Augier's held a large part of the export market, roughly 10 per cent. For the English trade, it appears to have been a dominant share. He had an especially active trade with the London house of James Hatch. His near 5,000 barriques in 1743 was probably the largest turnover by any house from 1721 up to the mid-1760s. Martell, on the other hand, in March 1743, lamented that he had had none of the favours of James Hatch for the past twelve months. His own business he regarded as an 'assez bonne tappe [*sic*] d'ordres, mais limittés', and a fleeting reference implied a turnover of 500 *pièces* (1,500 barrels).

The foreign trade crisis in Cognac, 1746–1753

The Augier business faltered again in the years between 1746 and 1752, when in contrast to successful management in 1739–41, things not only went badly wrong but from the very start. Augier had lost his hold on the London trade by 1753 as Lallemand, never one to understate a situation, boasted to a Dublin merchant that his own house was 'the chief loader for London and should expect the same thing in your place if they knew as well as they might good brandy'.[84] In 1747 Augier, discontented with his situation, seems to have represented his former income as 6,600 livres, which implies, converting commission into turnover, a business of 330,000 livres per annum.[85] These were for exporters years of unsurpassed difficulty: in 1748, 1750 and 1752 exports were the lowest for any recorded year before the late 1760s.

Why Augier lost out we do not know precisely. But we would guess that it was the English trade which posed the major problem. The years 1748 and 1751 were the low points in the trade with *Angleterre*, surpassed in peacetime only by even more legendary years of difficulty, 1740–1 and 1772. Almost certainly these years must have seen not only a passing loss of business, but a restiveness among the customers who directed some or many of their commissions to others in the hope of success. Augier was acutely discontented with his lot. Perhaps it was psychologically a repetition of the discontent he experienced as a young man in 1720. The outlook must have been all the more disturbing as English distillation was approaching its peak of expansion at the end of the 1740s, and the fall in trade could be seen as a result not only of adversity in the vintages but of crisis in English custom. Augier was a man with seven children to provide for, the eldest about to come of age, and he turned once more, on 23 May 1747, to his old friend Crommelin de la Villette. Significantly, on 24 June he referred to the 'multiplication des commissionaires'. Crommelin's reply to the first letter (of which we do not have a copy) gives us an idea of what was on Augier's mind:

Je sais que le commerce qui se fait dans votre ville et aux environs a bien des inconvénients que le défaut de récolte de vins le suspend et diminue en meme temps que les propriétaires des fonds perdent leur revenu, que vous etes pour ainsi dire bornés à cette partie de commerce. A l'égard des jeunes gens qui viennent se traverser par des manoeuvres c'est un mal assez général et qui s'est introduit par tout. Je compte, Monsieur, que cela dégoute ceux qui agissent sur des

---

[84] MAC, letter book 1753–4, 12 May 1753, to Dillon and Cahill.
[85] AAC, 24 June 1747. This figure is confirmed by the calculation of 53,116 livres for the period 30 January 1743–3 April 1749, or an average of 8,853 livres, which suggests even higher profits for the good early years of the run. AAC, 'Etat de mes affaires'.

bons principes et qui par leur ancienneté et capacité devraient etre préférés dans les affaires de commissions. Dans de pareils circonstances il est bien naturel de chercher à s'affranchir.[86]

Augier was equally influenced by the prospects of the Paris brandy trade which was draining off the brandy which might otherwise go abroad and which seemed to offer prospects as bright as those of the export trade were dark. Crommelin encouraged him in this, adding that 'il se fait beaucoup de consommation en l'eau-de-vie [à Paris]. Vous en feriez venir à mesure que vous en voiriez le débouché'.[87] Crommelin in later correspondence was more cautious about the proposal, and Augier characteristically raised a whole range of alternative possibilities in subsequent years, such as provisioning contracts for the navy and setting up a son in one of the major trading ports. In 1749 Augier was still lamenting that 'la misère ne s'est jamais fait sentir autant qu'aujourdhui. Cette province est regardée comme une des meilleures, sept des plus malheureuses récoltes l'ont mise si basse que je ne crois pas la revoir dans l'opulence avant de finir mes jours'.[88] Apart from taking refuge in the idea of making an easy living elsewhere, Augier's letter conveyed a sense of exaggeration beyond the facts. The bad seasons of the early and late 1740s were certainly real but they were interrupted by some outstanding seasons (the calendar year 1744 had the third highest recorded exports of the century). The diffuse character of his discontent, the vague or floating quality of his ideas and the fact that his correspondence with Crommelin de la Villette in these years erupted intermittently tells us something about the man. Perhaps in something as personal as character lies the ultimate explanation for the permanent shift of fortune from Augier to Martell's.

The cumulative addition between 3 May 1747 and 5 June 1755 to Augier's effects, which were calculated as the value of an inventory enlarged or reduced by profits or losses on his trade, was 1,300 livres. The house must have lived off its capital for some of the time as the value of effects which was 228,000 livres in May 1747 was down to 210,000 on 6 January 1750. The fact that the correspondence with Crommelin came to an end in 1751 suggests that things had begun to look up in 1751 or 1752. After 1751 there was a run of remarkably good vintages (excepting one single season) from 1752 to 1765. The internal logic of Augier's figures implies that he added 19,300 livres to his effects between January

---

[86] *Ibid.*, 6 June 1747, Crommelin de la Villette, Paris. He was in Paris for a season, but now lived in Muids in Normandy. Augier kept copies of some of his letters to Crommelin, though not of his letter of 23 May which appears to have been the opening shot in a correspondence which continued until 1751.
[87] *Ibid.*, 11 July 1747.   [88] *Ibid.*, 20 November 1749.

214 The brandy trade under the *ancien régime*

1750 and June 1755. In the four years to April 1759, 18,116 livres was added, which suggests that they preserved the position they had gained, but did not accelerate the rate of growth. Their invoices in 1756–7 show a little business with Ostend which was the channel in the first days of the Seven Years War, and suggests that the preceding uplift of business benefited them. They had acquired or reacquired several London customers by 1763.[89]

The Augier business in the 1750s and 1760s

The house of Augier, after some initial recovery, failed at first to benefit in full from the new trends in demand. While it acquired some Ostend orders in the first flurry of rerouted traffic in 1756–7 it did not succeed in holding on to them, and it also failed to retain the Paris business it acquired in 1757. However, the house did benefit from the intensified and speculative trade of the later stages of the war. Their fortunes then improved dramatically and in the five years 3 April 1759–20 February 1764, 58,584 livres were added to the inventory of assets, which suggests a significant recovery. These were, of course, very good years: there was a high level of foreign demand and a continuation of good vintages. One year (1761) witnessed the second highest exports of 1718–80, and only in one year between 1756 and 1765 did exports fall below 20,000 barriques.

Augier's business now became quite substantial, with very large orders from the two London houses of Gibson and Fontblanque and Thellusson, and several French houses in London. In 1763, in the heady conditions of peacetime trade, Augier occasionally got commissions from London customers, and acquired many temporarily in 1766–7 when Martell Lallemand's customers lost confidence in the house's ability to serve them in the quite novel conditions of those two years. In reality, 1766–7 apart, in the resumption of peacetime trade the Augier house lost much of its London custom, and became heavily dependent on the soaring Irish demand. In 1765 its business amounted to 60,123 veltes of which 36,964 were supplied to Galwey of La Rochelle and 13,884 to Pelletreau.[90] As Pelletreau was resident in Rochefort and most of the Irish vessels docked there not in Tonnay-Charente, these quantities must also have been intended for Irish vessels. The Galwey and Pelletreau invoices accounted for 80 per cent of the turnover (and much or most of Pelletreau's brandy may have been on Galwey's account), and the balance

---

[89] *Ibid.*, Invoices 18 November 1756–7 January 1764. These follow with a gap the invoices of 21 January 1736–29 January 1748 entered in a volume bearing at the back the title 'Comptes courants 1826–7'.   [90] *Ibid.*

supplied to overseas and French houses was a mere 9,165 veltes. The Augiers had only two London customers in 1765, one of whom, Smith and Harrison, was to prove a remarkably faithful customer for the best part of twenty years.

The profits as calculated by Augier were unique in 1764–7. They came to 64,000 livres from January 1764 to 12 August 1766. Half of this total (31,244 livres) seems to have been earned in the period 12 August 1765 to 12 August 1766. The following year was even better with 37,233 livres earned in one year. This was the end of their good fortune, however. From 22 September 1767 to 30 July 1769 the profits fell to 20,986 livres. The heavy reliance on a single house, Galwey, had a crippling effect because when high prices drove the Irish, like the Dutch at an earlier date, to other markets, the house had few alternative outlets. From 30 July 1769 to 13 December 1771 the profits, as calculated by the Augiers, were a mere 2,185 livres. In the two periods 1767–9 and 1769–71 they had speculated heavily on their own account: a half interest in 160 *pièces* in 1767–9, 141 *pièces* in 1769–71. The years 1764–8 were a strange Indian summer for the firm. Its vulnerability was, however, painfully evident. Philippe Augier himself lived until 1769 but he had withdrawn from business in 1764, and in the new partnership of Augier frères drawn up in 1764 'pour un temps indéfini' even the eldest son, another Philippe, seems to have been a sleeping partner, receiving a quarter of the profits for helping 'par ses conseils et sa plume au besoin'.[91] The contract provided for the 'retraite volontaire de notre frère Philippe Augier l'aîné pour etre continué entre Etienne Augier l'un de nous, Henry et Victor Augier ses enfants sous la raison de Augier frères et Cie'. The capital of the house was 75,000 livres augmented by 1779 by 30,000 livres lent by three sisters and a further 6,000 livres lent by Etienne Augier.[92]

The house, the oldest in Cognac and reinforced at a time when the trade was on the upturn by marriages with the Broussards and the Martells in 1757 and 1762 respectively, remained a highly respected one. When Edward Galwey on the death of his son wrote with some confidence to Augier about the affairs of his daughter-in-law in La Rochelle, he was taking Augier into his confidence. Etienne Augier was one of the arbitrators for the sale of John Saule's brandy, probably the largest quantity of brandy to come on the local market in a single batch at any time in the eighteenth century. In 1789 he was elected a deputy to the States General. But whatever the personal and social standing of the family, some revival of its fortunes still left it a secondary business in the

---

[91] *Ibid.*, letter of 15 Messidor an 11, or 4 July 1803, registered 29 December 1827.
[92] *Ibid.*, 'Etat des affaires de Philippe Augier fils ainé et Etienne Augier en société sous nom de Augier Frères'.

1780s. It slipped back again in the upheavals of the 1790s, and in 1798 had the smallest stocks of eight Cognac and Jarnac houses.[93]

The emergence of Martell dominance in the 1750s and 1760s

The decline of Augier's is the most marked single feature of the story of the brandy houses in the early 1750s. Its crisis of around 1750 is also the beginning of the ascent of the house of Martell to the commanding place which it acquired in the trade in the heady vintages of the late 1750s and early 1760s. Jean Martell, having arranged affairs with his creditors in Bordeaux in January 1727, had returned a year later to Cognac,[94] and he acquired some stake in the London trade in the course of Augier's later misfortunes. His personal success in business was modest; the secret lay in his second marriage to Rachel Lallemand in 1737[95] which brought to the house the support of his brother-in-law, Louis-Gabriel Lallemand. Lallemand seems to have been in Waterford in 1743 and in the spring of that year he was sent to London for a year.[96] These visits were to give him the confidence evident in his later years in dealing with both markets. It was, we may suspect, his backing (and London contacts he had made when abroad) which turned the fortunes of the house around in the late 1740s, and on the death of Martell on 23 January 1753, Lallemand became a formal partner of the house of Veuve Martell, Lallemand et Cie. The surviving letter book of 1753 reveals that the direction of the house was in his hands, and it was this powerful figure which put the house of Martell on the map. In a sense, the future of the Martell business was secured not because it was a Martell house but because it was a Lallemand one.

It was still a small business in the 1750s. However, as Augier's dominated the London trade up to the mid-1740s, they bore the brunt of resentment over the scarcity and high prices of brandy, and custom began to drift to Martell. In one sense it neither required great faults on the part of Augier to lose the business, nor great ability on Martell's part to acquire it. The Martell (or Lallemand) letter book and turnover in 1753 establish the existence of a clear-cut stake in London. The total shipments from the *généralité* to *Angleterre* were modest; the correspondence

[93] P. Butel, 'Quelques leçons sur le dynamisme commercial de Cognac à la fin du XVIIIᵉ siècle', in Huetz and Roudié, *Eaux-de-vie et spiritueux*, p. 35.
[94] Firino-Martell, *La famille Martell*, p. 64, quoting secondary authority.
[95] For details see *ibid.*, pp. 20–1.
[96] ADC, Angouleme, J215, Martell letter book 1742–3, 26 January, 4 March, 22 April 1743 to Eynard and Engel, London; to Le Febvre, 3 June 1743.

in the letter book itself was far from voluminous and business was at a low ebb. The success of the house in the 1750s is in part explained (ignoring the demand dimension) by two circumstances on the supply side. One was some inadequacy in Augier's, at the time the major house, to turn even recovery in the brandy trade to their advantage. The fact that the father was old, that the eldest son in 1764 did not head the new partnership, and that the house was in the hands of young successors, points to some obscure family or personality problems that may have contributed to their difficulties. The other circumstance which benefited the Martells was the retreat of Paris buyers from the central districts of Cognac, when the return of better vintages restored normal supply in regions closer to Paris. Even in the adversity of the early 1750s, Martell's seems to have become the leader in the London market; with good later vintages and competitively priced cognac, Veuve Lallemand and her partner-brother were even more dominant by 1762.

This development was facilitated by the fact that peripheral activities in Cognac business with the British Isles (the Isle of Man, Guernsey, and speculative buying ahead of sale) had contracted. The London market itself as opposed to a more diffuse and more speculative trade had probably reached a new height, a circumstance also evident in the fact that by 1763 even Augier's had re-established a modest niche in it. London was after 1768 the largest single European outlet for cognac brandy, which it had never been in the past; it was also price-insensitive, and its custom, in contrast to the fluctuating Irish business, was relatively unspeculative and directed towards the highest quality, which was more aged than the rawer brandies shipped for other markets. This characteristic is reflected in turn in the remarkably stable pattern of British brandy imports until the early 1780s.

The strength of Martell's business by the outset of the 1760s is revealed in the fact not only that it dominated the London market, but that it had an important custom in other English centres such as Bristol, Ipswich, Colchester and Leeds. Moreover, from little if any place in the Irish market, Martell's had built up a commanding place in the trade there when it soared in the late 1750s. In the early 1750s, outside England, the house's only contact of consequence in the brandy trade had been with the Dublin house of Anthony McDermott. These contacts, moreover, seem to have arisen out of McDermott's use of Martell's to sell Irish beef and butter on the Charente and some casual orders from McDermott for brandy. McDermott was probably the largest Dublin house trading beyond the British Isles. The fact that he chose Martell's to represent him on the Charente was itself confirmation that they were recognised abroad as the leading Cognac house. Lallemand had hoped that these ties would turn into more valuable business: letters to McDermott both in 1753 and again in the early 1760s were written in a tone of quite uncharacteristic obsequiousness. As late as 1774, in a short-lived upturn in the Dublin trade, respect for the McDermott house resounded in the Martell letters.[97] Martell's success in controlling the entire Irish trade for a while, apparently from the late 1750s, and more durably the London trade, left them open to the suspicion of being monopolists. Their dominance in 1757–61 prompted a challenge by Irish intrusion into the region. Judging by the timing it would seem to have been a wartime shortage of spirits, an upturn in prices and good French vintages which led to the first new Irish settlement in the region. In turn, when in 1766–7 frenzied Paris and Irish buying made it difficult for Martell to give satisfaction to their established London customers on price, quality and dispatch, the house was partly abandoned, and even London orders dispersed over other houses for a short period.

[97] MAC, letter book 1774–5, 19 March 1774, to Josias Cottin et fils, London.

8 External challenge in the 1760s: vicissitudes of old and new houses, 1762–1778

The Irish challenge to Martell Lallemand et Cie

Boom attracted outsiders as it did in the case of the Le Mesuriers and Martells at the end of the 1710s. A few figures occur at other times across the century, but the only concentrated influx to the Cognac region, exclusively Irish, was in the 1760s. Martell's advent in 1718 had been welcomed because the end of the 1710s was a boom period, and common interests and common religion outweighed rivalries. The 1760s were different. Though a period of boom, the more competitive conditions of the 1760s meant that the going was harder; the outsiders had over-reaching ambitions (and arrived expressly because they regarded the local houses as providing a declining quality at rising prices) and briefly also held a technical expertise in measuring alcoholic strength which locals lacked. At the end of the 1710s, there seemed to be a highly elastic market which could be shared with incomers. In the 1760s the incomers took market share immediately and directly from Lallemand. They were also with one exception Roman Catholic, and the fact that most Dublin brandy importers were co-religionists seemed to make the competition more ominous. To some extent Lallemand could countenance an alliance between an incomer and a local house happily enough. However, even the one Protestant incomer, James Delamain, was heavily backed by Catholic houses in Dublin. A persistent tension existed into the 1780s between Martell Lallemand and the Catholic houses, and though rancour as such was not evident in relations with Delamain, the overall pattern was one of two independent circuits – a Martell Lallemand one, differentiated in business and in social ties from the Hennessy/Saule/Delamain one. The Broussards and Augiers did not belong directly to either; they were linked by several marriages to the Martell family, but in business terms tended to gravitate towards the Irish interest.

James Delamain, a Dubliner and Protestant of remote Huguenot ancestry, was the first of the new group to appear. With rum scarce and bad harvests reducing whiskey distilling, brandy, a trade less dominated by established houses, may have offered a better opportunity for a young man to make a career as a merchant. On the evidence of the sole surviving journal of Isaac Ranson, Jarnac's leading merchant, a consignment of brandy to Delamain is recorded on 14 August 1759 as shipped on joint account with Robert Nevin in Dublin.[1] From the evidence of later orders, it had proved a success. It may well be that Ranson, looking for a wider market, turned to the services of Delamain, who in turn, as an under-employed young merchant already attempting to build up a business in wine (a charmed and capital-intensive commerce hard to break into), would be only too ready to undertake commissions to expand brandy business in Dublin. In the course of a passing visit in 1757, Delamain may have offered his services to help Ranson find a foreign market; the orders by Nevin may have been the first outcome, and a prelude to a more direct association between Delamain and Ranson. This had come into existence by late 1760. Marriage to Ranson's daughter and partnership both followed in 1762.

The marriage thus followed from rather than preceded a successful business relationship, but it cemented it, and made it a much more effective one. As the evidence from the *controle des actes* for Jarnac shows, the Ranson family were deeply imbedded in the business and social life of Jarnac. With Delamain's advent a unique business emerged: one with a large foreign trade and an established custom with Paris. The house had as many correspondents in Paris as it had abroad in the late 1760s. No other house in the region permanently combined foreign and domestic trade. In turn when foreign trade grew more difficult, dependence on Paris increasingly reasserted itself. Ranson's daughter's dowry at 7,000 livres might have seemed small in Dublin or Bordeaux terms, but it was as large as other dowries in the brandy trade in the bigger centre of Cognac at the time or in the preceding decades.

What Delamain had to offer as a young foreigner was essentially contacts and knowledge of an important outside market, and the assurances and backing of one or more of the new 'clubs' of importers emerging in Dublin with the purpose of making the ownership or chartering of vessels for Charente worthwhile. Delamain's personal ability was probably quite decisive. Ranson himself could confer no advantage on him either for the Dublin or the London market. Lallemand, the driving force in the Martell house, thought Delamain 'un brave homme', noting that 'I wont tell you may guess Messrs Delamain and Ranson acted wisely wanting each other'.[2] Activity quickly encroached on the established Martell position. As early as October 1762 Lallemand was reduced to writing to

---

[1] HAJ, journal of Isaac Ranson, October 1758–16 March 1761.
[2] MAC, letter book 1762–4, 15 May 1763, to S. Mitchell.

Anthony McDermott (or Dermott), his 'oldest acquaintance' there for support: 'Pray be our protector when ships are freighted to come over in our river. We find our friends in your place are hardly pressed to leave us which we cant help if such is their inclination.'[3] By December, he was forced to admit to McDermott that 'Ranson & Delamain have got the better of us. Pray tell ingeniously [sic] if they owe it to the quality of the goods or their protectors'.[4]

The discontent which accounted for Ranson and Delamain's initial success also prompted others to venture to Cognac (in Laurence Saule's case the germ of the idea might have gone back to 1759). The changes were prompted by growing dissatisfaction with the services of the buying houses in Cognac. As always in a boom, buyers ran into problems over price, quality or speed of dispatch. More persistent as a complaint was an alleged decline in quality or strength. How real the decline was is not apparent. As measuring instruments became commonplace in London and Dublin at this time, the barrage of complaints may simply have reflected a new-found sophistication in the appraisal of alcohol in both cities. For London the problem was not as acute as for Dublin because it had been customary to add spirit to cognac brandy to bring it up to a higher London standard, though similar complaints even occurred there, as Lallemand's letters show. To Thomas Egan in Dublin Lallemand laid the blame on 'too many hands . . . the reason that we get no brandy as strong as we used to do'.[5] As the dominant supplier of the Dublin market, Martell Lallemand bore the brunt of the recriminations from Dublin,[6] and this was inevitably reflected in business.

By June 1763 Lallemand had been reduced to lamenting to a fellow Huguenot outside Cognac that 'je ne suis aussi jeune et astuce que Monsieur Delamain'.[7] In the Dublin brandy boom by the time peace was in prospect, the importers had developed into competing clubs – at the peak there were at least four – to combine orders to a scale that would make the dispatch of direct vessels to load in the Charente economic, and Martell's first real business with Ireland came from them. The Dublin brandy 'clubs' owned their own shipping, often with a relative as master, and in fierce competition with one another became interested in establishing a foothold of their own in Cognac. From the outset James Delamain had Dublin backers, and Anthony McDermott seems to have encouraged the setting up of Antoine Galwey's business in La Rochelle,

[3] Ibid., 4 October, 1762. The reference to McDermott as their oldest acquaintance in Dublin is in a letter of 14 November 1763 to McDermott.
[4] Ibid., 6 December 1762.   [5] Ibid., 21 March 1763, to Thomas Egan.
[6] Ibid.., 13 June 1763, to Thomas Egan; 24 June 1763, to David Walsh.
[7] Ibid., 4 June 1763, to Charrier l'ainé, Rochefort.

not for personal interest but for the benefit of sons or relatives. The two groups made up the backbone of much of the Dublin market. These events lost Martell's much, although not all of their Irish business, which was in any event a very recent acquisition. Lallemand's Dublin business was decimated by 1766: he held the business of only one of the four important shipping groups, or 'clubs' as he had once called them, and by 1763 the prestigious independent merchants had entirely disappeared from his order book. The McDermott circle would appear to have ordered though Galwey and in the 1766–7 boom when Dublin orders soared and reliance on houses at the heart of the brandy region became useful, very probably were an added factor in the remarkable expansion of Laurence Saule's business.

As if this was not bad enough, Martell's hold on the London trade declined in 1766 and 1767. As they were better established in the London trade, high prices and disputes over quality were less likely to take a toll than in the Dublin trade. In January 1767 in the Leeds trade Lallemand was writing that 'we are surprised that your neighbour receives stronger spirits from Messrs Augier than what we have sent you'.[8] But quality was not a real issue in the London trade, as the addition of spirit to bring brandy for London up to standard was well established, and the houses paid the extra costs entered on the invoices. What seems to have been the decisive factor which cost Lallemand the custom of London houses, and that of the important house of Steele in particular, was the sheer difficulty of getting supplies as the Irish trade soared: vessels took a long time to load (coopering in particular proved a bottleneck), and, most damaging of all, brandy for some houses got to market later than brandy for rivals.[9] With a loss of confidence in Martell's on this score, orders were now much more divided among Cognac houses as a form of insurance of supply, and Lallemand lamented that 'the widow Martell & Lallemand are nowadays good for nothing, because they are no more in fashion'.[10]

Martell Lallemand lost ground over the period from 1762 to 1767. Faced in 1762 with the loss of their Irish business and with crisis even in their longer-standing London business in 1766–7, the letter books become uncommonly revealing. In the vivid prose of Lallemand the challenge was a real one, particularly in the Irish trade as opposed to the London trade where the crisis was short-lived. At that stage the powerful and fiery spirit of Lallemand comes across with more vigour and force than any other letter writer on the Charente in the eighteenth century. His drive built up the business in the late 1750s and he was to see off the chal-

---

[8] *Ibid.*, letter book 1766–7, 12 January 1767, to Hutchinson, Leeds.
[9] *Ibid.*, see especially letter of 2 March 1767 to Morgan Rice as illustrating the importance attached to this point.   [10] *Ibid.*, 30 March, 13 April 1767, to Morgan Rice.

lenge of the 1760s. He must be seen as the true creator of the standing and durability of the house, and his successful response to the challenge was arguably the largest part of his legacy to the firm.

The impact of the Delamain presence in the region, the first harbinger of challenge, was reinforced by Galwey's venture ordering from La Rochelle. Antoine Galwey first appeared in France in Saintes in 1757 to learn French. His status was reflected in his later marriage to a La Rochelle lady: her father was a Colonel Labadie, her dowry was very substantial, and her mother, 'the proud, the haughty Miss Butler formerly',[11] was one of the La Rochelle Butler family, long the city's leading business family, who had eventually forsaken the pinnacle of the city's commerce for a more aristocratic lifestyle. Galwey's place in the trade, ordering from La Rochelle through the Broussards in Cognac for direct shipment from the Charente, was well established by mid-1763. The virtual absence of orders from Anthony McDermott after 1763 and the slow realisation by Lallemand over four years that McDermott had also abandoned their house points to a source of Dublin orders for Galwey from the entourage of what was one of the most powerful houses in Dublin. Yet Galwey's activity engendered little of the emotional concern that others occasioned for him. If Galwey represented challenge, it was less serious than others. His business took the form of an alliance between an outsider, and an existing – and Protestant – house.

The advent of a third house, that of Saule and Jennings, was, however, quite a different matter from competition by Galwey which was organised through the agency of established local houses, or by Delamain who was in partnership with an existing house: such business had not disrupted established ties between shippers and sellers. Saule and Jennings were total outsiders, and were also (unlike the handful of German merchants who entered the region but remained in Tonnay-Charente as mere buyers from established native houses in the 1750s) involved in the trade with the British Isles, the only trade in which Martell Lallemand had a share. In contrast to the Galweys (from a Munster background) and even to Delamain (despite his close associations with Dublin Catholics), Saule and Jennings were from the central milieu of articulate Catholic merchants in Dublin, prominent in the Catholic Committee which emerged in the second half of the 1750s, and thus they counted on the backing of an expanding Catholic interest in the rapidly growing spirit market in Dublin. From the outset they expressly intended to dictate terms to the

---

[11] HAC, 12 August 1773, John Saule, La Rochelle, to Richard Hennessy. See also file on the de Galwey succession in ADCM, La Rochelle, notaire de la Vergne, no. 177. On the origins of the La Rochelle Butler house, see L. M. Cullen, 'Galway merchants in the outside world 1650–1800', in *Galway town and gown 1484–1984*, p. 66.

native suppliers. The earliest reference to the house is in a letter of 15 August 1763 to Lallemand's Dublin correspondent Matthew Stritch expressing surprise that: 'Gentlemen of great property beloved in Dublin and settled there can think of settling at Charente or even in any place in this country. I am sure I should incline to the reverse if I was in good circumstance enough to bear it.'[12]

Though an outsider, Jennings lost no time in striving to have a standard settled for the brandy shipped (by which he meant measurement by instrument rather than the hit-or-miss empirical 'proof') but 'we doubt of his success therein, and believe that everyone should be allowed to do his best for his friends' interest'.[13] As an erratic quality was, on Lallemand's own admission, one of the problems in the trade and dissatisfaction had promoted upheaval, he was on the defensive. The reference hints at the first appearance of the hydrometer in the region: it points to Jennings' efforts to buy brandy at its hydrometer strength, and Lallemand's less than enthusiastic attitude to the new instrument (though he was in fact quick to adopt it).

As late as 23 November, Laurence Saule had not yet been seen in person by Lallemand on the banks of the Charente. By that time he had, however, already appeared in the region, executing a master stroke in negotiating with success for all the supplies of the house of Gourg of Saint-Jean d'Angély in a rising market. Three years later Lallemand noted Saule's intention to overtake Ranson and Delamain.[14] Shortly afterwards, in the aftermath of the great expansion in the Dublin trade in 1767, the list of Saule's Dublin correspondents was impressive, larger than that of either Lallemand or Delamain.[15] In 1768 he had no less than fifty correspondents there. His seventeen Irish correspondents outside Dublin emphasise his place in the Catholic business world of the day, as they included some of the major Catholic merchants.

Fortunately for Martell Lallemand, Saule's expansion of his business coincided with soaring prices for brandy and emerging price resistance in Dublin, which in turn led into a falling market there in 1767. As Saule was the major shipper on the vessels that congregated in record numbers on the Charente in January 1767, he probably continued to hold that position in the following months. Of the ten vessels, Stritch, Lallemand's correspondent in Dublin, reported in mid-year that 'seven have given so

---

[12] MAC, letter book 1762–4, 15 August 1763, to Matthew Stritch.
[13] *Ibid.*, 7 November 1763, to Matthew Stritch.
[14] *Ibid.*, letter book 1766–7, 4 October 1766, to Matthew Stritch; 20 October 1766, to Richard Bennis.
[15] HAC, 'L. Saule's correspds. in 1768', in John Saule's hand, attached to James Tuke's letter of 7 November 1776. Delamain in the 1760s had thirty-six Dublin correspondents, Martell about thirty, and Hennessy only twenty-four.

much profit to their owners that they are now out of the trade'.[16] Martell
Lallemand and Co. escaped difficulty because their Dublin business was
now so low. Lallemand thought that Ranson and Delamain escaped too,
and the Ranson and Delamain letter book for 1767–8 reveals caution in
dealing with Dublin houses. The problem would have been less serious
for Saule if he had acted on the signals from Dublin. Making the mistake
of prolonging his huge expansion in 1766 into the more doubtful circumstances of 1767, Saule unwisely held on to the lead in the trade that he
had established for the first time in the spring of 1767. In October he was
the sole loader of a vessel,[17] probably the same vessel which, according to
Hennessy, had been consigned to 'a very principal house' and for which
the huge cargo of 200 to 300 puncheons was on hand.[18] At the end of a
difficult brandy season, such a very large stock, if acquired in anticipation
of Dublin orders, could only have been sold by abatements on the high
purchase price.

As there was remarkably little brandy in Saule's inventory of 1 October
1768, much of his brandy must already have been thrown on the market
at low prices. Price cutting on brandies purchased in anticipation of
orders was certainly in evidence in the spring of 1768. In May Delamain
noted that both Saule and Hennessy had invoiced brandy at lower prices
than he had.[19] Death, however, was even more effective in removing
Martell Lallemand's most serious rivals: Jennings died in late 1766, Saule
two years later in September 1768. Death also carried away Antoine
Galwey unexpectedly so that the two most serious Irish challenges by
Catholics, after a forceful impact, had melted away. Two others, Luke
Bellew and Richard Hennessy, had also arrived. Both were ex-army
officers, counting on success in the trade because of a network of immediate relatives in business in Ireland. However, after a fleeing appearance in
Charente in 1765, Bellew died in Britain in 1767 while setting up a rather
ambitious trade network. That left Richard Hennessy as the sole survivor
of the group apart from Delamain.

Hennessy's arrival was unobtrusive, and little reference occurs in the
archives of Augier, and more tellingly in the numerous letters received by
Broussard *fils*. Even in the sustained commentary by Lallemand in 1766

---

[16] MAC, letter book 1766–7, 1 June 1767, to Mathew Stritch. Dublin failures were noted as
early as 12 January in a letter from Lallemand to Stritch.
[17] DAJ, letter book 1767–8, 13 October 1767, to McLaughlin.
[18] HAC, letter book 1765–9, 5 October 1767, to Connelly and Arthur.
[19] DAJ, letter book 1767–8, 24 May 1768, to B. and J. Richard, Charente. This suspicion is
confirmed in a later admission by Hennessy that in May he had reduced his invoices 5
livres below the prices at which he had purchased in order to ship at the same price as
Saule and Ranson and Delamain. HAC, letter book 1765–9, 21 November 1768, to
Connelly and Arthur.

and 1767 his name recurs less frequently than that of the peripatetic Bellew and Bellew's putative partners, the London house of Wenman and Broughton. The only really positive reference was dismissive: 'la maison Hennessy a toujours peu de chose à charger. C'est ce que nous saurons mieux dans la suite'.[20] The style of the house was first Connelly, Hennessy et Cie (denoting the association with the Dunkirk house) and then Hennessy et Cie. Hennessy had no firm personal backing, and was later to resent the lack of practical support from his Galwey relatives in Bordeaux who first raised the question of his settling in Cognac. Unlike the other merchants he was relatively old at forty-one years of age, compared with Delamain who was twenty-three when he arrived in 1760 or John Saule (Laurence Saule's nephew) who was twenty-five when he finally formed a partnership with Hennessy in 1776. He had left the French army in 1753 and had spent the interval in Ostend, doing some business on his own account and hoping for a place in the Ostend business of his Hennessy relatives. Marriage to the widow of one of them in 1762 gave him a little capital, and encouragement from Bordeaux relatives provided the catalyst. Arriving at a time of crisis the house had few prospects and had little more than a vestigial role in the trade. Hennessy's thoughts turned early to the idea of leaving Cognac: the house barely made ends meet and from 1776 Hennessy lived in Bordeaux. Only Delamain's business had an uninterrupted existence, and that accounted for the respect both John Saule, without a business interest of his own, and Hennessy, trying to keep a small and struggling house afloat, had for Delamain, who from the start shouldered a patriarchal and helpful responsibility towards all Irish compatriots.

James Delamain's business

In 1762 Delamain's success in the trade was one of the dominant themes in the letters of Louis-Gabriel Lallemand. Though the vicissitudes of trade were such that Delamain never again occupied the place that he acquired so speedily in the first half of the 1760s, he was ever present in the story of the changing fortunes of the little world of the Irish settlers who arrived in the 1760s and in their social life. When Laurence Saule died in 1768 Delamain was executor of the estate. He helped to set up John Saule, Laurence's nephew, in La Rochelle in 1769 and supported him when he moved to Cognac in 1776. He provided support on several occasions for Hennessy in his disastrous business in Bordeaux between 1776 and 1788. When John Saule's death led to the insolvency of his firm,

[20] MAC, letter book 1766–7, 23 August 1766, to Gast Lallemand.

it was Delamain's introduction of a nephew, Samuel Turner, which put a new Hennessy house on its feet, since he must have provided Turner's share of the capital. If it was a godsend for the Hennessys, whose father was a business incompetent and whose son was still inexperienced, it was equally so for Samuel Turner.

James Delamain was a man of extraordinary personal authority, probably the most arresting person among the merchants on the banks of the Charente in the second half of the century though the circle included figures as captivating as John Saule or Richard Hennessy and as forceful as Louis-Gabriel Lallemand. As a young man of twenty-three years in 1760 and an outsider, he gained a central position, drawing a grudging admiration from Lallemand. Although he was a Huguenot by religion and married into the main trading family of the minor centre of Jarnac, he did not conform to the profile of merchants in a tight little world which had never reached beyond the narrow ties of family, religion and profession. Though all the settlers on the banks of the Charente were perforce rivals, he quickly befriended the newcomers from Dublin without exception. As early as 1768 we can trace them being invited to dine, and the friendships began earlier, because in that year he was already an executor of the estate of Laurence Saule.

Alone among the established merchants in the region his business correspondence sometimes strayed into wider events or a larger world. Even in writing of some legal nicety in 1789 (apparently the Regency crisis) he commented to an Irish merchant in London that 'your parliamentary debates are very extensive on a question most easy to resolve'. He went on to praise parliament and its prime minister William Pitt: 'on its steadfastness are founded the prosperity and liberty of the nation. We conclude the subject with most cordial wish that so upright so judicious a man as Mr Pitt may ever be at the head of affairs'.[21] The *donation entre vifs* (transfer of property between living parties) by his widow Marie Ranson in 1813 hints at the scale of the library he had left behind him: fifty-eight volumes of the *Encyclopédie*, six volumes of the Bible, 818 bound volumes and 212 soft-covered volumes (*broches*).[22] He was not the only well-read man among the merchants. John Saule probably surpassed him as a reader and book collector but Delamain's learning was matched by a maturity and authority which Saule lacked.

Like Hennessy and Saule, Delamain was a freemason, but while Saule took a childish pleasure in the rituals of the masons, it brought Delamain into contact with the social milieu of the region's great nobility. In

[21] HAJ, Delamain no. 2 letter book, 1787–9, 31 January 1789, to Thomas Gorman.
[22] Braastad archives, Cognac.

December 1778, for instance, unable to attend an assembly at Condac (Coudac?), near Ruffec, he asked for his respects to be conveyed to the comte de Broglie.[23] He had some contact with the duc de la Rochefoucauld. He obliged him occasionally with bills of exchange on Paris, on one occasion apparently in payment for brandy received. His most regular contact in this circle was with Charles-Rosalie de Rohan-Chabot, comte de Jarnac. The first known contact with him is in an intemperate letter from the count in 1767, which while it speaks well of Delamain makes clear the count's resentment of an attempt led, he believed, by Ranson to avoid the feudal obligation of baking bread in the manorial oven.[24] Subsequently the contact was closer and more harmonious. Before her marriage to the count at the end of 1776, Elisabeth Smith, the daughter of an Irish landowner, resided in Delamain's house,[25] and on occasion in subsequent years Delamain obliged the count in the matter of remitting money from Ireland to France. The count in turn took an interest in the affairs of the brandy trade. The representations at court which resulted in a reduction in duties on the export trade seem to have been made by the count. In April 1784 Delamain informed a Dublin merchant that 'Count Jarnac who has very great influence at court is now here, the writer is constantly employed with him finishing materials and observations to that salutary end and we shall have the first knowledge through this channel'.[26] Delamain's readiness to speak out on behalf of the trade of the region was in evidence again in 1789 when he wrote to Necker.[27]

The pace of events in July 1789 took Delamain by surprise, and in fact his business did badly in the 1790s, a result of his own caution or fear, and conflict with his sons, perhaps as a result of an authoritarian streak in his otherwise attractive personality. In turnover Delamain's trade was one of the two largest in the 1760s and 1770s and at some point in the 1760s probably the largest. However, with an exclusively Dublin background and no previous associations in foreign trade which could give him the London contacts that individuals from a more established mercantile background like Hennessy, Saule or Martell enjoyed, he had scarcely any London correspondence. His only sustained English business arose from the trade in flaxseed and return in coals which gave him a way into a brandy custom in Hull and Newcastle. The association was in particular very close with the house of Berry, later Knowsley. In 1789 Knowsley had in contemplation an even closer association.[28]

[23] HAJ, Delamain no. 2 letter book 1778–81, 8 December 1778, to de Mordieu.
[24] R. Delamain, *Jarnac à travers les ages* (2nd edn, Angouleme, 1954), pp. 163–4.
[25] *Ibid.*, p. 174.
[26] HAJ, Delamain no 2 letter book 1783–5, 17 April 1784, to Alley and Darby.
[27] *Ibid.*, Delamain no. 2 letter book,1787–9, 7 March 1789, to Necker.
[28] *Ibid.*, Delamain no. 1 letter book 1787–9, 12 September 1789, to Knowsley, Hull.

Delamain led Cognac in the number of his Irish correspondents. He was overshadowed only fleetingly in that market by Laurence Saule who unwisely expanded his business in 1767 at a time when Delamain sagely anticipated the adverse turn of the market. In June 1767 he told Pearl, captain of a Dublin vessel, that he was without fresh orders of any sort for Dublin.[29] In the Irish trade, when it contracted, he reassumed the leading position. As late as 1783 he was able to observe that 'from our first establishment here we believe we have done more business for Ireland than all the other houses in the country put together'.[30] What saved Delamain's business in the aftermath of the crisis in the Irish business in 1767 was their Paris trade. In August 1768, for instance, Delamain sent thirty-six circular letters to Paris.[31] In 1768 at the end of the great Irish boom, Delamain seems to have had more than one English-speaking clerk. By 1782, on the other hand, when Delamain took ill, the English correspondence had to be suspended because no one else in the house knew English.[32] Delamain's business is a fascinating one. Even Lallemand conceded in the early 1760s that Delamain's shipped a stronger brandy, and in 1799 Delamain wrote to a London house that 'we are surprised at what you mention that your friends complain the brandy they received from us was coarse. We have the reputation of shipping the best that leaves the country'.[33] Delamain made his own spirit for topping up his brandy, and this may have been a factor in guaranteeing quality. He had at various times eight to twelve stills manufacturing spirit,[34] and since it was located at the water's edge his distilling operation unlike much rural activity was never halted by a shortage of water.

Brandy distilling in Bordeaux

The later story of the little Irish colony, survivors of the upheavals of the 1760s, revolves around three individuals: John Saule, Richard Hennessy and James Delamain. In contrast to Delamain, both Saule and Hennessy made an inauspicious start to their business careers and neither held much of the Irish trade in the 1760s or 1770s. Most remarkable of the friendships was that between Hennessy and Saule. Saule was a nephew of Laurence Saule, and with Delamain's aid was fixed up with a partnership in a trading business in La Rochelle. The business of the La Rochelle concern was quite good. However, commission earnings did not admit of

---

[29] DAJ, letter book 1767–8, 27 June 1767, to Capt. Pearl.
[30] HAJ, Delamain no. 2 letter book 1783–5, 11 November 1783, to Alley and Darby.
[31] DAJ, letter book, 1767–8, letters of 23 August 1768.
[32] HAJ, Delamain no. 2 letter book 1781–3, 20 August 1782.
[33] *Ibid.*, Delamain no. 2 letter book, 1797–1801, 22 September 1799, to Yeats.
[34] Eight stills are mentioned in DAJ, letter book, 1767–8, 2 August 1768, to Bateson, Belfast. The higher figure emerges at a later date.

a large profit, once spread over three partners. Fortune hunting, he pursued a Cognac heiress, Victoire Bernard, for whose family his modest circumstances had little appeal. Hence, if he was to succeed it was necessary to think of a new business move. Richard Hennessy, whose business, after some modest recovery between 1773 and 1775, had not sustained its momentum, had entered once more into negotiations in Bordeaux, and was intent on moving there. Plans now began to take shape between the two friends: Saule would retain his interest in the house in La Rochelle, but would move to Cognac as a partner in a new firm of Hennessy and Co. to handle the brandy business after Hennessy's departure to Bordeaux.[35]

At the end of the year Saule finally moved to Cognac. But if the move in some respects helped Saule to press his suit more effectively (though against the opposition of the Bernard family), in other respects it was distinctly disadvantageous. The brandy trade was disastrously bad in 1777 and 1778, in part because with poorer vintages demand from Paris pushed prices up to a level which discouraged foreign buyers on whom all the *négociants* of Cognac depended. In the two years from 30 September 1776 to 14 December 1778, Saule shipped a mere 121½ puncheons of brandy, a figure which, converted to an annual basis, would have been a mere third of what Hennessy shipped in his worst years between 1766 and 1776. In other words his economic situation could only have further reduced his appeal for the family. Marriage to Victoire Bernard in 1778 did help him, and the volume of business recovered modestly, and finally in 1782 at 595½ puncheons it had reached a new peak for the house. Saule's better fortune had really set in by the spring of 1781: 120 puncheons were shipped off in a vessel in April 1781 and he was looking for a vessel to ship off another 100 puncheons.[36]

As for the reasons for Hennessy's move, the total quantities of brandy in his invoices tell the tale. Business which had picked up in 1773 and 1774 fell in 1775. At the end of almost ten years in Cognac, with a family and young children to support, Hennessy must have been in despair at his prospects. As far back as August 1775 he had had an interview with John Galwey, and by the end of November his intention of quitting Cognac was sufficiently well defined for Saule to refer to the proposal of his taking Hennessy's place in Cognac.[37] Business got even worse in the aftermath of the 1775 vintage. In 1776 Hennessy's turnover was halved. So desperate was he that he envisaged the possibility of setting up with Galwey's help in Cork or Le Havre. Bordeaux itself remained a possibility, and Saule advised Hennessy that it:

[35] There was a long and detailed run of letters from Saule to Hennessy on their projects at this time.   [36] HAC, 1 April 1781, Cognac.
[37] *Ibid.*, 24 August, 30 November 1775, La Rochelle.

would seem to me to suit you much better than any proposed plan as yet, should you be determined to quit Cognac. There your friends in Ireland could be of use to you, and Mr Galwey himself render you most essential service. There again you might reap still some advantage of your settlement in Cognac. You would only change places, the trade would continue the same, and he that gave satisfaction on the shipping cognac brandies [sic] may surely do as much in the Bordeaux brandy, beside other branches which may fall in your way.[38]

In a wider sense a factor influencing Hennessy to turn to Bordeaux rather than to try his luck in Cork or Le Havre was some upturn in Bordeaux's brandy trade in contrast to persistent problems in Cognac's foreign trade. Bordeaux's general volume of brandy business did not rise greatly, but there were encouraging signs, and Bordeaux expanded its markets in Russia and in the Guinea and colonial trades. The quantities shipped to Ireland in the *bureau de la balance du commerce* figures for Bordeaux, understate business, because as direct sailings from the Charente to Ireland declined, greater quantities of cognac brandy, recorded for statistical purposes in the trade returns of the La Rochelle *généralité*, were transhipped in Bordeaux. Relatively modest though the turnover in brandy in Bordeaux was, the absence of sophisticated distilling in its hinterland entailed a disproportionate rise in distilling in the port itself to raise the strength of brandy to the now-fashionable spirit strength. Over the 1770s the distilling and rectifying business prospered. Some Bordeaux brandy had even made an appearance on the London or Dunkirk markets, and some brandy in the Entre-deux-mers region was being distilled up to spirit strength.[39] A Dublin house claimed in 1772 that 'people here begin to relish it almost as well as the cognac', and in 1773 Hennessy's Bordeaux relative Galwey was sanguine about the quality of the new rectified brandies.[40] Dublin's preference for Bordeaux over Cognac was claimed encouragingly by a Dublin correspondent in late 1776.[41] In June Thomas Blake told Hennessy that the new methods in Bordeaux would cause a decline in cognac, and some parcels from Bordeaux to Dunkirk had been forwarded to England.[42] Hennessy's kinsman, James Nagle, encouraged him to move, adding that young McCarthy of Bordeaux maintained that 'you can not fail of making a fortune'.[43] There was not, as events proved, much basis to this confidence. It remained an inferior product, and its markets were marginal and fluctuating.

---

[38] *Ibid.,* 1 February 1776, Cognac.
[39] AAC, copy letters to English correspondents, 16 January, 6 March, 18 December 1769, to Smith and Harrison, London.
[40] HAC, 2 June 1772, Tom Egan, Dublin, to Hennessy; 11 June 1773, John Galwey, Bordeaux, to Hennessy.   [41] *Ibid.*, 7 November 1776, James Tuke, Dublin.
[42] *Ibid.*, 3 June 1776, Thomas Blake, Ostend, to Hennessy.
[43] *Ibid.*, 1 July 1776, James Nagle, Libourne, to Richard Hennessy.

Such marginal or exceptional demands in a year when supplies in and around Cognac were being absorbed by Paris created a false sense of bright prospects a hundred kilometres further afield in Bordeaux just beyond the reach of the greedy Parisians. Prospects were brightest in distilling itself. If demand rose, marginal and erratic supplies of the indifferent and weak brandy from the hinterland of Bordeaux, plus brandy from Mortagne, were rectified to spirit strength. For such a business distilling skill was at a premium, and the distilling operation in Bordeaux, not manufacturing in the hinterland, was the linchpin of the export trade from the Gironde. The distiller Hilary Andoe from Dublin had already settled there in 1774 and was to remain in the city for the next twenty years. Hennessy's move was into distilling, and he brought a distiller with him from Cognac. Thus, in theory at least, his experience as a *négociant* combined with the professional skills from Cognac should have equipped him to do well in the boom that the Irish circle optimistically read into the fickle demands of the 1770s. Hennessy finally set out in September.

Hennessy's problems were two-fold. The first – and more long-term one – was the erratic nature of Bordeaux brandy distilling. The second, and immediately more serious problem, was Hennessy's want of capital. Before going to Bordeaux he sought a partner, and even had in mind Roullet, a man with whom Saule had had a fleeting disastrous partnership at an earlier date. Saule dissuaded him from this step, and advised him, given the needs of his family, not to seek a partner at all.[44] However, Hennessy would have been quite unable to set himself up without some backing. Here, as on other occasions, Delamain came to the rescue. He seems to have guaranteed Hennessy's credit in Paris, and even provided 9,000 livres for his establishment in Bordeaux.[45] Thus from the outset Hennessy had difficulties in making a go of the business. This explains why, despite Saule's advice to the contrary, he took a partner, George Boyd, shortly after he had set himself up. When the partnership was concluded, the style of the firm remained Hennessy and Co. This was a typical case of a younger merchant, Boyd, making his debut with a supposedly more experienced partner. Boyd's attraction was the capital resources provided by his brother-in-law, David Skinner. Quite apart from any capital he may have provided, he was a guaranteed source of orders. Deeply involved in trade with Britain and Scandinavia, Skinner's interest in the distilling trade was no doubt similar to that of the Galweys: he provided both brandy and spirit for his foreign customers, and had rec-

---

[44] *Ibid.*, 9 July 1776, La Rochelle.
[45] *Ibid.*, 27 January 1778, Bordeaux.

tifying commissions to give out. At the beginning of 1777 the partnership was already in effect when William Coppinger observed to Saule that Hennessy's 'association with Boyd proves essential and good. They will do a great deal in the burning way'.[46] The reference to the 'essential' character of the association is in effect a comment on Hennessy's shortage of capital.

The Bordeaux distilling business, producing a brandy with little repute, was a marginal activity responding to vagaries in demand. In 1776 distilling was for the time being a prosperous business. In early 1777 these prospects had collapsed. The reason was in part the decline in Irish demand which had buoyed up Bordeaux distilling in 1776, and which was worsened by a sharp credit crisis in Dublin in the spring of 1777. In April 1777 Hennessy retailed the business failures in Dublin which helped to make 'brandy a very bad article there. God preserve our friends'.[47] So bad were conditions that Hennessy's stills were to remain unlit for two months.[48] Things then recovered a little but in February 1779 he lamented that 'I am again idle'. In some respects the situation was even more serious, because while the Dublin credit crisis (a by-product of financial stringency in London) had lifted, war produced a deepening one in Bordeaux, the true dimensions of which only gradually unfolded. On 10 May 1779 eighteen failures were reported in a single day, and many people had taken refuge in the countryside to avoid their importunate creditors.[49]

Things seem to have picked up again towards the middle of 1779, at least in the brandy trade.[50] By means of masked vessels the general commodity trade with Ireland remained relatively buoyant during the war; that meant that any upturn in demand for spirits would be quickly felt in Bordeaux, the more so as in wartime vessels were much scarcer in the Charente than in Bordeaux. By the end of the year, however, things were once more on the downturn, perhaps even more so than at any previous juncture. However, illustrating the speculative nature of the distilling business, the bad conditions of 1779 had turned into 'a terrible hurry' in the following April with six ships loading for Ireland at one time. From 18 February to 23 March 1780 Hennessy's twelve stills never stopped, and the partnership had purchased 400 *pièces* for rectification.[51] At the beginning of August six to ten stills were still working, and even as late as September, despite the cash shortage in Bordeaux, he reported that 'we will have a good deal to do for three Irish ships'.[52] New wine duties in

[46] *Ibid.*, 4 January 1777, Bordeaux, William Coppinger.   [47] *Ibid.*, 8 April 1777, Bordeaux.
[48] *Ibid.*, 10 June 1777, Bordeaux.   [49] *Ibid.*, 18 May 1779, Bordeaux.
[50] *Ibid.*, 29 June, 17 August 1779.   [51] *Ibid.*, 1 or 7 April 1780, Bordeaux.
[52] *Ibid.*, 1 September 1780, Bordeaux.

Ireland accounted for the upturn in the spring: some 3,000 tons of wine had been shipped for Ireland in a short space of time to beat the deadline.[53] A large number of vessels loading wine always generated some demand for brandy and the distribution of commissions to distil to the required strength. New legislation in Ireland which restricted distilling in small stills augmented the demand as well: in the long term the legislation simply encouraged clandestine distilling, but in the short term – into the mid-1780s – it created an artificial but real shortage in Dublin. However, news of the seizure of some of the masked vessels, filtering back to Bordeaux in July, threw doubts over this method of conducting trade.[54] Though the doubts were later resolved, the crisis halted the boom in the trade for Dublin. The Irish colony no longer had a means of escaping from the wartime depression in Bordeaux which was now reaching its peak. Although trade under masked colours was later able to continue in the knowledge that British war vessels were prepared to close their eyes to what was afoot, British or Irish shipping under masked colours remained fair game for French or American privateers.

By December 1780 a number of the Irish houses had halted payments: significantly the houses which did so were all deep into the Dublin wine trade. Hennessy commented: 'you can judge how those faileurs [*sic*] have hurt the credit of the factory particularly the young and striving part'.[55] By March 1781 things were even worse: 'the credit of the factory is now at the lowest ebb, there are not people wanting to say every house of them will stop'.[56] Hennessy's financial problems scarcely lessened in these times. In December he had noted that some had proposed supporting him, but then dropped the idea because of the badness of the times.[57] His brandy business too was now at a standstill.[58] There was subsequently a limited pick-up in business which helped to save Hennessy from utter disaster. But with brandy more freely available over the period, the Dublin market in February 1782 was said to be glutted.[59]

At the nadir of Hennessy's fortunes, as in 1772 and 1775, the question of abandoning France altogether came up. On this occasion, the prospect of setting up elsewhere arose in the context of an improvement in the prospective fortunes of his brother-in-law, Ned Barrett, who had virtually disappeared from Hennessy's correspondence in the mid-1770s, and now hoped to gain employment through the influence of their mutual relative,

[53] *Ibid.,* 29 May 1780, Bordeaux.
[54] There is an illuminating series of letters on the trade using masked vessels in State Papers Ireland, SP 63/470, f. 149, legal opinion of Patrick Duigenan, 1 July 1780, and ff. 151, 153, petitions of the owners of the cargoes of the *Nelly* and the *Providence.*
[55] HAC, 8 December 1780, Bordeaux.   [56] *Ibid.,* 23 March 1781, Bordeaux.
[57] *Ibid.,* 8 December 1780, Bordeaux.   [58] *Ibid.,* 3 July 1781, Bordeaux.
[59] *Ibid.,* 8 February 1782, Bordeaux.

the great Edmund Burke, fleetingly paymaster-general in a British government. Barrett suggested that Hennessy should go out with him, and settle in Barbados or one of the neighbouring islands. Hennessy expected that the sale of his interest in the business in Bordeaux would cover his debts. His personal expectations were modest: 'if there was a possibility of obtaining the management of a plantation in his or any of the neighbouring islands, I would think myself equal to it'.[60]

A post of overseer required no capital, and it was usually an outlet for a younger man of limited backing and prospects. That this was the hope of a man of fifty-eight shows how desperate Hennessy was, and how the horizons of his world had closed in. However, over the summer months the plans seem to have changed, as Hennessy did not sail with Barrett as the latter had proposed. The plan now was that after Barrett's arrival in the West Indies he would send for Hennessy's eldest son in the following year. But the plans came to nought, Barrett was shipwrecked, and by January 1783 was dead.[61] Mishap and death thus brought the plan for Hennessy's son to an end. Hennessy did not pursue his own plan of going to the West Indies any further. One reason for having already changed it in 1782 into a simpler plan of carving out a modest career for his son was that with prospects of peace in 1782 and a bad harvest in Ireland the fickle distilling business in Bordeaux staged an upturn.

Brandy business in Cognac in the 1770s

In essence the story of the 1770s is that overall foreign business in Cognac was too small to be profitable to more than a single house, and that, given the place it established in the London trade, only modest commissions were left for others, a situation which had devastating consequences for houses dependent on the large but short-lived Irish trade. The importance of Martell's business is evident in the shipments in 1774, the briskest year of the 1770s: 106,686 veltes or 3,952 barriques. This figure would be almost equalled by the turnover of Delamain at the time. Delamain's invoices totalled 80,477 veltes. However, Delamain's business with London was modest, and was dwarfed by his Paris dealings (19,251 veltes), his Irish trade (30,737 veltes) and by an English provincial custom. The latter consisted in part of business with houses which took walnuts or shipped coal. Thus not all his provincial customers were brandy merchants whereas Martell's seem to have been. The change in Martell's business is measured in their bank accounts. Martell's pioneered

[60] *Ibid.,* 20 August 1782, Bordeaux.
[61] *Burke correspondence*, ed. T. Copeland (10 vols., Cambridge, 1958–78), vol. V, p. 62, 62n. This correspondence refers to Barrett as Edmund, but it should be Edward.

the reliance on Bordeaux as their main banking centre at the time when their London business expanded in the late 1740s and early 1750s. The Martell account amounted to 721,515 livres for the period 25 March 1774 to 18 January 1775, and 475,649 livres for 18 January to 17 July 1775. For a period of twelve months this would come to 897,873 livres,[62] roughly three times the turnover of the early 1750s. In crude terms, at 170 livres a barrique f.o.b., the account total would suggest an outside brandy turnover of 5,082 barriques. This figure fits in neatly enough with the evidence of Martell Lallemand invoices. Their invoice figure of 3,952 barriques would suggest that they held a near-total stranglehold on the London market (only 4,404 barriques were shipped from the La Rochelle *généralité* to *Angleterre* in 1774) and that their business accounted for a third of total exports (12,741 barriques). Moreover, as much of the exports consisted of the novel rise in brandy demand by the slave traders of La Rochelle (5,293 barriques), Martell's would have shipped over half of the exports (7,448 barriques) destined for the entire European market. No other exporting merchant came near to rivalling them at this stage, and it was a unique dominance of the shipping business.

The Irish business now counted for little in the business of Cognac houses, and houses like Hennessy's or its successor Saule's, whose origins came from the Irish trade and which had a very modest stake in the London market, remained in dire difficulties. The Irish market had become small and erratic: 1774 was a particularly good year, and, except for years of short-lived upturn like 1774, direct shipments were rare. At that time Delamain remained the main house: his turnover for Dublin in 1774 was 30,737 veltes, Martell's 14,000, Hennessy's 11,377 veltes. That meant that demand in that year was large enough to warrant direct dispatch. Eight vessels loaded directly for Dublin, a record for the 1770s, whereas in other years the small quantities went to Bordeaux via Rochefort or Mortagne for dispatch to Ireland on the wine vessels.

The impersonal record of quantities invoiced and shipped reveals even more than the correspondence a virtual collapse of Hennessy/Saule shipments in 1777 and 1778. By January 1778 Hennessy noted that the Cognac house's credit with the Paris banking firm of Mallet was greatly overdrawn, and that the banker, whom he met in Paris, seemed uneasy.[63] Recovery in turnover was modest in 1779, 1780 and 1781. In 1781 at 416½ puncheons it was still below the level of the mid-1770s, itself hardly satisfactory. When Hennessy went to Bordeaux in 1776, he retained an

---

[62] MAC, accounts. For the period 26 July 1774–25 July 1775 the Paris account came to 282,926 livres. However, the accounts involve much double-counting, as bills were sold in whichever centre offered the most advantage, and arbitraging transfers took place between them.   [63] HAC, 13 January 1778, Bordeaux.

interest in the house which now traded under the style of Hennessy and Saule. Publicly that arrangement ended in September 1779 when Saule began to trade independently, under the style of his uncle who had arrived in 1763, as Saule and Co. The partnership had already effectively ended a year earlier in September 1778, though with Hennessy agreeing to let the old style of the house continue for the purpose of helping with its London orders.[64]

One reason for the change may have been the abysmal level of business in both Bordeaux and Cognac which left little profit in either centre. Another was Saule's marriage in 1778 and his need to provide for a household of his own. In the course of the extensive correspondence between the two friends in 1775 and 1776 which showed Hennessy's hopes for his Bordeaux venture, the joint interest in the Cognac house was probably less for the purpose of securing a profit to Hennessy than to retain an established name for the house in the first stages of a new merchant setting out on his own. In 1776 Saule was not only relatively young, but his name was unknown in business, not featuring even in the style of the La Rochelle house in which he was a partner. In January 1779, after the partnership had ended, Saule experienced difficulty in getting an account in his own name with a Paris banker. Saule attributed this to the jealousy of Lallemand. In 1779 he still had to make his mark. However, whatever the circumstances behind his problems, the fact is that the business had an upturn, however modest, in 1779. In June 1779, writing to the house of Connelly to whom he could speak frankly, he admitted that 'we are young beginners and are uneasy and constantly in dread of losing our customers'.[65]

The letter book reveals a keen interest in developing the London market at this time, and in the course of this year Saule proposed to Hennessy that they should both make a trip overseas (a proposal which came to nothing).[66] By January 1780 Saule was a little more sanguine and reported to Connelly and Co. in Flushing that 'we are gott in in a degree to the London trade'.[67] From the Hennessy business he had inherited the custom of the London house of Steele. As most big houses did, Steele divided their custom between several firms – Martell and Augier as well as Saule[68] – but regular commissions from such a house conferred a standing on Saule's. The business made little advance in 1780 and 1781.[69] In both years the two friends were in dire circumstances, neither

---

[64] *Ibid.*, letter book 1775–81, 16 September 1778, 18 May 1779, to Hennessy, Bordeaux.
[65] *Ibid.*, letter book 1775–81, 5 June 1779.
[66] *Ibid.*, 29 June 1779, Bordeaux; 30 June 1779, Cognac.
[67] *Ibid.*, letter book 1775–81, 15 January, 1780.
[68] *Ibid.*, 1 June 1780, Connelly and Co., Flushing.   [69] *Ibid.*, invoice book.

really able to help the other. Saule's situation improved somewhat in 1782, but Hennessy's, which we can only measure more impression-istically from personal letters to Saule, remained bad. The year 1783, however, bore fortune to him as well. The long dark business night of 1776–82 had ended, and both friends experienced a welcome relief from the almost unremitting cares of seven years.

9   The brandy business in Bordeaux and Cognac in the 1780s

Changes in the brandy trade

In the 1780s brandy had prospered through lower prices than the abnormally high prices of the 1760s and 1770s and this has created in the modern bibliography the mistaken idea that there was a price collapse in the 1780s. The near-decimated foreign market of the 1770s recovered; a deepening and widening market with more consumers ready to buy at lower prices meant that smuggling was once more active, now focused less on Ireland and the west of Scotland than on the ports close to London, the richest and largest market in Europe. Fitful in the past, smuggling was now big business especially at Dunkirk and Boulogne with the rising volume of activity supported by a French economic policy which dated back to the 1760s. Smugglers for the Irish and Scottish markets survived at Roscoff, Lorient and Guernsey, though as a secondary dimension of the business. However, in busy times, the Irish smugglers went as far afield as Bordeaux and even Charente. Thus the Bordeaux distillers dealing with them did well in 1783–5 though more fitfully in 1787–8.

Not only did the overland brandy route to Paris prosper, with Angouleme becoming a centre of some real economic force, but the coastal route also fared well. Thus all markets were expanding: foreign, inland and coastal. A consequence of an active coastal trade was that brandy flourished along the coast and at the mouth of the Garonne, and merchants there totally bypassed the La Rochelle buying circuit. In addition, further south, Armagnac became a well-defined product in its own right for the first time, and on the Mediterranean coast Sète became a major supplier of Paris, Dunkirk and the northern littoral of France. If this was the pattern, it is hardly surprising that relations between Bordeaux and Charente became closer, based both on an arbitraging movement of goods from the heart of Saintonge or from its fringes to Bordeaux and to distilleries in the port or on the northern shores of the Gironde, and on a close approximation of prices in the two centres. Distilling itself, traditionally a small-scale business waiting for rather than canvassing orders, became a more easily identified activity both in Bordeaux and in Béziers in the Languedoc: distillers dealt not only with local brandy *négociants* but often with the external buyers themselves, and in turn merchants moved into distilling. A sure sign of its new-found significance was that for the first time the Bordeaux distillers of consequence all seem to have been foreign – that is, Irish.

The impact of changes in the brandy trade on Bordeaux

As a result of the congruence of prices over a broad region and more movement of men, capital and even brandy from Cognac to Bordeaux, the broader economy of south-western France was more effective than ever: money moved in larger quantities and more regularly, and Cognac, especially as a source of bills on both Paris and London, was an important part of the payments network of Bordeaux. The exchange of letters between the two friends, Hennessy and Saule, has a major value as the closest surviving evidence of the nature of business ties between a satellite and a great port. Hennessy's circumstances in Bordeaux had so far been difficult, but in late 1782 his business experienced an upturn from the Irish market which continued at least into 1785. The reasons for the upturn were a combination of bad harvests in Ireland, a temporary clampdown on distilling, and the introduction, independently but coincidentally with the Irish harvest crises, of the rigid administrative regulation of Irish distilling. In November 1784 Hennessy was pleased to report that his house had got the custom of the major Barton house:

We have again got Messrs Barton's business – he began by giving us orders for 150 *pièces* ⅗ and 70 *pièces* double spirit but the time he gives us is short, that if we are not helped from you we must give up, as we have so many other customers who merit a preference though none so considerable as him.[1]

With a sudden upsurge in demand in the 1780s, assured supplies of cognac from either Rochefort or Mortagne were important to the maintenance of Bordeaux business. In the spring of 1785, Forster's were seeking cognac brandy. Boyd approached them to give Hennessy and Co. their custom, and when they did so, they commissioned Saule to buy for them in Cognac.[2] Some of this brandy was shipped round from Rochefort, but more of it came from well south of the Charente from the district between Pons and the Garonne. Smugglers often arrived in the river Garonne without advance notice, not only demanding brandy but spirit rectified to three-fifths strength or higher, degrees of strength executed only in

[1] HAC, 13 November 1784, Hennessy, Bordeaux, to Saule.
[2] *Ibid.*, 31 May 1785, Hennessy, Bordeaux, to Saule.

response to a sure demand. This caused sharp swings between idleness and bouts of frenetic activity. Thus, according to Hennessy in January 1784, 'since dispatching the above vessels, we have not had a still going, to-morrow we shall set 16 of them to work'. This was in response to the arrival of three vessels from Ireland, for which between 600 and 700 *pièces* of brandy for rectification were purchased in a single day.[3] By April, with four cutters loading the ankers beloved of smugglers, and 'traders' (meaning non-smuggling vessels) also loading for Dublin and Cork, all the stills were at work 'with an appearance of their continuing so some time if we can get brandy'.[4] A capacity of sixteen stills was impressive for the period, and it reflected the rather special circumstances of the Bordeaux business. At 30 to 40 veltes per still, this could amount to a total distilling capacity of 480– 640 veltes (or 960–1,280 gallons), which would have approximated to the size of a large Irish distillery of the 1770s (though not of the 1780s). When working to full capacity, this could amount to an output of 15 to 20 barriques of spirit a day. However, even such concentrated output would fail to meet the needs of vessels wanting to leave port at short notice with little loss of time. This explains why, when vessels arrived, orders spilled over to several houses.

At the end of 1784, with limited refining capacity in Bordeaux, it seemed to make sense to locate stills in the Mortagne region, or in the hitherto underdeveloped region to the west. Boyd, Hennessy's partner in the business in the new district of the Chartrons, immediately to the west of the city, not only opened premises at Royan further downstream than Mortagne, but contrived the first large still in the region at his new centre there. In December 1784 Hennessy advised Saule 'to wait the trial of the great still we are making which we hope to have up in the course of this month. The make of it I think must be better than the common ones'.[5] A month later he reported that 'we have got home this afternoon our new still, it has now 300 veltes water in it, and it will work'.[6] Prospect of continued success encouraged Boyd to erect yet a further large still: in September he was busy fixing it up at Royan, 'which is to be the Non such. It forms an oblong square with two worms'.[7]

Hennessy did not have a direct stake in the Royan distillery. While correspondence gives the impression that the Royan venture may have been at first an extension of the Chartrons business, it had or acquired a separate identity as it absorbed more of Boyd's time and, requiring capital,

3 *Ibid.*, 9 January 1784, Hennessy, Bordeaux.
4 *Ibid.*, 16 April 1784, Hennessy, Bordeaux.
5 *Ibid.*, 7 December 1784, Hennessy, Bordeaux.
6 *Ibid.*, 4 January 1785, Hennessy, Bordeaux.
7 *Ibid.*, 13 September 1785, Hennessy, Bordeaux, to Saule.

depended on a partnership with a more experienced merchant, Guiliory. A large and uncontrolled cash flow continued between the two centres, and while the Royan venture supplied badly needed spirit for sales in boom times in Bordeaux, the relationship between Hennessy and Boyd was in reality highly inequitable because, while the Royan venture used the working capital of the Bordeaux partnership, any profits in Royan went exclusively to Boyd.[8] The profitability of distilling was precarious: the truth of the matter was that the business was viable only when activity was at an absolute peak. The key market was Irish, partly smuggling but also from legal traders in Dublin and in Belfast. The fact that legal traders imported large quantities of spirit and that Belfast almost uniquely ordered double spirit suggests very extensive abuse in the Irish customs. However the market was highly speculative. When spirit prices were high in Ireland, the demand for spirits rose; it contracted at once when whiskey or alternative brandies became readily available at lower prices again. In the intervals between booms, prospects were poor. Boyd's Mortagne warehouse had to be closed down in 1786. A frantic Guiliory wrote repeatedly to Bordeaux about problems in October 1787. He proposed to sell the two small stills and to erect one of 60–80 veltes capacity.[9] A decision followed in the spring of 1788 to close the distillery in Royan. A new partnership was then established in Bordeaux, working from the premises that Hennessy had to relinquish to Boyd in late 1787, and hence relying on smaller and more flexible stills. The last letter from Royan was dated 4 March 1788. After the move to Bordeaux, the business continued to be conducted largely in spirits one-third and three-fifths, and in 1788 Boyd's new partnership did a respectable amount of business. A substantial business required turnover in both spirit and in brandy. However, any rise in demand which boosted redistillation into spirit in Royan or Bordeaux reduced the prospects of Bordeaux business in ordinary brandy, as a rise in the volume of trade made it more worthwhile to order cognac direct rather than indirectly through Bordeaux.

The economics of distilling

Hennessy's could fare well in the 1783–5 period when demand was at a peak and distilling capacity had not yet expanded to its limit. At that time the house made a handsome profit.[10] However, as capacity grew and demand failed to increase in proportion, in trying to keep to their old

[8] ADG, Bordeaux, journal 1788, 7B 1172; letter book of George Boyd and Co. of Royan 1785–8 and of Bordeaux 1788–9, 7B 1171; invoices 1788–9, 7B 1173; *acquits*, 7B 1174.
[9] *Ibid.*, 7B 1171, 11 October 1787, to Boyd.
[10] HAC, 14 September 1784, Hennessy, Bordeaux, to Saule.

rates for distilling, they found that they were undercut by other distillers, especially a large one like Andoe who was prepared to reduce his charges. In 1784 when capacity fell short of demand, and the gap between demand and supply was sharpest, the distilling commission was 30 livres per *pièce*. In later years Hennessy and Boyd were undercut, not irregularly, as in 1784, by operators such as 'the dirty little fellow Loche . . . picking up spirits . . . amongst the little bruleurs',[11] but by large distillers. Hennessy noted that 'that branch of business is getting into a Mr Andoe's hand who works at 9 livres per puncheon of spirits which none of the others think they can afford. Twenty livres was what I always got.'[12] Twenty livres itself was a decline from the rate of 30 livres for the smaller *pièce* (the Bordeaux *pièce* of 50 veltes compared with the puncheon of 64 veltes) in halcyon 1784. Saule upbraided Hennessy, stressing the advantages of lower returns on a larger turnover, saying with reference to Andoe that:

I suppose he is of the opinion I have adopted as much as I can, that its better gain in three operations three times three livres than to get but in one [operation] six livres . . . Its better for a man to get but 12 livres per day in working than to keep his still and himself idle. Rust gets in time in the mind as verdigrease does upon the copper.[13]

Measuring output by stray bits of evidence, at a guess Hennessy and Co. at their peak in 1784–5 must have distilled 2,000 puncheons a year, giving for a working year of about 300 days a daily output of about 12 barriques of spirit. A total of 2,000 puncheons, at 20 livres a puncheon, would have given them a gross income of 40,000 livres, or at 9 livres, a mere 18,000 livres. This figure would also be boosted by their commission of 2 per cent on total outlay where they serviced directly received foreign orders rather than distilled on commission which was more typical. Their rent alone amounted to 4,000 livres. To this should be added the wages of their distiller and workmen, costs of fuel, incidental costs of fabrication and some small overheads. Of course, the income would have to be divided between two partners, and for Hennessy at least, before arriving at a true profit, interest on borrowing would have to be deducted. At its peak in 1784, on several occasions single orders or batches of brandy for their stills ran as high as 700 *pièces*. At such times, the margin of income above their high rent was large, and Hennessy's attitudes became buoyant. They were probably the largest distillers in Bordeaux in the mid-1780s, very likely accounting for most rectification for the export market, before surrendering that position to another Irish house, Andoe, in the second half of the decade.

---

[11] *Ibid.*, 27 August 1784, Boyd, Bordeaux, to Saule.
[12] *Ibid.*, 6 November 1787, Hennessy, Cognac, to Saule.
[13] *Ibid.*, 5 January 1788, Saule, Cognac, to Hennessy.

A carelessness in bookkeeping was evident on both sides, and insofar as Boyd was the formal bookkeeper for the partnership with Hennessy as well as for his second business, his neglect was the worst of the two. Hennessy defended himself from the critical comments of his friends by alleging that other distillers were in the same plight, and were reduced to leaving their stills idle.[14] The large debt held against Hennessy in 1787 suggests that there was more involved than either Hennessy's spendthrift personal expenditure or Boyd's siphoning capital into his Royan venture. The fact that Boyd actually commissioned an accountant at the outset of 1787 suggests that he as well as Hennessy was already adrift. Hennessy himself conceded that their Chartrons business was ruinous in its want of profit, and attributed that to the partnership's high rent compared with Andoe's rent of 1,400 livres. His defence of the rent was simply that 'you'll say a less would serve but its very difficult to find a proper one for the business as many will not admit of a distillery in their houses'.[15]

Whatever the nature of the transactions between the Chartrons and Royan, and the degree to which one partner or other made free with the resources of the partnership, the general outcome was that, for a firm in difficulties, a rather handsome settlement was made with the creditors. In the short term, the loser was Hennessy who lost his interest in the distillery and who was now both without resources and was revealed more clearly and more publicly than ever as the ineffective businessman that he was. What was Boyd's benefit from the affair? In the short term, in early 1788, he gained the distillery in the Chartrons, either the largest in Bordeaux, or the second-largest next to Andoe's. In the longer term the situation was more problematic. The settlement had not been a cheap one for him (as in effect he made good the losses of the creditors of the former partnership with the help of his brother-in-law), and he was now short of capital. Like Hennessy he should be regarded as having, at best, emerged as an ineffective figure in business terms. Guiliory, already Boyd's partner in the old Royan venture, was partner in the new venture with Boyd.[16] In it Boyd's capital was 30,336 livres and Guiliory's 17,633. Guiliory himself was an honest and competent man, described by Saule as 'un homme plus qu'aisé'.[17] Guiliory's association was the typical case of a man of standing and resources lending his name and only some capital to a venture. It was his examination of affairs in October 1787, and the long letters that he wrote to Boyd at the time, that were the first stages of realism being forced on Boyd and the Royan enterprise being wound down.

[14] *Ibid.*, 17 July 1787, Hennessy to Saule.
[15] *Ibid.*, 28 June 1787, Hennessy, Bordeaux, to Saule.
[16] ADG, Bordeaux, 7B 1172, journal for 1788.
[17] HAC, letter book 1787–8, 12 April 1788, to Gastinel, Paris.

So straitened was Hennessy in 1787 that he gave up his living accommodation, and in October he had, for the second time in his Bordeaux career, retired to lodgings. Somewhat helplessly in November 1787 he reported Andoe's success.[18] Boyd, on the other hand, still working at the stills, set out to match Andoe's terms. He had no option if he was to survive and Saule in exasperation wrote to Hennessy that:

I see that Boyd's working upon same footing as Andoe deprives you of doing anything that way. But in the name of god, if Andoe gets a livelihood by it, why cannot you? This Andoe is not impoverished by his business, why should you? There seems something so strange to me in all this that I know not what to think or say.[19]

In 1788 Boyd, according to his own books, charged 5 livres 10 sols per *pièce* of 50 veltes for spirits one-third and 11 livres for spirits three-fifths. It was a heavy reduction on the preceding rates, and illustrates the price of survival in distilling in the late 1780s.

Distilling was not a large business. The write-down value of the two large stills and two small ones with their equipment at Royan, probably the largest distillery in France outside Béziers or Dunkirk, was a mere 16,800 livres in Boyd's new books. In other words, the fixed capital was a mere £700. This was a very small capital investment compared with much other manufacturing business. Rectifying, the most speculative branch of the brandy business, fell off sharply in the second half of 1787, itself a factor in determining the precise timing of crisis both in Hennessy's affairs and in Boyd's in Royan. While the brandy business at large recovered, reaching a peak, the largest since 1720, in 1789, the Bordeaux spirit business moved more fitfully, promising well in the spring of 1788, and running into difficulty again in 1789 when the counterdraw of London and Paris in putting up the price of brandy made things difficult for the rectifiers.

Vessels carrying spirit from Bordeaux were numerous in 1788, and smuggling vessels, a sure sign of the pick-up in the trade for marginal qualities of spirits, were in evidence among them. Boyd's new business thus maintained some momentum, profiting also from the custom of Hennessy's old buyers who withdrew in the course of 1787 and returned in some force to the market in 1788.Given the fact that a boom provided some marginal occupation in brandy buying even for Hennessy, it is easy to see why hopes of getting back into distilling lingered on. The prospects of a connection with Andoe were a mirage of late 1787, and later the hope of Samuel Turner, a nephew of Delamain's, joining him in Bordeaux was floated.

Boyd's turnover gained from the uplift in demand in late 1787 and

---

[18] *Ibid.*, 6 November 1787, Hennessy, Bordeaux, to Saule.
[19] *Ibid.*, 19 December 1787, Saule to Hennessy.

early 1788. However, business was far short of the probable turnover of the mid-1780s, and the underlying state of the distilling business was to be seen in the low distilling commission rates. In such conditions survival was, objectively speaking, impossible unless rents were low and borrowings limited, and it was only a matter of time before Boyd himself, like Hennessy before him, went under. Distilling costs were already pared to the bone, and the serious credit crisis in Bordeaux in 1789 first put at risk those houses which were already short of resources. Boyd's new and in a sense either brave or foolhardy venture crashed in the autumn. His turnover to September 1789 was only 626 *pièces*, well down on his turnover in the preceding year. Moreover, brandy or spirit supplied in ankers came to a mere 85 *pièces*, suggesting that the smuggling demand, a mainstay of the distilling business and one that had picked up in 1788, had contracted even more severely than demand at large. The crisis in Boyd's affairs seems to have come to light in July 1789. His partnership with Guiliory was dissolved the same month: the fact that business had for some time been close to a total halt is suggested by 'utensilles et effets en nature' making up 39,288 livres of the modest balance sheet total of 46,392 livres. The personal *bilan* or account of his affairs was handed in to the *greffe consulaire* on 23 September: assets which could be readily realised made up a mere 34,946 livres of the gross total of 114,878 livres.[20]

Bordeaux distilling had been more active in the 1780s than in the preceding two decades. However, speculative port distilling of this nature was squeezed between the problems of getting brandy for rectifying and a highly fluctuating demand. The problem was that the underlying strengthening of international demand during the decade created a persistent illusion that the business had a bright future, and that intermittent keen demand for the Irish market would become the basis of a wider custom. The reality was otherwise, simply a more dramatic repetition of the false hopes of the 1770s. Activity seems to have peaked in 1783–5, recovering again from late 1787 into 1788, and benefiting once more in the soaring demand for brandy in the second half of 1789. As early as 1787 the mirage of distilling profits seems to have prompted an expression of interest from Samuel Turner in Cognac as it did a year later from Thomas Knight in Bordeaux, and the prospect of support even fed Hennessy's illusion of re-entering the fray, if a partner were found. However, the prices of rectifying commissions, much lower than earlier in the decade, were pared to the bone; the bad business of the first half of 1789 made Boyd's failure inevitable, and two well-capitalised Irish businessmen who launched their business during the year failed to

[20] ADG, Bordeaux, 7B 538, Guiliory.

prosper. An export of 2,181 barriques of Guyenne *double* in 1789, even if concentrated in the second half of the year, does not suggest a rate of throughput which would make for profitability for the two or three Irish houses in business.

Looking back over the century, if the exports of Bordeaux in 1789 (19,656 La Rochelle barriques) and Bayonne (15,116 barriques) are aggregated, the south-west probably exported more brandy than in any year since the very outset of the century. However, the trade was made up of two contrasting segments: a highly speculative distilling of low-quality brandy mainly in the hands of foreigners literally on Bordeaux's foreshore, combined with heterogeneous and opportunistically acquired exports which were not rectified in the port; and a relatively compact and isolated inland region with its emerging quality Armagnac brandy. The decline in brandy distillation in the lands between Armagnac and Bordeaux and its own physical isolation helped to lay the basis for the emergence of a distinctive product. Armagnac's shipment through Bayonne was vital to its character and reputation. Over the century, the product had progressively freed itself from association with speculative purchasing by Bordeaux and Cognac houses who bought to gamble on price rises on the Dunkirk market. Such speculation by the end of the 1780s centred on Languedoc or Spanish brandy.

Saule's business in Cognac and Hennessy's return in late 1788

One solution to Hennessy's problems which had hovered in the wings was, as already mentioned, the prospect of an association with a nephew of Delamain's. This did not eventuate in Bordeaux as Hennessy had hoped, but it came up again unexpectedly after October 1788 when Saule died, and out of the resulting partnership the modern house of Hennessy grew. As Delamain had several sons of his own, there was no hope of a place for his nephew, Samuel Turner, who had come to France in or about 1781 to his uncle's house, and this meant that he was at something of a loose end. In August 1787 he seems to have proposed to James Hennessy, at the time a clerk in Saule's house in Cognac, that he should join Hennessy in the distilling business in Bordeaux if Richard could keep the business going in the interval.[21] Nothing came of it, probably because investigation revealed Hennessy's affairs to be desperate.

Saule's unexpected death, however, opened up an unforeseen avenue. The goodwill of the business was ceded by the widow to James Hennessy

---

[21] HAC, 14 August 1787, Saule, London, to Hennessy.

(Jemmy), but that did not make a start any easier. The question of partnership with Turner, though this time in a novel context, came up again, even as early as 20 October and James had apparently commented sanguinely on the prospect.[22] Perhaps it was with this prospect in mind that Richard finally decided to abandon Bordeaux and the house of Hennessy et fils emerged in December.[23] As far as Turner was concerned, the Cognac house, whose turnover on the prestigious and stable London market Saule had, during the decade of his ownership of the business, built up to very respectable proportions, was far more attractive than an uncertain distilling prospect in Bordeaux. Turner's joining the firm was somewhat protracted (he was at the time a partner in another business), but it was agreed in principle by May and in August 1789 the contract was signed.

The rivalry of Saule and Co. and Martell Lallemand

Turner and James Hennessy, in building up the house to new heights, did so on the foundations laid by Saule. The house had been of negligible proportions at the beginning of the 1780s. Saule's achievement during the decade was the basis of the rise. He shipped 596 puncheons in 1782, the highest figure attained by the house since its inception in 1765. The figure rose further to 945 puncheons in 1783, but it fell back in 1784 to 581 puncheons. Saule's growing London business prompted him to visit London in 1784, taking James Hennessy with him – the first true business visit abroad by a member since the foundation of the business in 1765. There were important consequences to the trip. The first was that, failing to find a place in London for James Hennessy, the young man entered Saule's house as a clerk. The second was that the long visit provided the basis of a large expansion in Saule's business. On his way he had been given letters of introduction by his Paris banker to the Arbouins of London.[24] This did not lead to great things, though Arbouin did order some brandy from Saule in subsequent years. More important was the acquaintance struck up with the house of Yeats and Brown, and especially with one member of the house, Tim Brown (nephew of the original proprietor of the business, Yeats). In 1787 Saule had seventeen London customers, and his volume of business with one, John and Walker Gray, was slightly larger than with Yeats and Brown. There were over sixty importers in London, usually giving their major custom to Martell

[22] *Ibid.*, letter book 1788–90, 20 October 1788, to John Mors, London; 3 November 1788, Murdoch, Dunkirk, to James Hennessy.
[23] *Ibid.*, letter book 1788–90, 6 December 1788, to Clancy and Parrant.
[24] *Ibid.*, 18 June 1784, Saule to Hennessy.

Lallemand and subsidiary orders to other Cognac shippers. Hence
Saule's place in the London market was somewhat restricted, and the
acquisition of a large house like Yeats and Brown was a stroke of fortune.
In some ways we may see it as a consequence of Saule's charm.
In his eagerness to expand business, Saule dealt with some of the Irish
smugglers who in the Irish spirit famine of 1783–5 came to Charente as
well as Bordeaux. Unfortunately, after four successful voyages over two
years by one of his Irish customers, he unwisely extended credit for a fifth
voyage in 1786, and ended up with a loss of £1,000. The loss was a
considerable amount for an individual brandy merchant, amounting to
about one-tenth of his turnover. It must have wiped out profits for the
year. Its impact was all the more serious as Saule was not only carrying a
large stock of brandy but an acute credit crisis set in in 1787. At the outset
of 1787 he had it in mind to go to London to further his business, and did
so later in the year. His invoices in 1787 at 1,470 puncheons were above
the previous year's level, and in 1788 (up to 1 September) rose further to
1,562 puncheons. This understates the expansion of business in 1788
because, having laid in large stocks in 1787, encouraged by the economic
and political news gleaned on his London visit, large amounts of brandy
were in his warehouse unsold in September 1788 and much of the stock
would have been sold in the remaining months of the year, had he lived.
The invoices to September plus stock he had on hand in his warehouses at
the time (450 puncheons) would amount to 2,000 puncheons. This
figure, the equivalent of 4,000 barriques, would mean that the business
was not far from matching Martell Lallemand's in turnover.
The significance of Saule's expansion, in contrast to the Broussards',
Arbouins' and Augiers' more modest recovery in the same decade, was
almost totally dependent on London. The tensions with Martell's arose
from the fact that they likewise, a few Irish orders apart, had an exclusively English and largely London custom. Over the decade Saule had a
string of successes. Even as early as 1780, the London house of Steele
divided their orders between Martell, Augier and Saule.[25] In the mid-
1780s Yeats and Brown switched their business from Martell's to Saule,
and in the short-lived upsurge in smuggling business, Saule's five cargoes
for the smuggling venturer, White, seemed to presage that there too he
might outshine Martell's in a field which was small and specialised.
Ever since the time of Lallemand's problems in containing opposition
in the 1760s, Martell's had shown resentment of the Irish challenge, and
no social contact existed between the Irish houses and Martell's before
the 1790s. Saule regarded them as hostile, and retrospectively attributed

[25] *Ibid.*, 1 June 1780, Connelly and Co., Flushing.

his failure as far back as 1769 to get a place with the Delaps, a Bordeaux Irish house, to them. The bitterness was already an established one in 1779 when Saule, referring to Lallemand, wrote that:

my lot is to find him everywhere. It was he who prevented my going to Mr Delap in 1769, he was the first informer against my wife and me, and now I dare say he has thrown me out of the way to obtain this small credit. I am sure the Augiers are incapable of doing me any prejudice, and I know full well that Lallemand is very sorry to see me doing anything this year, therefore if Messrs T. & B. wrote that house I am sure that they could not get from thence a satisfactory answer.[26]

In 1787 he told Richard Hennessy that he lost business through 'my envious neighbours, rich competitors who thought to crush me 'ere I could have wings to fly! They seem to love Hennessy now because he is not dangerous, but were he so, they would soon run him down.'[27]

The London visits were central both to Saule's success and to the profile of the house. His second visit, however, led him to give credence to rumours in England of war, which always had a positive impact on brandy prices. This visit was an extended one. Saule took his wife with him. They left at the end of June, and they did not get back until 1 November. The level of shipments rose somewhat in 1787. In leaving Jemmy in charge, Saule obviously had a good deal of confidence in him. Of course, this was the valley period before the new distilling season began. However, there would still be a good deal of business, and enquiries about the prospective trends in the new season in particular needed sensitive handling, as brandy importers maintained lines of communication with several *négociant* houses. Incompetence would be quickly detected and would prove damaging to the reputation of the house. On his return Saule wrote to Richard Hennessy on 7 November that: 'I hope and pray that my long absence four months must have done a great deal of good to your son, who was obliged to work on his own bottom. I have not had time to look over his operations as yet, but think they must be satisfactory.'

The first real expansion in Saule's business had come in the wake of his 1784 visit to London, and occurred as a result of the connection made with the Browns of London and Dunkirk at that time. By 1785 his turnover was almost three times the 1782 level, and from 1785 to 1788 it was never to fall below 1,398 puncheons. This was all the more creditable as conditions which had been brisk in 1785 were somewhat less so in late 1786. In early 1787 prices were not rising and there was stagnation in the trade.[28] Following the trade treaty with England which had raised hopes

---

[26] *Ibid.*, 23 January 1779, Saule, Cognac, to Hennessy.
[27] *Ibid.*, 19 December 1787, Saule.
[28] *Ibid.*, letter book 1786–7, 19 February 1787 to Bubbers; 19 February, 24 February 1787, to Arthur.

very high this was a little disappointing. However, the calm in early 1787 was largely artificial as there was delay in the application of the treaty: 'at present our trade is almost at a stand, until the treaty of commerce takes place'.[29] Hence the British trade was very much on Saule's mind. He had already intended to go to London at the outset of 1787 though this was deferred to mid-year. With the prospects of a larger trade in the wake of reduction in the duties, less brandy was likely to be sent to Dunkirk and in future brandy merchants would ship direct, taking brandy from Dunkirk only in the winter months.[30]

Brandy prices in early 1787 were only around 100 livres. They recovered thereafter and were 125 livres in November. Apparently from his contacts with Cherry, an admiralty official in London who was in the Yeats and Brown circle, and who might have revealed victualling plans which were often regarded as an indication of imminent naval action, Saule formed the idea on the eve of his return that a war was likely and speculated on a rise in brandy prices. The Browns had formed the same idea, no doubt from the same source, and their conviction can only have added to Saule's optimism. His speculative buying was all done in a very short period of time after his return and reflected a very sanguine estimate of the outcome. On 21 November, despite the fact that there was as yet little new brandy and a market trend had not established itself, he wrote: 'I gave 130 for large parcels at which I got about 400 puncheons.' Large purchases at this price would only fuel the expectations of sellers. Another 500 puncheons were purchased in a later splurge in a single week, and Saule admitted that 'we cannot save ourselves unless we charge 145'. Saule was in something of a frenzy. In the three weeks to 19 December 'I have not stirred out of the house but on Saturday markets and Sunday nights'. Immediately on his return from London, he had, he said, 'large orders'.[31] He had now 'near' 1,500 puncheons on hand (the bulk of it acquired in two separate weeks, some in very large lots) and he 'was knocked up with force of working constantly at it, and the making of cash and funds is not the easiest part'.[32] He boasted that 'we have thus almost in our hands all the old brandies which remain in the province.'[33] The London merchant Thomas Bevan, noting purchases by some London houses to lie in Cognac, in January thought it 'mad speculation'.[34]

The consequences of his buying were all the more serious for him as London brandy houses were to hold back in the course of 1788, regarding the prices as too high and gambling on a fall. Vessels were slow to arrive.

[29] *Ibid.*, 11 April 1787, Isaac Brown.   [30] *Ibid.*, 28 March 1787, Isaac Brown.
[31] *Ibid.*, 21 November 1787, Saule, Cognac.   [32] *Ibid.*, 5 January 1788, Saule, Cognac.
[33] *Ibid.*, 28 May 1788, Saule, Cognac.
[34] MAC, 25 January 1788, Thomas Bevan, London.

Even when they did, the London importers held back from purchasing. On 23 June Saule noted that 'we have this month past 3 London traders at Charente, but no orders for filling them up. I never remember to have seen the trade at such a dead stand. We have not bought a cask of brandy these last 6 or 8 weeks.' Little enamoured of *négociants* who by buying substantially ahead of orders were in effect speculating in brandy, the London houses were determined to break them. Hence, an undeclared war of nerves developed between the two sides, in which the London importers held back in a concerted fashion, confident that the market would break.

The irony of the situation is that *négociants* like Saule and Delamain did not at the outset fully appreciate that as importers had to combine to secure large vessels for the direct voyages, the necessity had created in effect a temporary ring among an influential circle within the London importers (a situation not wholly dissimilar from that created by Dublin clubs chartering vessels in 1762 when the prospect of peace restored the feasibility of direct shipments to Ireland). Even into August and September brandy stocks were not clearing. At the end of August some two- or three-year-old brandy had sold for 106 livres, and Yeats and Brown intimated to Saule that they had been advised to expect the market to fall to 65 and 70.[35] Given the fact that the London market in 1788 was holding off, the Paris trade was inevitably the most active market. Moreover, the Paris houses were quick to realise that, contrary to early expectations, the 1788 vintage would not be a good one, and they had enlarged their Cognac buying by the onset of autumn. These rising orders for Paris alone prevented a disastrous fall in prices at the end of the summer, and even Saule, who usually had little or no business with inland houses, in September sold 100 puncheons of brandy and 25 puncheons of spirit to Pierre Nouel of Angouleme: 'by this means I shall clear my stores of 100 puncheons brandy which you may judge I shall pick out of my hardest flavoured . . . This is a losing sale, but I am glad of it as I may buy new brandy in time much cheaper'. Saule was able to sell at a profit some brandy he had held in Dunkirk, but the loss on the deal with Nouel cancelled out that gain.[36] Paris demand, already the driving force in 1788, was still so into April and May 1789. When the expected fall did not come about, the London ring inevitably collapsed and a London-based rush to buy brandy had begun.

To add to this misfortune Saule took ill on 22 September and died on 5 October. Within days inspection of the books revealed a parlous state.[37] On Saule's death his widow and Hennessy formally approached Augier

[35] HAC, 3 September 1788, Yeats and Brown, London.
[36] *Ibid.*, 10 September, Saule, Cognac.
[37] *Ibid.*, letter book 1788–90, 20 October 1788, to John Mors, London.

and Delamain, and they eventually reported in somewhat more optimistic vein than Delamain had on 14 October. The house could cover 50
per cent of its engagement,[38] though his losses were estimated as at least
70,000 livres. Of this figure 24,000 livres were a consequence of the cargo
rashly provided on credit to White, 10,000 livres were miscellaneous
losses 'hereabouts', and the balance would represent the loss consequent
on sales or the prospect of sales below the price at which brandy had been
bought.[39] No doubt, if death had not intervened, the press of creditors
would not have been so great, and he could probably have warded off disaster. The straightforward nature of the failure is reflected in the fact that
a 50 per cent payment was made to creditors by the end of the year.[40]
Fortuitously the sale of Saule's brandy coincided with a rise in the
market, as Paris buyers were coming into the market strongly, especially
as they became aware of the likelihood of further price rises. Ten thousand livres more were realised for the creditors than had been anticipated.[41] Saule's brandy, purchased in haste at the end of 1787 and
apparently embracing all the older brandy available, proved 'of very
indifferent quality'.[42] Of one segment of 450 puncheons in Saule's stock,
160 were taken by Martell's, not on their own account, but to meet orders
in hand.[43] Good news though this turn of events was, the plague on
Saule's affairs persisted. If the brandy had been held off the market for
another few months, it would have realised much higher prices. As early
as the end of December Martell's were regretting that they had not made
a larger purchase of Saule's brandy. By late January prices taken at the still
had reached 120 livres, and the market price had climbed to 135 and 140
by late March. Allowing for some further premium for old brandy, sales at
those prices would have eliminated entirely or greatly reduced the losses
on the various parcels which made up Saule's stock. The decision of the
meeting of creditors on 8 November was registered on 22 January. The
only tangible personal assets he possessed were his furniture and books.
There were no buildings, and his wife was in danger of being turned out
of their rented house on his death. As mentioned, the payout at the end of
December was 50 per cent.[44]

Continuity in the story of the Saule house was provided by James

---

[38] HAJ, Delamain no. 2 letter book, 1787–9, 20 October 1788, to Yeats and Brown; no. 1
    letter book 1787–9, 21 October 1788, to Mallet, Paris.
[39] HAC, letter book 1788–90, 27 October 1788, to Tim Brown.
[40] MAC, letter book 1788–9B, 29 December 1788, to Yeats and Brown.
[41] HAJ, Delamain no. 1 letter book 1787–9, 18 November 1788, to Mallet.
[42] *Ibid.*, circular letter of 6 December 1788. In all Saule's remaining parcels, amounting to
    450 puncheons, realised prices of between 116 and 121 livres. *Ibid.*, 29 November 1788,
    to Knowsley, Hull.
[43] MAC, letter book 1788–9B, 29 December 1788, to Yeats and Brown.
[44] On the estate, see ADC, Angouleme, *étude* Imbaud, 2E 14272, inventory, 8 October–3
    December 1788; 11C 1481, controle des actes, 18 December 1788.

Hennessy, clerk to Saule and now partner to his own ageing father. To run the house, capital was necessary, something which the Hennessys painfully lacked. In default of matrimony (a theme which occurred in the correspondence), a partnership was the only hope for them. In 1789 the alliance with Turner was the best one that could be contracted in the region, and the drive and ability of the two young men was to lay the foundations of the mighty house of Hennessy which we know today. Letters from James Hennessy to Madame Saule when she accompanied her husband to London already reveal an ease of manner and a self-confidence, even if it was not the more showy one that would impress Saule. The year 1787 was not an easy one in any business and for Saule it was particularly difficult because Richard Hennessy's problems in Bordeaux combined with his son's presence in the Cognac house led some to suspect a hidden association between the two houses, and resulted in a reluctance to accept paper from Hennessy junior. In a postscript to a letter of 4 August James referred to the problem but in a casual and confident manner: 'you will easily conceive how disagreeable this is. Babin is continually about me for to know if Mr Pineau is paid. I want about 26,000 livres and as yet I can not get above 6,000 to 8,000. Patience'. In the correspondence of the first half of 1789, prior to the partnership with Turner, the driving force came from the son, not from the father. Nor was Hennessy *fils* dependent on a new partner for shrewdness. Even before the new partnership came into being, 'pestered all the morning by brandy sellers', he offered a low price on the ground that 'as they are Mr Augier's and Martell's customers they would not come here if them gentlemen gave them more'.[45]

As soon as the new partnership came into being in August, with demand soaring, James lost no time in visiting London, as Saule had done, to improve their business. Through his friendship with Tuffon (whose goodwill was another of the fruits of Saule's London sojourns), they acquired some custom from Timson's who had hitherto dealt with Martell's. Tuffon assured Hennessy that while the firm would continue to do business with Martell's, they would like to give some of their orders to Hennessy's. James apprised his father of how the orders should be executed, advising him to consult Saule's invoices to see how things were done for the London market. He described brandy from their house as 'foul and much too pale', and observed that rivals' brandy was in better condition.[46] The transition to a new house had posed problems in keeping up standards, and one London house at least complained of the

[45] HAC, 3 June 1789, James Hennessy, Cognac.
[46] *Ibid.*, 1 December 1789, James Hennessy, London.

brandy being inferior to what they had been accustomed to receive in Saule's time. The new partnership was, however, quick in getting on its feet. The ledger suggests that discounting 170 tierçons on hand at the outset, 1,036 tierçons and 11½ barrels were purchased in the period from 13 August 1789 to 30 September 1790. This is quite a good figure, given the fact that buying started in the high noon of Martell's ascendancy and in a buying season that became progressively more difficult. The massive London buying in the course of 1789, combined with the soaring prices caused by Paris buying meant that late in the year some brandy importers in England had left the French market, finding it more advantageous to buy in London.[47]

The rivalry bordering on hostility between Saule's house and Martell's, and which we might easily think to have existed only in Saule's head, was real in the perspective of James. In London he was shown a letter in which 'Mr Frederick – for I suppose he dictated it – throws some of his venom at us, but I hope the sting won't poison us'.[48] The house was also cementing its existing relationship with the London house of Shoolbred, and James actually lodged with them. A son of Shoolbred was staying with Hennessy *père* at the same time: indeed the son was in France from August 1789 to perhaps as late as March 1790. The liaison, while it had not hitherto loomed large in their business, was to be the key to their London wartime success in the late 1790s, based on trade through Hamburg.

Martell ascendancy in the 1780s

With some degree of boom in Bordeaux's distilling in the best years in the 1780s dispatch to Ireland, directly or indirectly from Cognac, never picked up greatly, even when spirits were short in Ireland. Thus in 1784 Delamain supplied a mere 9,913 veltes, Martell's 9,437 veltes, Saule 1934. On the Charente, Saule depended on London, a market which his friend and rival Delamain failed to penetrate. In 1784 Delamain had a mere four invoices for London. His business, his English provincial custom apart, was very largely one with Paris except for some fluctuating orders from Ireland. London dominated the export business of the Charente, and Martell's in turn dominated the London market. Their invoices in 1784 were almost twice the level of 1774 – 178,526 veltes or 6,614 barriques – and they kept up the momentum through the rest of the decade. While their accounts were not drawn up for regular accounting periods, the Bordeaux account can be crudely annualised:

---

[47] *Ibid.*, 12 November 1789, Dalton, Bury St Edmonds, to James Hennessy.
[48] *Ibid.*, 18 December 1789, James Hennessy, London.

Date	Livres
1786	644,535
1787	685,476
1788	932,436

There were, in addition, two lesser Paris accounts and a La Rochelle one. As much of these accounts were involved in arbitraging, their addition to the main account would inflate the commodity content. If the account is deflated by an f.o.b. price (crudely calculated as a rough average of prices increased by 20 per cent), turnover was 5,202 barriques in 1786, 4,896 in 1787 and 6,216 in 1788.

In 1789, calculated from invoice books, their shipments soared to 436,487 veltes or 16,165 barriques. The circumstances were unprecedented. In the first half of 1789 buying, though high, was not abnormal: for a year to mid-September a turnover of 631,321 livres suggests purchases of 4,041 barriques. This level suggests, moreover, that others had suffered more than they did by London buyers withholding orders, and that confidence in Martell's ensured that when, by May, Londoners belatedly realised that the vintage would be poor and supply would be short in the autumn, they gained disproportionately from the commissions rushed to Cognac. Buying soared. Delamain in the summer referred to 10,000 barriques being got ready for the export market at that time. Such concentrated purchases are most unusual, as buying usually tapered off from April. If one assumed that they were all made by Martell's, and that payments for them had not passed through their bank account by mid-September, their addition to the 4,041 barriques suggested by the account to that date would itself virtually account for all their shipments. In June prices, after touching 150 livres in April and then easing to 125 livres, began to rise sharply: already 180 livres in August, they reached 225 in October and 240 in November. What the pattern suggests is how dominant Martell's had become. Martell's turnover was still high in both late 1787 and in the first half of 1788. While there was a downturn in the trade, London importers reduced their commissions to other houses much more than to Martell, and that explains the refrain of curtailed buying which was so striking in Delamain's letters and up to the time of Saule's death. When the London importers panicked in mid-1789, they gave their orders to the Martell house. Martell dominance was enhanced by the death in October 1788 of Saule who had built his house up to sizeable proportions. While the house was re-established at the end of 1788, it took time to get on its feet: it kept Saule's customers but, despite the frenzy for brandy, it got commissions from few new London sources.

In the 1780s Martell's dealt with all the London brandy houses. No other house enjoyed such a position, and the letter books with their massive, though routine correspondence reveal their hold on the market. That gave Martell's a large bill trade on London, generated by a turnover of about 600,000 livres, in first-class bills on London. In other words in the 1780s, indeed from the 1770s, Martell's became a recognised force on the foreign exchange with London. If Theodore Martell's drive and ambition was a factor in the success of the house, in a circular fashion his standing itself relied on the bills, and the marriage of a Martell daughter to a Bordeaux Beyerman in 1778 reflected the commercial standing of the family. In turn, the ability to dispose of paper on London in Bordeaux showed that the house was independent of the Paris houses on which it relied. From the 1770s, Martell's were instructing their London and Paris correspondents to arbitrage the London–Paris exchanges on their account and for their profit. Theodore Martell was central to these events, and most tellingly of all to the marriage of James Hennessy to Marthe-Henriette Martell in 1795. As in 1720, speculation which had created ties between Martell on the Bordeaux market and Hennessy in common brandy and general commodity dealings was what dissolved old patterns. While speculation, the vagaries of Bordeaux's fortunes during unremitting war, and the hostility which successful merchants attracted from revolutionaries (Cognac was politically a safer centre for merchants in the anti-merchant phase of the Revolution than Bordeaux) sapped Theodore Martell's strength fatally in the end, the links he created for the Cognac house, which in the 1790s contracted through caution, were vital to its recovery post-1802.

Business in a changing economic and political environment 1789–1791

Even if there was a pause in the foreign brandy trade in the second half of 1788, the reduced duties under the treaty with England and the appearance of larger vessels to load full cargoes directly for London seemed to promise a bright future. The year 1789 seemed to bear out the fulfilment of the promise. Speculative as always, the distilling milieu in Bordeaux which Richard had left regained some of its confidence. Boyd held out the allurement of large commissions from his revamped house. Thomas Knight, one of Richard's Bordeaux friends, was ready to take a quarter-share in a new distillery if one was launched and if Samuel Turner, Delamain's nephew, also joined it.[49] This proposal came to nothing largely because of Turner's entry into the new partnership in Cognac. As

---

[49] *Ibid.*, Thomas Knight to Richard Hennessy, letters in March and April 1789.

the exceptional weather abated, social life seemed more than normally brilliant. Richard Hennessy reported from Bordeaux in February, of the pre-Lent festive season, that 'there is no time to talk to anyone of business. Balls, parties and dinners are all that is spoke of.'[50]

Despite difficulties and tight credit, foreign markets held up very well in 1789, not only in indigenous commodities like brandy but in re-exports of colonial produce, a key element in support of the level of the French livre on the foreign exchanges. A very poor vintage in 1789 in conjunction with a short carry-over of stocks at the end of a remarkable year ensured that by the spring of 1790 prices had moved beyond the previous peak of 1772. In late February they stood at 260 and 270 livres, and there was a shortage of both old and new brandy.[51] As early as the autumn of 1789 James Wood wrote to Hennessy and Turner that never in living memory had money been so scarce in Bordeaux. The credit crisis in Bordeaux, the main trading port of the kingdom, accounted for the emergence of an unprecedented gap between brandy prices in Cognac and Bordeaux. In Cognac, with the market in 1789 geared to a vigorous London demand, and hence to a degree insulated from the credit crisis, prices soared in the second half of 1789; in Bordeaux they stagnated between August and November in a band of 150–165 livres. In late October the price in Cognac, reflecting strong external and Paris demand, was 225 livres compared with a mere 160 in Bordeaux.[52] This development cut the ground from under the Bordeaux distillers or rectifiers, who were so dependent on brandy from the fringes of the Cognac region and who had been getting back on their feet. It was at this juncture that Spanish brandy really began to make an appearance in the region, and that distillers after a promising recovery earlier in the year ran into difficulties again. September was the month of Boyd's final failure in Bordeaux.

Foreign trade itself continued to hold up remarkably well into 1791.[53] Business and social life alike remained normal up to or beyond the declaration of war in April 1792. Thereafter the history of the brandy community and of the trade changed radically. The Revolution in its political excesses of 1793 into 1794 frightened older or more established figures. Even the Martell house lost ground, as did James Delamain who increasingly withdrew from business. It was younger men like Theodore

---

[50] *Ibid.*, Richard Hennessy, Bordeaux, letters in February and March 1789.

[51] *Ibid.*, letter book 1788–90, 1 March 1790, to Thomas Blake; 8 March 1790, to P. Arthur.

[52] HAJ, Delamain no. 1 letter book 1787–9, 27 October 1789, to MacCarthy frères; letter from MacCarthy frères, 11 November 1789.

[53] The economic conditions darkened slowly. See Cullen, 'History, economic crises', p. 643. Tonnage figures as a basis for establishing recession would overstate a downturn, and conditions in general were mixed: F. Crouzet, *La grande inflation: la monnaie en France de Louis XVI à Napoléon* (Paris, 1993), pp. 158, 198.

Martell in Bordeaux and James Hennessy and Samuel Turner who were not put off by regulation and dealt in state contracts on a large scale. Richard Hennessy himself gradually went to a life of retirement at La Billarderie. In May 1797 Delamain, who remained in constant touch with him, referred to him 'in health and spirits manually cultivating a pleasant property sixteen hours in the twenty-four'.[54] The old business world he had frequented in Bordeaux and Cognac was, however, fading away. The once abundant correspondence from Bordeaux was thinning and the Cognac letter books contained at times few letters to old friends, and none at all to the Bordeaux Irish. Perhaps that world – not only the Franco-Irish one but the *ancien régime* universe of commerce in which Cognac was a satellite to Bordeaux – expired with, or even before Richard Hennessy. Notarial documents in the 1790s show that Cognac houses handled more business procedures directly than through correspondents in the ports as in the past; they had much closer ties with Paris; and in the difficult conditions of trade in wartime in the late 1790s sent partners to represent the houses in Hamburg, in time of hostilities Europe's effective free port. Richard Hennessy died on 8 October 1800.[55] Delamain, patriarch of the brandy trade and his friend of thirty-five years from the first days of his arrival in Charente, preceded him by a few months, dying in May on the way to take the waters.[56] With these deaths the veil finally came down on the *ancien régime* along the Charente.

---

[54] HAC, 21 February 1797, 28 May 1797, Delamain.
[55] *Ibid.*, letter book 1800–1, 8 October 1800, to Behic.
[56] HAJ, Delamain no. 2 letter book 1799–1801, 17 May 1800, to Hutchinson, Altona.

Sources

As a result of the remarkable survival of the business records of many houses,[1] the brandy trade, a small commerce in the aggregate, is better documented for the eighteenth century than the much larger wine business of Bordeaux. In Cognac and Jarnac records survive in six modern houses (Hennessy, Hine, Delamain, Augier, Otard, Martell) and at the end of the 1980s, as some of the Delamain and Augier records were held in family possession, within eight locations in the region. These collections comprise all or part of the records of some twelve firms (thirteen if the Augier speculative partnership of 1719–20 is clearly distinguished), or eleven if we confine ourselves to records of business conducted within the region itself. In addition, some records of the distilling business survive in Bordeaux in the artificial 7B series made from business papers not reclaimed at the time from the legal jurisdictions of the *ancien régime*.

By far the richest collection is the Hennessy archives which contain, besides the complete records of the house (both bound volumes and correspondence received) and much of the personal correspondence of Richard Hennessy and John Saule, a letter book of the Tonnay-Charente house of Léon Régnier for 1735–6, an invoice book for a longer period, and a few strands of the records of Laurence Saule (for whose estate Hennessy was one of the executors). Legally, though to a lesser extent archivistically or economically, the main Hennessy records are the creation of five distinct businesses, four of them Hennessy houses or partnerships, from 1765 to 1789, one of them, the house of Saule and Co., a distinct business in substance for 1776–88, though in legal terms for the years 1776–8 a partnership with Hennessy. Strictly speaking the Hennessy records also contain a sixth corpus of business documents: a large but selected correspondence which Richard Hennessy brought back from Bordeaux in 1788.

[1] For an earlier and less complete summary of the records, see L. M. Cullen, 'Le réseau commercial du négoce du cognac dans les années 1760', in F. Crouzet, ed., *Le négoce international xiiie–xxe siècles* (Paris, 1989), pp. 153–4.

The Augier records contain, apart from letter books and other business documents mainly from the 1680s and 1720s, two letter books for the late 1720s belonging to Philippe Augier's sister, the Veuve Guérinet, who maintained a house in Tonnay-Charente, and a fairly substantial quantity of papers of the allied house of Broussard, especially for the late 1760s and early 1770s. The Augier collection is supplemented by a mass of papers and bound books about the traumatic bankruptcy of the family in 1722 (held separately from the main corpus of business records in the possession of Monsieur Jacques de Varenne). In the modern house of Delamain, a sole letter book of Ranson and Delamain survives, that for 1767–8, but the modern house of Hine, legal successor to the house of Delamain, contains the letter books of Ranson and Delamain from 1778, as well as the journal of Jacques Ranson, Delamain's father-in-law, for 1759–61 (the Delamain business was the continuation of the house of Ranson from 1762 under the new style of Ranson and Delamain).

The Martell archives contain, in addition to seven letter books for earlier business in Cognac (six volumes) and Bordeaux (one volume), an unbroken series from 1778 and a highly variable survival of correspondence received in individual years in the 1780s and 1790s. To these should be added a letter book not identified as such but which is a Martell letter book for 1742–3 in the Archives départementales at Angouleme. The house of Otard has a complete run of the bound volumes of its business from 1795, though no incoming correspondence.

Much, perhaps even most, of the outgoing correspondence in the early Augier letter books and in the sole Régnier letter-book is in Dutch, and a knowledge of Dutch is essential for their use. On occasion, Philippe Augier, in writing to his brother in Charente, also had the habit of putting particularly confidential remarks in Dutch. Reflecting the dramatic decline in the Dutch trade with Cognac, later correspondence is almost exclusively in French or English.

The trade is badly documented in the administrative records of the region, apart from two illuminating files, 5C5 and 5C6, of correspondence with the intendant in 1782–4 in the Archives départementales de la Charente in Angouleme, and the records of the chamber of commerce in La Rochelle. The latter records are unrivalled in completeness by those of any chamber of commerce on the west coast of France, and are the main source for the administrative history of the brandy trade at large. The intendant's correspondence was arbitrarily divided at the time of the Revolution and the Angouleme records are complemented by two small collections on the brandy trade (C186 and C188) in La Rochelle. As the controleur-général's correspondence in Paris is incomplete, policy regarding the foreign trade in spirits can be documented occasionally from the Correspondance politique Angleterre in the archives of the Ministère des Affaires étrangères and, fleetingly, in other sources.

The *états de la balance du commerce*, surviving for La Rochelle, Nantes, Bordeaux and the *généralité* of Rennes (which includes the important centres of Lorient and Roscoff) are supplemented by a detailed breakdown of trade for every port in France in 1789 (Archives nationales, F^{12} 1666). This volume almost uniquely distinguishes between the sub-divisions of ports or *bureaux* ('creeks' in British customs parlance) and between different strengths and provenances of brandy. Shipping movements, apart from those for Nantes, are poorly documented, because of missing or gapped Amirauté series: in particular, they are entirely missing for the *généralité* of La Rochelle. However, the *congé* series G^5 in the Archives nationales provide some of the missing information, most importantly for the key port of Tonnay-Charente.

The notarial records before the 1790s are not informative on the foreign or wholesale trade in Cognac. On occasion the *Controle des actes* is not only a guide to the notarial minutes, but a substitute, as it makes good missing documents or provides detail not given in the documents (an outstanding though untypical instance being the estate of John Saule, where the executors seem to have been in conflict with the agents of the *Controle* itself). For earlier years, however, the Cherpantier *étude*, the most maritime notarial *étude* in Tonnay-Charente, is very informative, as notarial acts relating to foreign trade were made by the agents there of the Cognac or Jarnac houses rather than by merchants in the town of Cognac itself. Practice began to change in the 1790s when the Cognac houses made themselves more centrally responsible for the management of their own affairs, and the minutes of Cognac notaries then begin to become useful for documenting the business activity of Cognac houses. Documentation of Hennessy's distilling business in Bordeaux or the distilling business of other houses, reflecting its small scale and rather passive dependence on commissions from Bordeaux merchants or the masters of Irish vessels, has not so far been found in extensive searches in the Bordeaux notarial archives (apart from a few and fleeting references, in the *études* of Guy and Guy fils, to Hennessy's long Bordeaux sojourn). The notarial records of La Rochelle are not informative on the brandy trade: even in the port's prime period of activity for brandy and commerce in general, the records of the main – and rich – commercial *étude*, that of Teuleron, throw little light on the trade in brandy. For the eighteenth century the notarial records for the town in general are in poor shape, with large gaps.

With the exception of the Martell records (which were already well organised at the beginning of the 1980s), the bulk of the research for this volume was conducted in physically difficult circumstances before

removal to new locations or listing of material. Even in the case of the
Hennessy archives, which though located off-site were fairly well stored,
the transfer to archival custody more recently has brought to light some
material missed in earlier researches. When the physically disorganised
Augier and Hine material is put in complete order, new finds and a possible misidentification of some material seen at an earlier date seem likely.
The modern rebinding of battered volumes has its own hazards for
searchers. By 1778 Delamain, in a highly systematic fashion, and by the
late 1780s Martell's (Hennessy's in the 1790s) maintained at least two
sets of letter books simultaneously to admit of two scribes copying letters
at the same time. In the case of Martell's and Hennessy's, letter books
were contemporaneously designated on the cover by a letter of the alpha-
bet. In the Delamain letter books, no clear distinction was made between
them (and this lack was continued in a more recent process of rebinding
the more damaged volumes), though the identification of letter books as
first and second in the sequence for each period is possible from internal
evidence: letter books are designated as no. 1 and no. 2 in the notes of this
book. In referring to the volumes, if a letter cannot be readily identified,
the searcher should seek it under the same date in the other volume for
the same chronological span.

Separate or independent businesses up to the beginning of the 1990s,
the Augier and Hine material has become part of the Martell and
Hennessy companies respectively in recent times, and that is currently
affecting their future archival history. Given the many changes, not only
archivally but in the legal ownership of companies, the details of location
in the bibliography are set out as at the time of inspection of the records,
mainly during the 1970s and 1980s.

Bibliography

PRIMARY SOURCES

ANGOULEME, ARCHIVES DÉPARTEMENTALES DE LA CHARENTE

5C5, 5C6, correspondence with intendant, La Rochelle, 1782–4
11C 1462, 1469, 1471, 1481, Controle des actes, Cognac, 1766–8, 1776, 1778–9, 1788–9
11C 1713, 1714, 1731, Controle des actes, Jarnac, 1766, 1767, 1788
2E 10894, Bardon repertories, 1760, 1767, 1779–91
2E 13511, Bernard repertories, 1732–52
2E 13545, Bernard notarial minutes, 1775
2E 13553, Bernard wills, 1754–82
2E 14272, 14273, 14275, 14276, 14279, 14294, Imbaud notarial minutes (1788, 1789, 1791, 1793, an 9)
2E 14416, Lauchère notarial minutes, 1778
J215, Martell letter book, November 1742–September 1743
J1631, accounts of Faure d'Ollivier, brandy merchant, Jarnac, 1750s and 1760s
L2451, Imbaud repertories, 1792–an 8

BELFAST, PUBLIC RECORD OFFICE OF NORTHERN IRELAND

Abercorn papers
Black papers
Castlereagh papers
Downshire papers

BORDEAUX, ARCHIVES DÉPARTEMENTALES DE LA GIRONDE

6B 47, 48, 49, 50, Passports for passengers, 1727–50
7B 537–538, failure of new Boyd–Guiliory partnership, 1787–9
7B 1169–1176, papers of Boyd–Guiliory partnership (George Boyd et Cie), 1780s
C 1072–1074, intendant's correspondence about 'Anglais' in Bordeaux, 1756–8
C 4268–4271, 4385–4390, *états de la balance du commerce* of the *généralité* of Bordeaux
Notarial minutes Guy, Guy fils

CASTLETOWN, CO. CARLOW (IN THE POSSESSION OF MRS AMY
MONAHAN)
Faulkner papers

COGNAC
Augier archives
Augier (various styles: Augier, Veuve Augier et Cie, Augier frères)
Accounts, 1686–90; miscellaneous accounts, 1723–6 (some on loose sheets);
    account book 1723–4; ledger 1724–41(with lacunae after 1735); foreign
    accounts 1727–8; ledger accounts 1742–53; *livre brouillon c.* 1730; *acquit*
    books, 1728–32, 1751–7; bill books, various dates
Correspondence with Crommelin de la Villette, 1747–51
Invoices, 18 November 1756–7 January 1764 (these follow with a gap invoices 21
    January 1736–29 January 1748 entered in a volume bearing at the back the
    title 'Comptes courants 1826–7'); invoices from 1764
Legal documents, sixteenth and seventeenth centuries; miscellaneous family
    accounts and papers, 1740s to 1780s
Letter books, 1681–6, 22 November 1717–21 August 1719, 3 August 1719– 6
    July 1720, 6 July–13 October 1720, 17 October 1720–24 October 1724,
    1724–6, 1726–7, 1727–8 (8 vols.); copy letters to English and Irish corre-
    spondents, 1768–82 (1 vol.)
Letter books, 1 June–18 December 1720, 16 March–2 December 1720; corre-
    spondence received from Paris and abroad, mainly on speculative business,
    1719–21; small soft-cover letter books and account books, relating to
    difficulties and bankruptcy 1720–3; letter book, Paris 1721, of Philippe
    Augier, and letters from Richard *l'aîné* to Paris 1721

Broussard papers
Letter book 26 April 1765–26 November 1766 (badly mutilated letter book,
    effective internal terminal dates 3 December 1765 and 1 November 1766;
    pages between 203 and 462 also missing in entirety)
Letters, mainly from mid-1760s to early 1770s (with some from 1730s and
    1780s)

Veuve Guérinet et Cie, Charente
Letter books, 1728–9 (2 vols.)

Hennessy archives
Hennessy (Hennessy et Cie, Saule et Cie, Hennessy and Turner)
Denizet, J., 'La famille et la maison Hennessy au XVIIIᵉ siècle' (typescript).
Letter books 1765–1801 (13 vols.); ledgers 1785–9, 1789–92, 1794–1800
Letters received, business and private, 1765–1800 (92 boxes to 1795), 1812–13
Miscellaneous Irish letters and accounts of Richard Hennessy, Ostend, 1753–65;
    small *carnet* entitled, in Richard Hennessy's hand, 'Copies of letters and
    accounts brought from Ostend'

Régnier, Charente
Letter book, 1735–6, invoice book 1737–50

Martell archives
Martell (Martell or Martell, Lallemand et Cie)
Account book 1782–93; ledgers 1749–53, 1773–89; journal 1720 (some months only, volume contains invoices from 1766); journal 1751–4, 1784–5 (in 1 vol.); journal 1782–93; bill books, invoice books and *livres de paye*, various dates
Letter books, 1720–1, 1721–2, 19 March–5 December 1753 (with a few later letters to 1759), 1762–4, 1766–7, 1774–5, 1775–6, 1778–90 (22 vols.)
Letters received, 1784–98 (few or none in some years)

Martell, Fiott et Cie, Bordeaux
Letter book, 1724–5

Otard archives (Otard and Dupuy)
'Généalogie de la famille O'Tard de la Grange précédée d'une notice historique et chronologique sur le Jarl Norvégien Ottard et ses descendants Barons de Gournay de Dunnottard et de la Grange par le Comte de Valls, gendre du généalogiste D'Hozier' (printed)
Invoice book 1796–an 9 (including accounts, 1 vol.)
Letter books, 1795–1802 (11 vols.)

CORK, CORK ARCHIVES COUNCIL
Hewitt letter books (in Irish Distillers' deposit)

DUBLIN
National Archives of Ireland
'A registry of reports by the Honourable E. Thompson Esq. Anno 1733'
Official papers (first series)
Rebellion papers
Wyche documents, 114/41, 'Some reasons demonstrating the prejudice that the importation of brandy occasions to Ireland'

National Library
Microfilm P.928, Hutchins papers

Registry of deeds
Memorials of deeds

University College
O'Connell papers

EDINBURGH, SCOTTISH RECORD OFFICE, GENERAL REGISTER HOUSE
Business papers (French trade with reference to brandy)
RH/59/5, RH/54/4, CS96/1575, CS96/3264, CS96/3309, CS96/3815

JARNAC

In the possession of M. Alain Braastad, Jarnac
Miscellaneous correspondence and papers of James Delamain, 1760s–1780s
Valette, La Rochelle, letter book, 1773–5

Delamain archives (Ranson and Delamain)
Letter book, 1767–8

Hine archives
Isaac Ranson et Cie
Journal, 1758–61
Ranson and Delamain
Letter books of Ranson and Delamain, 1778–1806 (17 vols.)
Invoice books from 1770; account book 1769–78; journal 1771–6; ledgers
  1773–85, 1785–9; *acquit* books, bill books, various dates
Legal papers of Hine family, 1796–1838

JEREZ, GARVEY AND CO.

Letter book, letters, accounts (incomplete, 1780s–1800s)

LONDON

British Library
Add. MS. 4759, Exports and imports of Ireland 1683–6

Public Record Office
Customs 1, Minutes of Revenue Commissioners
Customs 15, ledgers of exports and imports from 1698
Home Office papers, HO 100/43, ff. 251–67, c. March 1793[1]
Port books Ireland, E190/1345/1/16, December 1682–3
State Papers France, SP 78
State Papers Ireland, SP 63

LORIENT, ARCHIVES DU PORT

Archives of second French East India Company, correspondence, 1760s and
  1770s, especially IP283, IP286, IP286a, correspondence concerning purchases

NANTES, ARCHIVES DÉPARTEMENTALES DE LA LOIRE ATLANTIQUE

Amirauté, B4694[1], declarations by masters of outward vessels 1738
Série C, *balance du commerce* for Nantes and for Brittany

---

[1] I am indebted to Professor T. M. Bartlett of University College, Dublin, for this reference.

PARIS

Archives nationales
F¹² 51, 54, 55 Minutes of the *conseil du commerce* (council of trade)
F¹² 208, 'Nomenclature de différentes mesures applicable à plusieurs espèces de marchandises', n.d. (Revolutionary period)
F¹² 1646–50, report regarding the re-establishment of free ports, 9 Thermidor an 9.
F¹² 1666, *balance du commerce*, trade of French ports in 1789
57 AQ1–AQ8, Mallet archives, banking ledgers and journals
8Q 179, 217, 218, 230, 231, 239, Compagnie des Indes, archives of the 'third' company, ledgers, account books and letter books from 1785
G⁵ 47, 48, 50, 51, 62, *congés* for outward-bound vessels, Charente and Bordeaux
Serie Oi, *lettres de naturalité* and *lettres de reconnaissance de noblesse*

Archives du Ministère des Affaires étrangères
Correspondance politique Angleterre

Archives de la guerre
Personal file of Lieut.-Colonel Richard Hennessy
Yb 820, registre d'hommes de troupe 1752–7
IYC 258, registre d'officiers
AI 2770, nos. 76–93, 6 August–28 December 1730 (Richard Hennessy's mission)

RENNES, ARCHIVES DÉPARTEMENTALES D'ILLE-ET-VILAINE

Bourde de la Rogerie papers, 5 J 74, notes on Warren correspondence

LA ROCHELLE

Archives départementales de la Charente Maritime
B398, juridiction consulaire, 16 April 1755
C186, C188, intendance, 1729–64, 1775–7
Notarial minutes: Teuleron, 3E 1294–1319 (1645–81); de la Vergne
4J 2283, letter book of an unidentified Irish merchant, La Rochelle 1699–1707
4J 3630, account book of an unidentified merchant, Saint-Jean d'Angély, 1659–60

Bibliothèque municipale
MS 2703, Claude Claveau, 'Le monde rochelais de l'Ancien Régime' (contains summary statistics of brandy exports drawn from *balance du commerce* records, p. 767)

Chamber of commerce
Correspondence and records (including in cartons 21 and 27 the *états de la balance du commerce*), the richest administrative source for the French brandy trade

VANNES, ARCHIVES DÉPARTEMENTALES DU MORBIHAN
Lamaignère and Delaye papers

PRINTED SOURCES

CONTEMPORARY, AND LATER EDITIONS OF CONTEMPORARY RECORDS

Archivium hibernicum
Bang, N. E., ed., *Tables de la navigation et du transport des marchandises passant par le Sund 1497–1660* (Copenhagen, 1922)
Bang, N. E. and Korst, K., eds., *Tables de la navigation et du transport des marchandises passant par le Sund 1661–1783* (Copenhagen, 1930–53)
Burke correspondence, ed. T. Copeland (10 vols., Cambridge, 1958–78)
Calendar of State papers, Ireland, 1663–5
Conseil de commerce et Bureau de commerce 1700–1791: inventaire analytique des procès-verbaux (repr. Geneva, 1979)
Convert Rolls, ed. O'Byrne (Irish Manuscripts Commission, Dublin, 1981)
Correspondence of the Rt. Hon. John Beresford illustrative of the last days of the Irish parliament (2 vols., London, 1854)
George, J., *Mercuriales d'Angouleme, de Cognac et de Jarnac (1593–1797)* (Mémoire de la société archéologique et historique de la Charente, Angouleme, 1921)
Glasgow Journal
Golownin, V., *Narrative of my captivity in Japan during the years 1811, 1812, and 1813* (London, 1818)
Henry, W., rector of Urney, *An earnest address to the people of Ireland against the drinking of spirituous liquors* (Dublin, 1753)
Inventaire de la Série C (Archives départementales d'Ille-et-Vilaine)
Journals of the House of Commons (Ireland)
Kaempfer, E., *History of Japan* (London, 1727)
Kearney, H., 'The Irish wine trade 1614–15', *Irish Historical Studies*, 9, pp. 400–42.
The Kenmare manuscripts, ed. E. MacLysaght (Irish Manuscripts Commission, Dublin, 1942)
Le Normand, L. S., *Essai sur l'art de la distillation* (Paris, 1811)
Le royaume d'Irlande (late sixteenth-century printed map, in private hands)
Lewis, S., *Topographical dictionary of Ireland* (Dublin, 1838)
Madden, S., *Reflections and resolutions proper for the gentlemen of Ireland* (Dublin, 1738)
Munier, E., *Mémoire qui a concouru pour le prix proposé par la société royale d'agriculture de Limoges sur la manière de bruler ou de distiller les vins* (written 1766; published 1770) in B. Sepulchre, *L'Angoumois à la fin de l'Ancien Régime* (Paris, 1981)
Essai d'une méthode générale propre à étendre les connaissances des voyageurs ou recueil d'observations relatives à l'histoire, à la répartition des impots, aux arts, à la culture des terres, le tout appuyé sur des faits exacts et enrichi d'expériences utiles (2 vols., Paris, 1779) in B. Sepulchre, *L'Angoumois à la fin de l'Ancien Régime* (Paris, 1981)

Négociations de M. le Comte d'Avaux en Irlande 1689–1690, ed. J. Hogan (Dublin, Irish Manuscript Commission, 1934)
O'Rourke, J., *A treatise on the art of war* (London, 1778)
Old statistical account of Scotland
Reynolds, T., *Life of Thomas Reynolds*, vol. I (London, 1839)
Roche, J., *Critical and miscellaneous essays by an octogenarian*, vol. II (Cork, 1851)
Rozier, Abbé, *De la fermentation des vins* (Lyons, 1776)
Savary des Bruslons, J., *Dictionnaire universel du commerce* (1723 edn, 3 vols. in 4 parts; 1742 edn, 4 vols.)
Schelle, G., *Oeuvres de Turgot*, vol. III (Paris, 1919)
Scots Magazine
'Test book 1775–6', in *Fifty-ninth report of the deputy keeper of the public records in Ireland* (Dublin, 1962)
Williams, J. A., ed., *Post-reformation Catholicism in Bath* (2 vols., Catholic Record Society, London, 1975–6)
Wilson's Dublin directory
Young, A., *Tours in France and Italy during the years 1787, 1788 and 1789* (London, 1915)

MODERN

Aftalion, F., *The French Revolution: an economic interpretation* (Cambridge, 1990)
Ashton, T. S., *An economic history of England: the eighteenth century* (London, 1972)
Bernard, J., 'The maritime intercourse between Bordeaux and Ireland c. 1450–c. 1520', *Irish Economic and Social History*, 7 (1980), pp. 7–21
Bézaud, B., *Vignes, vins et eaux-de-vie* (Cognac, 1883)
Bouchary, J., *Les manieurs d'argent à Paris à la fin du XVIIIᵉ siècle*, vol. II (Paris, 1940)
Brady, J., *Catholics and Catholicism in the eighteenth-century press* (Maynooth, 1965), p. 319
Brodot, Abbé Mederic, *Tonnay-Charente et le canton: étude historique, géologique, archéologique, généalogique, bibliographique, religieuse et commerciale*, vol. I (Rochefort, 1901)
Bromley, J., 'Le commerce de la France de l'ouest et la guerre maritime, 1702–1712', *Annales du Midi* (1953), pp. 52–65
Butel, P., 'Contribution à l'étude de la circulation de l'argent en Aquitaine au XVIIIᵉ siècle: le commerce des rescriptions sur les recettes des finances', *Revue d'Histoire Economique et Sociale* (1979), pp. 83–109
La croissance commerciale bordelaise dans la seconde moitié du XVIIIᵉ siècle (Lille, 1973)
L'économie française au XVIIIᵉ siècle (Paris, 1993)
Les négociants bordelais, l'Europe et les iles au xviiiᵉ siècle (Paris, 1974)
'Quelques leçons sur le dynamisme commercial de Cognac à la fin du XVIIIᵉ siècle', in A. Huetz de Lemps and Ph. Roudié, eds., *Eaux-de-vie et spiritueux*
'Relations bancaires entre Bordeaux et La Rochelle au XVIIIᵉ siècle: correspondance du banquier bordelais Gabriel da Silva', *Recueil de la Société d'Archéologie et d'Histoire de la Charente Maritime*, 25 (1974), pp. 193–8

Carrière, C., 'Le commerce des eaux-de-vie à Toulon au xviiie siècle', *Provence Historique*, 12, fasc. 47 (January/March 1962)

Clark, J. G., *La Rochelle and the Atlantic economy during the eighteenth century* (Baltimore and London, 1981)

Clark, P., 'The "mother gin" controversy in the early eighteenth century', *Transactions of the Royal Historical Society*, fifth series, 38 (1988), pp. 63–84

Crouzet, F., *La grande inflation: la monnaie en France de Louis XVI à Napoléon* (Paris, 1993)

Cullen, L. M., *Anglo-Irish trade 1660–1800* (Manchester, 1968)

'Burke, Ireland, and Revolution', *Eighteenth-century Life*, n.s., 16 (February 1992), pp. 21–42

'Comparative aspects of Irish diet, 1550–1850', in Hans J. Teuteberg, *European food history* (Leicester, 1992), pp. 165–76

'The contemporary and later politics of Caoineadh Airt Uí Laoire', *Eighteenth-century Ireland*, 8 (1993), pp. 7–38

'The early brandy trade 1660–1760', in E. Aerts, L. M. Cullen and R. G. Wilson, eds., *Production, marketing and consumption of alcoholic beverages since the late middle ages* (Leuven, 1990), pp. 20–30

'The economic crisis of the end of the Ancien Regime', in J. P. Poussou, ed., *Crouzet festschrift*, forthcoming

'Galway merchants in the outside world 1660–1800', in D. O'Cearbhaill, ed., *Galway: town and gown* (Dublin, 1984), pp. 63–89

'History, economic crisis and revolution: understanding eighteenth-century France', *Economic History Review*, 46, no. 4 (November 1993), pp. 635–57

'The Huguenots from the perspective of the merchant networks of western Europe (1680–1720)', in C. J. Caldicott, H. Gough and J. P. Pittion, *The Huguenots and Ireland: anatomy of an emigration* (Dublin, 1987), pp. 129–49

'The Irish diaspora of the seventeenth and eighteenth centuries', in N. Canny, ed., *Europeans on the move: studies on European migration, 1500–1800* (Oxford, 1994), pp. 113–49

'Luthy's *la banque protestante*: a reassessment', *Bulletin du Centre d'Histoire des Espaces Atlantiques*, n.s, no. 5 (1990), pp. 229–63

'Merchant communities overseas, the navigation acts and Irish and Scottish responses', in L. M. Cullen and T. C. Smout, eds., *Comparative aspects of Scottish economic and social history 1600–1900* (Edinburgh, 1977)

'The overseas trade of Waterford as seen from a ledger of Courtenay and Ridgway', *Journal of the Royal Society of Antiquaries of Ireland*, 88 (1958), pp. 165–78

Princes and pirates (Dublin, 1983)

'Le réseau commercial du négoce du cognac dans les années 1760', in F. Crouzet, ed., *Le négoce international xiiie–xxe siècles* (Paris, 1989), pp. 153–68

'Smugglers in the Irish Sea in the eighteenth century', in M. McCaughan and J. Appleby, eds., *The Irish Sea: aspects of maritime history* (Belfast, 1989), pp. 85–99

'Smuggling and the Ayrshire economic boom of the 1760s and 1770s', *Ayrshire Archaeological and Natural History Society, Ayrshire monographs*, 14 (September 1994)

'The smuggling trade in Ireland in the eighteenth century', *Proceedings of the Royal Irish Academy*, section C, 67, no. 5 (1969), pp. 149–75

Delamain, R., *Histoire du cognac* (Paris, 1935)

Jarnac à travers les ages (second edn, Angouleme, 1954)

Delaye, G., *L'Angoumois au temps des marchands flamands (17ᵉ siècle)* (Paris, 1990)

Dermigny, L., *Sète de 1666 à 1880: esquisse de l'histoire d'un port* (Montpellier, 1955)

Dion, R., *Histoire de la vigne et du vin en France des origines au xixᵉ siècle* (Paris, 1959)

Enjalbert, H., 'Aux origines du cognac', in A. Huetz de Lemps and Ph. Roudié, eds., *Eaux-de-vie et spiritueux*, pp. 11–21

Faith, N., *Cognac* (Boston and London, 1986)

Firino-Martell, R., *La famille Martell* (Paris, 1924)

Fitzpatrick, W. J., *Ireland before the union* (sixth edn, Dublin, 1880)

Freche, G., *Toulouse et la région Midi-Pyrénées au siècle des lumières (vers 1670–1789)* (Paris, 1974)

Grand Larousse Encyclopédique

Guimera Ravina, A., *Burguesía extranjera y comercio atlántico: la empresa comercial irlandesa en Canarios 1703–1771* (Canaries, 1987)

Harvey, K. J., 'The family experience: the Bellews of Mount Bellew', in T. P. Power and K. Whelan, *Endurance and emergence: Catholics in Ireland in the eighteenth century* (Dublin, 1990)

Haudrère, Ph., 'Ravitaillement et ration alimentaire à bord des vaisseaux de la Compagnie Française des Indes en Asie au xviiiᵉ siècle', *Bulletin du Centre d'Histoire des Espaces Atlantiques*, n.s., 2 (1985), pp. 55–67

Hayes, R. J., *Biographical dictionary of Irishmen in France* (Dublin, 1949)

Henderson, W. O., 'The Anglo-French commercial treaty of 1786', *Economic History Review*, second series, 10, no. 1 (1957), pp. 104–12

Huetz de Lemps, A., 'Les eaux-de-vie et liqueurs en France vers 1825 d'après Cavoleau', in A. Huetz de Lemps and Ph. Roudié, *Eaux-de-vie et spiritueux*

Huetz de Lemps, A. and Ph. Roudié, *Eaux-de-vie et spiritueux* (Paris, 1985)

Huetz de Lemps, C., *Géographie du commerce de Bordeaux à la fin du règne de Louis XIV* (Paris, 1975)

Hufton, O. H., *Bayeux in the late eighteenth century* (Oxford, 1967)

The poor of eighteenth-century France 1750–1789 (Oxford, 1974)

Jamieson, A. G., *A people of the sea: the maritime history of the Channel Islands* (London, 1986)

Jeulin, P., *L'évolution du port de Nantes* (Nantes, 1929)

Jézéquel, J., *La Charente révolutionnaire, 1789–1799* (Poitiers, 1992)

Grands notables du premier empire (Paris, 1986)

Kléber, R., 'Le trafic des eaux-de-vie charentaises 1660–1775' (Travail d'étude et de recherche, University of Bordeaux, 1971)

Labrousse, E., *La crise de l'économie française à la fin de l'ancien régime* (Paris, 1944)

Esquisse du mouvement des prix et des revenus en France (Paris, 1933)

Lachiver, M., *Vin, vigne et vignerons en région parisienne du XVIIᵉ au XIXᵉ siècle* (Pontoise, 1982)

Lafon, R., J. Lafon and P. Couillaud, *Le cognac: sa distillation* (fourth edn, Paris, 1964)

Laveau, C., 'Le monde rochelais de l'Ancien Régime au Consulat' (1974), MS 2703, Bibliothèque municipale, La Rochelle

Lérat, S., 'Introduction à la connaissance du vignoble d'Armagnac', in A. Huetz de Lemps and Ph. Roudié, *Eaux-de-vie et spiritueux*

Le Roy Ladurie, E., *Histoire du climat depuis l'an mille* (2 vols., Paris, 1983)

Lyons, M., *France under the Directory* (Cambridge, 1995)

McCusker, J. J., 'Distilling and its implications for the Atlantic world of the seventeenth and eighteenth centuries', in E. Aerts, L. M. Cullen and R. G. Wilson, eds., *Production, marketing and consumption of alcoholic beverages since the late middle ages*

Rum and the American Revolution (New York, 1989)

McGuire, E. B., *Irish whiskey* (Dublin, 1973)

MacLysaght, E., *Irish life in the seventeenth century* (second edn, Cork, 1950)

Malcolm, E., *'Ireland sober, Ireland free': drink and temperance in nineteenth-century Ireland* (Dublin, 1986)

Malvezin, T., *Histoire du commerce de Bordeaux* (Bordeaux, 1892)

Martin-Civat, P., 'Le monopole des eaux-de-vie sous Henri IV et le départ du cognac', *Actes du 100e Congrès national des sociétés savantes* (Paris, 1977)

Matthews, G. T., *The Royal General Farms in eighteenth-century France* (New York, 1958)

Minchinton, W., 'The Canaries in the British trade world of the eighteenth century', in Francisco Morales Padron, ed., *IX Coloquio de historia Canario-Americana* (Las Palmas, 1990)

Mitchell, B. R. and P. Deane, *Abstract of British historical statistics* (Cambridge, 1962)

Murphy, A. E., *Richard Cantillon: entrepreneur and economist* (Oxford, 1986)

O'Connell, B., 'The Nagles of Garnavilla', *Irish Genealogist*, 3, no. 1 (1956), pp. 17–20

O'Connell, M. J., *Last colonel of the Irish Brigade* (1892; repr. Cork, 1977)

Pairault, F., 'Les expéditions d'eau de vie de Cognac par le port de Tonnay-Charente au xixᵉ siècle', *Revue de Saintonge et d'Aunis*, 11 (1976)

Parfouru, P., 'Les irlandais en Bretagne aux xviiᵉ et xviiiᵉ siècles', *Annales de Bretagne*, 9 (1893)

Pijassou, R., 'Quelques aperçus sur le commerce des eaux-de-vie en Angleterre au début du xviiiᵉ siècle', in A. Huetz de Lemps and Ph. Roudié, eds., *Eaux-de-vie et spiritueux*

Porter, R., 'The drinking man's disease: the prehistory of alcoholism in Georgian Britain', *British Journal of Addiction*, 60 (1985)

Poussou, J. P. et al., *Bordeaux et le sud-ouest au xviiiᵉ siècle: croissance économique et attraction urbaine* (Paris, 1983)

'Départ des irlandais depuis Bordeaux au XVIIIᵉ siècle' (unpublished paper, c. 1974)

'Le dynamisme de l'économie française sous Louis XV', *Revue Economique*,40 (1989), pp. 965–83

Ravaz L. and A. Vivier, *Le pays du cognac* (Angouleme, 1900)

Rodger, N. A., 'The victualling of the British navy in the seven years war', *Bulletin du Centre d'Histoire des Espaces Atlantiques*, n.s., 2 (1985), pp. 37–54

Royr, J., *Histoire de la franc-maçonnerie en Charente* (Paris, 1994)

Samuels, A. P. I., *The early life, correspondence and writings of the Rt. Hon. Edmund Burke* (Cambridge, 1923)

Schumpeter, E. B., *English overseas trade statistics 1697–1808* (Oxford, 1960)

Sepulchre, B., *Le livre du cognac: trois siècles d'histoire* (Paris, 1983)

Notes pour servir à l'histoire de la commune de Ségonzac ([Jarnac], 1984)

Sueur, L., 'La conservation des vivres et des boissons sur les vaisseaux au long cours appartenant au roi de France et qui se dirigeaient, à la fin du XVIIe siècle vers les Indes Orientales', *Revue Historique*, year 117 (January/March 1993)

Tarrade, J., *Le commerce colonial de la France à la fin de l'Ancien Régime* (2 vols., Paris, 1972)

Trocmé, E. and M. Delafosse, *Le commerce rochelais de la fin du xve au début du xviie siècle* (Paris, 1953)

The Wine and Spirit Journal (Toronto), 7, no. 3 (March, 1905), pp. 53–4

Index

Aigre, 3, 76, 119, 128, 170
  Aigriers, 147, 148, 149
  brandy output, 80, 121
  purchases for Paris, 112, 146
Alleret and Moynet (Charente), 210
Amsterdam,
  Augier in, 168
  complaints by merchants, 110
  decline in demand for brandy, 40
  foreign exchange, 52
  Huguenots, 20
  Janssens, 96
  taste for brandy, 115
Andoe, Hilary,
  arrives Bordeaux, 1774, 41, 178
  Bordeaux business, 232, 244, 245
  distilling commission rates, 243
Angouleme, 95, 112, 119, 123, 166, 170,
    172, 173, 239
  brandy buying by merchants, 119, 120,
    163, 172
  brandy market, 10, 19
  brandy prices, 163
  market for bills on Paris, 172
  paper industry, 167
  replaces La Rochelle, 52, 53, 153
  rise of, 3
  see also Nouel
Angoumois,
  brandy from, 42, 48, 138
  output, 121
  red wine used in distilling, 113, 123
  transit duties in, 133
Arbouin,
  Gernon partner, 174
  in London, 248
  in Pons, 169, 170, 177, 249
Armagnac,
  brandy, 9, 39, 42, 105, 247
  region, 2, 9, 156
Ashton, T. S., 21
Augier, 4, 57, 58, 81, 169, 182, 249

branch in Tonnay-Charente, 110
family (Cognac),
  Daniel, 175, 180
  Etienne, 59, 215
  Philippe (father and son), 18, 59, 96,
    110, 166, 168, 174, 187
  Pierre, 166, 187
  marriages, 59, 168, 169, 202, 215
  origins, 166–7
house,
  business of (1680s), 9–11, 74
  dealings with Martell's, 188, 197, 202,
    204; with Richards, 168, 188
  decline, 213–17
  difficulties and collapse (1721–2),
    191–3, 194
  recovery, 110–12, 195, 197, 207–8,
    209, 210–11
  renewed difficulties, 153, 212–14
trade,
  observations by Augier, 20, 105, 106,
    113–14, 115, 119, 147–8, 156
  with England, 176, 177, 205, 222
  with Guernsey, 187
  with Ireland and Irish houses, 214,
    252
  with London, 33, 112, 196, 206, 216,
    217
  with northern Europe, 175
  with Orleans, 147
  with Paris, 146–7, 156, 161–2
  see also Guérinet, Veuve
Aunis,
  dispute about brandy, 79, 87
  low strength of brandy, 72, 75, 76, 77,
    79–80, 83, 87
  output of, 10, 15, 23, 48, 103, 107, 120,
    122, 127
  province, 110, 124, 135
  shipments to northern France, 14, 125,
    139–40
D'Avaux, 42, 44

275

Printed in the United States
By Bookmasters